Wiltshire Record Society

(formerly the Records Branch of the Wiltshire
Archaeological and Natural History Society)

VOLUME 65

JUST 1/998A m. 41d. The writ sent to the justices during the 1268 eyre, instructing them how to deal with offences against the peace committed during the recent civil war (600). (Copyright TNA)

CROWN PLEAS
OF THE
WILTSHIRE EYRE
1268

edited by
BRENDA FARR
and
CHRISTOPHER ELRINGTON

revised and with an introduction by
HENRY SUMMERSON

CHIPPENHAM

2012

ISBN 978-0-901333-42-1

*The Wiltshire Record Society gratefully acknowledges the continued financial
support of Wiltshire Council.*

Typeset by John Chandler
Produced for the Society by
Salisbury Printing Company Ltd, Salisbury
Printed in Great Britain

CONTENTS

PREFACE

Before she died on 4 January 2007 Brenda Farr had prepared a transcript and translation of the crown pleas of the Wiltshire eyre of 1268. She had started work on the edition by 1981 and had taken it to an advanced stage before illness prevented her from completing it. In 2008 her daughter Jane Farr passed a typescript of the transcript and translation to Christopher Elrington, who was able to check the transcript against photographic copies of the original manuscript, and modified the translation in the light of his decision to publish that alone, without a full transcript of the Latin text. Professor Elrington also compiled drafts of the indexes of persons and places, in both of which he was greatly assisted by Mrs. Farr's earlier work, and of subjects. But circumstances made it impossible for either of this text's primary editors to compose an introduction to it, and that task has therefore been performed by Dr. Henry Summerson, who also revised the translation and extended the annotation. The Society is grateful to Mrs. Farr, the editor of *The Rolls of Highworth Hundred, 1275–87* (volumes 21 and 22), to her daughter for extracting her mother's work from a mass of papers, and to Mrs. Jean Elrington for passing on the text to the editors. The Society is also grateful to the donor, who wishes to remain anonymous, of the gift in memory of Professor Elrington which paid Dr. Summerson to write a scholarly introduction, and to Dr. Summerson for revising and completing the edition.

Dr. Summerson wishes to record his thanks to Steven Hobbs, Virginia Bainbridge and Alex Craven for undertaking the revision of the indexes, to John Chandler for overseeing the provision of illustrations, and to all four for support while work on the edition was in progress. And he gratefully acknowledges the scholarly foundations laid for this volume by Mrs. Farr and Professor Elrington.

This translation of a Crown-copyright record in The National Archives is published by permission of the Controller of Her Majesty's Stationery Office.

BRENDA MARION FARR, NÉE TIDMAN (1923-2007): an appreciation by Jane Farr

Brenda Marion Farr (née Tidman) was born in Eastbourne, Sussex on 31st August 1923. Her father, Frederick Tidman, worked for the Co-operative Society and her mother Eva Pike came from a family of bakers. Brenda was awarded a scholarship to Eastbourne Grammar School, and passed her Higher Certificate in June 1941. She gained a place at the University of London to study Classics, and graduated in 1944 with a First Class Honours Degree. Her first job was with the university as an assistant teacher of Classics at Royal Holloway College. In 1950 Brenda took the Diploma in Archive Administration at the University of London School of Librarianship and Archives. Brenda studied Medieval Latin and Anglo-Norman French on the course. She was described as an outstanding student, and awarded the Churchill-Jenkinson Prize. Here Brenda met fellow student Michael Farr, whom she married in 1952, following her work placement at the William Salt Library, Stafford. The couple lived first in Stafford, where Michael worked at Staffordshire County Record office, and settled in Warwick in 1955, where Michael was Assistant County Archivist and later County Archivist.

Once the early years of rearing their three children were passed, Brenda returned to work as a part-time Classics teacher in local schools and joined Michael in the study of Wiltshire medieval records. Michael published *Accounts and Surveys of the Wiltshire Lands of Adam de Stratton*, ed. M. W. Farr (WRS 14, 1959). Brenda published *The Rolls of Highworth Hundred 1275–87*, ed. B. Farr (WRS 21-22, 1966, 1968). Following her retirement from teaching, Brenda resumed her study of Wiltshire medieval records, working on the *Crown Pleas of the Wiltshire Eyre, 1268*. She greatly enjoyed translating the documents and the stories they told of people's lives. Brenda died on 4 January 2007 and Michael on 25 June 2009. Sadly they lost their son Simon in 1986, but are survived by their daughter Jane and son Andrew. Brenda is remembered as a woman of gentle character, great personal strength and academic excellence.

CHRISTOPHER ROBIN ELRINGTON (1930-2009), by Negley Harte and Kenneth Rogers

Christopher Elrington devoted the whole of his professional life as a historian to the *Victoria County History*, that magnificent encyclopaedic work attempting to provide fully researched and properly referenced historical accounts of all the counties of England and their more than 10,000 individual parishes. Some 250 large red volumes of the *VCH* have appeared since the endeavour began in 1899. Elrington had an increasingly influential hand in all the volumes that have appeared in the last fifty years.

He was General Editor of the whole enterprise from 1977 until 1994, having been Deputy Editor from 1968, and before that County Editor for Gloucestershire from 1960 to 1968, and originally assistant to the General Editor from 1954 to 1960. His first contributions were published exactly fifty years ago in 1959 – he compiled the index to the excellent economic history volume IV of the *VCH Wiltshire*, and in the same year he wrote three succinct articles about aspects of the University of Cambridge in the *VCH Cambridgeshire,* volume III.

The *VCH*, originally a private enterprise, had been based at the Institute of Historical Research at the University of London since 1933, entrenched in the old-fashioned if 'modern' Senate House since the Ministry of Information faded away at the end of the war. Elrington brought a breath of fresh air when he arrived in 1954, combining, as he did, a twinkling irreverence with a scholarly commitment and a gift for encapsulating complex matters in a simple elegant phrase.

Christopher Elrington was born in 1930, perhaps the best year in the twentieth century in which to be born (– Discuss, as we say in examination questions…) He was the son of a military family, his father a brigadier, and educated at Wellington before himself undergoing national service, and then going to University College, Oxford, where he graduated brilliantly in history and took his MA. He then went to Bedford College in London and took a real MA, producing a thesis based upon detailed medieval research.

Elrington's predecessor as General Editor of the *VCH* was the austere R.B. Pugh, whose crab-like movements and old-fashioned buttoned-up bachelor suits had intimidated generations of research students at the Institute of Historical Research since 1949. Pugh and Elrington were – to use appropriate Wiltshire terminology - chalk and cheese. But Elrington always paid generous tribute to his mentor; certainly they shared a scholarly concern for precision and clarity of provenance. In due course Elrington also succeeded Pugh as the President of the Wiltshire Record Society in 1984, the Society founded in 1937 by Pugh and described by Elrington (before he became its President) as 'probably the very best' of the local record societies.

When I moved to Wiltshire in 2004 Elrington said with great enthusiasm 'You have chosen the best county'. Soon afterwards I invited him to come as my guest to a dinner of the Essay Club in London, writing to explain that he did not need to write an essay, or – worse – listen to one being read, but that the name of the Club was a pun upon the Society of Antiquaries, the members being chosen from among the Fellows of that Society. 'Yes, yes', he rang to say; 'I know all about it, I've been before. Delighted to come, so long as you don't expect me to become a member'. He hated joining clubs, he added by way of explanation.

He enjoyed the evening, evidently quite at home with the erudite scholarly gossip and banter, but he generally preferred to be at home, or exploring and travelling with his family. He had, after all, a very lively and charming wife (Wiltshire-born), whom he had married in 1951, when she was involved in her first job of helping Sir Hugh Casson to construct the Festival of Britain. Jean Elrington was a working architect of great taste and style. They had a very happy marriage and a very happy family life with their twin son and daughter, and later grandchildren.

He was a Fellow of the Society of Antiquaries (elected 1964) and of the Royal Historical Society (1969), neither society requiring clubbiness. The only period he spent away from the *VCH* was a short period as a visiting scholar at the Folger Library in Washington in 1976. He received a wonderful accolade in 1994 with the publication of a *Festschrift* edited by the two Chrises, Currie and Lewis, with chapters systematically considering the historians of all the counties of England, a volume that should be on the shelves of all local historians.

In view of Elrington's distinction, the University of London in 1992 conferred upon him the title of professor (though he never taught in any formal sense); after his retirement in 1994 he became an emeritus professor, a style which suited him admirably.

Christopher, for all his sympathetic writing about parishes and medieval thought and practices, was a sensible and intelligent atheistic rationalist. Confronted by the diagnosis of pancreatic cancer, he chose to die quietly and all too quickly at home, sadly a few months before his 80th birthday. He left his body for medical research. His places – the meetings in Wiltshire, the teas at the Institute of Historical Research, the laughter in Lloyd Baker Street, WC1 – will no longer for many be quite the same.

Christopher Robin Elrington, historian and editor: born Farnborough 20 January 1930; Victoria County History: editorial assistant, 1954-60, editor for Gloucestershire, 1960-68, Deputy Editor, 1968-77, General Editor, 1977-94; Hon. Editor 1962-72 and President 1983-2009, Wiltshire Record Society; President, Bristol and Gloucestershire Archaeological Society, 1984-85; married 1951 Jean Buchanan (one son, one daughter (twins)): died London 3 August 2009.

[The above obituary was published in the *Independent* on 1 September 2009. It was written for a general and national audience by Dr. Negley Harte, before he knew he was to succeed Professor Elrington as President of the Wiltshire Record Society. A further tribute to Professor Elrington's contribution to the work of the Wiltshire Record Society is added by Mr. Ken Rogers, a long-standing member of the committee.]

Professor Christopher Elrington, copyright VCH, IHR, University of London.

Christopher Elrington's connection with Wiltshire, begun with his marriage in 1951, must have been enhanced as soon as he joined the *VCH*. Ralph Pugh, an honorary Wiltshire man with family at Devizes, was not only general editor but also editor of the Wiltshire series, which began its stately and still-continuing progress in 1937. Pugh was also founder, and at that time Chairman, of the Records Branch of the Wiltshire Archaeological & Natural History Society, as the Wiltshire Record Society was then called. Elrington must have been editorially involved in the production of the Wiltshire *VCH* general volumes, and wrote the parish history of Woodford for volume VI.

Involvement with the Record Society was inevitable. Elrington was general editor of its series from 1962 until 1972. During that time eight volumes were produced, and of these it is known that at least one required a very notable input from Elrington himself. He left ten more volumes in stages of preparation. In 1974 the only volume he actually edited, *Abstracts of Feet of Fines for the Reign of Edward III*, came out.

In 1983 Elrington became President of the Wiltshire Record Society. From then until his final illness he hardly ever missed a committee meeting or an A.G.M. Those of us who served on the committee will never forget his experience. He was an essential link between us and the world of academic scholarship. His knowledge of the whole field of record publication all over England and of the people involved in it seemed universal. He could always suggest someone to consult, a volume to look at, and, sometimes, a grant-giving body to approach. He seemed familiar with the most abstruse archives. Yet his quiet humour made the meetings a pleasure to attend.

But his contribution to the Society's work went much further. As a typical example, I quote from the introduction to volume 54, *The First General Entry Book of the City of Salisbury*. 'The translation and interpretation of this difficult manuscript have been immeasurably improved by the painstaking labour of Professor Christopher Elrington, who has not only examined the text in its entirety, but has also prepared the index of persons, and contributed to the index of places and subjects and the introduction.' He provided similar input to the second volume of the *Hungerford Cartulary*, left unfinished by John Kirby's death, and was working on the present volume, also left unfinished, almost until the day of his death.

At the Commemoration for him I spoke these words: 'In his novel *Anglo-Saxon Attitudes*, Angus Wilson draws a contrast between the wise and cultured Professor Middleton, whom we are to admire, and the narrow and humourless Professor Clun, whom we are to despise. Middleton feels that detailed scholarship such as Clun favours is insufficient, disreputable, crossword puzzle work. But, wait a minute, that's what record societies and the *VCH* do. I, and I think most people here, are on Clun's side, and we aren't narrow and humourless. If ever, in all my acquaintance, anyone ever demonstrated that the contrast drawn by Wilson is false, that man was Christopher Elrington.'

INTRODUCTION

The eyre, its record and its organisation

The text which follows is a translation from Latin into English of the record of the crown pleas section of the eyre which took place in Wiltshire between 14 January and 1 March 1268.[1] An eyre (a word ultimately derived from the Latin *iter*, meaning a journey) was a periodic visitation of a county by royal justices, usually as part of a circuit involving several counties. Deriving its authority from the premise that all government was ultimately the king's, it divided its proceedings into two sections, comprising civil and crown pleas. The former involved civil litigation, largely over property. The latter were primarily concerned with what today would be regarded as criminal proceedings, covering what were categorised as felonies – serious offences like homicide, theft, arson and rape – along with any other transgressions allegedly accompanied by breach of the king's peace. But they also had a significant administrative and fiscal dimension, for not only did the justices hear about acts of violence and robbery, but they also reviewed the performance of local mechanisms of law enforcement, and penalised inefficiencies, delinquencies and corrupt practices, both by individuals and by whole communities. Punishment almost invariably took a financial form, as did infringements of royal rights, whose maintenance, and where necessary recovery, constituted another of the justices' responsibilities. But although the crown pleas section of any eyre undoubtedly made an important contribution to the king's revenues, and although its record invariably has a marked fiscal bias, it would be wrong to regard it as primarily an agency of royal finance. Despite its intermittency, in the thirteenth century the eyre constituted the single most important link between the central government and the shires. A powerful manifestation of royal authority, it brought a multitude of men and women together to investigate, observe and participate in the maintenance of the king's peace, a peace which was also their own.

That is not to say that an eyre was always welcomed by the shires to which it was sent. On the contrary, it was commonly regarded as intrusive, disruptive and exacting, and by the 1260s it was claimed, and largely accepted, that it should be held only at seven-year intervals.[2] The previous Wiltshire eyre had taken place in April and May 1256. Another had been planned for early 1263, but the outbreak of war in the Welsh marches, and then nationwide political disturbances, prevented its taking place.[3] Only after the end of the

---

1   D. Crook, *Records of the general eyre* (Public Record Office handbooks 20, 1982), 134-5.

2   H. Cam, *Studies in the hundred rolls: some aspects of thirteenth-century administration* (Oxford studies in social and legal history 11, 1921), 83-8.

3   *CR 1261-1264*, 236.

Barons' War, and the restoration of peace, could another judicial visitation be organised. Justices were formally appointed on 7 December 1267,[4] for a circuit which was intended to begin in Wiltshire and then cover much of southern England and East Anglia, but it seems clear that planning had begun earlier, for by the time the commission was issued one of the original justices had been replaced, while writs had been issued around 22 November excusing a number of landowners from attending.[5] When the eyre opened, on 14 January 1268, the four justices were Nicholas de Turri, Master Richard of Staines, Henry de Wollaveston and Henry de Montfort. Robert de Briwes, who had originally been a member of the panel, stayed at Westminster to replace Turri in the court *coram rege*, and Henry de Montfort, a previous sheriff of Wiltshire and lord of the manor of Farleigh Hungerford on the eastern edge of Somerset, took his place.[6] Since Turri and Staines are recorded as giving judgment together on a civil plea at the Norfolk eyre which they held later in 1268,[7] while Montfort is recorded as pardoning two poor litigants in a Wiltshire crown plea (**268**), it may be assumed that Turri and Staines also held the Wiltshire civil pleas, with Staines acting alone when Turri, as parson of Grittleton, litigated on his own behalf,[8] and that Montfort and Wollaveston presided over the pleas of the crown.

The record of their proceedings survives as TNA, JUST 1/998A, a roll of forty-two membranes stitched together at the head. The fact that marginal notes of fiscal relevance are regularly struck through suggests that it was made for the use of Nicholas de Turri, since this was customarily done in the principal justice's roll.[9] The first twenty-three membranes contain the civil pleas, which are followed by a further nineteen containing the crown pleas. Tears and creases on five membranes of the latter[10] have blurred or eradicated some words, but the loss is rarely such as to make the affected passages incomprehensible, and usually the text can be read without difficulty. It is written in three principal hands, with a few annotations and corrections in at least one more. The first clerk, responsible for almost all of membranes 24 recto to 37 dorso (**1-509**),[11] wrote in a neat and regular hand with an occasional penchant for the use of the old-fashioned runic 'thorn', representing 'th', and 'wen', which he used variously to replace 'w', 'wh' and 'y'. The second clerk, who took over on m. 38 recto, and was responsible for all but the last of the remaining membranes (**510-600**), neglected almost entirely to use paragraph signs, and wrote in a slightly larger, freer, and more characterful hand, one which was also employed to record civil pleas. The concluding

4   *CPR 1266-1272*, 172.

5   *CR 1264-1268*, 494-5.

6   JUST 1/998A m. 1.

7   W.H. Dunham, jr., *Casus Placitorum and reports of cases in the king's courts, 1272-1278* (Selden Society 69, 1952 for 1950), 9-10.

8   JUST 1/998A m. 5.

9   *Wiltshire crown pleas, 1249*, 109.

10   JUST 1/998A mm. 24, 25, 32, 38, 39.

11   Another hand was responsible for nos. **64-5, 216, 370, 426-31**.

membrane, mostly devoted to New Salisbury's crown pleas (**601–625**), was written in a small, careless and rather unpleasant hand, often cramped and with no pretensions to elegance.

Taken as a whole, the roll has few visual charms. Doubtless drawn up at the end of the eyre from notes made in the course of it (several membranes conclude with jottings of names, presumably *aides-mémoire* in the task of compilation – **27, 50, 283, 305, 364, 598**), there are signs throughout that it was written up carelessly and in haste, in a process that must have been complicated by the need to translate into Latin a record of proceedings originally conducted either in Anglo-Norman French or in English,[12] and sometimes probably in both together. In several cases there were unresolved issues awaiting attention, and spaces were left for additional material, which, however, was not forthcoming (**10, 12, 167, 173, 216, 363, 364, 540, 541, 609, 625**). In others, spaces were left within entries for names and other details (e.g. **18, 74**). One entry broke off after a false start and was begun again, and this time completed, elsewhere (**118, 130**). Others were simply left incomplete (**115, 127, 137, 542**). In a striking example of negligence, the clerk overlooked one of two connected actions relating to the same affray, finally adding it to the roll only two membranes later (**133, 216**). Errors of omission (**520**), of grammar (**269, 581**) and of dating (**541**) all occur. Erasures and insertions are very numerous, usually involving only one or two words, but occasionally whole sentences, which were not always added in the right place (**359**) and might be so badly composed as to make little or no sense (**135, 614**).

The extended period of disorder which preceded the eyre may help to account for the no less disorderly compilation of its record. It is also possible that insufficient time was allowed for the eyre's preparation, especially as it took place in winter, when roads would have been bad and communications slow. There is no record of when the sheriff of Wiltshire was notified of the impending visitation and instructed to make the necessary arrangements. Foremost among his tasks was that of ensuring the attendance of all those people without whom the eyre could not proceed. In this respect the eyre commanded great, perhaps all-encompassing, authority. In February 1268 the sheriff of Wiltshire was ordered to produce the bailiffs of Wilton in the exchequer of the Jews, to answer a charge of preventing a distraint from being taken in that borough. But the justices there refused to allow them to go to Westminster, even though the plaintiff was no less a figure than the Lord Edward, the heir to the throne, and the case had to be adjourned to a later date.[13]

As this case shows, foremost among the men who presence was required were past and present officials, who had to attend with their records. Two previous sheriffs, John de Vernun and Ralph de Aungers, had died and were represented by their sons, who were not only required to answer for money

12   For some comments on the language of the courts see P.A. Brand, *Observing and recording the medieval bar and bench at work* (Selden Society lecture, 1999).

13   J.M. Rigg (ed.), *Calendar of the plea rolls of the exchequer of the Jews i: Henry III, A.D. 1218-1272* (Jewish Historical Society of Engand, 1905), 192.

owed by their fathers (**287, 459, 539**) but were also – as was conventional – treated as answerable for the latter's shortcomings in office (**57, 61, 349**). Also summoned were landholders great and small; representatives of boroughs and townships; litigants awaiting the trial of their lawsuits; prisoners and anyone who had previously been arrested and released to bail; all the numerous men and women who had been in some way caught up in the mechanisms of law enforcement and therefore had to come now before the king's justices. And in addition the sheriff had to make ready the premises needed to contain proceedings which from start to finish must have involved several thousand people. The main session of the eyre was held at Wilton, as the county town – Wilton Abbey has been suggested as the venue.[14] There were also two subsidiary sessions, at Marlborough and New Salisbury. A case is recorded as being in progress at the latter on 6 February (**609**), but as another was expected to be concluded at Wilton on the 24th (**598**), it would appear that at some point the justices adjourned their proceedings from Wilton to Salisbury, and made the short journey back again afterwards. It is not known when they sat at Marlborough.

There is no evidence for any opening ceremony, or for the kind of feasting known to have preceded other eyres.[15] The bishop of Winchester, the local magnate probably likeliest to have laid on a banquet for the justices, as he did in 1249, was in Italy by 1268, and died there while the eyre was in progress, and although Abbot Colerne of Malmesbury recorded laying out £100 at the 1268 eyre, this money was most likely spent on litigation.[16] So once the justices had arrived at Wilton, and demonstrated their authority by reciting the royal writs empowering them to act, they may then have launched the eyre in a matter-of-fact way by proceeding directly to the selection of juries, an essential element in the hearing of crown pleas. In 1268 the county was divided into fifty presenting areas. Thirty-seven consisted of hundreds, the ancient administrative units into which the county was divided. Salisbury was represented by two juries, one for the castle – in effect what is now known as Old Sarum – and the other for the recently-established city of New Salisbury. There were also juries for seven boroughs, three townships (a fourth, Chippenham, united to answer with the hundred of that name), and the royal manor of Rowde, near Devizes. All had provided juries in 1249, but the township of Corsham, which answered separately in that year,[17] did not do so in 1268, having been absorbed by Chippenham (**593-4**).

It was the task of the serjeant or bailiff of each area to choose two leading men from its inhabitants, who in turn were to select the rest of the jurors. The juries were usually twelve strong, but the smaller communities of King's Barton and Longbridge Deverill had only six each, while Rowde was represented by eight. The only formal qualification for election was to be 'free and law-abiding', but Rowde, where the jury was described as

14   *Wiltshire crown pleas, 1249*, 23.

15   *ib.*, 13-14, 17.

16   J.S. Brewer and C.T. Martin (eds.), *Registrum Malmesburiense: the register of Malmesbury Abbey*, 2 vols. (Rolls Series, 1879-80), ii, 361.

17   *Wiltshire crown pleas, 1249* no. 98.

consisting of 'three free men and four men and the reeve', may have departed from this rule – the office of reeve was one commonly performed by villeins, and the four men who accompanied him at the eyre probably shared his status, explaining their differentiation from the free men. The requirement that jurors should be law-abiding was taken seriously, and the electors of the Branch hundred jury who chose a man accused of robbery were penalised for doing so (**334**). It was not unknown for men to secure election to a jury in the hope of influencing its verdict. In 1249 John of Netheravon contrived to be chosen a juror for Elstub hundred so that he could speak up for his son Stacey, who was accused of battery and robbery,[18] and it may have been for a similar reason that in 1268 William de Bacham, a clerk, intruded himself among the Dole jurors, although he had not taken the requisite juror's oath (**341, 348**). But in ordinary circumstances nomination to a jury was no more invariably welcome in the thirteenth century than it is today, and Richard of Woodborough, selected for the Damerham jury, let it be known that he did not wish to serve and did not come to the eyre. He was therefore put in mercy – in modern parlance, fined (**90**).

Presentments, indictments and trials

Richard was one of the few jurors whose name was recorded, because the kalendar listing the juries has not survived. Had he attended as required, he and his associates would have had two principal tasks to perform before proceedings began. The first was to prepare, within a limited time (in 1289 the Dunworth jurors were amerced for taking ten days to do this),[19] answers to a set of questions embodied in articles handed to them by the justices, the so-called *Capitula Itineris*. These have been studied in detail by Helen Cam and C.A.F. Meekings, and it is unnecessary to reproduce all their findings.[20] By 1268 there were about sixty articles, but the Wiltshire juries did not return answers to all of them, and several had become effectively obsolete. Consequently only the articles to which they did respond in 1268 are given here, along with references to the relevant cases among the pleas of the crown and the numbers given to them in Cam's list.

> 1 Of old crown pleas, pleas begun at the previous eyre but not completed there. No presentments as such, only the New Salisbury jury is recorded as making a formal statement that it had nothing to report under this heading. **601**. (Cam no. 1)
>
> 2 Of new crown pleas, crown pleas that have occurred since the previous eyre. A very high proportion of the eyre's criminal business will have originated in presentments under this heading, which, however, is only once referred to, again by the New Salisbury jury, no doubt because its relevance was otherwise taken for granted. **602**. (Cam no. 2)
>
> 3 Of ladies in the king's gift, and whether they are marriageable, or married.

18 *Wiltshire crown pleas, 1249* no. 240

19 JUST 1/1011 m. 54d.

20 Cam, *Studies in the Hundred Rolls*, especially 92-4; *Wiltshire Crown Pleas, 1249*, 27-33.

The right to dispose of the hands in marriage of the daughters or widows of tenants-in-chief (landowners holding directly of the crown) was a valuable instrument of royal patronage. **214, 382.** (Cam no. 5)

4 Of churches. The king held the advowsons of numerous churches, which were particularly useful for rewarding the services of the many royal agents who were clerics. **33, 36, 134, 343, 495.** (Cam no. 6)

5 Of escheats. Escheats were lands which had become available to the king by the death or forfeiture of tenants-in-chief, and were thus available for exploitation or redistribution by him. **73, 496.** (Cam no. 7)

6 Of serjeanties. Serjeanties in this context were lands granted in return for the performance of particular services to the king, sometimes military but more often administrative or domestic, which were sometimes commuted for money payments. The presence in Wiltshire of several forests and a number of royal palaces and castles made serjeanties numerous there. **29, 37, 52, 64, 140, 157, 258, 278, 304, 335, 344, 384, 414, 435.** (Cam no. 8)

7 Of purprestures. A purpresture was an encroachment on the rights or lands of the crown. The justices were expected either to recover them, if they were found to be detrimental to the interests of the king, or indeed of anyone else, or to fix a rent for them, payable in future to the crown, if they were not. **135, 212, 279, 449.** (Cam no. 9)

8 Of infringements of the assize of cloth. An assize, or ordinance, issued in 1196 and confirmed in 1215 by Magna Carta clause 35, had stipulated that no cloth should be sold that was not two yards in width. **484, 498, 620.** (Cam no. 11)

9 Of infringements of the assize of wine. Regulations for the sale of wine were periodically issued. In 1243 it was declared that in the ports at which it was landed French wine should not cost more than 6*d.* per sester (defined in the late thirteenth century as four gallons),[21] and wine from other countries more than 8*d.* In 1223 it had been allowed that more could be charged in inland towns (Marlborough and Cricklade were among those named) to cover the cost of transport,[22] but this concession does not appear to have been repeated later. **32, 69, 222, 280, 286, 297, 422, 485, 497, 579, 621.** (Cam no. 12)

10 Of forgers and clippers of money. Outside a very few highly privileged areas, only the king had the right to issue coins, and the preservation of their integrity was fundamental to his authority. **509, 619.** (Cam no. 19)

11 Of malefactors, burglars and those who harbour them in peacetime. The substance of this article was often subsumed within no. 2, new crown pleas, and presentments under it were uncommon, but **261** may be an example. (Cam no. 21)

12 Of markets shifted from one day to another, or newly introduced, in either case without royal licence. Numerous markets were held by prescription, as existing from time immemorial. By the thirteenth century a royal charter was required for a new market, not least in order to prevent its establishment proving detrimental to existing ones in its neighbourhood – a distance of just under

21   *CR 1242-1247*, 104.

22   T.D. Hardy (ed.), *Rotuli litterarum clausarum i: 1204-1224* (Record Commission, 1833), 563-4.

seven miles was usually regarded as needed to prevent injurious competition.[23] **31, 390, 502**. (Cam no. 24)

13 Of new customs. An article designed to protect the king's subjects from misgovernment, it was used at many eyres to complain of innovations which entailed financial exactions even when they were not overtly extortionate. **147** and **285** may be examples. (Cam no. 27)

14 Of defaults by those summoned to the first day of the eyre who did not come A wide range of people were summoned to attend the eyre, including all the freeholders in the county and representatives of every township, but not all did so. Magnates with estates in several counties might obtain royal writs granting them exemption from attendance, but many men and women, of all ranks, and also some communities, simply did not trouble to come, finding payment of the modest amercements imposed for their defaults less inconvenient that the journeys required to avoid them. Presentments under this article are consequently very numerous. **28, 53, 63, 65, 72, 87, 97, 104, 128, 158, 172, 186, 200, 211, 248, 257, 274, 298, 305, 312, 317, 324, 336, 342, 361, 383, 397, 415, 423, 436, 453, 475, 518, 528, 535, 540, 571**. (Cam no. 28)

15 Of those who hold pleas involving approvers without warrant. The approver was the medieval equivalent of queen's evidence, and the right to hold proceedings arising from his accusations was very largely a royal monopoly. **426** may be a presentment under this article. (Cam no.30)

16 Of escapes by thieves. An article intended to seek out and punish shortcomings in a crucial area of local law enforcement, and perhaps also to ensure that the usual penalty imposed for escapes from custody, a £5 amercement, was duly demanded and paid. Escapes were commonplace, from both the county gaol and the stocks maintained by townships., and several presentments were made under this article. **88, 136, 284, 313, 367, 377, 490, 593, 625**. (Cam no. 32)

17 Of those who do not allow the king's bailiffs to enter their lands to make distraints. The taking of distraints to enforce payment of debts or compliance with instructions was one of the most resented activities of the agents of royal government, not least because those affected could expect difficulties in recovering what was taken (most often livestock), and was often resisted. **19, 142, 454, 580**. (Cam no. 35)

18 Of those who have withdrawn suits from public courts. Every court had its suitors – landholders and representatives of communities who were required to attend it in order to make presentments, give judgments, and by their presence maintain the authority and prestige of the assembly. Suit could be shirked as burdensome, however, while powerful lords were apt to reinforce the standing of their own courts at the expense of the king's by preventing their tenants from attending the latter, and particularly the courts of those hundreds over which the crown still possessed lordship. (The recovery of suit to the many hundreds which had passed into private hands was the responsibility of their lords, who

23   C. Dyer, *Making a living in the middle ages: the people of Britain, 850-1520* (New Haven and London, 2002), 191.

could bring a civil action for the purpose.) **132, 143, 159, 173, 249, 299, 320, 346, 425, 455, 588, 591**. (Cam no. 38)

19 Of those who hold pleas of replevin. Replevin (also known as *vee de naam*) arose from the processes of distraint. The distrainee who offered security ('gage and pledge') for the performance of the duty or payment of the debt for which his goods had been taken was entitled to recover them, and by the action of replevin to sue the distrainor who refused to surrender them. Only the greatest lords claimed the right to hear such cases, which were otherwise strictly reserved to the royal courts. **86, 143**. (Cam no. 39)

20 Of officials who have taken bribes from squires for not compelling them to become knights. By the mid-thirteenth century there was a perceived shortage of knights, who were needed for administrative as well as military purposes, and from 1242 men aged twenty-one and over who possessed either a whole knight's fee (the estate thought sufficient to maintain a knight) or lands worth at least £20 were liable to be distrained to become knights. Some paid fines to the crown to avoid, this, others gave bribes to be left alone to local officials, who might also solicit them. **287**. (Cam no. 40)

21 Of squires who have not become knights. The corollary of the previous article, inquiring as to landowners who had qualified for knighthood but had not become knights. **281, 347, 578**. (Cam no. 41)

22 Of those who fish with kiddle-nets. A kiddle-net was a weir built across a river with a gap in the middle fitted with nets. Resented for obstructing navigation, and probably also for reducing the number of fish available to poor people, the device was formally prohibited in Magna Carta clause 33 (23 in later reissues). **282**. (Cam no. 51)

23 Of officials who take bribes for releasing suspected killers to pledges. People arrested and imprisoned for homicide should not have been released to pledges except on the authority of a royal writ, whereas those charged with lesser offences could be released on finding sureties willing to guarantee their subsequent appearance in court. There are numerous cases of officials who took money for releasing suspects to pledges, either out of greed or to relieve pressure on prison-space. **213**, perhaps **360**. (Cam no. 52)

24 Of officials who have arrested suspected thieves and taken bribes to release them. Like the previous article, directed against misuse of powers of arrest and imprisonment. **575**. (Cam no. 53)

25 Of mainpernors who undertook to produce people at the beginning of the eyre and failed to do so. Mainpernors were sureties who had guaranteed, or mainprised, to produce in court men and women whose alleged offences did not require their detention in prison. This article, like its two predecessors, was concerned to tighten up procedure relating to imprisonment and bail. **623**. (Cam no. 55)

As well as compiling the documents, known as *veredicta*, which recorded their answers to the articles of the eyre, the jurors were also required to indict, to make secret accusations against, the men and women whom they suspected of serious crimes, so that they could be arrested. They did so by drawing up lists of names, usually known as *privata*, which were submitted to the justices and then passed on to the sheriff.[24] It was this process which Richard of Chiseldon described in 1281, when he complained that two members of the Thornhill jury had indicted him by means of 'schedules' which they submitted to Richard of Boyland, one of the justices, accusing him of 'extortions and robberies' for which he would have suffered loss of life and members had he been convicted.[25] Indictments did not necessarily originate with the jurors. They received accusations from many sources – two women are named in a single entry as having made indictments of homicide which must then have been passed on by the Marlborough jury, leading to the arrest of the three men accused (**493**) - and when suspects came into court the charges against them often turned out to have stemmed from malice or even rumour; Roger le Parmenter of Amesbury was suspected of killing Robert Cod because the two men had once quarrelled, though in the end it was found that Robert had died a natural death (**8**).

Roger had run away to avoid arrest. Suspects who came into court were asked how they wanted to be acquitted, and at this eyre they invariably opted for jury trial (clerics put up a show of resistance to being tried in a secular court, but were nevertheless required to submit to a jury's verdict). This usually meant trial by the presenting jury, probably augmented by representatives of the four townships nearest to the scene of the crime, but in several cases the seriousness of the alleged offence or the status of the suspects led to larger juries being convoked. Thus three juries acquitted William Scut, who had been charged with harbouring his son, a thief, and also revealed that the indictment had originated in malice (**202**), while for the trial of the many men accused of killing John de Cumbe in Quidhampton in 1261, the Branch jurors were joined by the whole of the Cawdon jury, eight men from each of the Cadworth and Dole juries, and representatives of the townships of Fisherton, Bemerton, Ditchampton and Harnham, 'with each township being carefully examined by itself ...' (**327**). As this case and others show, the justices were not always silent observers of proceedings, but could become actively involved in efforts to discover the truth about what was presented before them. Thus the Whorwellsdown jury was asked which bishop a clerical killer had been handed over to (**292**), while the Chippenham jurors who had presented the accidental killing of one nine-year-old boy by another were asked 'if there was any discord between them', and replied that there was not (**568**). When the Selkley jury presented the killing of Thomas le Forester, they must have done so in a way which made the justices feel the need for further information, as a result of which the jurors were brought to describe how the two suspects had encountered Thomas in the act of burglary and killed him in self-defence (**114**). It was probably questioning by the justices which led to the disclosure that two men acquitted of killing Thomas Costard had nonetheless been involved in the dispute which lay behind the deed (**431**). The repetitive formulae of the eyre roll cannot entirely conceal the extent to which the proceedings they record involved challenges, questions and exchanges.

24   *Wiltshire crown pleas, 1249*, 92-8.
25   JUST 1/1005/2 m.161d.

Wiltshire in 1268

The county in which the justices held their sessions in 1268 was, and is, entirely land-locked, placed between Berkshire to the east, Gloucestershire and Oxfordshire to the north, Somerset to the west, and Dorset and Hampshire to the south, but with easy access to the ports of London, Southampton and Bristol.[26] The county was moderately prosperous at the time of Domesday Book, and its population grew and the area under cultivation expanded, especially in the twelfth century but continuing thereafter – the process may well have reached its apogee around the time of the 1268 eyre, helped by favourable climatic conditions (vineyards were recorded at Seend and Stert on either side of 1300).[27] Although the spread of cultivation was theoretically inhibited by a ring of royal forests along the county's boundaries, these were coming under steady pressure from both lords and peasants seeking to bring more land into agricultural use, and alike inside and outside the forests the landscape had come to have a mostly well-settled look; the grant of forty acres of woodland in Melksham forest to Lacock Abbey in 1260, for instance, did not define it in terms of trees and clearings, as one might have expected, but of hedges and ditches.[28]

The landscape of medieval Wiltshire was one of considerable variety, but although exceptions can be found to every generalisation, in terms of economic usage it can be divided into two basic types. South and east of a line following, and continuing, the vale of Pewsey, the terrain was dominated by chalk downlands intersected by rivers, creating a countryside of nucleated villages practising what has been characterised as a 'sheep-and-corn' economy. Seen in the context of their surrounding territories, such villages often had a long and narrow profile, resulting from their being commonly sited in river valleys, along with their valuable hay-producing meadows; above them on the lower slopes of both the flanking hillsides stretched their common fields, which in turn gave way to downland pasture, rough grazing for sheep and cattle. The north and west of the county, by contrast, was dominated by low-lying expanses of clayland which were hard to drain, and so were better suited to dairy farming than to the cultivation of arable. Communities were smaller and more scattered in this half of the county than in the other, and there was more woodland. This is not to say that arable farming was never practised there. In fact crops were grown wherever suitable ground could be found, or even where it could be created, by the making of lynchets, artificial terraces set into the sides of hills.[29]

26   For the county in general I have relied particularly on *VCH Wiltshire, passim*; J.H. Bettey, *Wessex from A.D. 1000* (1986); J. Chandler, *Devizes and central Wiltshire* (East Knoyle, 2003); *ib.*, *Marlborough and eastern Wiltshire* (East Knoyle, 2001); M. Aston and C. Lewis (eds.), *The medieval landscapes of Wessex* (Oxbow monograph 46, Oxford, 1994).

27   Chandler, *Devizes and central Wiltshire*, 200, 209.

28   K.H. Rogers (ed.), *Lacock Abbey charters* (Wiltshire Record Society 34, 1979 for 1978) no. 22.

29   Bettey, *Wessex from A.D. 1000*, 46. But see also A. Reynolds, 'The Compton

Arable farming, in fact, provided the essential subsistence of the county, but its wealth came above all from sheep. The county magnates, lay and ecclesiastical, owned large flocks, but so did humbler people, and those of the townships often outnumbered those of their lords.[30] Pasture might be plentiful, but such was the demand for it that care had to be taken not to overburden it – in 1243 it was found that a hide of land (roughly 120 acres) in Christian Malford could not be expected to support more than sixteen oxen, four cows, two stots, fifty sheep and six pigs[31] – and access to it might be bitterly disputed. Robert of Earlscourt, acquitted at the eyre of killing William Wykeman (**362**), was found in 1262 to have been maliciously indicted by the bishop of Winchester's men of Little Hinton as a result of a dispute over pasture rights which had lasted for eleven years.[32] Sheep were prized above all for their wool, but they were also valued for their meat, and for their manure, which was particularly prized on chalkland soils which were easily cultivated but needed constant re-fertilising. To ensure that their manure went where it was needed they were often confined in moveable pens made of hurdles – the death of ten-year-old Adam son of Robert, killed when a hurdle fell on him in a gale, doubtless occurred in one of these contraptions (**355**).

The wool of Wiltshire's sheep made a substantial contribution to the county's economy. Much of it will have been exported, but it also supplied the raw material for a developing cloth industry which presumably afforded a livelihood to men like Peter le Tuckere, a fuller on the evidence of his name (**589**), Adam le Burler, a maker of coarse burrel cloth (**189**), and Walter the weaver of Lydiard (**404**). Agriculture in all its forms prospered sufficiently to maintain a growing population, which itself furthered economic growth. Twenty-four new place-names were recorded between 1190 and 1280,[33] while forty-three places of varying size received grants of markets and fairs, separately or together, between 1199 and 1268, some of them complementing or replacing ancient prescriptive rights but most of them for the first time.[34] Providing additional opportunities for exchanges of produce – the mid-thirteenth-century custumal of Brixton Deverill, in south-west Wiltshire, recorded the tolls which the lord was entitled to take from the serfs when they sold oxen and horses, 'excepting at a fair'[35] - the geographical spread of these grants was wide. Most were in the south and west of the county, but the

Bassett (Calne) area research project – first interim report', *University of London Institute of Archaeology Bulletin* xxxi (1994), 169-98, at 180-5.

30   *VCH Wiltshire* iv, 18-21, 28-9.

31   A. Watkin (ed.), *The great cartulary of Glastonbury* iii (Somerset Record Society 64, 1956), 667-8.

32   C 144/5 no. 32.

33   H.E. Hallam (ed.), *The agrarian history of England and Wales ii: 1042-1350* (Cambridge, 1988), 212-17.

34   Samantha Letters, *Online Gazetteer of Markets and Fairs, England and Wales to 1516*, http://www.historyac.uk/cmh/gaz/gazweb2.html>:[Wiltshire] (last updated 15 July 1210).

35   J.R. Pierrepont, 'The manor of Brixton Deverill: a custumal and an extent of

beneficiaries also included such places as Sherston and West Kington in the north west, Hannington in the north, Great Bedwyn near Wiltshire's eastern border, Chitterne and Tilshead on the central expanses of Salisbury Plain, and even Fifield Bavant, near the county's border with Dorset. The same forces must have been a reason for the extension or rebuilding of a number of churches during the thirteenth century, for instance at Ashton Keynes in the north of the county, Baydon in the east, Chilmark in the south-west, Heddington and Yatesbury on the edge of the Marlborough Downs, and Figheldean and Milton Lilbourne on Salisbury Plain.[36]

The growing prosperity, it hardly needs saying, was not universally shared. The enlarged churches still exist, but some communities which came into being under the pressure of population growth failed to survive the economic down-turn of the later middle ages, for instance one at Wroughton Copse on Fyfield Down, which seems to have lasted for little more than a hundred years in the thirteenth and early fourteenth centuries.[37] Not every community granted a market or fair prospered as a result, indeed, some charters simply triggered off disputes with neighbouring townships, resentful of competition (**31, 502**). Stone bridges improved communications wherever they were built – the prosperity of Salisbury owed much to one which Bishop Bingham laid across the Avon at Harnham in 1244[38] – but some rivers could still only be crossed on planks (**512**), or at fords (**96, 295**), in either case at some risk. At the 1281 eyre it was reported that Richard of Lambourne had drowned in the Avon near Patney when he fell from a wooden bridge 'because it moved'. Its value was assessed at just 6*d*.[39] The examination of human remains from a cemetery in Trowbridge led to the conclusion that in the eleventh century, at least, the available food supply was sufficient to feed the existing population of Wiltshire.[40] That may have remained the case in the thirteenth century, but there were certainly some who drew no benefit from the existing resources, like the unknown man whose body was found near Uffcott, where he had died of hunger and cold (**187**).

That wretched stranger was one of the very lowest members of a profoundly hierarchical society, one represented, moreover, in all its ranks among the 1268 crown pleas, from Henry III downwards. Mainly through his

the thirteenth century', *Wiltshire Archaeological and Natural History Magazine* 78 (1984), 55-61, at 57-8.

36   I have used *VCH Wiltshire, passim*; J. Chandler and D. Parker, *The church in Wiltshire* (East Knoyle); N. Pevsner and B. Cherry, *The buildings of England: Wiltshire* (2nd. edition, Harmondsworth, 1975).

37   H.C. Bowen and P.J. Fowler, 'The archaeology of Fyfield and Overton Downs, Wiltshire', *Wiltshire Archaeological and Natural History Magazine* 58 (1963), 98-115; C. Taylor, *Village and farmstead: a history of rural settlement in England* (1983), 195

38   Bettey, *Wessex from A.D. 1000*, 58-9.

39   JUST 1/1005/2 m. 144d.

40   D.A. Hinton, 'The archaeology of eighth- to eleventh-century Wessex', M. Aston and C. Lewis (eds.), *The medieval landscapes of Wessex* (Oxbow monograph 46, Oxford, 1994), 33-46, at 42.

possession of several residences in Wiltshire, Henry was in a position to have a
greater impact there than in most other parts of his realm. Not only was he a
great landowner in the county, and the lord of eleven and a half hundreds, but
he was also a frequent visitor to Clarendon Palace and Marlborough Castle,
who spent large amounts of money, and provided a good deal of employment,
on works at both (he also spent smaller but still significant sums on Devizes
and Ludgershall castles), while his outlay on food, drink and all the other
amenities of residence was also considerable.[41] Business and pleasure alike will
have attracted people to his court – the king of France's messenger, allegedly
robbed of his strong-box in Marlborough, must have been unusual only in
the eminence of his employer (**492**). Henry III was a generous benefactor to
the church, who was lavish in his support for Amesbury and Marlborough
Priories,[42] and above all for the building of the new cathedral at Salisbury, to
which he contributed 'bountifully' and which was dedicated in his presence
on 30 September 1258.[43] And he did not forget his obligations to the poor, to
whom he made regular distributions of alms – in 1245 he ordered the sheriff
of Wiltshire to make 'a penthouse for the poor' along the wall inside the
great gate of Clarendon Palace, presumably to give them shelter while they
waited for a royal hand-out.[44] When around the end of 1260 Bishop Bridport
transmitted to the religious houses of his diocese the king's request for prayers
for the safe delivery of his daughter Margaret, then near to childbirth, and 'for
the peace of holy church and of our realm',[45] it is easy to imagine a fervent
response, and perhaps not only within conventual walls.

The king's position in the county was further strengthened by his ability
to grant lands and favours to members of his family like Queen Eleanor (**7**),
his brother Richard (**544**) and his half-brother William de Valence (**588**), and
to courtiers like Mathias Bezill (**541**). Of the magnates of the county, the
greatest under the crown was arguably the bishop, alike as a major landowner
and by virtue of his office. Both Giles of Bridport and his successor, Walter
de la Wyle, probably also enjoyed the respect that came from their being
active resident diocesans, who had, moreover, been elected without the king's
interference (unlike Bridport's predecessor William of York, a former royal
justice, whose election Henry III was reported to have secured by threatening
to force the canons to move their cathedral back to its original site).[46] Whether
those monasteries and nunneries which were either situated in Wiltshire or

41   For the king's residences and castles see A. Richardson, *The forest, park and palace
     of Clarendon, c. 1200-c. 1650* (British Archaeological Reports, British series,
     387, 2005), T.B. James and A.M. Robinson, *Clarendon Palace* (Reports of the
     Society of Antiquaries of London 45, 1988); R.A. Brown, H.M. Colvin and
     A.J. Taylor, *The history of the king's works: the middle ages*, 2 vols. (1963).

42   *VCH Wiltshire* iii, 244-6, 316-17.

43   Matthew Paris, *Chronica majora*, ed. H.R. Luard, 7 vols. (Rolls Series, 1872-
     1883), iii, 189-90; v, 719.

44   *CLR 1240-1245*, 291.

45   *EEA, Salisbury* no. 184.

46   Matthew Paris, *Historia Anglorum* ed. H.R. Luard, 3 vols. (Rolls Series, 1866-9),
     iii, 14.

had important estates there, like Shaftesbury and Glastonbury Abbeys, were similarly well-regarded it is hard to say. Their status as religious did not protect two Shaftesbury nuns against highway robbery (**521**), or prevent the prior of Ivychurch from being accused of homicide (**327**). But like the king, the county's religious houses were influential in ways which went beyond their ostensible function, as lords of lands and men, and as employers of labour – the nuns of Lacock, for instance, needed 'a small army' of servants to run their house and its property.[47]

Among secular magnates, by far the most powerful was Gilbert de Clare, earl of Gloucester and Hertford, fully the inheritor of the 'might' which made his father a usurper of royal rights (**249**). In Wiltshire the earl and his officers made a determined effort to extend his chase of Cranborne northwards, 'so that whatever is in Wiltshire from the boundaries of Dorset to the river Nadder he claims is his forest.'[48] In support of these claims Gilbert's foresters were alleged to have taken unwarranted tolls from men crossing Harnham bridge just outside Salisbury, and even to have seized one John Hoyhod at Martin, on the border between Hampshire and Wiltshire, and carried him back to Cranborne, where they hanged him, 'without any cause', subsequently making a series of raids into Wiltshire in pursuit of John's chattels.[49] But the earl's principal interests lay elsewhere, and the same was true of some of the other barons who had estates in Wiltshire, for instance Walter de Dunstanville and Robert Tregoz. The lords of manors, and fractions of manors, could be men of significant influence in Wiltshire, either as landowners or as the sheriffs, coroners, justices and tax-collectors who did so much of the king's business there, but neither they nor anyone else, singly or together, constituted an effective rival to the authority of King Henry within the county.

The king's government

Every lord had a part to play in the maintenance of peace and order. The king's own role was largely symbolic, in that it was his peace which was upheld, but he could become directly involved, in his own omni-competent *coram rege* court, which could be constituted wherever he happened to be. It must have been in this court that the appeal of robbery against Walter Escamel or Scammel, a royal clerk who became bishop of Salisbury in 1284, and many others was concluded *coram domino rege* (**167**), and here, too, that shortly after the 1268 eyre a suspected robber was brought before King Henry in person, to be acquitted by the same jurors who had just indicted him – Henry was so angry that he imposed a £5 amercement on them. As this second case shows, the king's traditional duties were not yet ones from which elements of personality could be entirely excluded – hence also the pardon granted to an outlawed killer at Henry's daughter's request (**23**) – but by the mid-thirteenth century they were largely mediated through the government which functioned in his name.

47   Bettey, *Wessex from A.D. 1000*, 73.

48   E 163/2/30A m. 3d.

49   *Rot. Hund.* ii, 243, 249, 253; JUST 1/1005/2 m. 148d.

As far as peace-keeping was concerned, there were several ways in which the king's government at Westminster could impinge on a county like Wiltshire, of which the eyre was only one. Actions could be removed by royal writ into the central courts (**12, 494**), and commissioners could be appointed to inquire into difficult cases, for instance the killing of Roger le Schyreve (**266**). There was now a standardised procedure for obtaining grants of bail and pardons in cases of homicide, so that the former could be made if an accusation was shown by a formal inquest to have been ill-founded or malicious, the latter if the deed was found to have been accidental or committed in self-defence.[50] Eyres were held only at extended intervals, but justices – usually local men, sometimes with administrative experience as sheriffs or coroners - were much more often appointed to deliver the county's gaols. A number of townships are recorded as having had lock-ups, but these rarely seem to have been more than a pair of stocks, so that it was advisable to transfer suspects to more secure custody as soon as possible. Wiltshire's county gaol was at Salisbury, in the old castle above the new city, which in fact contained two prisons, one inside the main structure and the other probably in the outer bailey.[51] There are also thirteenth-century references to royal gaols at Marlborough, Mildenhall, Wilton and Ludgershall,[52] but except for a single commission for Marlborough, all the commissions of gaol delivery issued during the period covered by the eyre were for Salisbury, so presumably prisoners from other gaols, like those held in village stocks, ended up being taken there for safe-keeping and eventual trial. In fact transferring prisoners from one gaol to another was a far from simple matter (**487**), and keeping them in Salisbury castle once they were there was not easy either. A number of escapes from it were recorded in 1268, one of them by four men who killed the gaoler first (**57, 61, 136, 349, 593**)

Gaols in thirteenth-century England were essentially places where men and women awaited trial, custodial sentences for lesser offences were limited to convicted poachers. Badly-maintained buildings, and the likely temper of inmates facing the prospect of hanging, combined to make medieval gaols insecure, along with the fact that prisoners were maintained from outside, either by charity – in 1275 a desperate thief tried to borrow 6d. from his former employer for his sustenance, and accused him of homicide when he refused[53] – or by kinsfolk and associates bringing them food and drink. In 1287 a mass break-out resulted when a man bringing victuals to his brother, a prisoner in Salisbury Castle, contrived to make the gaolers drunk and incapable, after which the two men killed their keepers and fled with some twenty other inmates, though most of them were later rounded up by the

50 *Wiltshire crown pleas, 1249*, 47-8; R.B. Pugh, *Imprisonment in medieval England* (Cambridge, 1968), 204-5.

51 *VCH Wiltshire* vi, 59.

52 Pugh, *Imprisonment in medieval England*, 83-4, 268 (Salisbury, Marlborough and Wilton); *CR 1264-1268*, 69, 421 (Mildenhall and Ludgershall). Ludgershall gaol is also referred to in no. **625**.

53 C 144/14 no. 57

sheriff.[54] Pressure on space and a desire to prevent escapes together made it highly desirable that prisons should be cleared of their occupants at regular intervals. That they were so cleared is attested by the twenty-two hangings, one burning, one conviction of a cleric[55] and nine acquittals which were specifically attributed to gaol deliveries at the 1268 eyre.

Passing references to executions and acquittals give no idea how many sessions were involved, and it is impossible to be certain how often any gaol was delivered – commissions, as enrolled, are seldom dated, and some may be duplicates. In Wiltshire the 1256 eyre probably left the county gaol with few or no occupants, and perhaps it was slow to fill up again, for no gaol delivery was commissioned until around May 1257.[56] Two commissions were issued during 1258, one in 1259, two in 1260 and one in 1261. None have been noticed for 1262, and something of a crisis may have resulted, for not only was a commission issued in January 1263, but it was followed by another barely a month later, and then by a third in May. The next delivery would appear to have been ordered around the end of the year, its successor in July 1264. In 1265 commissions for Salisbury and Marlborough (to a single justice) were issued in January and February respectively, but only around the beginning of December was another gaol delivery arranged for Salisbury, for which a single commission was also issued in each of 1266 and 1267.[57] When the justices came to Wiltshire in January 1268 the county gaol may well have been uncomfortably full of prisoners.

The sheriff and his staff

In the context of county administration, the royal gaols were among the many responsibilities of the sheriff, the king's principal officer in the administration of the shire. The sheriff's activities were never likely to make him popular, but in the mid-thirteenth century he became controversial as well, the target of complaints for extortions and malpractices. In the reforming legislation of the baronial government of the late 1250s it was ordained that he must be a local man, who should not retain his place for more than a year, and was not to hold it on terms which made him little more than an agent of fiscal oppression on behalf of the exchequer.[58] In fact Wiltshire may have suffered less than other counties from the central government's determination to maximise its revenues.[59] John de Vernun, who had been sheriff at the time of the 1256

---

54   JUST 1/1011 m. 63.

55   There may have been two more, but the record of no. **506** does not say if the accused were convicted or not.

56   C 66/71 m. 11d.

57   Details of gaol delivery commissions have been taken from C 66/72 mm. 9d, 14d (1257/8); C 66/73 mm. 2d, 13d (1258/9); C 66/74 m. 12d (1259/60); C 66/76 m. 6d (1260/1); C 66/77 mm. 2, 2d, 13d (1261-3); C 66/81 mm. 8d, 20d (1263/4); C 66/83 mm. 23d, 27d (1264/5); C 66/84 mm. 16d, 44d (1265/6); C 66/85 m. 21d (1266/7).

58   *Documents of the baronial movement*, 108-9.

59   The brief account of the sheriffs of Wiltshire which follows is heavily indebted to *VCH Wiltshire* v, 10-12.

eyre, was a landholder in the county who had also held a number of lesser offices there, and must have been just the sort of man the barons looked for to administer the shires. As the new policy dictated, he was replaced late in 1258 by Godfrey de Scudamore, a man of similar background, but was reappointed as sheriff a year later, a sure sign that he was acceptable to the county and *persona grata* to the central government. Indeed, in the king's eyes Vernun probably came to seem insufficiently royalist, for when Henry III regained lost authority in July 1261 and ordered a general replacement of sheriffs, the shrievalty of Wiltshire was entrusted to Ralph Russel, also a landowner in the county, though his principal interests lay in Somerset. At Midsummer 1264, following the battle of Lewes, a further replacement of sheriffs led to Russel being in his turn superseded by Ralph de Aungers, another local man with administrative experience – he was nominated to almost every Wiltshire gaol delivery commission between February 1258 and the end of 1263 – who can hardly have been a diehard Montfortian, since he remained sheriff after the battle of Evesham, and died in office around the end of February 1266, when his place was briefly occupied by his son John.[60] Appointments were now back in the hands of the crown, but there was little obvious change in the sort of men chosen to administer Wiltshire. At Easter the same year Henry de Montfort, one of the justices in 1268, became sheriff, and served for a whole year, before giving way to Richard of Worcester, a rare example, as his name implies, of an outsider to the county. But Richard only served for six months, and his successor, William le Dun, appointed in November 1267 and sheriff until May 1270, was another local man, with property at West Harnham. In April 1267 Dun, Worcester and Montfort were all nominated to a commission to deliver Salisbury castle gaol.[61]

The fact that the 1268 crown pleas have relatively little to say about these men and their subordinates may indicate that on the whole they carried out their work at a reasonable level of efficiency and honesty. It is not surprising that jurors should not have criticised William le Dun, since as the man in office he could have been a dangerous enemy, and on later occasions he was charged with unspecified extortion and with bilking labourers at Clarendon Palace of their wages.[62] But although there was nothing to be gained by concealing the failings of John de Vernun and Ralph de Aungers, who had both died before the eyre, very little was said to their discredit, or, indeed, to that of any sheriff. In other shires complaints of dishonesty and abuse of office constitute a valuable source for the activities of sheriffs and their underlings, but without them it is often hard to tell what these men did. As far as sheriffs were concerned, the crown pleas contain numerous references to their responsibility for the financial issues of the eyre, above all for the money due from criminals' chattels. But how far they involved themselves in day-by-day police activities is unclear. There is record of one (unnamed) sheriff investigating a man's death, or trying to (**227**), and arrested suspects were twice said to have been delivered into the custody of John de Vernun

60   *CPR 1258-1266*, 565.

61   C 66/85 m. 21d.

62   *Rot. Hund.* ii, 243, 276, 280; JUST 1/1005/2 m. 147d.

(240, 242). But the fact that more is reported of their subordinates probably indicates that these men did most of the work.

The number of officials active in the county probably grew as the thirteenth century progressed, perhaps as an inevitable response to the rise in population and spread of settlement. In 1281 it was a matter for complaint in Chippenham hundred that whereas its lord formerly employed only two beadles who made their rounds on foot, now they went on horseback, with three servants in attendance, which 'overburdened the country to its great loss'.[63] By then Calne hundred had acquired a catchpoll, who made himself offensive by extorting money from poor people.[64] Such men might face resistance when they tried to collect money due either to the sheriff or to the king, or take distraints, or make arrests, understandably, since all were processes unpopular in themselves and also liable to abuse (19, 142, 249, 454, 580). People feared imprisonment, and in order to avoid it they were willing to give bribes to the men who controlled it. Thus Martin of Leigh, deputising for Ralph Russel as his undersheriff, was said to have taken half a mark apiece from three men, allegedly harbourers of thieves, for leaving them in peace (66). Every hundred had its bailiff, with responsibilities for peace-keeping. The unnamed bailiff of Knoyle was only doing his job when he held an inquest into a burglary in his hundred at which Henry the smith and William le Flemenge were indicted – William was subsequently hanged (519). But others exploited their office for personal gain. John le Pek, bailiff of Kingsbridge, was found to have taken 10s. from three suspected killers for releasing them to bail, though having received the money he then kept them in prison until the next gaol delivery (213). Robert Stoket, the bailiff of Chippenham hundred, was charged with arresting the mother of a suspected thief and keeping her a prisoner in his own house in Chippenham until she gave him cattle and sheep worth a total of 21s. to be released, an accusation he could not deny (575). He seems to have been a man of bad reputation. Accused of homicide at the eyre, he was acquitted, though a man said to have associated with him in the deed was hanged (576), but in 1281 Robert was less fortunate. Charged with another killing, this time he was convicted and hanged, while his wife fled to Chippenham church and abjured the realm for homicide and harbouring thieves.[65]

The sheriff had a clerk as well as bailiffs, in fact he probably had more than one. When they presented their accounts at Westminster for the county's revenues, several successive sheriffs were represented by John of Upton, who as their clerk answered for them to the exchequer almost continuously from 1263 until at least 1271.[66] As sheriffs came and went, John of Upton must have represented continuity in the fiscal administration of the county. But individual sheriffs seem also to have had their own clerks to act with and for them. Thus Adam of Codford was said to have been John de Vernun's clerk,

63   JUST 1/1005/2 m. 135.

64   *ib.*, m. 136.

65   JUST 1/1005/2 m. 135.

66   E 159/39 mm. 8, 8d; E 159/41 m. 9d; E 159/43 mm. 13, 18; E 159/45 m. 22d; E 159/46 m. 21.

and to have misused his position to extract a total of 60s. from three men on a trumped-up charge of homicide – their alleged victim was shown to be still alive (**360**). Presumably Adam's position on the sheriff's staff gave him the authority to make arrests, or to threaten to do so.

The coroners and their responsibilities

Subordinate only to the sheriff in the administration of the county were the coroners, of whom Wiltshire had three in 1268. Eight are listed at the head of the crown pleas (**1**), but two of them were dead, a third had been removed from office, on unspecified grounds, and two others had retired. One of these last was Walerand of Blunsdon. In September 1260 order was given that a successor be chosen for Walerand because he was too frail to continue in office;[67] the position was an exacting one, and perhaps no-one could be found willing to take it (at the 1289 Wiltshire eyre one Robert de Lucy paid 40s. not to be appointed coroner),[68] for twelve months later the order had to be repeated.[69] The coroners were county landowners. To meet the demands of their unpaid office they needed resources and leisure, and also good health, since the work entailed much travelling. Not only did they have to attend the four-weekly county court at Wilton, where they kept a record of matters relating to pleas of the crown which had an authoritative status exceeding that of the court's own record, kept by the sheriff – it was to the coroners' rolls that recourse was had when the details of the elaborate action known as the appeal of felony, which was always prosecuted in the county court, needed to be checked (**327, 364**) - but a coroner's presence was also required when a felon took refuge in a church and abjured the realm (a procedure described below), and above all whenever anyone was found suddenly, violently or suspiciously dead.

When this happened, a representative of the community where the corpse was found was required to notify the nearest coroner, who before he came to the scene was expected to convoke the four nearest townships to act as the jury at the inquest he intended to hold. In the mid-thirteenth century this meant their entire adult male populations, a burdensome and arguably unnecessary requirement which aroused such resentment that in 1259 the baronial government declared that it was sufficient that 'enough men come to enable such inquests to be made properly'.[70] But the relief was short-lived, for although the Statute of Marlborough of 1267 repeated the ordinance of 1259 for inquests into felonies like robbery and arson, it excepted 'inquests concerning a man's death, when all who are twelve ought to appear unless they have reasonable cause of absence'.[71] As a result, amercements on communities for failing to come 'fully' – or even at all - to a coroner's inquest occur frequently among the 1268 crown pleas. Deciding whether or not a

---

67 *CR 1259-1261*, 120

68 JUST 1/1011 m. 57d.

69 *CR 1259-1261*, 439.

70 *Documents of the baronial movement*, 146–7

71 H. Rothwell (ed.), *English Historical Documents iii: 1189-1327* (1975), 391 (clause 24).

township had been adequate in its attendance was one of the coroner's tasks when he held his inquest.

Townships were occasionally found to have buried a dead body before it could be viewed by a coroner – the case of five-year-old Agnes daughter of Robert, drowned at Seend Head and surreptitiously buried by four neighbouring townships, is one such (**269**). It is impossible to say if such concealments were common, though they would probably have been hard to organise in the face of all the measures, discussed below, which had been devised precisely in order to uncover and publicise suspicious and unlawful actions. But even if most deaths were properly examined by the coroners, it is often hard to tell how far the local townships were involved, for it is clear from other eyre records that more accidental deaths, in particular, were discovered and investigated than were finally enrolled among the crown pleas. Where no felony was involved, deaths were only recorded when the crown's financial interests were concerned, which often meant when townships were amerced for insufficient attendance before the coroner. The death of Christian, wife of William Everard, is mentioned in a single sentence tacked on, like an afterthought, to another entry recording a man's violent death; the subject of that sentence, however, is not Christian's tragedy but the amercement imposed on Hawkeridge vill for failing to come to the inquest (**302**). Just as there were other entries in which only one or two townships were penalised for such failings (e.g. **124, 207, 296, 331**), implying that the remaining two or three had appeared as they should, so there will have been inquests into deaths by misadventure to which all came as summoned and whose findings therefore went unrecorded on the eyre roll, a consideration which needs to be set against the many cases of reported non-attendance.

When the coroner held an inquest into a death, the official and the men of the townships, whatever their number, were expected to identify the dead person (something they often could not do) and determine the cause of death. If it resulted from felony, then they were to discover the killer, if they could. In many cases this proved impossible, but failure did not necessarily result from any lack of diligence. Much will have depended on the local knowledge of the townships, their awareness of quarrels and enmities within communities. The quarrel between Gilbert le Blechere and Roger Horn, arising from a fight between their dogs which turned into a set-to between their owners, in which Gilbert knocked Roger down with his staff and was consequently accused of killing him because he died shortly afterwards, was probably common knowledge in Bodenham, where the two men came to blows (**80**). When death was not been instantaneous, neighbours must sometimes have been able to question a dying man or woman and then circulate what they learnt. The Chippenham jurors presented that one evening six unknown thieves had attacked the house of Edith of Bowden in Lacock, where they killed her daughter, mortally wounded her son and carried off the contents of the house (**550**). That unknown criminals had committed the crime it hardly needed a coroner's inquest to discover. Their number, and the time of the attack, must have been revealed by its sole survivor before he died of his injuries.

Sometimes there may have been scope for detailed examination of the circumstances of a death. Hence cases like those of Jordan son of Herbert of Shaftesbury, who was apparently deliberately dragged to his death by a tether tied round his arm (**103**), and John son of John of the wood, whose body was found to have been hung on a tree by his killer, presumably in an attempt to make his death look like suicide (**373**). But when death had been accidental, or when no killer could be identified, usually all the coroner could do was attach the first finder of the body and the four nearest neighbours to the spot where it was found – that is, arrange for them to find sureties for their future appearance at the next eyre. In cases of accidental death, the material cause – an untamed horse (**458**), for instance, or a stone falling in a quarry (**517**) – must also be secured and arrangements made for it, or its value (which was several times misrepresented at inquests, e.g. **5, 43, 192, 225**), to be produced at the eyre. Where there had been bystanders, they, too, should be attached (**170**), while anyone found to be a suspect was to be arrested and handed over to the sheriff (**240, 242**). One justification for the large attendance required at a coroner's inquest must have been the opportunity it provided for telling a whole neighbourhood about a killing and anyone suspected of it, thereby improving the chances that arrests would be made.

The same consideration applied to an abjuration, an extension of the right of sanctuary which enabled a suspect to take refuge in a church and send for a coroner, before whom he could return to the king's peace or, as usually happened, make a detailed confession of his offences and swear to leave the realm, departing within forty days from a port which the coroner prescribed. If he returned without a royal pardon his confession would be held against him, and he would be hanged. Wiltshire was prosperous and well-inhabited enough to contain many churches, and abjurations were numerous. When a fugitive entered a church, the local community had to watch over it to ensure that he stayed there. Thus the safe-keeping of Richard of Westwood, who had fled to Fittleton church, became that township's responsibility, and it was amerced when he escaped, even though he was unable to flee very far, finally taking refuge in the neighbouring church of Netheravon and abjuring the realm there (**71**). He probably made his departure before a large assembly, for it was common practice for the neighbouring four townships to be summoned to attend an abjuration, as for an inquest. The utility of, and need for, their presence is shown by a case like that of John Maheu, said to have abjured the realm in Tisbury for burgling a house in Knoyle on 2 November 1262 (**514, 520**). It is possible that he went abroad and later returned, but more likely that he left his road long before he reached the coast, and thereafter led a bandit's life in and around Knoyle. In 1281 the Knoyle jury recorded how justice eventually caught up with him, when he was arrested after a failed burglary and summarily beheaded 'as he had previously abjured the realm at Tisbury in Dunworth hundred'.[72] The record of, and publicity given to, his felony together brought him to a violent end, and always threatened to do the same for other abjurors who made an illicit return.

The Wiltshire coroners, like the sheriffs and other officials, emerged from the 1268 eyre with a fairly clean bill of health. Their shortcomings

---

72   JUST 1/1005/2 m. 122.

were few and relatively unimportant, and there were no reported instances of corruption among them. It was a coroner's clerk, not his employer, who was the principal offender, when he conspired with the neighbouring townships to bury a suicide without an inquest (**441**). Less than a decade later the coroner Roger Pypard, who was in office by 1268, and then and later seems to have been active in the north of the county, was alleged to have demanded money on four occasions for coming to hold inquests on corpses, and also to have taken 6s. 8d. to allow a suspected killer to escape after an inquest, and similar charges were made against other coroners.[73] Such malpractices were common, and the temptation to resort to them must have been great. Perhaps fear of detection at the eyre, and, in the period of baronial reform, the prevailing stress on maintaining good standards of conduct among officials, worked together for a while to discourage extortion and peculation.

Forests and franchises

The sheriffs and coroners, and their subordinates, were not the only officials, royal or otherwise, to be found in thirteenth-century Wiltshire. Another significant presence in the county was that of the foresters, verderers and regarders who administered the royal forests there. The upkeep and protection of the latter, and of the animals which lived in them, were reviewed in separate forest eyres – rolls survive for those of 1257, 1263 and 1270. Comparison of these with the 1268 crown pleas show a degree of overlap, but no obvious clashes of jurisdiction. In 1268 several deaths were attributed to malefactors lurking in the forests (e.g. **177, 246, 371, 585**), but these were clearly treated in exactly the same way as deaths elsewhere, requiring a coroner's inquest and the usual attendance by the neighbouring townships. Two deaths in Clarendon forest recorded in 1263, those of Maud of Alderbury, struck by a falling branch, and an unknown man found with his hands tied and throat cut, cannot be found among the 1268 crown pleas,[74] but in Maud's case that may well be because it was finally decided that she had died of sickness and not from her injuries. Although the stranger's death should have been presented to the eyre, it was not alone in having been apparently passed over, and the omission is as likely to have resulted from forgetfulness or neglect as from administrative confusion.

Also under the jurisdiction of the eyre for common pleas were those who killed or stole within the woods and parks of private individuals, however powerful. These, too, had their officials, men like Richard of Blandford, Henry de Lacy's forester, who killed Neil Edwyne of Purton in Braydon forest, having probably caught him trespassing in his lord's wood (**433**). The employees of many landowners, ecclesiastical and secular, had a role in the administration of the county through the powers of government, or franchises, which had accrued to the estates of their lords, whether by royal grant or by virtue of ancient tenure, and gave them a privileged status, along with what could be valuable revenues. It was one of the functions of the eyre to check on the lawfulness of these liberties, as they were known, in case they originated in an

---

73   *Rot. Hund.* ii, 244, 258, 271, 276.

74   E 32/199 mm. 9d, 10.

unwarranted usurpation of royal rights, and also to ensure that they fulfilled their functions by contributing to the government of the realm – lords who did not exercise their franchises as occasion required, or who used them improperly, alike risked losing them. For their part, lords had to be ready to defend what they claimed were their rights – the bailiff of Knoyle hundred, which belonged to the bishop of Winchester, was paid 20s. for spending six weeks at the 1268 eyre, 'for defending the bishop's liberties'.[75]

Liberties (which could also be whole communities, in the case of boroughs) varied considerably in their powers, depending on the status of their holder and the extent of his franchises. At their greatest they could effectively exclude the sheriff and his subordinates, through their entitlement to return of writs, which enabled them to receive and execute the king's mandates without the involvement of royal officials.[76] The number of lords exercising this right in 1268, whether in individual manors or in whole hundreds, is unclear. Evidence from Edward I's reign shows that claims were neither made nor recorded with complete consistency, and that in any case some were abandoned or over-ruled. In 1281 Walter de Pavely was alleged to have return of writs in Westbury hundred, but himself disclaimed it, as did another seven lords of manors, while the earl of Cornwall, the king's cousin, lost this franchise when challenged over his right to it in his hundred of Mere.[77]

Many Wiltshire hundreds had passed into private hands by 1268 – it has been calculated that in 1281 only eleven and a half out of thirty-eight were still held by the crown[78] – but not all of them were held on terms allowing their possessors to debar the king's officers. One lord who was so privileged, however, was the abbot of Glastonbury, who had return of writs throughout his lands, and a presentment made in 1268 shows him consolidating his rights, in a process which was not without complications. Glastonbury had a cluster of manors in the north of Chippenham hundred which were eventually amalgamated to form North Damerham hundred. Until the early 1260s arrangements for routine business within them, like making distraints and organising assizes, had been handled by the bailiffs of Chippenham, who usually did what was required themselves but sometimes – possibly in occasional deference to the abbot's claims – instructed the men of the townships to act. In proceeding thus the bailiffs were following the instructions not of the sheriff but of Geoffrey Gacelyn, who was farming the hundred from the crown and claimed extensive rights within it. In 1281 these were presented as including return of writs, but when he was challenged by the king's attorney he confined his claim to the hundred, and when the issue was raised again in 1289, his son recited a long list of franchises to which he

75   E 352/61 m. 6d.

76   See M.T. Clanchy, 'The franchise of return of writs', *Transactions of the Royal Historical Society* 5th series 17 (1967), 59–82.

77   Details from W. Illingworth (ed.), *Placita de Quo Warranto temporibus Edw. I, II, et III* (Record Commission, 1818), 796, 800-1, 801, 802, 805, 807 (Walter de Pavely), 807-8 (earl of Cornwall), 809.

78   *VCH Wiltshire* v, 51.

said he was entitled, but did not mention return of writs among them.[79] It would thus appear that the bailiff was exercising a right which he probably did not possess, in manors whose lord should have been able to keep him out. From Glastonbury's point of view this cannot have been a satisfactory situation.

Then in 1261 Ralph Russel became sheriff, and not only was he himself a landowner in Somerset, where he became sheriff in 1265, but he employed as his deputy one Martin of Leigh, who was a tenant and retainer of the abbot of Glastonbury, and clearly willing to act as the latter's agent in maintaining or extending the monastery's privileges. As under-sheriff, Leigh now proceeded to send royal writs directly to the abbot's bailiffs, bypassing the bailiffs of Chippenham. This set a precedent, and thereafter when the latter tried to make distraints they were repulsed (**580**). The king was hardly the loser, since of late his agents had apparently had only intermittent access to the lands which made up Chippenham hundred. Indeed, although one may doubt if this was Martin of Leigh's motive in acting on the abbot's behalf, the administration of the area may have been improved by the establishment of direct links between the king's government and the abbey's administrative network. More generally, the case further illustrates the value of the eyre, as a means both of keeping an eye on officials who might otherwise be tempted to give local interests precedence over royal ones, and also of clarifying the chains of command which ensured that the king's orders were obeyed and the king's business done.

Lords with the franchise of return of writs were substantially outnumbered by those who claimed the right to private gallows, enabling them to hang thieves caught on their lands in the possession of stolen goods and confiscate their chattels. This was not a privilege which could be exercised without due formality. By the mid-thirteenth century two elements had become required to justify such executions – the thief must have been arrested in possession of stolen goods, and he must be prosecuted for them by their owner. The liberty of Ludgershall was taken into the king's hand in 1268 because the townsmen had arrested and hanged Robert le Webbe on charges of homicide and theft; they had no jurisdiction over homicide, and since Robert 'was not arrested with stolen goods and nor did anyone sue against him' they had no right to hang him for that either (**370**). Sir Mathias Besille's court at Sherston erred similarly because in 1256 it hanged one William of Liddington after he admitted theft and mortally wounding the man who tried to arrest him. It had no powers in cases of homicide, and except when authoritatively set down in a coroner's roll a suspected thief's confession had no validity. William should have been remanded to gaol for eventual trial before justices of gaol delivery; because he was not the Sherston liberty, too, was taken into the king's hand (**541**).

Frankpledge

Lords with the franchise of gallows often also enjoyed the privilege of holding their own view of frankpledge. This last brought the liberty which had it into the workings of a system of law enforcement which operated

79   *Placita de Quo Warranto*, 803; JUST 1/1011 m. 49d.

throughout the lower levels of medieval society. Frankpledge was a system of mutual responsibility whereby all the males in a community over the age of twelve, with certain exceptions, became sureties for one another's good behaviour.[80] Women were excluded, and so were free men, clerics, and men in the households, or 'mainpasts', of lords and gentry who were expected to keep their underlings law-abiding and were amerced if they failed to do so. A man entered frankpledge by joining a tithing, a term with more than one meaning. In much of southern and central England a tithing was a group of ten men defined by its head, or tithingman, (e.g. **34, 597**), but in parts of the south and south west it was a whole community, often coterminous with a township. In 1268 both kinds were found in Wiltshire, but the latter greatly outnumbered the former. There was similar variety in the larger boroughs, where the basis of frankpledge was the aldermanry. In Marlborough this was a personal grouping (**490**), while in Malmesbury (**567**) and Salisbury (**607**) it was a territorial subdivision. In the 1280s, at least, the eight aldermanries of Wilton (**476**) seem to have been named from both people and areas.

A youth joining a tithing or aldermanry, however constituted, swore a solemn oath that he would be neither a thief nor the associate of a thief, and that he would not conceal thieves or acts of theft, but would 'reveal it to those whom it should be revealed ...'.[81] To the medieval mind theft had associations extending beyond the stealing of other people's goods, it encapsulated what today would be called crime, and covered every kind of offence against property and public order. Fundamental to its prevention and punishment was the raising of the hue. Traditionally made 'with both horn and mouth' (**327**), it was a call to action against any breach of the king's peace, and should bring everyone within earshot to the scene; townships which failed to respond could expect to be punished (e.g. **559**). But it was not only a public summons to action against lawbreakers, for every action which resulted in the raising of the hue was also the subject of repeated presentment to public courts by tithingmen, who in this context were regarded as the representatives of their townships.[82] At the lowest level this meant the three-weekly hundred court. At a session of Kinwardstone hundred court held around the time of the 1268 eyre, for instance, the tithingman for Collingbourne 'Abbot's' presented how 'John the hayward, Ralph the parson of Collingbourne's servant and Henry the clerk fought together, and blood was drawn and the hue raised',[83] and in the 1270s and 1280s presentments of affrays involving the raising of the hue were part of the routine business of Highworth hundred court.

Brawls and punch-ups in themselves came within the ordinary jurisdiction of the hundred court, which by dealing with them may sometimes have been able to defuse quarrels and prevent further violence. Far more

---

80   The standard treatment of frankpledge is W.A. Morris, *The Frankpledge System* (Harvard Historical Studies 14, 1910).

81   F.W. Maitland and W.P. Baildon (eds.), *The Court Baron* (Selden Society 4, 1891 for 1890), 76-7.

82   Pierrepont, 'The manor of Brixton Deverill', 59 – *pro villa respondere ubique sicut tedingeman.*

83   SC 2/209/6 *recto.*

important were the six-monthly sessions of the hundred court, held after Easter and after Michaelmas, when the sheriff made a circuit of the county, known as his 'tourn', collected some customary dues, and received presentments of offences against the peace, communicated by the tithingmen to a jury made up of 'the most sage, lawful and sufficient men of the whole hundred'.[84] He also reviewed the maintenance of frankpledge. In about half the hundreds of the county these functions were performed by the lord or his steward, but procedure remained the same. It had much in common with that of the eyre, with presentments being made in response to a set of articles, and covering largely the same ground – in 1268 the Melksham jurors complained of the way that the officials of the countess of Devon, one of the county magnates entitled to exercise the sheriff's jurisdiction on these occasions, were amercing tithingmen and tithings 'if they do not answer to all and each of the articles put to them' (285). Like the king's justices, the sheriff also received indictments of suspected malefactors, so that they could be arrested if possible (for hundreds from which he was excluded such details would have to be passed on to him by their lords), and he reviewed peace-keeping arrangements as well. Among the offences which the tithingmen were expected to report were any involving the raising of the hue, which might signal no more than disorder, but could also follow more serious violence, which would thus be in less danger of concealment or oversight. Sheriffs' accounts for the profits of the county in the late 1250s and mid-1260s show them imposing amercements for raising the hue, for raising the hue and not following it, and for raising the hue 'foolishly' – presumably unnecessarily.[85]

Offences like these, and others relating to local law enforcement, could be dealt with at once by the sheriff or by lords with his jurisdiction, at the enlarged sessions of the hundred court, known as 'lawdays', which followed closely after the two tourns – the right to hear such cases, and to impose amercements for breaches of regulations like the assizes which fixed the prices of bread and ale, were the essential components of the franchise of view of frankpledge. Very little direct evidence survives for proceedings at the tourn in cases of felony. It may well be that William Hyldulf, indicted for theft by the Cricklade jurors in 1268, had previously been indicted at the tourn, since he was said to have fled from the peace eight years earlier (424), just as it is very possible that at least some of the men briefly mentioned as having been hanged had been arrested following indictment at the tourn, to be executed following trial and conviction at gaol deliveries. That has to be speculation. It is probably less risky to surmise that the few cases dealing with felonies in the surviving records of ordinary sessions of hundred courts either originated in or led to presentments or indictments at the tourn. It seems likely, for instance, that the amercement imposed on Littleton tithing in 1258 or 1259 for not arresting John Thurbern followed from John's having been indicted at the tourn.[86] He was said then to have absconded, and it would appear that

84   F.M. Nichols (ed.), *Britton*, 2 vols (Oxford, 1865), i, 178-9. For a full description of the tourn see H. Cam, *The hundred and the hundred rolls* (1930), 118-28.

85   E 389/136, 137.

86   E 389/136 m. 4.

he became aware that he was now a marked man because he did not come back - in 1268 he was indicted for theft by the Rowborough jurors (**396**).

At Highworth hundred court's lawday of 16 November 1276 order was given for the arrest of two men said to have been involved in the killing of William the carter, while the tithingman of Hampton was amerced for failing to produce William Wydie and William Purnele, described as being of ill fame.[87] These charges, too, probably resulted from indictments at the recent tourn, indictments which were followed up afterwards, albeit with differing results. In 1281 William the carter's death was described as the work of unknown criminals, suggesting that the suspects of 1277 were cleared by subsequent investigations, but William Wydie and William Purnele, like John Thurbern earlier, had made themselves scarce and were indicted again at the eyre.[88] On another occasion a presentment in a local court may have *preceded* an indictment at the tourn. On 22 January 1276, when the next tourn would have been more than two months away, Geoffrey the carter and four others were presented by the tithingman of Lydyard as having stolen pigs from the parson of Lydyard, and order was given for their arrest.[89] Either the tithing captured him, or indictment at the tourn followed, along with action by the sheriff, for in 1281 Geoffrey was reported to have been seized and put in the stocks, though in the event he managed to escape and abjure the realm.[90] On all these occasions local courts, with the tourn as their focus, were used for the exchange of information between communities and officials, resulting in action against suspected malefactors.

John Thurbern, William Purnele and Geoffrey the carter were all said to have been in tithings, and their indictments may have originated within these, in the resolve of their fellows to take action against law-breakers in accordance with their oath. Inevitably such a system lent itself to misuse, and the malicious indictments attributed to the tithingmen of Clyffe Pypard and Buttermere in 1268 may also have originated within the communities these men represented (**215, 386**), among men anxious to be rid of trouble-makers, rather than in individual ill-will. Such charges underline the fact that frankpledge had an implicitly exclusive as well as an explicitly inclusive function, in that as well as aiming to secure the good behaviour of those within it, it allowed no lawful place in a community to those who did not join it, or remain within it. Those who were admitted to townships must be completely absorbed. In February 1277 order was given in Highworth hundred court for the attachment of Robert and Adam Wakerild, who were not in frankpledge – the marginal note 'Sunt in theþinga' records the outcome, clearly a satisfactory one, since neither man was subsequently recorded as disturbing the peace.[91] William of Bristol and his wife Amice had been lodging at the house of Robert Richer for three weeks when they killed Robert's wife Gillian and fled. They had

87   *Highworth hundred rolls* i, 51.
88   JUST 1/1005/2 mm. 117, 117d.
89   *Highworth hundred rolls* i, 25.
90   JUST 1/1005/2 m. 117.
91   *Highworth hundred rolls* i, 56.

been staying in Downton, which in 1268 was amerced for having harboured them outside a tithing – even for that short period, it would appear, William should have been brought into the township's network of mutual responsibility (**78**). Naturally the same was true for people harboured outside frankpledge for longer periods, men like Alexander of Dean, who had been living outside a tithing in Bremhill for six months before he killed John the miller (**543**). Conversely, when in September 1283 Moredon tithing not only failed to produce two disreputable brothers in Highworth hundred court but also let it be known that 'it does not wish to have them in future',[92] it was probably trying to have them ejected from the township, and thereby reduced to a status like that of Stephen le Bloys of Upton, one of a pair of thieves described in 1268 as 'not in a tithing, but ... paupers wandering through the country' (**474**). Judging by his name Stephen had originated in a Wiltshire township, but now he had no place in it, and was condemned instead to a vagrant life.

The enforcement of regulations concerning the receiving of strangers was no easy matter, when the roads were full of people on the move. Monitoring those who harboured strangers, and reporting them at the tourn, was one of the responsibilities of the tithingmen, and court rolls of the 1270s and 1280s contain numerous presentments of delinquencies, which in turn shed light on the difficulties involved. Many incomers must have wanted no more than temporary accommodation, and perhaps the chance of employment. The latter was most likely to have been forthcoming at certain times of year, when, indeed, the demand for labour was doubtless very great. Hence the amercements imposed in Sevenhampton manor court in 1281 and 1283 on those who 'harboured strangers in autumn'.[93] The offenders were nearly all women, who may well have been poor and for that reason supplemented their incomes by accommodating the men who came each year to help with the harvest. Less regular in their appearance, but surely no less valued for their services, were travelling craftsmen like the anonymous tinker given shelter in 1279 by James Rolves, a man of substance in Highworth hundred.[94] Men like that tinker doubtless constituted the strangers referred to in November 1283 by the tithingman of Hampton, when he described them as 'accustomed to come by night to the house of certain women'[95] – women, it may be surmised, who were no better than they should have been. There must have often been more to draw outsiders into the townships than the possibility of shelter and work.

The watch and the enforcement of outlawry

Reinforcing frankpledge as an agency of exclusion was the watch. As far as those who lived in the townships were concerned, the watch's main task was probably ensuring the observance of the curfew, but overall its principal function was controlling the movements and activities of outsiders. An

92   *ib.* ii, 246.

93   R.B. Pugh (ed.), *Court rolls of the Wiltshire manors of Adam de Stratton* (Wiltshire Record Society 24, 1970 for 1968), 68, 80.

94   *Highworth hundred rolls* i, 126

95   *ib.* ii, 251.

ancient institution, in 1268 it was regulated in accordance with instructions promulgated in 1242, and re-issued and in some respects elaborated in 1253, which ordered the keeping of watches at night throughout the summer months, and placed close restrictions on the harbouring of strangers.[96] A case from the 1249 eyre shows the watchmen of Cowesfield acting as they should, in trying to arrest an unknown man who entered the township by night, though he disappeared into the woods when he was challenged.[97] Like frankpledge, the watch in Wiltshire was organised at the level of the tithings. During his tourn in August and September 1265, Ralph de Aungers amerced tithings in several hundreds for failing to keep watch[98] – perhaps he was responding to the political crisis of those months – and in the 1270s and 1280s the tithings of Highworth hundred were regularly penalised for the same reason. On 27 June 1278, for instance, the tithingman of Stratton St Margaret was amerced for concealment 'and because he did not keep watch well with the wardstaff with the whole tithing.'[99] The wardstaff, which seems to have been a symbol of the watchman's office, was kept by the tithingman, and probably handed by him to those members of his tithing to whom he deputed his authority.

Since the watchmen of Cowesfield were said to have raised the hue on the stranger, the incident should in due course have been presented both to the hundred court and to the sheriff's tourn. In many shires the county court, too, regularly received presentments by townships of matters relevant to the pleas of the crown, including raisings of the hue. No evidence has been found that Wiltshire county court did so when it met every fourth Tuesday at Wilton, but it would still have become well informed about acts of violence and theft through its essential role in the prosecution of offenders, both personally, through the appeal of felony, and in the king's name through the process of exigent. The appeal is discussed further in a later section, and it is sufficient to say here that it was an action brought in an elaborate prescribed form by one or more accusers against a named defendant, or defendants, alleging a specific felony or breach of the king's peace. If the accused did not come to answer, the appeal could be continued to a further four sessions of the county court, at the end of which the defendant who neither attended nor found pledges for his future appearance would be outlawed – in 1268 the justices called for judgment on the county court for failing to outlaw four men who had been appealed of homicide at five consecutive sessions (**12**). The procedure of exigent, which was usually gone through only after an eyre, was much the same, only substituting the king for a private prosecutor. If the accused failed to surrender to the peace after repeated summonses, again he would be outlawed, or in the case of women, waived

The outlook for the outlaw, or waif (a term also applied to stray cattle), was bleak. He was every man's enemy, and should be arrested on sight, or killed if he fled or resisted capture. In 1281 John le Haver, who had been outlawed both for poaching and for killing Nicholas le Forester, was described

96   *CR 1237-1242*, 482-4; *CR 1251-1253*, 492-3.

97   *Wiltshire crown pleas, 1249* no. 496.

98   E 389/137 mm. 10, 12, 13; JUST 1/1005/2 m. 147.

99   *Highworth hundred rolls* i, 100.

as having been spotted when he came to East Grimstead; he ran for his life, but the man who had tried to arrest him shot him down 'as he fled from the king's peace', and subsequently received a pardon for the deed.[100] It is not surprising that John was recognised, for his status should have become widely known, thanks to the operations of a system of repeated presentments in public courts, culminating in the process whereby he was outlawed. The raising of the hue when Nicholas was killed should have been presented at the hundred court, and John may well have been named at the coroner's inquest held shortly after the death, or indicted at the next sheriff's tourn; while once his responsibility was established his crime would have been further publicised by proceedings against him in the county court. The conditions of medieval life made it difficult (though by no means impossible) to secure arrests, but if a suspect could not be caught then he could be identified, and excluded from the society in which he had previously moved – treated, in fact, like all the other outsiders whom the townships were required to keep at arm's length. His chattels, moreover, would be forfeited, so that his life became that of a pauper, a pauper whose life could lawfully be cut short at any moment.

There was always the possibility that the outlaw, like the abjuror, might try to settle elsewhere among the law-abiding. Both the risk, and the way it could be counteracted, are illustrated by a case from the 1289 Wiltshire eyre. A certain Roger de la Forde had been put in exigent following indictment at the 1281 eyre for a burglary in Bradford hundred in which a woman was killed. Subsequently outlawed, he made his way to Chippenham, where he was 'many times harboured by night' at the house of one Payn Dabel, who had since died. But Roger's crime had evidently not been forgotten in the neighbourhood where he had committed it, and word that he was still at large filtered back to Bradford hundred, where his return was reported to the sheriff at his tourn. As a result the case came before the king's justices, who amerced the townspeople of Chippenham of twenty marks for failing to arrest the outlaw in their midst, while Roger, it may be assumed, returned to the hopelessness and danger of an outlaw's life.[101]

The system of law enforcement which detected the misdeeds, and then the return, of Roger de la Forde was one which made great demands on everyone involved in its workings, requiring unfailing vigilance, attention to duty, and where necessary courage, since suspects might stand and fight instead of running away (**541**). Indeed, one could argue that it required more than those concerned could reasonably be expected to deliver, in maintaining both a rigid separation of the townships from the perilous world outside them, and a continuous scrutiny of the behaviour of kinsfolk and neighbours, along with a readiness to report suspicions of them where necessary. When Walter le Burgeis's mistress Alice raised the hue on her lover after he had broken out of gaol and fled to her house, she was doing what the law required of her (**593**), but others clearly found themselves unable to follow her example, men like William Pumerey, who died in prison after being arrested for harbouring his son, hanged for theft in Hampshire (**606**). The forces of sympathy, fear and

100   JUST 1/1005/2 m. 146d.
101   JUST 1/1001 m. 49d; JUST 1/1005/2 m. 126.

indifference need to be set against those of dutifulness and discipline when evaluating the contents of a record like that of the 1268 Wiltshire eyre.

Of its nature any judicial record is always much more likely to report the crimes of violence and theft which were committed than those which for any reason were not, making it very hard to assess how far a society was able to restrain those inclined or tempted to lawlessness. But where the detection and punishment of offenders were concerned, it will be argued below that the officials and communities of Wiltshire probably did as well as the prevailing conditions allowed. That this should have been so is testimony to the conscientiousness, however imperfect, of the men who acted as officials, though often unpaid, and of those who shouldered the burden of manning tithings, raising and following the hue, attending coroners' inquests and sheriffs' tourns. But it also bears witness to the importance of the eyre, which by detecting and penalising failures and delinquencies did much to ensure that a complex and onerous network of courts and inquests continued to function. Standing at the apex of the existing system of law enforcement, the weight of the eyre, though only periodically exerted, was largely responsible for keeping the parts below in place.

The effects of civil war

The task of keeping the peace had recently been greatly complicated in every part of England by the outbreak of a civil war whose effects were still very much in evidence in 1268. Wiltshire, dominated as it was by the king and his allies, appears to have escaped relatively lightly, but there had still been disturbances in the county, and the justices seem at first to have been uncertain as to how to deal with them. It was probably accepted from the first that as at the beginning of Henry III's reign, crimes committed in wartime should not be treated as ordinary breaches of the king's peace. But it was not as easy now as it had been after the hostilities of 1215-17 to decide when the country had been at war and when at peace. The opponents of Henry III had begun to take action against the king's supporters long before Henry himself took the field against his baronial enemies, and the consequent fighting had been far from continuous. When Henry was defeated and captured at the battle of Lewes on 14 May 1264, it must have looked as though the war was over, but the fighting began again in 1265, and despite the decisive royalist victory at Evesham on 4 August continued intermittently for another two years. For the justices at Wilton the issues raised by the Chalke jury's presentment of the forcible taking of a horse, apparently by a group of Dorset men, from brother Adam of St Nicholas's hospital, Salisbury, 'after the battle of Lewes, and after peace was proclaimed' (**106**), presented real difficulties – it was far from clear, for one thing, that peace *had* in any meaningful sense been proclaimed in 1264 – and they remanded the case, and others similar to it (**66, 105**) for discussion, not so much among themselves as with the central government.

On 4 February, three weeks after the beginning of the eyre, the government sent a considered reply, laying down, apparently for the first time, how offences committed during the civil war were to be handled (**600**). There was to be an amnesty for all felonies committed between 4 April 1264 and 16 September 1265, a period in which the war was deemed to have 'lasted continuously'; instead, the justices were to use their discretion in treating them as in effect civil trespasses. However, this core period was to be extended at both ends, to cover the hostile deeds of the barons from 4 June 1263 onwards, and also the activities of the followers of the earl of Gloucester when he occupied London between early April and mid-June 1267, in a move which more than any other brought the civil war to an end. But only participants in these latter events were to benefit from this broadening of the amnesty – felonies perpetrated by anyone else during the months in question were to be treated as committed in peacetime. And opponents of the king who had continued in their resistance after the battle of Evesham were to enjoy no protection outside either the terms of the Dictum of Kenilworth laying down the conditions on which they might recover their lands (a copy was sent to the justices), or individual charters re-admitting them to the king's peace.

How many killings and robberies went unrecorded on the eyre roll after the receipt of these instructions it is impossible to say, but it seems certain that some were, occasionally with the help of a little chicanery. On 20 January 1264 order was given that John Walerand, imprisoned at Marlborough for the death of Reginald of Stitchcombe, should be released on bail.[102] Reginald's death went unmentioned in 1268, but in 1281 Sir Thomas de Turberville (later notorious for treason against Edward I) was charged with it, as allegedly committed 'in peacetime in Selkley hundred'. At first Turberville refused to plead, but the case was remanded to parliament, where it was testified that Reginald had been killed 'in the fifty-first year, that is, when the earl of Gloucester had occupied London ...', and he was released.[103] The order for bail, issued in 1264, and the testimony of 1281, dating the death to 1267, are chronologically irreconcilable. Since Stitchcombe was clearly dead by the beginning of 1264, it may well be that he was killed in an affray near Marlborough (in Selkley hundred), arising from competition between royalists and Montfortians for control of the castle, and that the deed was left out of the eyre roll because it could be construed, with some stretching of the facts, as committed in time of war. By 1281, in part *because* there was no record of the case among the 1268 crown pleas, those 'facts' could be stretched again, to relocate the death in time and so secure Turberville's release; by the following year he was a knight of the royal household.

References to the disturbances of the mid-1260s are rare among both the crown and the civil pleas of the 1268 Wiltshire eyre, though where the latter were concerned their number must already have been reduced by the sessions *de terris datis*, hearing actions under the Dictum of Kenilworth, known to have been held in the county before Nicholas FitzMartin (no record of their proceedings has survived).[104] Perhaps unsurprisingly, only a few of the county's landowners were active as rebels, and except for Simon de Montfort himself (**73**), whose principal interests lay in other counties, and John FitzJohn, the lord of Woodborough,[105] none of them were men of notable stature. Henry

102   CR 1261-1264, 334

103   JUST 1/1005/2 m. 161.

104   KB 26/186 m. 25.

105   *Calendar of Inquisitions Miscellaneous i: 1219-1307* no. 934.

de St Maur followed Sir Henry Hastings into the Montfortian ranks, and forfeited his manor of Rowden for doing so, though he subsequently recovered it.[106] Gilbert de Neville lost his manor at Durrington for the same reason, but paid sixty marks to have it back.[107] Robert le Chamberleng (a member of the family which gave its name to Compton Chamberlayne) and Thomas de St Martin, who also opposed the king, were pardoned, in Robert's case after he had successfully pleaded that he had been coerced into joining the rebels (it was said on Robert's behalf that in reality he had supported the king 'with mind, soul and counsel', and had sent 'his best and favourite esquire' to join the royalist army for the Evesham campaign).[108] Bishop de la Wyle had been a Montfortian, but since a fine of 100 marks sufficed to remit the king's rancour,[109] he was probably less committed to the baronial cause than some of his fellow bishops. It may be significant that after 1265 only two Wiltshire men were said to have been beneficiaries of the cult of Simon de Montfort.[110]

Pleading in the Westminster courts, a few Wiltshire litigants alleged that wrongs done to them had been perpetrated 'at the time of the disturbance of the realm'.[111] It is always possible that such references to the civil war were essentially rhetorical, made in the hope of winning the sympathy of the court, though in the case of the justice Nicholas de Turri, complaining that his goods had been taken at Lacock and Grittleton, it is at least credible that a prominent royal servant should have been targeted by the king's enemies.[112] The Jews of London suffered severely at Montfortian hands, and those of Wilton seem to have done the same – on 22 December 1265, moved by 'compassion for the losses which the Jews of their town have sustained by occasion of the disturbance had in the realm', Henry III appointed a number of the burgesses to act as their 'guardians and defenders'.[113] Perhaps the Jews of Salisbury were targeted as well – in March 1266 order was given for the release on bail of John Rocelin of Wilton, arrested for the death of a Jew named Jospin of Fisherton (**610**).

Just as Jews were vulnerable in a Christian society, so civilian populations always faced harassment and pillage when war broke out. The amount of actual fighting which took place in Wiltshire during the Barons' Wars was probably very limited – there is very little reference to hostilities in the bishop of Winchester's pipe rolls, for instance.[114] Salisbury castle was believed to be in danger of capture by rebels in 1263, but the garrison was reinforced and

106 KB 26/207 m. 8d; JUST 1/1005/1 m. 58d.

107 *CR 1264-1268*, 358.

108 *CR 1264-1268*, 216-17; *Calendar of Inquisitions Miscellaneous* 1 no. 932.

109 E 372/110 m. 7d – the bishop owed 300 marks (£200) in all, but 200 marks were due for failing to provide troops for the king's army.

110 J.O. Halliwell (ed.), *The chronicle of William de Rishanger of the Barons' Wars: the miracles of Simon de Montfort*, Camden old series 15 (1840), 100.

111 KB 26/175 mm. 5d, 7; KB 26/177 m. 17; KB 26/184 m. 11d.

112 KB 26/175 m. 14.

113 *CPR 1258-1266*, 521.

114 N. Vincent, 'The politics of church and state as reflected in the Winchester

no attack followed.[115] But there does seem to have been some skirmishing around Marlborough in 1264, when the castle was taken into Montfortian hands after the battle of Lewes, and retaken for the king shortly afterwards by soldiers from Bristol.[116] It was probably these events which the sheriff was later instructed to investigate, when the castles of Marlborough and Ludgershall were seized and looted, and the men of Roger Clifford, the royalist keeper of Marlborough, attacked at Easton, and some of them killed.[117] The impact of hostilities on the county is probably more truthfully conveyed, however, by the action found among the 1268 civil pleas in which William of Bingham sued two men who he claimed owed him twelve marks (£8) for two palfreys which he had sold them at Marlborough on 1 August 1263. The defendants denied the charge, saying that they had taken the horses and other goods of William's because at the beginning of hostilities he had refused to come into the castle, but had behaved as an enemy, and that when the barons had the upper hand he had threatened them with arrest and imprisonment, thereby causing them to subscribe a bond for the sum demanded. This defence William rebutted, saying that he had always been loyal to the king, that he had been robbed of his palfreys for that reason, and that the defendants had freely made him their bond after he complained to the king when peace was restored following the battle of Lewes. The case was adjourned, and its conclusion is not recorded.[118] But its claims and counterclaims are probably authentic in suggesting that the county suffered less from outright devastation and the clash of arms than from the incidental accompaniments of war, from the activities of garrisons and the movements of troops, and the insecurities these aroused.

Garrisons were enlarged where necessary. Salisbury castle was held by thirty soldiers in the summer of 1263, but by seventy in the following spring.[119] Marlborough castle was still being held by seventy-four men from March to June 1266,[120] and had probably contained many more a year earlier. The methods by which these bodies of men were maintained during the war were probably all too often indistinguishable from those employed after it by the keeper of Salisbury castle, when he sent a servant to Whiteparish who carried off the parson's goods (**66**), and indeed by the king himself. In 1281 fifty-six oxen were found to have been seized on Henry III's behalf 'at the time the king was at Stratford and besieged London', that is, during the occupation of the capital by the earl of Gloucester in 1267.[121] In December 1264 the royalists at Bristol surrendered the castle and made their way to Salisbury, where three of them were among the members of the garrison later recorded as poaching

pipe rolls, 1208-1280', R. Britnell (ed.), *The Winchester pipe rolls and medieval English society* (Woodbridge, 2003), 157-81, at 176-7.

115   *VCH Wiltshire* v, 11-12.

116   *VCH Wiltshire* xii, 166.

117   KB 26/178 m. 13d.

118   JUST 1/998A m. 13.

119   E 372/110 m. 7d.

120   *Calendar of Inquisitions Miscellaneous* i no. 319.

121   JUST 1/1005/2 m. 140d.

in the king's forests.[122] Men from the garrison of Marlborough did the same, either for food or amusement, or both.[123] The fact that the men from Bristol who recaptured Marlborough in September 1264 were fighting for the king did not prevent their pursuing his deer in Savernake forest, while John Giffard, another royalist and an almost fanatical huntsman, went after the deer in the forests of Clarendon (where he was particularly active during the months between the battles of Lewes and Evesham), Braydon, Grovely (with 'a great multitude of men'), Savernake, Selwood, Melksham and Chippenham, both during the civil war and after it.[124] For his part, the king exploited the forests for timber for works on his castles,[125] and while he besieged the Montfortian die-hards at Kenilworth in 1266 received supplies of salted venison from Clarendon, Melksham, Chippenham and Savernake.[126]

Except locally, the ravages endured by the king's forests probably had no equivalent elsewhere in Wiltshire. Indeed, although gatherings of troops could pose a threat to crops and properties, they might also present opportunities to those with food, clothes and other appropriate wares to sell. It may be significant that the violent affray involving Walter Hyon, Henry Leggegode and others took place on Saturday, 14 March 1265, as Walter and Henry were coming from Marlborough (**133, 216**) – they had probably been attending the town's market, which took place on Wednesday and Saturday each week, and which may well have been flourishing thanks to the demands of the garrison. The county court was later recorded as meeting as usual in the early months of 1264 (**12**), and a number of hundred courts continued to meet at three-weekly intervals throughout the spring and summer of 1265. No sessions are recorded from July, possibly as a result of that month's intense political and military crisis, but Chilmark fair was held on the 21st, its accustomed day.[127] If the civil wars posed anything more than a passing threat to law enforcement in the county, it was probably less by undermining the routines of government than by fostering habits of mind which were relatively indifferent to the maintenance of public order, in people who had learnt to live with the danger of violence and rapine, and whose respect for the processes of law is unlikely to have been fostered by the amnesty granted to such as had recently disregarded them. Thomas Tartarin, who killed John le Crispe in a mock joust, probably not long before the eyre, was a member of the household of Sir John Giffard, a warrior who had fought for Simon de Montfort at Lewes and against him at Evesham (**170**). Thomas's willingness to fight, even in sport, could well have been learnt from, or encouraged by, the recent deeds of his lord. As late as March 1269 Bishop de la Wyle found it

122   *CPR 1258-1266*, 397; E 32/200 m. 6d.

123   E 32/200 m. 11.

124   *ib.*, mm. 6d, 8, 8d, 11d, 12d, 14d. Two of the bishop of Winchester's yearlings at Fonthill were recorded in 1268 as having been savaged by Giffard's dogs, Hampshire Record Office, MS 11M59/B1/32 m. 4d.

125   E 32/200 m. 4d.

126   E 372/110 m. 5; E 372/112 m. 18.

127   E 389/137 m. 13.

necessary to administer a stiff rebuke to the dean and chapter of Salisbury for permitting disorderly gatherings of knights in the cathedral close, perhaps for tournaments, where they had disrupted services and harassed the clergy[128] – it seems at least possible that they were simply occupying themselves as they had done four or five years earlier. There must have been a serious danger that attitudes learnt in wartime would be carried over into times of peace.

Homicide

Of the felonies covered by the 1268 Wiltshire eyre, homicide was the most important, and within the record as a whole the most prominent. Under the heading of new crown pleas, the justices ought to have heard about every killing and accidental death to have taken place in the county since the previous eyre, in 1256. To be regarded as felonious, a killing should have been committed either with malicious intent or in circumstances seen as making the deed a culpable one. It was lawful to kill in self-defence, if the slayer was himself in danger of death when he struck down his assailant, and lunatics (**365**) and children under the age of twelve were regarded as incapable in principle of committing felony. The treatment of the latter varied. They risked being outlawed if they fled, and probably also if the circumstances of their deeds suggested that they had acted deliberately. Although John of Brinkworth was too young to be in a tithing, it must have been held against him that he had struck Henry son of Thomas a fatal blow in a dispute over sheep and then made off (**237**). But in the case of Richard son of William, killed when William of Shaw fell on him as they wrestled in play, not only were the protagonists only nine years old, but the Chippenham jurors were emphatic that Richard's death had been accidental. So although William, too, had run away, the justices gave him permission to return to the king's peace (**568**).

Outside these restrictions, the issue of intention was seldom raised. Thirteenth-century courts did not distinguish between murder and manslaughter, and though the recorded circumstances in which many killings took place were not such as to suggest that they had been premeditated, these were usually treated by the justices in exactly the same way as homicides which were cold-blooded murders (a word used at the eyre only in a fiscal sense – it is discussed in a later section). Juries developed the practice of representing deaths resulting from spontaneous quarrels and fights as committed in self-defence, thereby justifying a pardon,[129] and it is possible that the violent death of Thomas le Forester, allegedly killed in self-defence by two men he attacked in the house he had just broken into, was such a case (**114**). The justices made a note to refer it to the king, as they did with the death of John le Mouner, accidentally killed when wrestling with Walter the smith, which the Knoyle jurors were insistent had not occurred from 'any spirit of evil intent' (*animo malingnandi*) (**523**). But in neither case is a pardon recorded as having been granted, and on other occasions when killings were presented in terms which

---

128   *EEA, Salisbury* no. 259.

129   T.A. Green, 'The jury and the English law of homicide, 1200-1600', *Michigan Law Review* 74 (1976), 413-99.

suggested that they, too, had been essentially accidental (**60, 170**), there is nothing to suggest that the justices regarded them as other than felonious.

The jurors who presented particulars of deaths to an eyre were expected to do so on the basis of their own knowledge, and recollections, of events within the areas they represented. What they said would be checked against official records at the disposal of the justices, above all the coroners' rolls, but they were not themselves required to consult those records, indeed, cases from other eyres show that they would be amerced if they were found to have done so. In a case like that of John the chaplain of Preshute, where there was no coroner's inquest because his body was never found, the jurors would have had no choice but to look elsewhere for information – one of John's killers was later hanged, and may have confessed to the crime before his execution (**126**). In a very few cases (**510-12, 519-20**) the provision of exact or approximate dates may indicate that a written record of some kind had been drawn upon, perhaps that of the inquest which the bailiff of Knoyle is described as holding in one of these cases (**519**), or Sherston manor's court roll for the events leading up to the hanging of William of Liddington in 1256 (**541**). But for the most part the jurors appear to have relied on their own memories, and on information supplied by townships and boroughs.

It has been argued that for the presenting jurors 'the preparation of their *veredictum* can have presented little difficulty'.[130] But as far as homicide is concerned, there are many indications that the record of the 1268 Wiltshire eyre is incomplete. The evidence for its imperfections is provided by Wiltshire cases from other courts and by grants of pardons or bail to people imprisoned in Wiltshire gaols. It is possible that some of those grants related to killings in other counties, but the names of those involved, either as victims or suspects, suggest that this was rarely, if ever, the case. In all either sixteen or seventeen cases, involving nineteen or twenty deaths (the killing of Peter of Wooton is uncertain, it may have been presented by the Staple jury, though with a different suspect from the man who was pardoned for it, **429**), were apparently not presented at the eyre. Thus in April 1267, less than a year before proceedings began, three separate commissions were issued to inquire whether Walter of Wike had killed Philip of Edington and his wife Christian by misadventure or felony,[131] yet nothing was said of this case at the eyre. It may well be that Walter was cleared, but one would still expect these presumably recent deaths to have been presented, and the suspect named, if only to clear him. Even closer in time were the pardon granted on 20 December 1267 to Richard Fysse, found to have killed John Antegoyn of Wilton in self-defence,[132] and the grant of bail issued on 26 December 1267 to Hugh son of Geoffrey le Berker, imprisoned for the death of Peter le King of Ludgershall[133] – none of these men were mentioned at the eyre.

It is possible that deaths which occurred in the late 1250s and early 1260s were sometimes simply forgotten. The earliest omission, the death of John

130   *Wiltshire crown pleas, 1249*, 34.

131   *CPR 1266-1272*, 72, 134, 135.

132   *ib.*, 175.

133   *CR 1264-1268*, 421.

Colstan, for which Thomas de la Hele was to be released to bail, took place some time before 4 December 1257.[134] Probably in 1258 Emma, widow of Henry Wyking, appealed Walter Nutel and three other men in the county court of the death of her husband; early in 1259 the case was brought into the bench, where Emma declined to continue her action, no doubt because Walter had been granted a pardon, on the grounds that he had killed Henry by misadventure, on 4 February. Another appellee had been released to bail on 28 January.[135] Nothing was said about any of them in 1268, though any appeal made in the county court should have been recorded there by the coroners, and thus brought to the attention of the justices at the next eyre. The appeal which Agnes, widow of William de Enesbyre, brought in the bench in Michaelmas term 1261 against two men for the death of her husband, killed on 3 May 1261, was also ignored.[136] She claimed that they had ridden him down with their horses, raising the possibility that this death, too, had been accidental, but there is no way of telling, for there is no reference to it among the 1268 crown pleas. As already observed, the killing of an unknown man found with his throat cut in Clarendon forest in 1262 was presented before the king's forest justices, but not before royal justices itinerant. Grants of bail were made for a further seven alleged killings of which no trace can be found in the eyre roll – two in 1260,[137] one in 1261,[138] two in 1262,[139] and one apiece in 1266[140] and 1267.[141]

It is possible that some violent deaths were omitted because by 1268 they had come to be regarded as covered by the amnesty granted to felonies committed in the Barons' Wars (**600**). The deaths of John de Tronmere, his son John and John Attestaple, for which three men were bailed on 21 August 1265 following an inquest which named a fourth as culpable,[142] may have been one such case, the killing of Reginald of Stitchcombe, commented on above, was very likely another – neither case was recorded in 1268. It is noteworthy that although some killings which resulted in pardons or grants of bail, going back at least to 1259 (**266, 321**), *were* entered on the eyre roll, there are none datable to the years between 1263 and 1265. However, it is the number, rather than the fact, of deaths going unrecorded in 1268 which is surprising, the total of four deaths resulting in grants of bail which were passed over at the 1249 Wiltshire eyre was probably much more typical.[143] Any assessment of Wiltshire's homicide rate between 1256 and 1268 needs to take into account

134   *CR 1256-1259*, 168.

135   KB 26/162 m. 36; *CPR 1258-1266*, 11; *CR 1256-1259*, 357.

136   KB 26/171 m. 45.

137   *CR 1259-1261*, 129 (Edward Binethebrok), 325 (William de Everwiksire).

138   *CR 1259-1261*, 341 (William le Flemingisman).

139   *CR 1261-1264*, 23 (John son of Stephen), 39 (Alice daughter of Christine).

140   *CR 1264-1268*, 169 (William de Anne)

141   *ib.*, 319 (Ellis Marmiun).

142   C 144/5 no. 48; *CR 1264-1268*, 69.

143   *Wiltshire crown pleas, 1249*, 48.

the consideration that the actual number of killings during those years was almost certainly significantly higher than the eyre's record shows.

Without the killings shown to have been probably omitted, the 1268 crown pleas record a total of 248 deaths which the justices treated as felonious. This figure includes the small number of killings whose perpetrators were put in exigent even though their deeds had been presented as unintentional or committed in self-defence, and also the death of Ralph of Collingbourne, killed in Gloucestershire after he had himself slain John le Broke at Sopworth, although John of Norton, who pursued and dispatched him, was not put in exigent, and may have been seen less as a felon than as an agent of justice (**566**). But the deaths of Thomas Avenel, killed by a lunatic (**365**), and of John le Mouner and William of Shaw, which the court accepted had been accidental (**523, 568**), have been excluded from the total. In a number of cases men and women stood trial for homicide and were acquitted, without anyone else being named as guilty, raising the possibility that the deaths involved had been natural or accidental, or even that nobody had died at all (**360**). But as juries were clearly willing to state that allegedly felonious killings had in fact been natural deaths (**80, 388**), cases where they did not do so have been treated as homicides.

These figures may be compared with the total of 181 homicides presented at the 1249 Wiltshire eyre, the same criteria having been applied. Without the survival of coroners' rolls it is impossible to show fluctuations in the annual death rate, all that can be done is calculate an average for the periods covered by the two eyres. The 1249 eyre covered almost exactly eight years, and therefore heard of an annual average of 22.5 allegedly violent deaths during that time. Figures for the 1268 eyre are more difficult to establish. It covered just over eleven and a half years, but of that period nearly eighteen months were a time of civil war, and so excluded from consideration by the amnesty granted afterwards. If the time remaining be treated as a round ten years, then the average annual homicide rate during that decade was nearly 25. If the known omissions are also borne in mind, then it was probably somewhat higher.

An increase of three or four killings per annum across an entire county is significant but can hardly be regarded as cataclysmic, especially when the likely effects of political instability followed by outright conflict are taken into consideration. Given the evidence for population growth during the thirteenth century, a rise in the homicide rate was probably to be expected. It was unevenly distributed, but steep rises in Selkley from seven killings (one of them in fact a natural death) presented in 1249, to thirteen in 1268, in Whorwellsdown (from one to seven), in Warminster (from five to ten) and above all in Chippenham, where the borough and hundred together recorded fifteen killings in 1249 but thirty-two in 1268, are consistent with other evidence for a continuing expansion of settlement within the county. Perhaps Marlborough castle, at the heart of Selkley, acted as a lure to people seeking employment; more people were drawn to Warminster and Whorwellsdown by the prospects offered in the west of the county by forest clearances and the development of the local cloth industry; perhaps the mixed farming previously found mostly in central and south-east Wiltshire was now encroaching on the clay-lands of the north west, dominated by Chippenham, at the expense of its dairy farms and dispersed settlements.

The rise in homicide cannot be attributed to habitual criminals, to bands of robbers who haunted the roads and broke into houses to rob and kill. In 1249 sixty-four killings had been presented as the work of such men, described as 'unknown malefactors', amounting to roughly one in three of the total. Even numerically the total in 1268 was lower, standing at sixty-one, or about one in four of the total, while in terms of annual averages the fall was steeper still, from eight each year to around six. It would thus appear that the watch, while unable wholly to exclude bandits from the townships, had remained vigilant against them. As for felonies committed *within* townships, the number of killers who abjured – testimony by their taking sanctuary to communal alertness and readiness to pursue evildoers – remained almost unchanged, with eighteen recorded in 1249 and nineteen in 1268. And although arrests and executions remained relatively uncommon – twenty-two killers were recorded as hanged in 1249, either at the eyre itself or in proceedings since its predecessor, compared with twenty-five in 1268 - courts and inquests enjoyed a fair measure of success in identifying felons and circulating information about them. In 1249 twenty individuals had brought appeals of felony against alleged killers, twenty-seven of whom were found to have been outlawed or waived. In 1268 the total of appeals was only one lower, but the figure is misleading, as seven of those actions related to a single death (**327-8**), and the number of outlawries fell to thirteen. Personal actions were increasingly giving way to public prosecution through the process of exigent; eighty-four suspected killers were put in exigent in 1249, but 159 in 1268. Possibly juries were less precise than individual appellors in targeting offenders, and more inclined to name every possible suspect, so helping to explain why the number of acquittals also rose sharply, from sixty-three to 127.

Even more than in 1249, the men and women identified as killers in 1268 were predominantly poor and unfree – only one man was said to have free lands (**185**), compared with five in 1249. But 130 of them were recorded as having no chattels, as against sixty-one in 1249, while a further thirty-eight had chattels valued at less than 3s. 4d., the sum which would have made them liable to national taxation (in 1249 the equivalent total had been fourteen). Seventy-eight had been in tithings, eighteen more than in 1249, while twenty-eight had been harboured in townships without becoming enrolled in tithings, and no fewer than thirty-eight were described as strangers (the equivalent figures for 1249 were twelve and fourteen). The number of women involved in homicide fell, but only from eight to seven, while that of clerics rose in almost identical measure, from eight to ten. Those who came to violent ends did so at predominantly male and secular hands. It should be acknowledged, however, that figures in which outlawry, or orders for outlawry, feature so prominently need to be treated with caution, and seen in a somewhat provisional light. The guilt of abjurors, who confessed their felonies before leaving the country, can be assumed, and the same *ought* to be true of suspects who were convicted in court. But with men and women who were in effect convicted *in absentia* it is always possible that they had left the neighbourhood unaware of the charges against them, perhaps following acquittal at a gaol delivery (**375**), or had been accused on the basis of rumour, or out of ignorance or malice (**266, 380**), or were in some other way the victims of corruption or dishonesty. During the extended proceedings over the death of John de Cumbe (**327-8**), killed in what was described in 1268 as an outbreak of violence involving nearly fifty men and women, John of Langport was alleged to have collected 30s. from the men of Quidhampton and paid it to three men 'so that they should take John's death upon themselves'.[144] Those three men were indeed reported to have been outlawed by the time of the eyre (one of them was also said to have abjured the realm, **612**), and though nothing was said then to suggest that they had been unjustly treated, it must remain possible that they had been chosen, or persuaded, to act as scapegoats for their community. It would be rash to assume that no other attempts were made to manipulate the processes of outlawry, or that those which were made never succeeded.

When all provisos have been entered, however, it can at least be said that the impression conveyed by the entries relating to homicide among the 1268 crown pleas is both plausible and consistent, especially when details of some of the sixty-seven deaths said to have been accidental or natural (some were at first presented as felonious, or at least suspicious) are also taken into account. They reveal a society in which life was insecure, materially straitened and physically hard, in which men and women living in close proximity, and required, moreover, to keep one another under observation, were easily set at odds, and in which tensions were quick both to develop and to explode into violence. Homicide as recorded in 1268 was predominantly committed by the poor, often the very poor. In 1281 John of Monmouth, a wealthy landowner who served at least three times as a gaol delivery justice, was hanged for killing a chaplain in Wilton,[145] while Sampson Foliot, lord of the manors of Draycot Foliat and Chilton Foliat, was put in exigent for killing his own son, and though he managed to secure a pardon he may have forfeited his chattels, valued at a total of £106. 8s. 2d.[146] But in 1268, as in 1249, the rich and powerful were said to have been involved in acts of violence mainly through the misdeeds of their dependents (**130, 196, 430, 431, 468**). Except in the case of criminals who broke into houses to kill and rob, poverty is not often likely to have been a direct cause of homicide, but the effects of insecurity arising from want, or the fear of want, on men and women already living near to destitution, should not be under-rated. If the people of thirteenth-century Wiltshire appear all too often to have been touchy, choleric and resentful, that could well have been because there was little in the circumstances of their lives to make them anything else.

The growth of population and spread of cultivation mostly benefited landlords. John Hugh, a tenant of the bishop in Ramsbury, found that he could no longer afford to pay a rent of five marks per annum for his holdings there, and so 'he left them and went out of the country and never afterwards

---

144   KB 26/171 m. 13.

145   JUST 1/1005/2 m. 118; C 66/97 m. 11d; C 66/98 mm. 14d, 26d.

146   JUST 1/1005/2 m. 132.

returned to them ...'.[147] His prospects thereafter were probably bleak, but even at the best of times men like John Hugh lived under constant threat. There is nothing in the 1268 eyre roll to match the death of Richard Urnawey, who was said in 1289 to have been killed in Stoke Farthing field by a freak hailstorm,[148] but the more ordinary hazards of life are everywhere apparent in it, as when it records deaths while crossing rivers, or by falls from trees, or from sudden sickness, as with the Salisbury widow who 'died suddenly in her own house' (**603**). Several men were killed by the workings of water-mills, Adam Alwyn was struck dead by the sailyard of a windmill as he tried to grease its axle (**352**). Wood was medieval society's principal building material, and obtaining it, or working with it, could prove fatal. Alwin de Wygeton was struck dead by the branch he was cutting (**85**), William le Syur crushed by the beam he was trying to move (**50**). But working with stone could be no less hazardous – Peter of Bemerton was killed when a stone fell on him as he dug in Fonthill quarry (**517**). Working with animals was even more dangerous: a number of men died by falling as they rode, others were struck dead by horses – Hugh Bulymer, for instance, fatally kicked by the colt he was trying to catch (**458**) – or crushed by horse-drawn carts.

But it was when dealing with their fellow men and women that the people of the Wiltshire townships were at greatest risk, and not least when working in the fields. The opportunities for tension were all the greater because arable farming was essentially communal, in expansive open fields, with individual holdings scattered among them (**92, 237, 314, 325, 365, 586**). When Glastonbury Abbey conveyed a property in Badbury to Walter Buche and his wife in 1269, it included sixteen acres of arable land in no fewer than twelve portions, ranging in size from half an acre to two and a half acres.[149] A task like cutting hay brought villagers together in a substantial collective effort - in 1289 Richard de la Knolle was found to have fatally injured John Osmund by gashing his shin as the two men scythed side by side in Wanborough meadow[150] – and the same was true of harvesting, when every able-bodied person might be pressed into service, women included. Probably in 1250 Sybil the wife of William Prude came under suspicion of burgling a house in Stanton St Quintin precisely because 'a very great infirmity of her eyes' had made it impossible for her to join the others in the fields at autumn, so exposing her to suspicion when criminals raided what was probably a largely deserted township.[151]

Several deaths took place over a week after an act of violence. In the case of William son of Christine, knifed in the arm by William son of Giles, the Chippenham jurors could only say that he died 'within a month' (**562**). The homicide rate was certainly inflated by the inability of medieval medicine to treat wounds which would often be easily curable today. In 1281 the Cawdon

147   JUST 1/1002 m. 25.

148   JUST 1/1011 m. 63.

149   A. Watkin (ed.), *The great chartulary of Glastonbury* iii (Somerset Record Society 64, 1956), 682-3.

150   JUST 1/1011 m. 56d. *Wiltshire crown pleas, 1249* no. 181 records a similar case.

151   C 144/3 no. 42.

jury presented the suicide of Gilbert de Cumbe, described as a doctor.[152] His chattels were valued at £14. 6s. 9d., suggesting that he had a profitable practice, but his skills, and those of others like him, were insufficient to prevent cuts turning gangrenous and internal injuries developing fatal complications. As it was, when men came to blows, death all too often resulted. Perhaps an awareness of this gave an additional urgency to the efforts which some men made to contain acts of violence, sometimes dying themselves in the process **(60, 614)**.

Although the circumstances behind killings are rarely recorded, the evidence suggests that the people involved in them were commonly quick to take offence and easily moved to violence, in outbursts which were all the more dangerous because people could easily lay hands on weapons of some kind, whether staffs, or knives (even a lunatic was able to obtain one, **365**), or dangerous tools like flails (**314**) and spades (**586**). Confrontations on roads (**15, 16**), or on a bridge (**231**), or in a mill (**166**) could all have disastrous consequences. Insults were resented; they might be prosecuted in local courts,[153] and no doubt often had more sinister outcomes. It was probably with good reason that the steward and bailiff of John Giffard took over £11 from the men of Longbridge Deverill for offering insulting words (*verba contumeliosa*) to Laurence Kyx at a wrestling match;[154] in 1281 the justices thought the sum excessive, but the officials may have taken a strong line in order to quell bitterness and prevent uproar. If so, they could be regarded as wise, given the way disputes which arose from seemingly trivial causes could end in bloodshed and death. When Thomas the miller of Chalke came to his mill and did not find his servant in it, the resulting quarrel ended in Thomas striking the man down with a stake (**100**). Thomas Faukes was so enraged when he found Philip Sueteblod fishing in the Avon that he dealt him a fatal blow with a stone (**69**). A fight between the dogs of Gilbert le Blechere of Odstock and Roger Horn led to a fight between their owners, in which Gilbert knocked Roger down and was subsequently accused of killing him, though at the eyre a jury decided that Roger had died naturally (**80**).

The processes of distraint, themselves often violent, were always apt to lead to disorder and worse. A dispute over suit of court between Margery of Uffcott and the chancellor of Salisbury cathedral, during which Margery beat off successive attempts at distraint, culminated in the chancellor's officer occupying her house in full armour and overseeing its demolition (**189**). Distraints were commonly taken in the form of livestock; men understandably objected to their loss, not least because they would probably have to pay to receive them back, if, indeed, they recovered them at all, and often resisted their seizure. A number of townships in Chedglow hundred, distrained for arrears of money owed to the sheriff, 'with force and arms hindered the king's bailiffs from distraining them, and took their animals from them ...', an offence which cost the men of Hullavington, which had been prominent in

---

152   JUST 1/1005/2 m. 122d.

153   *Highworth hundred rolls* i, 87; Pugh, *Court rolls of the Wiltshire manors of Adam de Stratton*, 138 – in both cases the alleged insult was calling the plaintiff a thief.

154   JUST 1/1005/2 m. 149.

resisting, ten marks (**249**). Distraints taken in the form of pledges for future recompense were no less contentious. John le Messor of Compton, presumably that township's hayward, and as such a man of local consequence, was killed by Robert Palling, who gave him 'many wounds' with a staff when he tried to take a pledge from him (**179**). But in other cases it was the would-be taker of the pledge who turned to violence, for instance Henry Grom, who tried to take a pledge from Thomas le Kake when he found him fishing in the Wylye, presumably where he had no right to be, and when Thomas ran away pursued him and struck him dead with a pick-axe (**447**).

Men often seem to have been made more quarrelsome by drink. Medieval Englishmen were notoriously partial to ale.[155] Until around 1261 the men of Stert, in Studfold hundred, paid 4s. per annum at the sheriff's tourn. Twenty years later it was revealed that although the money had gone on being collected, the men of the township had stopped giving it to the sheriff, preferring instead to spend it on booze-ups (*potationes*) at the tavern.[156] In 1281 this disclosure may have made the court smile, but the justices would probably have found such a presentment less amusing in 1268, when a dozen killings were said to have been committed either in taverns (**251**) or by men who had just come out of them (**117**), with one quarrel claiming two lives (**121**).

Many men and women were killed in their houses by criminals who had broken into them in pursuit of plunder, while a smaller number perished at the hands of those who shared their homes. Seven men are recorded as having killed their wives, Ralph Ful killed his daughter as well (**393**). Presentments in local courts suggest communal disapproval of violence by men against their spouses – in April 1282, for instance, William Saillefest was amerced in Highworth hundred court 'because he drew blood from his wife',[157] and in May 1284 William Castle was amerced in Highworth portmoot 'because he ill-treated his wife'[158] – and there is record of attempts to prevent it, though these did not always end happily. John Smalred, setting about his wife, fatally injured his stepmother when she attempted to stop him (**587**). Similarly when Richard le Marchaunt of East Martin beat his wife Clarice, her brother Peter intervened to protect her, so forcefully that Richard allegedly killed him in self-defence (**95**). In two cases the roles were reversed, and wives killed their husbands, on both occasions with the support of outsiders. The relative scarcity of such a crime may have been at least partly due to the severity of the penalty for it. The wife who killed her husband committed petty treason, and therefore risked being burnt alive – the fate suffered by Christian, the wife of David of Medbourne, following her conviction at a gaol delivery (**349**). Isabel, the wife of John Page, who killed her husband in Salisbury with the help of Felice la Grosse, was more fortunate, and the two women made their escape (**617**).

155   Thomas of Marlborough, *History of the Abbey of Evesham*, ed. and trans. J. Sayers and L. Watkiss (Oxford Medieval Texts, 2003), 354-5 and note 2.

156   JUST 1/1005/2 m. 144.

157   *Highworth hundred rolls* ii, 204

158   Pugh, *Court rolls of the Wiltshire manors of Adam de Stratton*, 146.

The strains which underlay these acts of violence can seldom even be guessed at. It is probably significant that Robert of Cowley, a Buckinghamshire man who killed his wife and threw her body into the Avon, should have had the assistance of one Christian le Fys, presumably his mistress (**551**). After Thomas Blaunchard had killed his wife Gillian and fled, his mother Agnes, who was in the house when the crime was committed, came under suspicion of it and had to face trial at the eyre. She was acquitted, and the accusation was found to have been malicious, but that it was made may point to a local belief that there had been ill-will between wife and mother-in-law which contributed to the former's death (**380**). On four occasions men were said to have killed their brothers. Again, the circumstances are usually mysterious. The eyre roll contains nothing to explain why, for instance, John le Kyng of Catcomb killed his brother Robert as they went through Lyneham fields (**207**). But in one case there are clear signs of severe family tensions. Thomas, the son of Walter de la Leghe, became so angry with his father that he tried to strike him, and then went for his brother Richard who had come to their father's aid, whereupon Richard felled Thomas with an axe (**407**). Parricide was a heinous crime in a patriarchal society like that of medieval England, and like the killing of husbands by wives, and for the same reason, could be regarded as petty treason. Although it is impossible to say why the Leghe family was so afflicted, the attack on Walter, and the violence of Richard's response to it, offer a rare and fleeting glimpse of a family riven by discord which erupted in fierce violence.

As recorded, attacks on the very young were similarly rare. Children could be caught up in domestic violence – in an action in Highworth hundred court in 1279 Alice de Wydya was alleged to have thrown her child at the man from whom she was claiming maintenance for it[159] – and they were no more immune than anyone else from the asperities of a rough society. In 1249 a boy named Adam was said to have run away when he was threatened with a beating for failing to keep sheep properly, and was never seen again.[160] In the later middle ages infanticide seems to have been increasingly left to the church courts,[161] but in the thirteenth century it fell within the remit of the eyre, and was prosecuted like any other form of homicide, at least where it could be shown where responsibility for it lay. The man who threatened Adam came to the 1249 eyre, but was cleared of harming him. In 1281 the Bradford jurors told how Isabel of Bradfield bore a male child to Robert Hudde, and when he was a year old she carried him to Robert's house in Clevancy. But Robert refused to accept him, so she left the baby on the village street, where he died in the night 'for lack of keeping'.[162] Probably she intended to shame Robert into providing for his child, though it is possible that she hoped some stranger would adopt the infant – earlier in the century Bishop Poor's statutes had included a clause ordering the baptism of abandoned babies, clearly a problem

---

159   *Highworth hundred rolls* i, 116

160   *Wiltshire crown pleas, 1249* no. 508.

161   R.H. Helmholz, *Canon law and the law of England* (1987), 157-68.

162   JUST 1/1005/2 m. 139d.

which the priests of his diocese might have to deal with.[163] In this case the jury pronounced the death accidental, but the justices amerced Robert and Isabel, and also the township of Clevancy, because they 'so left the infant that he died by their negligence'. The justices in 1268 clearly took very seriously the death of four-year-old Roger, son of Robert le Taylur, who died a few weeks after being injured at play; they accepted that he had died by misadventure, but still inspected his alleged slayer in court, even though John Turgys had himself been only five when Roger died (**491**). Calculated infanticide must often have been concealed, if not always successfully – the 1249 eyre heard the sad case of a Wraxall girl who buried her new-born child in a ditch, only for a dog to disinter it and carry the little body down the village street[164] – but still seems to have been rare. The 1268 eyre roll contains only one example, the death of an unknown child for which John Atteberton was put in exigent (**136**), and it was no more commonly presented at later eyres.

One case that did come to light was presented at the 1281 eyre, when William of Newton was described as having 'found a one-year-old female child in his house in Coulston, and as he found the child weeping he killed her ...'.[165] It was probably impatience and sudden anger, rather than deliberate brutality, which moved William to his savage act, and the same must be true of many of the homicides recorded at the 1268 eyre. But some men and women undoubtedly killed neighbours and associates out of malice aforethought. In 1281 a fatal quarrel between Richard le Fotour and Richard of Grittenham was said to have arisen 'out of ancient hatred between them' (*pre antiquo odio inter eos habito*),[166] and though none of the killings among the 1268 pleas was presented in such terms, it is likely that some of them could have been, perhaps when spouses slew one another, or when servants killed their masters. The death of the rector of Fonthill, for instance, killed by his servant with an axe as he slept in his hall one evening, can hardly have been other than premeditated (**524**). The horrible fate of Jordan son of Herbert of Shaftesbury, 'apparently dragged to his death by a tether tied round his arm', would seem to point to considered cruelty on the part of his anonymous killers (**103**). But it is worth observing that it was not always necessary to use force to bring a man to his death, and that malicious accusations could also be directed to lethal ends. In 1249, in a vivid illustration of the way tensions could develop within a family, Robert of Bodenham, a tenant of the bishop of Winchester's manor of Downton, had done his utmost to secure the deaths of his own wife and two sons on a charge of theft.[167] And at the 1268 eyre it was discovered that Ralph of Poulshot, lord of the manor of Poulshot, had had his tenant Peter Enok charged with the killing of Roger le Schyreve for no better reason than that he wanted to recover the land which Peter held

163   *Councils and synods* i, 70. See also J. Boswell, *The kindness of strangers: the aban-donment of children in western Europe from late antiquity to the renaissance* (1988), chapter 9.

164   *Wiltshire crown pleas, 1249* no. 189.

165   JUST 1/1005/2 m. 141d.

166   *ib.*, m. 134.

167   *Wiltshire crown pleas, 1249*, no. 166 and note.

from him. That the land was worth one mark per annum gives some idea of the value which Ralph placed on Peter's life – had the plot succeeded, Peter would have been hanged for Roger's death (**266**). The king's justices were required to examine indictments with great care, in order to ensure that innocent men were not convicted on false charges.[168] Despite their efforts such charges went on being made, and it is impossible to be certain that none ever achieved their malevolent purposes.

Suicide

Suicide, too, was a felony, one committed against oneself – hence its invariable designation in the eyre roll, *felonia de se ipso*. Seven suicides were recorded in 1268, compared with four in 1249; the differences are too slight for any certain meaning to be read into them, though the smallness of the figures has its own significance. Like homicide, suicide was a mortal sin, but unlike homicide it was never allowed any secular justification - it could not of its nature be committed accidentally, or in self-defence. As a felony, suicide entailed forfeiture of free lands and chattels. Where confiscation was involved, the treatise *De legibus* once attributed to Bracton distinguished between suicide committed by a felon desperate to avoid conviction and the self-destruction of an invalid or depressive, but legal practice ignored the distinction, at the 1268 eyre as elsewhere.[169] The chattels of Roger le Bewr, who killed himself at the second attempt (**110**), were forfeited as comprehensively as those of Adam the miller of Downton, who escaped from prison after being arrested for theft and threw himself into the Avon (**82**). The motive for suicide is very rarely given. For Edith Husful, who stabbed herself after being arrested for setting fire to a house (**531**), her fears may have been multiplied by a particular dread of punishment, since in some quarters burning was regarded as the appropriate penalty for arson. Nicholas de Kyngebure and Serlo de Bernake were both recorded as having no chattels, and perhaps made away with themselves for that reason. John Ive, who drowned himself in the Were, and whose chattels were described as consisting solely of twenty-five acres sown with crops, may have despaired of holding out against hunger and want until harvest-time (**547**).

It is possible that other suicides went undetected, perhaps misrepresented as accidents or the work of brigands. A pressing motive for disguising them thus was to avoid the forfeitures which suicide entailed, as ruinous for the dependants of the self-slayer. Hence, no doubt, the false valuation of the chattels of Adam of Downton – the three townships responsible must have wanted to salvage something for Adam's widow, recorded as having discovered his body. But there was probably also a stigma attached to suicide, resulting from the religious sanctions against it, which relatives or communities will have wanted to avert. The death of Hugh the chaplain of Codford, who hanged himself in his house, prompted the most determined attempt at concealment recorded in the entire eyre roll (**441**). It seems likely that a cleric's suicide

168 *ib.*, 95-6.

169 H. Summerson, 'Suicide and the fear of the gallows', *Journal of Legal History* 21 (2000), 49-56.

was regarded as particularly shameful, and covered up for that reason. Indeed, the stigma of suicide was probably one that people sometimes tried to add to a death, in order to make it more disgraceful. Perhaps Thomas de la Slade hoped to conceal his own responsibility for the death of John, son of John of the wood, when he killed him and hung his body up on a hazel tree, but it seems that he also wanted to make his victim appear contemptible, and to injure his family, by making John's death look like suicide (**373**).

Theft

Theft became a capital felony when the goods stolen were worth more than 12*d.* – reckoned to be the amount a man or woman needed to stay alive for a week.[170] In 1249 a woman convicted of petty theft was ordered to find pledges for her future good conduct,[171] and at a gaol delivery in 1280 a man found to have stolen wool worth 3*d.* was ordered to leave the liberty of Chippenham,[172] but no parallel cases were recorded in 1268. As with homicide, intention was important. When John Harding absconded with a horse, surcoat and book belonging to his brother, the Chippenham jurors assured the court that his purposes had been positively high-minded – 'he did this not with any intention of stealing (*non animo furandi*), but only because he wished to go to the schools at Oxford', and would return the goods once he was there (**577**). It is impossible to tell how many acts of theft were committed in Wiltshire during the period covered by the eyre. Burglaries which also entailed homicide, and alleged robberies which gave rise to private prosecutions, were recorded individually, but otherwise the justices were more concerned to identify suspected thieves than to learn about their individual misdeeds.

The number of men and women put in exigent on suspicion of theft, nearly all under the heading *De indictatis*, was in fact lower in 1268 than it had been in 1249, falling from 130 to 115. But there are grave problems with the latter figure, in that the number of indictments made by juries varied sharply, and, indeed, implausibly, with several presenting areas naming few or no suspects. In particular, it is impossible to believe that the combined jury for Chippenham borough and hundred knew of only one malefactor, or that no fewer than twelve hundreds, along with the boroughs of Malmesbury, Wilton and New Salisbury, contained no suspected evil-doers at all. It is also noteworthy, and presumably connected with the unevenness of the indictments, that very few people were hanged for theft in 1268 – only eight, compared with twenty-one in 1249. These inconsistencies and gaps in coverage suggest either serious problems in the organisation of the eyre, perhaps arising from insufficient time for preparation, or perplexities among those involved in its workings. It is possible that the amnesty for offences committed in the civil war, once it became known, had again created difficulties – if a thief was not to be charged with felonies committed in 1264 or 1265, was it proper, or even reasonable, to accuse him of identical crimes perpetrated in 1263 or

---

170   *Britton* i, 56 note i.

171   *Wiltshire crown pleas, 1249* no. 116.

172   R.B. Pugh (ed.), *Wiltshire gaol delivery and trailbaston trials, 1275-1306* (Wiltshire Record Society 33, 1978 for 1977), no. 155

1266? Whatever the cause, the 1268 eyre's record of thieves and thefts, as of homicides, is even on its own terms manifestly incomplete.

That is not to say that it is without value. That thieves had continued to frequent the county, and probably in greater numbers, is clearly shown by the striking increase in recorded abjurations, from thirty-one to seventy-one, and probably also by the higher number of recorded hangings at gaol deliveries and on private gallows, twenty-five compared with eleven. If the latter rise is due in part to there having been more gaol deliveries in the years since 1256 than in the 1240s, that in itself must at least partly reflect a greater need for such sessions. These figures also show that communal alertness against criminal activity, along with a readiness to pursue suspects and fugitives, was being maintained in the townships, and also in the countryside beyond, where the goods targeted by thieves must often have been found. Those goods are not in fact often defined, but they included sheep (**17, 107, 446**), pigs (**426**), cattle (**313**), deer (**544**) and horses (**525**), and also corn (**102**) – the varied products of a society which seldom specialised in its agricultural practice, though sheep, as a major source of wealth at every social level, were probably especially liable to be taken. In 1281 William le Rous of Fyfield was recorded as having stolen twenty-three sheep and four lambs in Hampshire and then driven them to Selkley hundred, where their owners caught up with him and killed him as he resisted arrest.[173] The small flock was worth fighting for, and sheep were evidently thought worth killing for as well – hence the slayings perpetrated outside Thomas of Canford's sheep-fold and the bishop of Salisbury's sheepcote (**51, 394**). Cloth, too, was stolen – linen as well as woollen (**261**) - and so were clothes (**589**).

Much theft must have been essentially opportunistic, and as such could prove ill-judged, as when Stephen de Wynterburneforde made off with Nicholas Royrun's horse and cart, only to find that he could not flee fast enough with his booty to escape Nicholas's pursuit, and had to take sanctuary in Coombe church and abjure the realm (**252**). The sort of pilfering recorded in the Highworth hundred court rolls, involving things like tools, poultry and items of clothing, was probably also often done on the spur of the moment, and in response to a pressing need. Such offences must have been common, reflecting a widespread poverty. They were beneath the attention of the eyre, but the thieves recorded there, along with many of the known killers, came from the same indigent milieu. The number of them with no chattels rose from 103 in 1249 to 125 in 1268, of those with chattels worth less than 3s. 4d. from eighteen to forty. More of them were women, often found together with their husbands – seventeen female abjurations or exigents were recorded in 1268, compared with nine (and one conviction of petty theft) in 1249. Of the men, the number of thieves in tithings had declined, from ninety-seven to seventy-nine, but there were many more described as strangers, with an increase from fifteen to fifty-six. Since only seven men were described as having been harboured outside a tithing, as against twenty-four in 1249, while the number of reported burglaries, with or without homicide, fell from twenty-nine to twenty-one, at first glance it would appear that the separation

---

173   JUST 1/1005/2 m. 118.

of those whose place in the life of townships had been consolidated by their membership of tithings, from the rest, who were excluded from every aspect of communal life, was still being successfully maintained, and may even have improved. Potential or would-be criminals, it could be argued, were being either kept away from the world of the law-abiding or detected and pursued when they penetrated it. There may be an element of truth in this (it is supported by the higher number of abjurations), but it is also likely that the number of those illicitly harboured was seriously under-recorded – the eyre roll often does not say whether a thief was in a tithing or not, and in such cases most of the men concerned were probably either strangers or had been received into townships without being compelled to join tithings. Consequently it would probably be safer to conclude only that the existing system of law enforcement continued to function, despite the threat posed to it by a rising tide of homelessness and vagrancy.

In 1276 Bishop Wickhampton appropriated Purton church to Malmesbury abbey 'for the sustenance of guests and of the needy, of whom a countless multitude has flowed almost continuously to them ...',[174] and that this was not just rhetoric is suggested by the will of Robert de Cardevill, treasurer of Salisbury cathedral, who at his death in 1264 made bequests of sums ranging from 20s. to £20 to the poor of nine parishes, instructed his executors to buy rents which, among other good works, would suffice to give 100 poor people a farthing a day for ever, and ordered that a third of his otherwise undistributed goods should be given 'to the poor and wretched – widows, the sick and the infirm ...', in the form of food, clothes and shoes.[175] The hospital of St John in Cricklade had been founded to meet the needs of poor wayfarers, probably in the 1220s.[176] By the 1260s such birds of passage were becoming numerous, as the 1268 eyre roll amply demonstrates. It is not surprising to find it recording killers and thieves from the neighbouring counties, from Gloucestershire (**218, 272, 378, 431**), Somerset (**529, 561**), Oxfordshire (**372, 481**) and Berkshire (**356**). But the county also attracted evildoers from the Welsh marches, from Monmouthshire (**46**), Herefordshire (**395, 402, 408**) and Shropshire (**465**), and from Wales itself (**428**), from midland counties like Warwickshire (**7**) and Northamptonshire (**584**), and from still more distant shires, from Lincolnshire (**48**), Derbyshire (**308**) and Yorkshire (**405**). Of the last of these, Richard of Pontefract, it was superfluously noted that he had not been in a tithing because he was a stranger, and the same could have been said of the man he killed, John of Ireland.

Some of these outsiders had probably come to Wiltshire in the retinues of lords with possessions elsewhere – Roger le Wodewarde, a Devonshire man in the mainpast of Hugh Peverel, who had important interests in both Devon and Wiltshire, must have been one such (**430**). Recent disturbances in Wales and its marches may have dislodged some people and sent them on

174   Brewer and Martin, *Registrum Malmesburiense* i, 421–4

175   W.R. Jones and W.D. Macray (eds.), *Charters and documents illustrating the history of the cathedral, city, and diocese of Salisbury in the twelfth and thirteenth centuries* (Rolls Series, 1891), 342–6.

176   *VCH Wiltshire* iii, 335.

travels which brought them to Wiltshire. Others could have been drawn to that county by the opportunities for work provided by royal castles and palaces, or by Salisbury cathedral. Mobility in itself was unremarkable in thirteenth-century England, people moved about freely, and over long distances. Gillian, the wife of an Amesbury carpenter named William Gyffard, came into court at the 1281 eyre suspected of the death of her husband, who had disappeared. She declared that William was in fact still alive, and that fearing for his prospects because he had failed to finish work on a barn, he had gone to Ireland. This was largely corroborated in letters patent sent by the mayor of Bristol, though he reported that William had not in fact reached Ireland, having died a natural death at Haverfordwest in Pembrokeshire.[177] There was clearly nothing implausible about Gillian's story of her husband's departure, and she was acquitted.

William Gyffard, it may be surmised, had been a respected craftsman when he set off for Ireland, but there were increasing numbers of people at large of whom that could not have been said. Not everybody who lead a vagrant life in fact came from outside Wiltshire, some were described as strangers even though they were named in terms of townships in the county. John Grym of Westwood, for instance, who abjured the realm for theft (**174**), was presumably known in his own neighbourhood, but had either been unable to join a tithing or had been expelled from one. There must have been many others like him, suspicious characters, perhaps, long before they crossed the line dividing disreputability from actual felony. No doubt there were many vagrants who stayed within the law, or at any rate tried to, by finding work or subsisting on alms, just as there were some for whom a wandering life was a necessary element in their employment, pedlars and tinkers for instance, and also travelling entertainers. Roger Hobyhors and Ranulf le Taborer, both said to have been hanged sometime before 1281,[178] must have been men of this sort, along with William of Hereford, a bear-keeper (*ursarius*) who was hanged for killing Griffin Grosmund, described as leading an ape.[179] William left chattels worth 7s., which may well have been the value of his bear.

The insecurities of a vagrant existence, without frankpledge and other societal constraints to keep them from going astray, must often have led men like William of Hereford into evil courses, so justifying, and intensifying, the contempt, and also fear, with which they were regarded in the townships through which they passed. It was impossible to keep them away completely. Extra arms might be needed at harvest-time, and individual beggars may sometimes have been regarded as harmless, though if they were given shelter it was probably often in shacks and outhouses, like the 'old building', part of Thomas of Woodford's house, whose fall killed John de Anesy, described as a beggar (**545**), and perhaps the barn in which an unknown man was found killed in Wroughton (**195**). But those who accommodated strangers did so literally at peril of their lives (**486**), helping to explain why wandering strangers were readily identified with 'thieves', a term which was generally

177   JUST 1/1005/2 m. 138.

178   *ib.*, mm. 141, 149

179   *ib.*, m. 130d.

applied to evil-doers more formidable than mere pickpockets and raiders of hen-runs - 'bandits' would be a more fitting description. The law-abiding went in dread of them – Henry III's charter for New Salisbury of 1227 had empowered the bishop to enclose the new settlement in ditches 'for fear of thieves' (*propter metum latronum*)[180] – and with good reason.

It is not surprising that such people were rarely identified – juries representing townships which were required to keep them at arm's length can seldom have been in a position to discover their names. The best source, though a tainted one, for the world of criminal vagrancy is appeals made by approvers, the medieval equivalent of queen's evidence. The approver was himself a felon who in the hope of saving his life confessed his crimes to a coroner and accused others of associating with him in them. If he secured enough convictions, either by defeating the people he accused in judicial duels or through convictions by juries, his life was spared and he was allowed to abjure the realm.[181] Very few achieved this, however – jurors were well aware that approvers had every reason to lie, and almost invariably disbelieved them. The only approver recorded in 1268 was Nicholas Gangy of Shorncote, who appealed three men, apparently before the earl of Gloucester's bailiffs, of associating with him in theft. They were subsequently acquitted, whereupon the bailiffs let Nicholas go (**426**). This was an anomalous case in every respect, since the right to conduct proceedings involving approvers was usually reserved to the crown, and there is no evidence that the earl possessed it. But the justices were probably reluctant at this time to challenge a man so powerful, and therefore adopted the simple expedient of treating Nicholas like any other fugitive felon, and had him put in exigent. A few more conventional approvers were recorded in other sources from the period covered by the 1268 eyre. One of them, John le Brazur, was taken to Newgate in 1260 at a cost of 10s.,[182] and will have made his accusations there, probably alleging crimes committed in many counties besides Wiltshire. But others stayed in prison at Salisbury, and brought their appeals there. Approvers were maintained by the crown, at the rate of 1d. a day, and sheriffs accounted for payments to these men, along with the cost of equipping them for duels, and of 'doing justice' afterwards, that is, organising executions, either of the approvers or of the men they had accused. In 1264, for instance, two approvers were paid a total of 9s. 6d. for a total of fifty-seven days, a single duel cost 6s. 3d., and a further 4s. 1d. was spent on doing justice.[183]

Although the 1268 eyre roll records no appeals made by approvers besides Nicholas Gangy, it contains enough material - particularly when it is reinforced by cases from later eyres - to make it possible to say something about the shadowy world inhabited by men and women who were either full-time criminals or well on the way to being so. Many of the burglaries recorded at the 1268 eyre, which juries could attribute only to 'unknown

180   Jones and Macray, *Charters and documents ... of Salisbury*, 176.
181   H. Summerson, 'The criminal underworld of medieval England', *Journal of Legal History* 17 (1996), 197-224
182   *CR 1259-1261*, 71; *CLR 1260-1267*, 110.
183   E 372/108 m. 11.

criminals', must have been the work of such people, breaking into houses to slaughter their occupants and steal whatever they could carry away. They attacked churches, too, and to no less deadly effect – when an attempt to break into Foxley church was foiled by the parson's son, his intervention cost him his life (**235**). But thieves were no less dangerous in the fields and woods, and certainly no more merciful. Maud the daughter of Simon le Brewere was killed in the fields near Penleigh by unknown malefactors, no doubt for the oxen she was driving (**301**). Several anonymous killings were perpetrated in woods and forests. In some cases the victims were themselves unknown, like the two men found killed in Norridge wood, 'having many wounds' (**460**), and both killers and killed could perhaps have been numbered among the evildoers who shot arrows at gamekeepers – such as those who killed Philip le Parker in Conrish park (**530**) - or were described as having been robbers (*depredatores*) as well as poachers.[184] In others only the attackers were robbers. A woman named Wenciliana was fatally wounded in Chippenham forest by criminals who stole her cloak (**585**), while Thomas Trepas was killed in Braydon forest, and his wife Emma wounded, by men who carried off their clothes (**246**). It is quite possible that burglaries, too, often ended in the stripping of dead bodies.

Woods could provide cover for attacks on wayfarers, as when three men stole the tackle of two Shaftesbury nuns as they passed through the bishop of Winchester's wood near Knoyle (**521**). But thieves did not need such protection to make the roads dangerous, and their operations clearly made some places notorious – Bishopstone parish, on the boundary between Wiltshire and Berkshire, contained both a Rogues Way and a Thieves Way.[185] An unknown man was killed on 'the king's highway of the Fosse', on the western county boundary (**241**), while Richard le Marchaunt was killed by unknown malefactors on 'la Rigweye'.[186] In 1281 the approver James Horn (who secured a number of convictions, suggesting that his testimony was unusually reliable) described an attack in a valley called 'la Bysse', apparently on the road to Bristol, in which a man with a horse loaded with apples was killed.[187] Criminals probably often lay in wait outside major towns. Thus Walter son of Aunger was killed as he travelled from Devizes to Rowde (**35**), three men were cut down at Puthall, on the approaches to Marlborough (**507**), and an unknown man was found killed in the road outside Ludgershall (**624**). Perhaps he had been going to Ludgershall market, as Richard le Ferur of Avebury was doing when he was attacked by two strangers, who tried to rob and kill him (**115** – the entry was left incomplete). Markets and fairs presented opportunities for theft which criminals exploited. One gang of unknown malefactors killed Walter le Cok as he came from Heytesbury fair (**315**), another did the same for Thomas le Deveneis as he made his way home from Bradenstoke fair, waylaying him in a wood between Stanton and Christian Malford (**569**). James Horn told how on 1 November 1280 he and

184   E 32/198 m. 14.
185   *VCH Wiltshire* xii, 3.
186   JUST 1/1005/2 m. 132d.
187   *ib.*, m. 160.

at least two other men had lain in wait outside Westbury to rob men coming from Warminster fair (perhaps they were travelling in a group for security's sake),[188] while in 1289 criminals were described as infesting Heytesbury fair, where one of them cut a purse containing 5s.[189] – a valuable prize, equivalent to several weeks' wages for an agricultural labourer.

A few of the people suspected or convicted of felony bore names suggestive of their milieu. William Dychewater (**74**), Maud Bareleg (**284**) and Agnes Shakepurs,[190] for instance, and also Adam le Beggere, who killed Agnes of Bristol in Chippenham forest, and was unsurprisingly described as 'a stranger and vagabond'.[191] Henry Evelbred was a member of a tithing when he was put in exigent in 1281 for killing a man in Braydon forest,[192] but once outlawed he would probably have had little choice but to live up to his name. In 1305 a man was indicted as the leader of 'a great company of thieves',[193] but in earlier decades felons seem usually to have operated in modest-sized groups, of no more than four (**234**) or six (**550**) men. Such bands were no less dangerous for being small, their ferocity being perhaps intensified by their separation from conventional society and the dread they inspired within it. When unknown malefactors came one night to burgle the house of Peter Walerand in Highworth hundred, one of them managed to get inside and open the door, whereupon his associates took him for Peter and killed him instantly.[194] The whole tithing of Studley turned out to lie in wait for two robbers in Chippenham forest; one of them was arrested and later hanged, the other, described simply as a stranger, put up a fierce resistance and wounded many of his assailants before he was captured, half-dead, and carried in that state to a cross nearly half a mile away, where he was beheaded.[195] Although it was lawful to kill a felon in self-defence, or when he was resisting arrest, in this case the justices must have felt that the stranger's helplessness made such summary justice unnecessary, and the Studley men had to pay 40s for inflicting it. But for the villagers, who had disposed of a social scourge, the sort of man they were positively required to treat with suspicion if not outright hostility, perhaps the money was regarded as well spent.

Appeals of felony and breaches of the peace
Thieves were usually prosecuted at the king's suit, through the process of indictment. There was an alternative process which could be used against them, as there was in cases of homicide, in the form of the appeal of felony.[196] But whereas juries were also required to name those who killed or stole in their

---

188   *ib.*, m. 162.

189   JUST 1/1011 m. 53d.

190   JUST 1/1005/2 m. 148d.

191   JUST 1/1011 m. 49.

192   JUST 1/1005/2 m. 120.

193   Pugh, *Gaol delivery and trailbaston trials*, no. 781.

194   JUST 1/1005/2 m. 116d.

195   *ib.*, m. 136.

196   *Wiltshire crown pleas, 1249*, 69-74.

veredicta or *privata*, and were penalised if they failed to do so, accusations of rape (discussed separately below), assault, mayhem, unjust taking of goods and similar offences against the peace were usually only brought to the attention of the king's justices when an injured party chose to sue by way of an appeal, bringing the case within the remit of a royal court by the claim that felony had been committed and the king's peace broken. Appeals continued to be made throughout the thirteenth century, but their use declined steadily, in Wiltshire as elsewhere. Thirty appeals made by thirty-four people alleging offences other than homicide and rape were heard at the 1268 eyre, compared with fifty-two appeals by fifty-seven people in 1249. The number of appellees remained almost constant – 137 in 1249, 131 in 1268 – but the 1268 total is seriously distorted by the single action in which four men united to appeal no fewer than fifty men of robbery, in a case stemming from a dispute over Bradford-on-Avon church (**167**). In 1268, as in 1249, there were appeals which alleged burglary, robbery and theft, and some of them clearly involved genuine felonies (e.g. **609**). But most appeals at both eyres were concerned less with offences that could have brought those who had supposedly committed them to the gallows, than with non-felonious wrong-doings of the kind later classified as torts, and in the middle ages referred to under the general heading of trespasses.

It is very likely that torts were prosecuted in the county court; its records have disappeared, but the sheriff of Wiltshire's account for 'perquisites of the county' in 1258/9 included a payment of 4s. by Roger of Purbeck 'for trespass done to William of Berwick'.[197] More certainly, the records of Kinwardstone hundred court in 1262 and Highworth hundred court in the 1270s and 1280s contain numerous actions alleging just such offences. These often employed an appeal-like formula, but the peace supposedly broken was that of the lord of the hundred – the earl of Leicester or Adam of Stratton - not the king's. The Highworth court dealt with such issues as disputes over pledges and distraints, insults (on one occasion arising from an attempt to collect a royal tax), and assaults, some of them violent. When Henry Arnald sued William the deacon in 1282 for breaking into his house and attacking him, it was decided that this offence amounted to felony and should be prosecuted in the county court. But Henry evidently decided that this would be too much trouble, for three weeks later William was amerced of just 6d. 'for trespass done to Henry Arnald'.[198] This settled the case, which went unmentioned at the 1289 Wiltshire eyre.

The obvious alternative to the appeal, for anyone wanting access to the king's courts, was the writ of trespass, but in the 1250s and 1260s this was still in process of development, and only seven actions of trespass are recorded among the 1268 civil pleas.[199] Like the appeal (**581**), trespass could be prosecuted in the Westminster courts, and a few cases show this happening. In 1258, for instance, Arnulf de Maundevill prosecuted Walter Giffard (a future archbishop of York) and others in the bench for assault and carrying

197   E 389/136 mm. 4d-5d.

198   *Highworth hundred rolls* ii, 223-4, 226.

199   JUST 1/998A mm. 9d, 11d, 13, 13d, 14, 15, 17d.

off goods which included his strong-box, in what was said to have been a quarrel arising from a game of dice at Boyton.[200] In 1266 Richard of Bedford, who was convicted at the eyre of ordering an attack at Milston in which the householder was beaten up and his corn taken (20-22), himself brought an action in the *coram rege* court alleging that four men had broken into his house at Rockley and removed goods worth £40. Richard renewed his action at the eyre, but among the civil pleas,[201] and as far as the crown pleas were concerned the incident might as well have never happened. A similar silence covered proceedings in the exchequer court involving offences allegedly committed against royal officials, for instance the claim made in 1260 by Adam de Aroges, an exchequer clerk, that William le Someter of Upham and others had attacked his carters and beaten and wounded them.[202] As with homicide and theft, though even less surprisingly, the record of breaches of the king's peace which fell short of felony is demonstrably far from complete, indeed, it never aspired to completeness.

Given its disadvantages, the survival of the appeal may seem surprising. It was an antiquated action which had to be made in an elaborate set form, setting out the time, place and circumstances of the alleged offence in minute detail, and recording that the hue had been raised, the neighbouring communities alerted, and the case formally prosecuted in the county court, where appellor found pledges that he or she would make suit – in 1281 the county court was amerced for allowing a plaintiff to proceed without having done this[203] – and where the coroner enrolled it (e.g. 595). If the accused then appeared, he would be either imprisoned or attached by pledges, depending on the seriousness of the offence, in order to ensure his appearance at the next eyre. If he did not, the appellor was then expected to repeat his appeal at the next four sessions of the county court, at the last of which the appellee who remained contumacious would be outlawed (or, if a woman, waived). Assuming both parties came to the eyre, the appellor must then repeat his accusation, in exactly the same words used to lodge it in the county court, and unless he was maimed, over the age of sixty, or a woman, he was required to conclude by offering 'to prove against him as against a felon to the king by his body as the court shall decide' – in other words, offering to fight.

Trial by combat, except where approvers were involved, was discouraged in English courts by the 1260s. It remained a possibility, as a homicide case at the 1268 eyre demonstrates (598 – there is no evidence that the proposed duel took place), but the king's professional justices clearly disliked it, and litigants seldom showed much enthusiasm for it either – four appellors described themselves as maimed, and so unable to fight (20, 133, 508, 595). Appellees were for their part no keener on battle, and to avoid it, as well as to cast doubts upon the accusations against them, would usually subject the charges against them to rigorous scrutiny, pointing out formulaic inadequacies and also discrepancies between appeals as they were made in the county court

200   KB 26/160 m. 37d.
201   JUST 1/998A m. 13.
202   E 159/34 m. 1.
203   JUST 1/1005/2 m. 157.

and at the eyre. Naming another place as the scene of an attack, or failing to identify the exact part of a field in which an assault took place, or even not specifying which bone had been allegedly broken (**133, 595**), would be sufficient to enable the justices to quash an appeal. This did not bring proceedings to an end, however, for the king's peace had supposedly been broken, the matter still had to be investigated, but proof was supplied by a jury's verdict – something likely to have outweighed the inconveniences of the appeal for many litigants.

Those inconveniences extended beyond a cumbersome and verbose procedure. The inability of women to fight was regarded as giving them an unfair advantage over men, and their ability to proceed by appeal was accordingly severely restricted - in theory a woman could only bring an appeal for the killing of her husband 'in her arms', for the rape of her virginity, and (in 1268 a recent innovation) for an assault which had caused her to miscarry. A woman might use an appeal to allege some other offence, but the appellee who responded by claiming that her accusation extended beyond the customary limits could expect to see his objections upheld, the appeal quashed and the appellor amerced (**189, 345**). A further disadvantage of the appeal was its failure to provide damages - the best an appellor could hope for was the restitution of his property if he was alleging robbery or theft.

Very few of the thirty appeals had an untroubled passage in court. In no less than twenty-one cases the appellor either failed to attend the eyre or came but declined to prosecute, while a further seven appeals were quashed on technical grounds. Seventy-four appellees were convicted, on at least part of the charge – a figure distorted by the forty-nine men found to have forcibly occupied Bradford-on-Avon church and seized a coffer in it (**167**) – and six more either had been, or were to be, outlawed. Twenty-five were formally acquitted. Of the rest, some had died, but in a number of cases no clear verdict was given. The nature of the offences varied; sometimes a single trespass or felony was alleged, but in several cases two or three were prosecuted together. Thus four appeals alleged mayhem, with two of them involving attempted arson as well, while one action involved a charge of arson alone (**276**). Three appeals alleged violent attacks, defined variously as assault, beating and wounding, upon the accuser, and eight brought charges of robbery, burglary or theft, but fourteen prosecuted combinations, in various degrees, of robbery with personal violence.

What appellors hoped to achieve will have varied according to circumstances. Some will have wanted justice, or revenge, perhaps with the encouragement of their communities when serious breaches of the peace were at issue. In some cases charges were obviously inflated, particularly by the addition of robbery to the accusation, perhaps in the hope of forcing an out-of-court settlement, something the justices always inquired into. Actions in lower courts were frequently settled by arbitration. The love-day, whose avowed purpose was the reconciliation of disputants, was a regular feature of proceedings in Highworth hundred court. But the eyre was different, at least where the crown pleas were concerned. Presumably the courts had decided that royal justice should not be exploited for private ends, and that allegations of breach of the king's peace, once made, must be thoroughly investigated and authoritatively concluded.

The possibility of such treatment must in fact have been one reason why some litigants chose to bring appeals – their disputes involved complex issues, and sometimes also important people, and could only be satisfactorily handled in the king's courts. No doubt they could have sued at Westminster (in at least one case they did, **581**), but there was an obvious convenience in being able to litigate closer to home, to add, perhaps, to the possibility of exerting greater pressure on the jury. The appeals which Richard of Milston and his son brought against Richard of Bedford and others, for instance, alleging violent assault, attempted arson and the removal of corn, arose from what was plainly a serious breach of the king's peace in itself, and one that was also potentially complicated by reason of its date, four days *before* what was eventually decided (though not, it would seem, until after this appeal had been made) should be the official conclusion of the recent civil war (**20–22**). Alexander of Trowe's appeal against Richard de Bahuse, for robbery committed 'after peace had been proclaimed in England', seems to have presented similar difficulties, and the justices put it to one side for discussion (**105**). By contrast the appeal which Margery of Uffcott brought against three men, one of them the chancellor of Salisbury cathedral, claiming that they had destroyed her house and removed her livestock and valuables, proved to be related to an action of novel disseisin which Margery had been prosecuting simultaneously, and that both actions stemmed from attempts to distrain her to perform suit of court. The complexities of the case, which are vividly demonstrated by the confused state of the manuscript recording it, were such that a double jury was needed to resolve them (**189**).

Margery was herself an appellee in what seems to have been essentially a property dispute (**191**). Her action against the chancellor of the cathedral was probably one which could have been plausibly brought only in a royal court, Heigham having been too important and influential a man to be prosecuted anywhere else. The same is true of Walter Scammel, a royal clerk, archdeacon and future bishop, who was the principal defendant in the appeal made by Robert le Franceys and three others, alleging that they had been robbed of £200. The sum turned out to have been greatly exaggerated, but the importance of the case is shown by its having been concluded *coram domino rege* (**167**). The appeal made by Henry Heleman, reeve of Coombe Bissett, shows a relatively humble man getting caught up in a quarrel between his own lord and Hugh de Plessis, a local grandee who was the son of the earl of Warwick. Threatened with violence by Hugh's men, Henry did not dare to continue his action after the two landowners settled their dispute, and he failed to prosecute it in 1268, but his appeal, once made, remained on the record, and the case was therefore investigated at the eyre, where the justices decided that it should be discussed further (**259**). The outcome is unknown, but Henry's appeal, though it cost him one mark, at least ensured that the affair was not swept under the carpet, with its serious repercussions for lesser folk ignored. In this last case an appeal of felony alleging robbery and arson, although the appellor had in reality been the victim only of attempted assault, was the means of bringing to light a potential threat to public order, while a jury's verdict established the background to events in a way which trial by combat could never have achieved.

However, there was one other way of proceeding available to litigants, namely the plaint, the straightforward demand for justice addressed to the king or to his representatives.[204] The use of the plaint was normally limited to particular circumstances, notably to recently-committed offences, but its potential for litigation had been widely publicised in the years on either side of 1260 by its employment as an agency of political reform,[205] and it was occasionally exploited by men and women who would otherwise have had to prosecute appeals, or perhaps been unable to sue at all. Ralph Pycot had begun an action against Robert of Hampton in the county court as an appeal, alleging mayhem, assault and robbery, but at the eyre he abandoned all the formulas of his action and continued his suit 'in complaint' (*conquerendo*), with a simple statement of the alleged offence. Robert objected to this departure from the usual protocols, Ralph's action was quashed, and the case went to a jury, which found that the two men had fought together, and that Robert had wounded Ralph in self-defence. Both parties were therefore taken into custody (**508**). In this case perhaps it was nothing more than the relative simplicity of the plaint which made Ralph change his manner of prosecuting. But in another case the plaint was the only method used, when Agnes of Hilperton and her daughter complained of robbery and assault at Melksham. The offence was said to have happened more than ten years earlier, on 11 June 1257, a lapse of time which could have invalidated their complaint. On the other hand, as women they were liable to be barred from proceeding by appeal. At the end of the case, when the accused had been acquitted, the plaintiffs were pardoned an amercement by Henry de Montfort, one of the justices, on the grounds that they were poor (**508**). If the continued use of the appeal illustrates the adaptability of an ostensibly outmoded form of action, the possibility of recourse to the plaint underlines the way in which the eyre could provide an access to royal justice which legal formalities might otherwise have denied.

Rape

Rape was a felony, albeit one hedged by qualifications, which in turn probably arose, at least in part, from problems of definition, for the same word – *raptus* – was used to describe both sexual assault and forcible abduction.[206] The clearest example from Wiltshire of the latter comes from the 1281 eyre, where three men were arrested, and acquitted, for having allegedly ravished – *rapuisse* – a nun from Wilton Abbey.[207] But the appeal which Cecily, the widow of Richard le Frankeleyn, brought against Walter son of Roger of

204   Discussed by H.G. Richardson and G.O. Sayles (eds.), *Select cases of procedure without writ under Henry III* (Selden Society 60, 1941).

205   Primarily under the first clause of the Provisions of Oxford: *Documents of the baronial movement*, 98–9.

206   J.B. Post, 'Ravishment of women and the statutes of Westminster', J.H. Baker (ed.), *Legal records and the historian* (1978), 150–64.

207   JUST 1/1005/2 m. 152.

Charlton in 1268 (**334**), may well provide another instance, since although all women were in principle protected by the king's peace against rape, it had become accepted doctrine that a valid appeal was limited to the rape of virginity, and a widow who made one might find herself non-suited as a result.[208] The fact that Cecily did not attend the eyre, however, makes the circumstances of this case unknowable. Until 1275, moreover, when the first Statute of Westminster of 1275 raised the possibility of arraignment at the king's suit,[209] rape, however understood, was almost invariably prosecuted by an appeal, which itself could only be brought by the self-proclaimed victim. This created difficulties for a would-be appellor, who had to publicise the loss of her virginity, several times, starting with the raising of the hue and other formalities demanded of all appeals, continuing in the county court, and culminating (if she persevered long enough, and if the appellee could be arrested or attached) in a formal accusation at the eyre, where she would have to persuade a male jury of the truth of her allegations, knowing that conviction could in theory lead to the accused being blinded and castrated. Unsurprisingly, the number of appeals of rape made at any eyre was seldom great, while the conviction rate was invariably low.

The way in which appeals of rape were made and treated can be better illustrated from the 1249 eyre than from that of 1268, since the former heard many more of them, nineteen to the latter's five (including Cecily's referred to above). Of the appellors in 1249, one was a widow and one a wife, while one had died. One was a servant, while nine were defined not by place-names but as the daughters of a parent, usually a father, suggesting that they were young women. Of the twenty men they appealed (one was accused as an accessory), two had already been outlawed, one woman was licensed to continue her action against a defendant who failed to come to the eyre, and two appellees were put in exigent; of these last, one had confessed his guilt in the county court and was attached to come to the eyre, which he failed to do, while the other had been sued at the previous eyre, in 1241, and put in exigent there, but had returned to the peace before absconding for a second time. Another fugitive appellee was found to have been accused by his lover, but was still put in exigent as a suspected thief. In three cases no verdict of any kind was given, either because one of the parties was dead or because neither came into court. Six appellees were formally acquitted, though one was said to have made an agreement with his accuser. Of three more men who did the same, no verdict was given on two, but the third was convicted. He had been appealed by a widow who failed to prosecute at the eyre, which may explain why he was allowed to make fine by one mark. In one case the settlement took the form of marriage, which also concluded the single case in which an appellee came into court and was convicted. The fact that the appellor had withdrawn her action may have mitigated the sentence, but it is also possible that the justices were influenced by the doctrine laid down in

208   H. Summerson (ed.), *Crown pleas of the Devon eyre of 1238* (Devon and Cornwall Record Society new series 28, 1985), xxxvii–xxxviii.

209   Rothwell, *English Historical Documents iii*, 400 (clause 13).

the treatise *De legibus*, that a woman could save her rapist from mutilation by consenting to marry him.[210]

The details of the 1249 eyre do much to explain why appeals of rape were rare (the total from this eyre was in fact much higher than usual) and seldom resulted in convictions. The penalty for rape was potentially very severe, and of a kind which male jurors are unlikely to have wanted to see inflicted on other men. That the prosecution of rape could in any case be regarded with indifference or hostility by men is shown by the difficulties which confronted Margery, daughter of Walter, when she prosecuted William de Cattesdene for raping her. William, who was eventually outlawed, was the prior of Winchester's hayward, and as such probably an important figure in Bushton, where the attack probably took place, which may explain why, when Margery first pursued him after the attack, she was seized and imprisoned by five men, presumably more concerned to protect an employer or associate than to see justice done to his victim.[211] The process of making an appeal must have been both embarrassing and burdensome, while the consequences of an unsuccessful action could have been distinctly injurious, since the accuser had admitted to being no longer a virgin but had failed to show that this had been involuntary. A summons to appear in the rural chapter on a charge of fornication might well have resulted. The inevitable result was that the women who brought appeals were often of low social status – one was a servant, three were poor, one was prosecuting a lover who was himself a thief, and nine were probably very young, raising the possibility that they were acting under the influence of parents and kinsfolk – which in turn made convictions even harder to obtain. Consequently respectable women must often have been reluctant to risk losing their good names by prosecuting their assailants.

How reluctant they might be is surely demonstrated by figures like the very low number of appeals of rape brought at the 1268 eyre – five at the most. The pattern was much like that of 1249, with three actions being brought by women described as daughters, and so probably young; one of them was also said to be poor. In four cases the appellor did not come to the eyre (in two of them the appellee did not attend either). Edith, daughter of William de la Cote, who had begun her appeal against Philip de Wyxsy seven years earlier, did at least prosecute in 1268, but her appeal was quashed, while her claim of rape was found to be no more than a bloody nose suffered when Philip 'threw her to the ground when playing ...', an offence which cost him 6*s.* 8*d.* (**364**). In the case of John Balriche, appealed by Maud of Hungerford of robbery as well as rape, the jury similarly found that he only 'threw her to the ground against her will', an offence against the peace described as a 'trespass' (**264**). In three of the cases in which the appellor absented herself the jury stated that there had been no agreement between the parties, showing that either they or the justices were aware that an appeal of rape could be used to force a settlement of some kind. One of these was the only appeal, that of Alice daughter of Richard le Frye against John de la Punde,

---

210   *Wiltshire crown pleas, 1249* no. 517; *Bracton De Legibus*, ed. and trans. S.E. Thorne, ii (Cambridge, Massachusetts, 1968), 417 (fol. 148).

211   *Wiltshire crown pleas, 1249* nos. 273-4.

to result in a conviction, inasmuch as the jurors found that John 'forcibly lay with her' (*vi concubuit cum ea*), a rather equivocal expression which may have been intended to suggest that John had imposed himself on Alice as his mistress rather than raped her as a stranger (**359**). The justices ordered John's arrest, and nothing further was said of the case. Of the case of Maud daughter of Walter le Paumer, who had appealed Thomas le Thecher, nothing was said at all. Neither party came, though both had found pledges, and no verdict was called for (**109**).

It seems wholly improbable that only five women were raped in Wiltshire between 1256 and 1268. The soldiery recorded as moving about the county at the time of the civil war is unlikely to have been any less rude and licentious than armed men have been at other times – the appeal of rape which Maud the wife of Richard le Cupere made against Warin, the constable of Devizes' man, in 1249,[212] at the very least bears witness to the threat which men in garrisons could be seen as posing to the civilian populations they were intended to protect. It is certainly possible that the civil war amnesty had caused appeals to be dropped, either when it related directly to offences committed during the relevant period, or because it created uncertainties as to which accusations should be proceeded with, regardless of when the offences in question had occurred. But it seems just as likely that the procedure involved in the appeal of rape, with its unwelcome publicity and potentially dire impact on the appellor's reputation, had become such that few victims of rape were prepared to make use of it.

The church and clergy

Among the constraints which could have inhibited men and women from acts of violence and dishonesty were the moral values and religious sanctions proclaimed by the Christian church, which constituted a powerful presence in thirteenth-century Wiltshire. The most important man in the county after the king was arguably the bishop of Salisbury, whose spiritual office, supported by a large, wealthy and distinguished cathedral chapter, gave him the command of a network of parishes covering the whole of his diocese. These he could supervise directly, if intermittently, through visitation, while exercising a continuous jurisdiction over priests and people alike through a hierarchy of courts whose competence included such matters as wills, perjury, marriage, and sexual morality generally, all closely affecting the lives of the laity. Discipline was enforced through excommunication, a formidable weapon in itself, in that it left its victim isolated and without rights, and made potentially more effective by the bishop's ability to call on the king's government to act against those who refused to submit to it.[213] Thomas de la Forde, sued *coram rege* for trespass allegedly done to Jordan de Cotele late in 1269, was cleared when he showed that he had been sent by the sheriff to arrest Jordan as an excommunicate, and had otherwise done him no harm.[214] The bishop also had his own gaol, for the confinement of miscreants like the two clerks recorded

---

212   *Wiltshire crown pleas, 1249* no. 207.

213   R.N.Swanson, *Church and society in late medieval England* (1989), 179-81.

214   KB 26/201 m. 5d.

in 1249 as having been imprisoned for possessing forged papal bulls (possibly they were men of the sort denounced in Bishop Bingham's statutes, as using false apostolic letters to raise money under the pretence of collecting alms).[215]

The bishop of Salisbury was a great landowner, the lord of three and a half hundreds, while the bishop of Winchester, who had two hundreds, was likewise a powerful figure in parts of Wiltshire. Alongside the secular church, moreover, there was a large religious establishment, which under Henry III's pious leadership was still increasing in number and wealth. In 1268 it consisted of thirteen monasteries and nunneries, one Templar and possibly one Hospitaller preceptory, a Franciscan and a Dominican friary, six cells dependent on overseas monasteries, fifteen hospitals, and two collegiate churches.[216] Some of these houses were very ancient, long predating the Norman Conquest, but others were recent foundations – Easton Priory and Wilton's house of black friars in 1245, De Vaux college in Salisbury and Wootton Bassett hospital in 1262 and 1266 respectively. In addition, a number of houses outside Wiltshire owned substantial estates within it, notably Glastonbury, Shaftesbury and Romsey abbeys and Winchester cathedral priory.

It was observed earlier that many Wiltshire churches were enlarged during the thirteenth century, and there seems no doubt that the number of secular clergy in the county increased as well. Not only was there more work for the latter to do as the population expanded, but there was also a need for additional priests to staff private chapels and chantries. These were usually founded by wealthy landowners, like the wooden chapel which Ralph de Thony was licensed to build in the courtyard of his house at Britford in 1236,[217] or one which Sir Richard of Havering founded and equipped at Wilton in Great Bedwyn parish in 1258; he and his wife, with their family and household, were permitted to attend a daily mass in it, but in all other respects the rights of the mother church at Great Bedwyn were upheld[218] – a proviso calculated to ensure that the establishment at the latter was not affected, numerically or otherwise, by Sir Richard's foundation. But people of lesser means might also cooperate to the same end – in 1264, in a striking act of communal piety, the vicar of Bishops Cannings and fifteen of his parishioners clubbed together to give lands and rents to endow a daily mass in their church.[219] Yet others may have supported a hermit or recluse, like the female recluse (*incluse*) whose barn at Wroughton was found one day to have a dead body in it (**195**).

With the wealth, manpower and buildings at its disposal, the church was in a good position to propagate its message in Wiltshire. This was not just a matter of preaching that homicide, theft and acts of violence were mortal sins, or of using the confessional to induce penitence in those who had committed them. There are also clear signs, in the statutes of Bishops

---

215   *Wiltshire crown pleas, 1249* no. 565; *Councils and Synods* i, 386.

216   Details from *VCH Wiltshire* iii.

217   Jones and Macray, *Charters and documents … of Salisbury*, 232-3.

218   *EEA, Salisbury* no. 173.

219   *ib.*, no. 207.

Poor, Bingham and Bridport, that the clergy (to whom they were mainly addressed) were required to act in ways which could have had a significant effect both on attitudes towards criminality, and on the sort of behaviour which could lead to it, within lay society as a whole. Thus the statutes of Richard Poor, bishop between 1217 and 1228, urged parish priests to act as peacemakers between members of their flocks and to give alms to the poor. They were not to grant absolution to self-confessed thieves until they had returned what they had stolen. Homicide, and other crimes like setting fire to churches and the debauching of virgins and nuns, were major sins, for which only the pope or his legate could grant dispensation. Condign penance was to be enjoined upon those whose perjured testimony may cause others to lose life or member, 'as often happens'. Perjurors, along with sorcerers, incendiaries and common brigands (*raptores publici*), were to be solemnly excommunicated three times a year.[220] This last clause was taken up by both Bingham and Bridport, and extended to all who disturbed the king's peace and the tranquillity of the realm.[221] Bridport, believing like his predecessors that the clergy would be better able to influence for good the behaviour of the laity if they distinguished themselves clearly from them, in both appearance and behaviour, ordered the priests of his diocese to proclaim their clerical identity by having their heads tonsured and by wearing clothes of becoming simplicity, without superfluous ornaments. He also forbade them to hold secular offices or engage in trade, to attend performances by players and jesters, to play at dice and to frequent taverns. Bridport also ordered parsons to forbid their parishioners to attend the communal drinking parties known as 'scotales', and to withhold the sacraments from those who persisted in going to them.[222]

There is no reason to suppose that Bridport's efforts to limit his flock's drinking rights were popular, and indeed, the clergy's attempts to raise standards of morality and behaviour among the laity may often have seemed intrusive and unwelcome. Whether they were therefore ineffective it is hardly possible to say, since there is no way of knowing what people might have done, or even intended to do, but were stopped from doing by religious considerations. Vagrants and paupers, people with no settled place in any community, were probably largely immune to ecclesiastical influence. Even if they sometimes benefited from the alms which priests and monasteries were expected to distribute, they were more likely to regard churches as sources of valuables than as places of religious instruction. The silver chalice, vestments and books which Richard of Havering undertook to provide for his chapel would have been highly attractive to men like the unknown malefactors who attempted to burgle Foxley church, and cut down the parson's son when he raised the hue on them (**235**). In 1281 a man was hanged for robbing Wilton abbey church, possibly the same crime, described as 'robbing St Edith's shrine of the gold and silver with which it was covered', for which a chaplain was

---

220 *Councils and Synods* i, 64, 73, 74, 76-7.

221 *ib.*, 387, 567.

222 *ib.*, 560, 565.

put in exigent at the 1289 eyre.[223] Another man was put in exigent then 'for stealing wax in the great church of Salisbury'.[224] He had no chattels, and the wax candles used in the cathedral, so much more valuable than the tallow ones which burnt in most houses, must have constituted a temptation he could not resist.

The effectiveness of religious constraints on people with a more secure place in society is hard to assess. Bishop Poor ordered his clergy to warn women every Sunday not to risk overlying their babies by taking them into their beds, not to leave them alone in houses containing a fire, and not to allow them to go near water.[225] The fact that some women took these risks (**6, 250, 269**), does not mean that his admonition was always ignored. The violent quarrel which erupted between Walter del boys and Stephen Mouhan on Trinity Sunday 1267 shows how anger and the urge to revenge could lead to the desecration of what should have been a holy day (**595**), not that people under emotional pressure were invariably impervious to considerations of time and place as these were enjoined by their religion. Despite the church's avowed hostility to sexual immorality, the sin of lust inevitably continued to lead to men and women assaulting and killing one another. Robert of Cowley's slaying of his wife, in which he had the assistance of a woman who appears to have been his mistress (**551**) may be one example; the case from the 1281 eyre in which two brothers killed the man they found in bed with their mother is more certainly another.[226] But the number of such cases, even allowing for the frequent silence of the records concerning motivation, may have been genuinely low, and the same was probably true of suicide.

Members of the clergy, both secular and regular, made a number of appearances at the 1268 eyre, as both perpetrators and victims of crime. By this time the church's claim to jurisdiction over its own members, which had been central to Henry II's dispute with Thomas Becket a century earlier, had a settled form, in the 'benefit of clergy' which men in orders were entitled to claim when they appeared in royal courts on charges of felony. It was not an entirely unqualified right, however. The procedure as it had become established by 1268 can be illustrated from the case of Adam le Clerk, one of several men appealed of killing Nicholas Marmyun (**265**). On coming into court, Adam's first response to the accusation was to refuse to answer it, on the grounds that he was a clerk, after which the bishop of Salisbury's official – no doubt after he had presented the bishop's letters patent authorising him to act, as he did in another homicide case (**327**) - formally claimed him for the church courts. The record is silent as to whether Adam was obliged to prove his clerical status, though a reference in 1249 to a man who 'pretended to be a clerk and was later hanged' certainly suggests that a claim to be a cleric was liable to be scrutinised.[227] Later in the thirteenth century a man pleading

223   JUST 1/1005/2 m. 151; JUST 1/1011 m. 59d.
224   JUST 1/1011 m. 62d.
225   *Councils and Synods* i, 70.
226   JUST 1/1005/2 m. 138d.
227   *Wiltshire crown pleas*, 1249 no. 288.

clergy would either have to pass a reading test or show his tonsure (in 1289 a suspected thief presented a freshly-shaven crown by way of evidence, but it turned out to have been the work of his gaoler).[228] But in any case Adam was not handed over immediately. The king's courts had been steadily asserting their right to jurisdiction over offences against the king's peace, even when these involved people whom they were unable to judge, and under a formula seemingly introduced in 1247, 'in order that it may be known what sort of man is to be handed over to him', the case was referred to the country, that is to a jury, the same one convened to try the other defendants. All were acquitted, and the justices ended the case by declaring that there was no need for Adam to be handed over to the bishop. Perhaps this was standard practice before 1268, but this eyre appears to be the first at which such a statement was made, and it may have aroused some ecclesiastical discontent, by emphasising the extent to which the lay courts now controlled procedure involving members of the clergy.

A clerical suspect convicted at an eyre or gaol delivery was handed over to the bishop for confinement in the latter's prison while he awaited the opportunity to clear himself in accordance with ecclesiastical practice, and meanwhile any chattels he had were confiscated on the crown's behalf. When he came into the bishop's court, he was not required to clear himself of the specific offence of which he had been convicted before the king's justices, but instead had to undergo the process known as purgation, which involved finding at least twelve men willing to swear to his good reputation. If he achieved this, he could claim to have established his innocence, and therefore apply for the return of his chattels – a process which might take some time. During the spring of 1257 the exchequer was notified that a priest named Richard Makerel, who had been accused of homicide, probably at the 1256 eyre, had duly purged himself of the crime, for which he had forfeited chattels worth £7. The diocese of Salisbury was vacant at the time, and although its keeper was ordered to return his chattels to Richard, they had been sold and the proceeds accounted for at the exchequer. So the best that could be done was to order the keeper to pay Richard the £7 out of the money he had received from the issues of the bishopric, which he seems to have done piecemeal - Richard was still owed 35s. 1½d. in October 1258.

Richard, who must have been a man of substance, was possibly the man of that name amerced with other freeholders of Elstub hundred for failing to attend the 1268 eyre (**72**). Nothing was said of him to suggest that he was the incumbent of a parish. Such men were more likely to appear in eyre records as the victims than the perpetrators of crime, the fate recorded in 1249 of one of the cathedral's vicars-choral,[229] and in 1268 of the rector of Fonthill, killed by his servant as he slept in his hall one evening (**524**). A comparison of the two eyres shows a slight fall in the number of clerical felons between 1249 and 1268. The details for the 1249 eyre are sometimes rather obscurely recorded, but at the most ten men described as clerks were put in exigent, five each for homicide and theft, while one more had already been outlawed. One

228   JUST 1/1011 m. 67d.

229   *Wiltshire crown pleas, 1249* no. 552.

man was convicted in court of burglary and homicide, and two of robbery, while four were acquitted of homicide. Two clerks were convicted on an appeal of assault and wounding, while no verdict was given on three men appealed of other offences, when their accusers failed to prosecute. The 1268 eyre heard how one clerk had abjured for homicide (**461**) and two had been outlawed (**267, 328**), while two were put in exigent for burglary accompanied by homicide (**93, 229**) and one for theft (**55**). John Cogligan, described as 'not in a tithing because he was formerly a lay-brother in Gloucestershire' (**429**), was probably also in some sense a cleric. One man was convicted of homicide at a gaol delivery (**565**), but the verdicts on three more suspected killers handed over to the bishop at gaol deliveries were either unknown to the jurors in 1268 (**292**) or went recorded at the eyre (**506**). Three men who pleaded clergy when charged with homicide were acquitted in 1268 (**265, 327**). Members of the clergy, both religious and secular, were among the accused in six actions alleging violence and the taking of goods (**167, 189, 259, 268, 307, 581**); an appeal of wounding was to continue against one of them, but of the rest only one (no less a figure than the chancellor of the diocese) was convicted on any part of the charge.

Chancellor Heigham and the prior of Ivychurch, who was appealed but acquitted of harbouring the killers of John de Cumbe (**327**), stood out among the clerical suspects of 1268 in being men of standing in society at large. All the others seem to have been members of a large ecclesiastical proletariat, consisting of men who were clerics primarily in the sense that they had taken orders and received first tonsure; with little prospect of being presented to a benefice, they made a precarious living at best, manning chantries, acting as assistants to parish priests, and serving chapels in outlying communities. In around 1260 fifty-six people were recorded as owing a total of 10s., made up of sums ranging from 1d. to 4d., to maintain a chaplain at 'Stoke' in Westbury.[230] Such, perhaps, was the livelihood of a man like Robert, the servant of the parson of Keevil, who was handed over to bishop Bridport at a gaol delivery after being charged with homicide (**292**). The chattels of these men, when mentioned, were usually worth little or nothing. Philip Reyner, convicted at a gaol delivery of killing William de la Hyde, was unusual in having goods worth £1. 13s. 4d. (**565**), and he may in fact have been fortunate to be allowed benefit of clergy, since he was said to have been in a tithing, which clerics as a rule were not (**229**). Much more typical were men like Walter de Straford, in exigent for theft (**55**), Nicholas le Jeu, outlawed for homicide (**267**), and Roger Glendy of Wilton, who abjured for killing Adam Selyman (**461**), all of whom were paupers.

Such men, and their equivalents from the 1249 eyre, constituted both a source of constant embarrassment to the medieval church and a problem of ecclesiastical discipline which it never came near to solving. If it can at least be said that matters did not become worse in this respect between 1249 and 1268 (possibly due, at least in part, to the opportunities provided for unemployed clerics by the chapels founded by landowners like Ralph de Thony and Richard of Havering referred to above), there are signs that

---

230   J.H. Stevenson (ed.), *The Edington cartulary* (Wiltshire Record Society 42, 1987 for 1986), no. 314.

the clergy were becoming more involved in secular quarrels and disputes relating to worldly interests during those years. There is nothing among the 1249 crown pleas to parallel the sheer scale of the quarrel over Bradford-on-Avon church between Walter Scammel, who was already an archdeacon and later became bishop of Salisbury, and Ralph de Englescheville, one which drew dozens of other people in its wake (**167**), or the intensity of Margery of Uffcott's dispute with Ralph of Heigham over suit of court (**189**). Two clerics were recorded as having died by violence in 1249, but six in 1268. The circumstances are usually obscure, but the death of John the chaplain of Preshute, killed by three men in the household of the archdeacon of Wiltshire, can reasonably be assumed to have originated in tensions among members of the clergy (**126**). Ecclesiastics may also have been more often targeted by thieves, either in their persons, like the two Shaftesbury nuns waylaid on the road near Knoyle (**521**), or in their property, like Stanley abbey's grange at Richardson, which was broken into one night (**120**).

It is extremely difficult to assess the church's position, and influence, with regard to criminality. Its place in society was arguably always an ambiguous one, owing to its pursuit of incompatible aims – it aspired simultaneously to retain its status as the first estate of the realm, to keep itself unspotted from the world, and to engage with secular society in order to fulfil its mission to save souls. How hard it was to instill the standards of behaviour required of the clergy even among its own members is vividly illustrated by a case from the 1281 eyre, in which William of Grinstead, a clerk, was described as having killed John of Seaford, also a clerk, as they made their way through either East or West Grinstead on their way from a service of ordination in Salisbury.[231] Probably they had only just been ordained, but this did not prevent their coming to blows.

The right of sanctuary embodied in individual churches may have proclaimed a message of mercy, but it must also have sometimes suggested that the church's concern for its privileges outweighed its responsibilities to uphold that very peace which was professedly among its most urgent concerns. In 1281, and again in 1289, laymen were prevented from pursuing thieves into Salisbury cathedral close by 'clerks of the close' and the janitor, who would not allow them to go further than the gates, with the result that the fugitives could not be guarded properly and subsequently escaped.[232] The contradictory positions which the church's various objectives obliged it to adopt, together with the frailties of some of its ministers, probably did have the effect of vitiating its religious message. But at the same time the low number of recorded suicides, taken together with the evident piety of some among the laity, suggests that its voice could be heeded when it was raised against violence and rapine, at least by those in a position to hear it.

The Jews

One section of thirteenth-century Wiltshire society that was unlikely to pay much attention to the voice of the church was that consisting of the

231   JUST 1/1005/2 m. 146d.
232   *ib.*, m. 155; JUST 1/1011 m. 62d.

county's Jewish communities. These were situated in Marlborough and Wilton,[233] and there are also references to Jews living in Salisbury (**137, 610**) and Chippenham.[234] Religious differences and their association with usury made the Jews resented, and often hated, by their Christian neighbours (their mistreatment at the time of the civil wars was mentioned earlier, and may have been the occasion of the killing of Jospin the Jew in Salisbury – **610**), and their separation from the rest of society was accentuated by their relationship with the crown, which administered Jewish affairs through an exchequer department dedicated to them.[235] This exchequer of the Jews was staffed by justices who exercised jurisdiction over nearly all lawsuits involving Jews and most accusations against them. But although charges of felony against Jews were rarely brought before justices itinerant, some were recorded at the 1268 Wiltshire eyre, helping to illuminate the involvement of Jews in criminality, as both perpetrators and victims.

The crimes most commonly alleged against Jews involved the clipping and forging of coins. In that respect Deulegard the Jew of Marlborough, who was outlawed for forgery, was a typical offender (**509**). Later in the century other Wiltshire Jews were charged with similar misdeeds. Salomon, a Chippenham Jew, was said in 1281 to have been appealed of theft by an approver. Having escaped arrest through a conflict of jurisdictions, he fled to London and was hanged there for clipping money, possibly a victim of the mass executions of 1279.[236] At the same eyre the Branch jury told how one John le Tumbere was arrested at Stockbridge in Hampshire for clipping money, in the company of an unnamed Wilton Jew, who was also said to have been hanged.[237] John's arrest is a reminder that clipping and coining were not a Jewish monopoly. Late in 1257 William Isemberd of Wilton, a member of a powerful family in that borough and formerly its mayor, was recorded as having been hanged in London for an unspecified crime involving 'fraud and malice' – a choice of words which makes it highly likely that he was convicted of an offence against the coinage, which was a form of treason. He had acted in partnership with Abraham Russell, a Wilton Jew who had earlier engaged in money-changing transactions, and who had managed to flee overseas (his wife was able to pay twenty talents for licence to return).[238]

Hake the son of Deulecresse of Wilton had no reported accomplices when he was put in exigent for theft in 1268 (**337**), but Michael Feghin, a Jew of Old Salisbury who was put in exigent for harbouring thieves (**137**), clearly found men to associate with him in crime, as did Koc the Jew of Marlborough, hanged some time before 1281 for a burglary at Lambourn in Berkshire which he committed with one William of Wilcot, presumably

---

233   *VCH Wiltshire* vi, 12; xii, 208.

234   *Rot. Hund.* ii, 250.

235   P.A. Brand, *Plea rolls of the exchequer of the Jews* vi (Jewish Historical Society of England, 2005), 6-16.

236   *Rot. Hund.* ii, 250; JUST 1/1005/2 m. 133d.

237   JUST 1/1005/2 m. 153d.

238   *CR 1256-1259*, 357.

at least a nominal Christian.[239] Neither Koc nor William had any chattels, suggesting that a shared poverty might draw men of different religions into evil-doing together. Perhaps Isaac the Jew, whose house in Marlborough was robbed by two men (**490**), was a man of means, but it is equally possible that he was no better off than the pawnbrokers in the Wilton Jewry to whom William Planche was said in 1249 to have offered 3s. worth of stolen clothes.[240] The animosity towards them may have meant that the Jews, even more than the rest of society, came under pressure to refrain from offences against the peace, for fear of the consequences for their communities at the hands of watchful and hostile neighbours. But the Wiltshire evidence, meagre though it is, also suggests that those who transgressed, except in apparently showing a propensity for offences against the coinage, offended in much the same way as others did, in response to identical motives.

The king's rights

The king's interest in the Jews, which in theory extended to the right to take everything they possessed, was mainly safeguarded by the exchequer of the Jews. But numerous presentments recorded in 1268 show how the eyre played an important part in maintaining royal rights, primarily financial – the king stood to lose money owed to him if his bailiffs were prevented from making distraints (**19, 142, 454, 580**), or if his property was encroached upon (**135, 212, 279, 499**). The crown also lost financially when suit was withdrawn from royal hundreds, as a number of presentments attested, but the quality of local government, too, might be impaired if attendance dwindled at local courts, and especially if this affected the view of frankpledge and sheriff's tourn (**173, 249**). More generally, the king's prestige was apt to suffer if he could not hold on to what was his – in the aftermath of a civil war in which the earl of Gloucester had played a decisive role in both securing victory for Henry III and then bringing about a satisfactory settlement, the king could ill afford to be seen allowing the earl's 'might' to prevail over his own right with impunity (**425**). Similarly the earl's new gallows at Sutton Mandeville were as much a threat to the king's authority as to his coffers, which in fact do not appear to have suffered from their erection, since the chattels of a man hanged on them were secured for the crown (**145, 147**).

Other royal rights which came to the notice of the justices similarly combined fiscal with political significance, stemming from their value as instruments of patronage. Lands which had escheated to the crown, either through forfeiture or from a lack of male heirs (**73, 496**), marriage to an heiress or widow (**52, 214, 382**), the wardship of an under-age heir (**52, 435, 578**) – all provided the king with the means to win support and reward service, and were kept under supervision accordingly. Churches were safeguarded for the same reason, since they could be given to members of the king's ecclesiastical retinue, (**33, 134**), or awarded to royal clerks, to provide them with an income (**343**). When the diocese of Salisbury fell vacant at the end of December 1262, Henry III quickly took the opportunity to present to St

239   JUST 1/1005/2 m. 149d.
240   *Wiltshire crown pleas, 1249* no. 166.

Peter's church in Marlborough, a living otherwise in the gift of the bishop
(**495**). His ability to grant manors like Sherston (**541**), West Kington (**578**)
and Sopworth (**588**) to his servants and kinsmen constituted a valuable asset.
The large number of serjeanties in Wiltshire could serve the same purpose. In
1268 Robert Walerand, one of King Henry's ablest and most versatile agents,
was holding two of them, each with a manor, or part of a manor, attached.
Longford had been granted to him by its former holder, a transaction which
the king later confirmed (**258**), while a quarter of Chelworth came to him
along with the wardship of one of the heirs to a forest serjeanty, given to
Robert in 1266 (**435**). Although the serjeanties were mostly attached to estates
of modest value, they were liable to close supervision by royal justices, and
their holders constituted a body of lesser landlords who were closely linked
to the crown, attentive to its interests, and able when necessary to give a lead
to others of like rank.

The issues of the eyre

The eyre's concern with the profits of justice is discernible in almost every entry
on the roll, recording the crown's claims to criminals' chattels, forfeited lands,
and all the fines agreed upon and amercements imposed for misdeeds, failures
and infringements of all kinds. It is also implicit in omissions from the roll, for as
already observed, it seems clear that more cases were presented than were finally
recorded, especially accidental deaths – when an inquest was held, attended by
everyone summoned to it, and misadventure was found to be the cause, then
there was no need to record it at the eyre. With exclusion went abbreviation,
as represented by the single entry recording two unrelated abjurations for theft
in Purton church (**428**), almost certainly presented separately, and in greater
detail, by the Staple jurors. In 1268 all that was recorded was that neither had
chattels, the man was not in a tithing, and most significantly the township had
failed to arrest either of them and could therefore be amerced. To save space
on the roll the two cases were run into one.

   In cases of homicide there was the possibility of an additional charge, on
top of amercements for failing to pursue killers or attend inquests, in the form
of the murder fine.[241] Introduced in the years after 1066 in order to protect
French soldiers and settlers against attack by resentful natives, it was originally
a penalty imposed on townships which were unable to demonstrate that the
victims of murderous attacks had been English. Presentment of Englishry,
the process whereby such demonstrations were made, varied from county to
county – in Wiltshire it required the attendance at the coroner's inquest of
two paternal and one maternal kinsmen of the dead man or woman (**3**). In the
only case to provide details, Englishry was presented on Walter son of Philip
of Studley, killed by unknown malefactors in Chippenham forest, by two of
his brothers, along with a relation of his mother (**582**). During the twelfth
century the murder fine had come to be applicable to all deaths, accidental as
well as felonious, and to be imposed on hundreds rather than townships, but
the provisions of Westminster of 1259 had ordained that in future it should only
be incurred where death resulted from felony, and this was confirmed by the

241   *Wiltshire crown pleas, 1249*, 61-3.

statute of Marlborough of 1267.[242] At the 1268 Wiltshire eyre the distinction was observed (the justices may have decided that further discussion of the murder fine imposed for the killing of Jordan son of Herbert of Sherston was called for because the cause of death was uncertain, **103**), as it had not always been at eyres held shortly after 1259, though it may well have been felt that the justices sometimes interpreted felony over-literally – a murder fine was imposed when John Ive was presented as having drowned himself in the river Were, presumably because suicide was a felony, even though in this case it was one which the killer had inflicted on himself (**547**).

As other historians have noticed, there are problems relating to the applicability and presentment of the murder fine.[243] In 1268 it was imposed on a total of forty-four killings, in twenty-two of which, exactly half, the victim was unidentified. In such cases there can have been no possibility of kinsmen making themselves available to present Englishry, and a murder fine was accordingly to be expected. But it seems strange that no Englishry was presented in cases like those of Walter son of Aunger of Rowde, killed near Devizes (**35**), and John the weaver, killed in Seend (**273**), when the finding of their bodies by their father and brother respectively shows that there were kinsmen of the dead men available, and no less surprising that a murder fine was imposed for the killing of John the chaplain of Preshute, when the removal of his body by his killers made it impossible for anyone to present Englishry upon it (**126**). The reason for the apparent inconsistency must lie in the standing of the men and women slain (fines were imposed for the deaths of six women, one of them killed with her husband). John the chaplain, as a man in orders, almost certainly had the rank of a free man, and the same was probably true of John Ive, who held twenty-five acres of free land at his death. Clerics and freeholders might well have inherited the status of the Frenchmen whom the murder fine was originally intended to protect, making it not only pointless but even socially improper to present Englishry upon them. As for people of lower rank, the fact that villeinage was widespread in thirteenth-century Wiltshire did not necessarily make it acceptable, still less welcome. If presentment of Englishry implied recognition of unfree status, it would not be surprising if people were reluctant to undertake it, especially when the resulting fine might be shared out among the townships of an entire hundred, limiting its incidence upon individuals.

The disappearance of the estreat, the full record of the financial issues of the eyre, makes it impossible to tell how the murder fine was calculated except in a few individual cases entered elsewhere. Three fines were imposed on Downton hundred (**78, 81, 83**), which paid a fine of £3;[244] a single killing in each of Cawdon and Branch hundreds led to their being required to pay 40s. apiece (**255, 332**);[245] and Knoyle hundred, which also had one

242   *Documents of the baronial movement*, 146-7; Rothwell, *English Historical Documents* iii, 391 (clause 251).

243   *Wiltshire crown pleas, 1249*, 62-3.

244   Hampshire Record Office, MS 11M59/B1/32 m. 2.

245   E 372/114 m. 3d; E 372/116 m. 17.

fine imposed (**522**), was assessed at 26s. 8d.[246] No doubt the relative sizes and
resources of these hundreds mattered at least as much as the number of fines
to which they had become liable when these sums were calculated – it is not
surprising that Knoyle, as the smallest of them, should have been expected
to pay the lowest fine. But all were modest-sized, and larger hundreds like
Kinwardstone, Selkley and Chippenham probably paid more. In the cases of
Cawdon and Branch the fine was said to have been due from the hundred
'except liberties'. Many lords, lay and ecclesiastical, had obtained exemption
from the murder fine. Immediately after the eyre Humphrey de Bohun, earl
of Hereford, successfully claimed exemption from a demand for 16s. 4d. for
murder, 'of which the earl claims quittance by the liberty of sitting at the
exchequer ...' – a marginal note of 'constable' reveals the basis for the earl's
claim.[247] Others had been granted charters, which, however, had the effect of
exempting them from contributing to murder fines when these were levied
on hundreds, rather than from the fines themselves. Thus it was 'because it
does not participate with the hundred' that the bishop of Salisbury's liberty
in Rowborough, which constituted half the hundred of that name, had to
bear a murder fine imposed upon the whole of it after two men were found
killed near the bishop's sheepcot (**394**).

   Murder fines might no longer be levied upon deaths by misadventure,
but there was another levy which was so exacted, in the form of deodands.
Also known as 'banes', these were the material causes of accidental deaths, so
named because they were given to God, to propitiate Him for the men and
women they had killed, and the money raised from their sale did not go into
the exchequer but benefited an appropriate institution named by the king
– for the 1268 Wiltshire eyre this was the newly founded Merton College
in Oxford.[248] They came in every form, mostly livestock, but sometimes
carts which overturned on people or ran over them, boats from which they
drowned, mill wheels which crushed them, trees from which they fell, and
also included the stone which fell on a man as he dug in a quarry at Fonthill
(**517**), and the lead cistern which a man drowned in when he took a bath on
a mid-December day (**510**). Identifying deodands, having them appraised,
and ensuring that their values were accounted for at the eyre formed part
of the coroner's responsibilities. It was no easy task, for the loss of chattels
or gear was clearly sometimes resented. After Walter Peree drowned in the
Avon while trying to open the sluice-gate of Bradford mill, three townships
tried to conceal the deodand, in the form of the sluice-gate – perhaps they
claimed he had simply fallen into the river (**164**). In this case it is unlikely
that they were anxious to avoid financial loss – its estimated value was only
3d. – so much as the inconvenience of having the mill stopped and part of
it removed and sold. But in other cases deodands were found to have been
deliberately undervalued (**5, 43**), while when a servant of Alice de Beauchamp
– the widow of a Somerset baron – drowned in Semington Brook, she had
the horse from which he fell removed before the coroner caught sight of it

246   Hampshire Record Office, MS 11M59/B1/32 m. 3.
247   E 159/42 m. 16d.
248   *CR 1264-1268*, 510.

(**295**). It was a valuable animal, said to be worth £5, and she did not wish to lose it. The total value of the deodands recorded at the eyre came to £14. 1s. 6½d., but cases like this suggest that it should have been somewhat higher.

Most of the issues of the eyre came from forfeitures of chattels and lands, amercements and fines, the last being in effect settlements reached between the justices and either individuals or communities as to the money the latter should pay for their particular shortcomings or offences. Nearly all fines were recorded on the eyre roll, but not, however, the largest one, the 'common fine' made by the whole county to cover all its shortcomings as these were revealed before the justices. Entered on the 1268 pipe roll, the annual record of accounts presented by sheriffs and other royal officers, it amounted to 100 marks (£66. 13s. 4d.), the same as at the two previous eyres.[249] Such fines were a usual accompaniment to any eyre, and the justices never had any difficulty in finding grounds for them. The 'trespass' for which this one was said to have been incurred was probably the county court's failure to proceed to outlawry against four men appealed of homicide by Herbert of Knighton, which obviously aroused the justices' displeasure (**12**). Responsibility for paying the common fine would have been shared out among townships and boroughs; how this was calculated is unknown, but the prior of Winchester is recorded as owing 60s. (less some unspecified sum owed to the queen) for his lands in Wroughton.[250]

The fines which *were* recorded at the eyre, together with the forfeited chattels and lands entered on the roll, amounted to £129. 0s. 2d. Chattels – which were also liable to concealment and misrepresentation (**48, 358**) - did not involve only moveable goods. Those of Walter Burgeis of Corsham, who abjured for theft, consisted of a horse and a cow, three acres of land sown with oats, worth 7s., and debts totalling 8s. 7d., for all of which the sheriff was expected to account (**593**). Walter was in a tithing, and therefore unfree. Had he been a freeholder, his land would have been taken into the king's hand and its issues taken for a year, at the end of which it would have been stripped of everything saleable on it. Such was 'the king's year and waste', which when William Hyldulf of Cricklade was put in exigent for theft was valued at a total of 6s. 8d. William had apparently been first indicted eight years earlier, and had then absconded, whereupon his estate was seized by its immediate lord, who sold it. Its issues in the intervening period (to which the king was also entitled) amounted to 16s., suggesting that it was worth 2s. per annum, and that the 'waste' which the king finally received from it came to 4s. 8d., more than double the rental value (**424**). It should be added that fleeing from the king's peace was sufficient to justify the confiscation of a suspect's chattels, regardless of whether or not he was outlawed or convicted in court afterwards. Benedict of Soley, who was said at first to have absconded when he came under suspicion of killing Geoffrey son of Agnes, and therefore had his chattels confiscated, was later recorded as having been arrested, and when he was acquitted at a gaol delivery probably recovered his chattels by showing that he had never

249   E 372/112 m. 3.

250   A.W. Goodman (ed.), *Chartulary of Winchester Cathedral* (Winchester, 1927), no. 212.

run away (**375**). Far commoner were cases like that of Roger le Parmenter of Amesbury, who made himself scarce following the death of Robert Cod, with whom he had quarrelled. Roger forfeited chattels valued at 11*s.*, and although a jury found that Robert had died naturally, there was no suggestion that Roger, who was still on the run, should have his goods back (**8**).

The bulk of the issues of the 1268 eyre came from amercements, of which no full record survives. They were assessed at the end of proceedings, following consultations between the justices, county officials and others, and a list of them, and of all the other debts arising from the eyre, would be sent to the exchequer.[251] It did not, however, include the sums owed by inhabitants of those few liberties whose holders were entitled to receive them; these were expected to obtain royal writs to the sheriff, ordering him to provide them with particulars of the money in question, after which it was up to them to collect it. The record of the money received by the bishop of Winchester from the eyre suggests that many amercements proved to be more nominal than real. The pleas of the bishop's hundred of Knoyle record a total of four amercements on tithings, five on townships, and one apiece on the hundred's jury, an appellor who failed to prosecute (along with his two pledges), and a defaulter from the eyre, together with one murder fine and 8*s.* for a fugitive's chattels (**519-528**). The defaulter was the bishop himself, who died in Italy while the eyre was in progress, and was in any case unlikely to be summoned to contribute to his own finances. Of the other debts, the bishop's pipe roll for 1267/8 shows that just four debts were summoned – the hundred's murder fine, its jury's trespass, and two from Upton, as both a township and a tithing (in the former capacity it may have been confused with Knoyle, which was put in mercy at the eyre for failing to pursue, as Upton was not, though in the pipe roll that was the latter township's offence).[252] There was a similar shortfall for Downton hundred, where again many more amercements were imposed than can be shown to have been collected. It is possible that some were shared between neighbouring communities, in a way which left no mark on the records. But it may still have been the case that the justices intended to raise more money than could be collected.

The process of collecting the money raised by the eyre was not always straightforward. The township of Wingfield was amerced of 6*s.* 8*d.* for harbouring a killer outside a tithing (**171**), but when the king's bailiffs came to raise the money, they were kept out by the earl of Gloucester's bailiffs.[253] And when the money owed was collected, there was no certainty that it would end up in the exchequer. In 1281 the constable of Marlborough was said to have taken £3 from six men for amercements at the 1268 eyre (they probably originated in the civil pleas), but to have failed to give them the tallies which proved that they had paid, with the result that the exchequer had set about raising the money from them a second time.[254] But such difficulties notwithstanding, the pipe rolls

---

251   *Wiltshire crown pleas, 1249*, 107-9; C.A.F. Meekings, *Studies in thirteenth-century justice and administration* (1981), chapter 2.

252   Hampshire Record Office, MS 11M59/B1/32 m. 3.

253   JUST 1/1005/2 m. 125.

254   *ib.*, m. 119; see also *Rot. Hund.* ii, 262.

of the king's exchequer show that the sheriff was able to account for the first time for the issues of the 1268 eyre later in that year, when he answered for a lump sum of £333. 8s. 6d., and also for twelve individual debts totalling £134. 3s. 4d.,[255] which included a number of major fines – 100 marks from the whole county, thirty marks (£20) from Richard of Bedford (**20**), ten marks (£6. 13s. 4d.) from Ralph of Heigham and Adam le Butiller (**189**), and – from the civil pleas - the fine of forty marks (£26. 13s. 4d.) made by Henry Huse of Harting, a substantial sum for what seems to have been a relatively slight offence, and one which was later reduced to £5.[256]

There was no Wiltshire account in 1269, but in 1270 William le Dun, who had been replaced half way through the year, answered for a further £57. 11s. 8½d., along with another seventeen individual debts amounting to £13. 10s.[257] As late as 1286 the sheriff accounted for 46s. 8d. from the issues of the eyre,[258] but otherwise between 1270 and that year only individual debts were entered – one in 1272 (£2), six in 1276 (£14. 3s. 4d.), four in 1277 (£1. 10s.) and one in 1278 (6s. 8d.).[259] As accounted for at Westminster, the total issues of the eyre amounted to £559. 0s. 2½d. They would have been greater had it not been for the sums claimed by liberties, but only in the case of the bishop of Winchester is it known what these were – later in 1268 the bishop received £9 from Downton hundred, £3. 10s. from Knoyle hundred, and 16s. 8d. from the township of Fonthill, £13. 6s. 8d. in all.[260] In 1256, when the see of Salisbury was vacant, the exchequer is known to have received £46. 16s. 6d. from that year's eyre which would otherwise have gone to the diocesan, raising the possibility that the issues of a Wiltshire eyre brought larger gains to the bishop of Salisbury than to his brother of Winchester. It would not be surprising if this were so, and would add strength to the suggestion that up to 10% of the proceeds of any eyre ended up being paid into private coffers.[261]

The recorded individual debts constitute only a small sample of the whole, but still suffice to give an idea of how the justices treated some of the offences presented or discovered at the eyre. Nearly all of them originated among the crown pleas, which at this as at other eyres made a much larger contribution to the king's revenues than did the civil pleas. Only one amercement was of a sum below the usual minimum of 6s. 8d., when John le May was charged with 40d. 'for flight' – probably he was the tithingman in North Tidworth penalised for failing to arrest two killers (**10**). But some offenders were amerced in groups, so that individually they would have paid only modest sums – five of Dunworth hundred's twenty-two defaulters, for instance, were required collectively to pay a total of 10s., implying a contribution of 2s. apiece (**518**). Five amercements of hundred juries are

255 E 372/112 m. 17d.

256 JUST 1/998A m. 3; *CR 1264-1268*, 471.

257 E 372/114 m. 3.

258 E 372/131 m. 4.

259 E 372/116 m. 17; E 372/120 m. 11d; E 372/121 m. 18; E 372/122 m. 9.

260 Hampshire Record Office, MS 11M59/B1/32 mm. 2, 3, 4d.

261 *Wiltshire crown pleas, 1249*, 112.

recorded, and these, too, would have been shared out among their members. The four recorded on the royal pipe rolls, three as penalised for concealment and one for trespass, are identified only by the names of their leading members, so that for lack of a kalendar it is impossible to say which hundreds they represented. Each jury had to find 20s., not much of an imposition for a dozen men of local eminence. The Knoyle jurors were amerced of 26s. 8d. for the concealment recorded on the eyre roll (**526**); perhaps their offence was regarded as more serious, but its consequences seem unlikely to have weighed much more heavily on the men who committed it.

When a suspect escaped from custody a standard amercement of £5 was exacted from the township responsible, regardless of its size, as it was, for instance, from both Fittleton (**71**) and Chelworth (**429**). But otherwise amercements on communities were assessed according to the latter's wealth and importance as well as to the seriousness of the offence. The substantial sum of £5 exacted from the borough of Ludgershall, for its trespass in hanging a man for theft when he was not arrested with stolen chattels and when nobody made suit against him (**370**), probably shows an important township suffering on both counts. While Amesbury had to pay £2 for failing to arrest a thief (**4**), and Durrington had to find the same sum for valuing a deodand falsely, Little Amesbury paid just 6s. 8d., for an identical offence, only a sixth as much (**5**). The cost of failing to attend a coroner's inquest varied similarly, and for the same reason - it could be 6s. 8d., as it was for Purton (**198**), or 10s., demanded from Elston (**341**), or 13s. 4d., levied from Collingbourne Valence (**365**). Lockeridge's offence in harbouring the killer Nicholas Quintin (**121**) might well seem more serious than staying away from a coroner's inquest, but presumably its amercement of 6s. 8d. was reckoned to be all that a modest-sized community could afford to pay. A few amercements are mysterious. Maddington township was amerced of 10s. 'because it did not come', although no entry recording such a failing can be found on the eyre roll. The *township* of Heytesbury was required to pay 26s. 8d. 'because it did not come and for other trespasses'. Again the record of the eyre contains nothing relevant, but it is possible that in reality the offence was that of the jurors of Heytesbury *hundred*, of whom it was noted at the beginning of the civil pleas that they and the jurors of five other hundreds were in mercy for an unspecified reason[262] – perhaps they had been slow to attend at the beginning of the eyre, or inefficient in preparing their veredicta or indictments. The carelessness which has left its mark all over the record of the eyre may also have extended to the details of its financial issues.

The issues of the 1249 Wiltshire eyre (excluding the sums paid to liberties) had amounted to £673. 4s. 5½d., of which the sheriff answered for £596. 11s.[263] Those of the next Wiltshire eyre, in 1256, were slightly less profitable, totalling £565. 10s. 1d. – the yield would have been lower had the county not been mulcted twice, once of 100 marks (£66. 13s. 4d.) 'for several trespasses', and once of sixty marks (£40) for a defective outlawry.[264] Given

262   JUST 1/998A m. 1.

263   *Wiltshire crown pleas, 1249*, 111.

264   E 372/100 m. 11d; E 372/102 m. 9.

the likely impact of recent events, it is not surprising that the issues of the 1268 eyre, at £559. 0s. 2½d. should have been no higher than its predecessor's, even though it covered a considerably longer period (eleven and a half years, compared with seven). It should be said, however, that not all the money that was formally entered in the records of the exchequer was actually paid in there, for a number of payments were made out of the proceeds of the eyre before they were accounted for at Westminster. Even before the eyre began, on 21 December 1267, the sheriff of Wiltshire was ordered to pay Nicholas de Turri his yearly fee of £40 out of the issues of the eyre, while on 15 March 1268 another writ commanded that the same amount be paid to Henry de Montfort.[265] Four days earlier the sheriff had been instructed to pay £60 to one of the purchasers for the king's wardrobe, as his salary for eighteen months,[266] while on 27 March he was directed to pay £100 to Robert Walerand, 'of the king's gift', and £134 to two Italian merchants 'for cloths of silk and fine linen.[267] Three years later the exchequer was told that when William le Dun presented his account, he was to be allowed the sum of 411 marks (£274) which he had paid into the wardrobe, again for payment by its purchasers to Italian merchants.[268] This last sum may well have included the £134 which William was ordered to hand over in 1268, while Henry de Montfort seems to have received only ten and a half marks (£7) out of the £40 allocated to him.[269] Even so, the amount finally paid into the treasury would still have been reduced by £347, considerably more than half the nominal receipts.

That this should have been so is not necessarily evidence of royal extravagance or financial mismanagement. In 1268 the king needed cash at a time when other revenues were scarce, making it natural that he should exploit the issues of the Wiltshire eyre as and when they became available. He had done the same after the 1256 eyre, and on an even larger scale, diverting over £450 to his servants and creditors.[270] Henry III's ability to anticipate his income in this way illustrates the value of an eyre to the king's finances, and in the process illuminates the economic life of a county like Wiltshire, whose townships and boroughs clearly had ready access to the coin they needed to satisfy the justices' demands. By 1281 both the country and the king's authority had recovered from the strains of the mid-1260s, and their revival is reflected in the issues of that year's Wiltshire eyre – in his first two accounts the sheriff answered for a total of £1171. 15s. 8¼d.[271] As a demonstration of the reach of the central government, and as a source of revenue, the eyre remained a potent instrument of royal authority until the last decade of the thirteenth century.

265   CLR 1267-1272 nos. 59, 199.
266   ib., no. 189.
267   CLR 1267-1272, nos. 217, 223.
268   ib., no. 1570.
269   ib., 336.
270   CLR 1251-1260, 294, 309, 330, 346, 368.
271   E 372/127 m. 20d; E 372/128 m. 18.

ABBREVIATIONS

Book of Fees, *The book of fees commonly called Testa de Nevill*, 2 vols. in 3 (HMSO, 1920-31)

CCR, Calendar of Close Rolls

CChR, Calendar of Charter Rolls

CIPM, Calendar of Inquisitions Post Mortem

CLR, Calendar of Liberate Rolls

CPR, Calendar of Patent Rolls

CR, Close rolls of the reign of Henry III

Councils and Synods, F.M. Powicke and C.R. Cheney (eds.), *Councils and Synods with other documents relating to the English church ii: 1205-1313*, 2 vols. (Oxford, 1964)

Documents of the baronial movement, R.E. Treharne and I.J. Sanders (eds.), *Documents of the baronial movement of reform and rebellion, 1258-1267* (Oxford Medieval Texts, 1973)

EEA, Salisbury, B.R. Kemp (ed.), *English episcopal acta, xxxvi-xxxvi: Salisbury, 1229-1297* (Oxford, 2010).

Highworth hundred rolls, B. Farr (ed.), *The rolls of Highworth hundred, 1275-1287*, 2 vols. (Wiltshire Record Society 21-2, 1966, 1968)

ODNB, H.C.G. Matthew and B.H. Harrison (eds.), *The Oxford Dictionary of National Biography*, 60 Volumes (Oxford, 2004), and subsequent online releases

PNS, J.E.B. Gover, A Mawer and F.M. Stenton , *The place-names of Wiltshire* (English Place-Name Society xvi, Cambridge, 1939)

Rot. Hund., W. Illingworth (ed.), *Rotuli Hundredorum temp. Hen. III et Edw. I*, 2 vols. (Record Commission, 1812-18)

VCH, The Victoria County History of England

Wiltshire civil pleas, 1249, M.T. Clanchy (ed.), *Civil pleas of the Wiltshire eyre, 1249* (Wiltshire Record Society 26, 1971 for 1970)

Wiltshire crown pleas, 1249, C.A.F. Meekings (ed.), *Crown pleas of the Wiltshire eyre, 1249* (Wiltshire Record Society 16, 1961 for 1960)

CLASSES OF DOCUMENTS IN THE NATIONAL ARCHIVES: PUBLIC RECORD OFFICE CITED

C 144, Chancery, patent rolls

C 66, Chancery, criminal inquisitions

CP 25/1, Court of common pleas, feet of fines

E 32, Exchequer, treasury of receipt, justices of the forest

E 159, Exchequer, king's remembrancer, memoranda rolls

E 163, Exchequer, king's remembrancer, miscellanea

E 352, Exchequer, pipe office, chancellor's rolls

E 372, Exchequer, pipe office, pipe rolls
E 389, Exchequer, lord treasurer's remembrancer, sheriff's accounts
JUST 1, Justices in eyre, rolls and files
KB 26, Court of common pleas and king's bench, early plea and essoin rolls
SC 2, Special collections, court tolls

BIBLIOGRAPHY

Bibliography of selected plea roll publications and other studies relevant to the eyre and to law enforcement generally.

M.T. Clanchy (ed.), *The roll and writ file of the Berkshire eyre of 1248* (Selden Society 90, 1973 for 1972-3)

A. Harding (ed.), *The roll of the Shropshire eyre of 1256* (Selden Society 96, 1981 for 1980)

A.M. Hopkinson (ed.), *The rolls of the 1281 Derbyshire eyre* (Derbyshire Record Society 27, 2000)

C.A.F. Meekings and D. Crook (eds.), *The 1235 Surrey eyre*, 3 vols. (Surrey Record Society 31-2, 37, 1979-2002)

C.A.F. Meekings (ed.), *Crown pleas of the 1249 Wiltshire eyre* (Wiltshire Record Society 16, 1961 for 1960)

J. Röhrkasten (ed.), *The Worcester eyre of 1275* (Worcestershire Historical Society, new series 22, 2008)

S. Stewart (ed.), *The 1263 Surrey eyre* (Surrey Record Society 40, 2006)

H. Summerson (ed.), *Crown pleas of the Devon eyre of 1238* (Devon and Cornwall Record Society, new series 28, 1985)

H. Cam, *The hundred and the hundred rolls* (1930)

D. Crook, *Records of the general eyre* (Public Record Office handbooks 20, 1982)

A. Harding, *The law courts of medieval England* (1973)

J. Hudson, *The formation of the English common law* (1996)

R.F. Hunnisett, *The medieval coroner* (Cambridge, 1961)

N.D. Hurnard, *The king's pardon for homicide before A.D. 1307* (Oxford, 1969)

R.B. Pugh, *Imprisonment in medieval England* (Cambridge, 1968)

The ease of access to medieval legal records afforded by the AALT website is acknowledged in the commentary on editorial method. Invaluable information has also been provided by three other websites: The Henry III Fine Rolls Project, accessible at http://www.finerollshenry3.org.uk; *The Oxford Dictionary of National Biography*, accessible at http://www.oxforddnb.com; *The Gazetteer of Markets and Fairs in England and Wales to 1516*, compiled by Samantha Letters, accessible at http://www.history.ac.uk/cmh/gazweb2.html.

EDITORIAL METHOD

Although Brenda Farr originally undertook this edition intending that it should consist of a Latin transcript accompanied by an English translation, a change of plan has led to its being presented, like its precursor, *Crown Pleas of the Wiltshire Eyre, 1249*, edited by C.A.F. Meekings, in an English translation alone. It differs, however, from Meekings's notable edition in some important respects, particularly where the presentation of place-names is concerned. These are given in their modern forms where they can be identified. Many which can be identified in their basic modern forms have suffixes in the text which have since disappeared. In such cases the modern form of the place-name is used, along with the obsolete suffix in inverted commas – Bulford 'Abbess' is an example (**69**). Unidentified place-names are also set within inverted commas where they occur in running text, but where they constitute toponymic surnames they are preceded by 'de' rather than 'of', the latter being used for toponymic names which have been identified. Thus the same case contains Herbert of Knighton and Adam de Katelby (**12**). Occupational and descriptive surnames have been translated when presented in Latin, but not when written in Norman-French or English; hence 'Adam the baker' but 'William le Warener' (**167**).

Personal forenames are translated where there is a recognizable English equivalent.

Italic type is used to indicate words that are repeated or added in the margin; where the words are only in the margin and not in the body of an entry the edition places them in round brackets. Words supplied editorially to clarify or comment on the text are enclosed in square brackets. Angle brackets are used to enclose words which cannot be read but can be inferred and also for blank spaces where the words can be neither read nor inferred. A few Latin words in unusual forms are given in footnotes, as are significant interlineations and obvious mistakes.

Numbers are expressed in the MS. variously in words and in roman figures. The edition renders them in words or arabic figures as seems appropriate.

Throughout this book monetary values are expressed in terms of the system in use in England in 1268, one familiar until 1971 as that of £.s.d., under which a pound sterling consisted of twenty shillings, each of which contained twelve pennies or pence. However, the pound and shilling, and also the mark (valued at 13s. 4d., or 66 pence in decimalized currency), were essentially units of account, and the silver penny was the only coin in general circulation.

Numbers in bold type are used throughout to refer to individual cases among the crown pleas.

Unless otherwise stated, all unpublished documents cited are in The National Archives (formerly Public Record Office), Kew, London. The translation of this one is freer than might otherwise appear suitable because the original text is easily, and freely, accessible to anyone wishing to consult it through the remarkable digital archive of legal records in The National

Archives which has been assembled by Robert C. Palmer and Elspeth K. Palmer as 'The Anglo-American Legal Tradition', available at www://aalt. law.uh.edu/AALT.html. It is for this reason that the numbers of the AALT images are supplied for each side of every membrane of the crown pleas. Editorial work has been greatly eased by the ready access to original documents which AALT provides.

ILLUSTRATIONS AND MAP OF WILTSHIRE

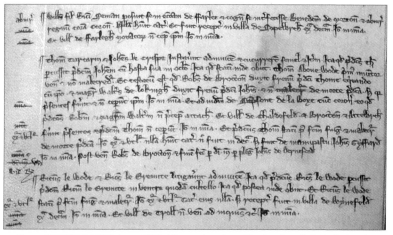

Part of JUST 1/998A m. 28d, illustrating the roll's first hand. It includes the death of John le Crispe, killed by Thomas Tartarin in a mock joust (170). (Copyright TNA)

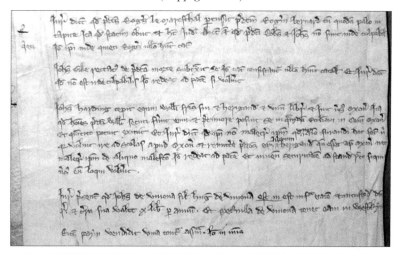

Part of JUST 1/998A m. 40, including the record of John Harding's making off with some of his brother's goods in order to fund his own education at Oxford (577). (Copyright TNA)

Map of Wiltshire hundreds and principal places referred to in the text. This map was completed by Christopher Elrington for this volume and submitted less than a week before his death in August 2009.

CROWN PLEAS OF THE WILTSHIRE EYRE, 1268
JUST 1/998A, m. 24 (IMG 0355, 0356)

1. These were the coroners after the last eyre of justices itinerant in this county: Stephen of Woodfalls who has died, Robert Drueys, Walerand of Blunsdon, Richard Pypard who has died, Ralph of Poulsholt who was removed [from office], William le Droys, Sa[m]pson of Box and Roger Pypard, who are now coroners.

2. These were the sheriffs after the same eyre: John de Vernun, Godfrey Eskydemor, Ralph Russel, Ralph Dangers, Henry de Montfort, Richard of Worcester and William le Dun who is now sheriff.

3. The whole county records that Englishry is presented in this county by two on the father's side and one on the mother's, and this both on males and females killed feloniously.

THE HUNDRED OF AMESBURY COMES BY TWELVE

4. Alice de la Rochelle fled to Amesbury church, admitted theft and *abjured* the realm. She had no chattels. It is testified that she was in the company of William of Sandwich and Simon Pryk, who were accused of theft and later arrested and imprisoned in Salisbury castle. Amesbury township did not arrest her, so it is in *mercy*. Let it be inquired more fully of *Salisbury*[1] township concerning William and Simon, what became of them, and of their chattels.

5. John son of Robert Cade was struck by a horse which was pulling a cart belonging to the abbess of Romsey, so that he died instantly. Robert Cade, the first finder, has not come, and he was attached by Amesbury tithing,[2] which now does not have him, so it is in *mercy*. No one is suspected. Judgement *misadventure*. The value of the horse (*deodand*) *2 marks*, William le Dun, the sheriff, to answer. Little Amesbury, Brigmerston, Amesbury and Durrington townships valued the horse falsely before the coroner, so they are in *mercy*. Ralph the carter was present and now he does not come. He is not suspected. It is testified that he has died.

6. John son of William le Nywe, aged one-and-a-half, was found drowned in a ditch in his father's garden. His mother Agnes, the first finder, has not

---

1 *Sarum* in the margin is written in a different, larger hand.

2 *thethingam*, a term occasionally substituted, for no obvious reason, for the more frequently used *decenna*.

come, and she was attached by Robert son of Hugh of Fifield[1] and Humphrey le Newe of the same, who are in mercy. No one is suspected. Judgement *misadventure*.

7. Robert of Baynton[2] [of Warwickshire] fled to Cholderton church at the pursuit of the men of Ludgershall, and there he admitted theft and *abjured* the realm before the coroner. His chattels *12d.*, the sheriff to answer. Cholderton township did not arrest him when this happened in daytime, so it is in *mercy*. The chattels were delivered to Cholderton tithing, which now does not have them, so it is in *mercy*. And it is testified that John of Radnor, Robert's associate, was arrested at Amesbury by the same men's pursuit,[3] and was hanged there by judgement of the court of Amesbury, which was then in the queen's hand.[4] His chattels *4s.*, the sheriff to answer.

8. Roger le Parmenter of Amesbury has made off under suspicion of the death of Robert Cod, because it was alleged against him that at one time they quarrelled together. He has made off out of fear and does not come now, but he is not suspected of Robert's death nor of any other evildoing, so he may return if he wishes, but his chattels are confiscated for his flight. His chattels *11s.*, Amesbury township to answer. He was in the tithing of Adam le Muker in Amesbury, who does not now have him to right, so he is in *mercy*. No one is suspected of the death because he died from natural causes.

9. An unknown woman was found killed in Sheepbridge wood, having many wounds. John de la Barre, the first finder, comes and is not suspected, it is not known who killed her. No Englishry is presented. Judgement *murder*, upon the hundred.

10. Isabel of Tidworth appealed Walter le Noreys and William Brun in the county court of the death of her son Reynold, so that by Isabel's suit they were outlawed in the county court. Walter's chattels *2s. 10d.*, William's *10d.*, the sheriff to answer. They were in the tithing of John le May in North Tidworth, which is in *mercy*. Isabel does not come now, and she was attached by William Walerand of Tidworth and Adam Attetuneshende of the same, who are in *mercy*. The jurors made no mention of this appeal in their *veredictum*, so they

---

1 Altered from *Ficeldon*. Faintly in the margin is written in a different hand, apparently in relation to the entry, *de hund' de ellest'*. Fifield and Fittleton are in neighbouring Elstub hundred.

2 Written in a different hand above *Itchington*, which is struck through, but through scribal carelessness 'of Warwickshire' was not cancelled as well.

3 *per sectam* – this expression could mean 'by pursuit', as it seems to do at its first appearance in this entry, or 'at the suit', meaning 'by prosecution'; in the second case it could mean either, or even both together.

4 Queen Eleanor held the manor from 1257 until 1268 during the minority of the heir: *VCH Wiltshire* xv, 30.

are in *mercy*. William Pepercorn, accused of the death, has made off. Tidworth township does not come to answer before the justices, so it is in *mercy*.[1]

11. Maud la Bere and two strangers were lodged at the house of William Beufiz, and the two strangers got up in the night and killed Maud and fled immediately. Their chattels, tithings and names are unknown because they were strangers. No one else is suspected. Hindurrington township did not pursue them, so it is in *mercy*. Amesbury, Durrington, Alton and Brigmerston townships did not come fully to hold an inquest before the coroner, so they are in *mercy*. No Englishry is presented. Judgement *murder*, upon the hundred.

12. Herbert of Knighton appealed Robert le Ku of Tidworth, John Pacok, Adam de Katelby, Henry Brun, John le Fulere, Walter de Rycold, Roger and Simon sons of Ellen of Tidworth, Ralph Crok, Gilbert son of Christian of Tidworth, Adam of Sulby, Walter Doleman, John le Messager, John le Hauekere and John le Careter in the county court of the death of William the miller of Knighton. Herbert does not come now, so let him be arrested, and his pledges for prosecuting are in *mercy*, namely William Kynt of Knighton and William Gerbert of the same. Robert and the other appellees do not come. It is testified that the king commanded by his writ that he [the sheriff] cause this appeal with all the attached persons to come before the justices at Westminster on the morrow of the Ascension in the 48th year [30 May 1264], and that writ came to the fifth county court after Herbert began his appeal against them. On the day appointed for them in the Bench the justices did not sit by reason of the disturbance then suffered in the realm.[2] Notwithstanding the writ, Herbert prosecuted his appeal against Henry Brun, Ralph Crok, Gilbert son of Christian of Tidworth and Adam of Sulby, who were not mentioned in that writ, up to the fifth[3] county court, at which the court did not proceed to any outlawry, although they [Henry Brun and the other three] were not mainprised. It is testified by the coroners and their rolls that they held a county court on that day, and the county[4] likewise attests this, so to judgement upon the whole county. Henry and the others do not come, and it is testified that nearly all of them are from Hampshire. So the sheriff

1 The entry is followd by a space wider than usual, presumably to record the completion of unfinished business. Faintly in the margin is *alibi*; see below, **23**.

2 Because of the disorder in the realm, there seem to have been no sessions in the Bench in Easter and Trinity terms 1264, while Trinity term 1265 was brought to a premature close on 1 July. C.A.F. Meekings and D. Crook, *King's Bench and Common Bench in the reign of Henry III* (Selden Society supplementary series 17, 2010), 291, 293.

3 Although the process against the principal appellees had been transferred by the king's writ to Westminster, Henry Brun and the other three men not named in the writ were still liable to exaction and outlawry, as having not appeared in the county court, which was therefore at fault for having failed to carry out the process.

4 i.e. the suitors of the court.

of Hampshire is ordered to have their bodies etc. (*Let there be a fuller discussion concerning the whole county*).[1]

13. Henry Attestyle and William son of Walter le Hayward quarrelled together, and William struck Henry in the right side with a knife so that he died seven days later. William fled immediately after the deed and is suspected, so let him be *exacted and outlawed*. He had no chattels and was in the tithing of Robert le Newe in Netheravon, which is in *mercy*. Ablington township did not arrest him when the hue was raised, so it is in *mercy*. Ablington, Figheldean and Brigmerston townships did not come fully to hold an inquest before the coroner, so they are in *mercy*.

14. John son of Serlo of Amesbury was crushed by a cartwheel which fell on him, so that he died instantly. John Golding was present, and immediately afterwards he fled to Amesbury church, where he stayed for two days and subsequently escaped from the township's custody. John does not come, but he is not suspected, so he may return if he wishes. He had no chattels, but he was in the tithing of Thomas Elys of Durrington, which it is in mercy.[2] No one is suspected. Judgement *misadventure*. The value of the wheel (*deodand*) 2s., the sheriff to answer.

15. William Stake was coming from New Salisbury when he encountered Adam of Lydiard, and a quarrel having arisen between them, Adam struck William with an axe below the knee so that he later died. Adam fled immediately after the deed and is suspected, so let him be *exacted and outlawed*. His chattels and tithing are unknown, but let there be a fuller *inquiry* of Blackgrove[3] hundred.

16. Richard, Thomas of Canford's miller, and Walter le Escriveyn encountered John le Tapiner of Boscombe on the king's highway outside 'la Forde', and a quarrel having arisen between them Richard and Walter gave John bloodless wounds[4] so that he later died.[5] Immediately after the deed Richard and Walter made off, and they are suspected, so let them be *exacted and outlawed*. Richard's chattels 2s., and Walter's 12d., the sheriff to answer. They were not in a tithing in this hundred, but Richard was in the mainpast of [Thomas] of Canford, who is in *mercy*. Walter was received outside a tithing in Winterbourne Earls township, [which is in mercy]. Amesbury, Boscombe, Allington and Newton

---

1 *est loquendum plenius* is written in the margin in the hand of the entry and *de toto comitatu* in a different hand. There is a space of about eight lines before the next entry.

2 The amercement is not noted in the margin.

3 Adam evidently came from Lydiard Tregoze in Blackgrove hundred.

4 *orbos ictus dederunt.*

5 The foot of the membrane is worn and torn, and illegible in places.

townships did not come fully to hold an inquest before the coroner, so [they are in *mercy*.]

m. 24d (IMG 0436, 0437) *Continuing Amesbury hundred*

17. Peter Bole of Hindurrington and William Wyvere, accused of theft and many evil deeds, come and deny theft and all, and for good and ill put themselves on the country. The jurors say on their oath that Peter is not guilty of any evildoing, so he is quit. Of William they say that he is guilty of stealing three sheep, so etc. [hanged]. His chattels *8s.*, Bulford township to answer.

18. As Peter Kene was coming at night from Ludgershall towards Tidworth, he encountered Adam Baghye of Tidworth and Hugh Coppe of the same, and an argument having arisen between them they [Adam and Hugh] killed Peter and fled immediately and are suspected. So let them be *exacted and outlawed*. Their chattels ( ).[1] Adam was in a tithing in the fee of Henry Hosee in 'Tudeford',[2] so [the tithing] is in *mercy*. Hugh was received in Collingbourne township, so let his tithing be inquired of from Kinwardstone hundred. Maud Kene, the first finder, has not come, and she was attached by Ralph Kene of Ludgershall and Peter the shoemaker of the same, who are in *mercy*. And Tidworth, Biddesden, Cholderton and Newton townships did not come fully to hold the inquest before the coroner, so they are in *mercy*.[3]

19. Concerning those who do not allow the king's bailiffs to enter their lands to levy what is due to the king, they say that William of Durnford does not allow the king's bailiffs to raise *5s.* a year for sheriff's aid and has withheld that money for three years. John son of Aucher has likewise withheld from the king 3s. a year owed for sheriff's aid, and has withheld them for two years.[4] Henry of Candover has likewise now withheld 3s. 4d. for eight years and more, but he comes and says that he was enfeoffed by the king with the land which owed that service for 6d. a year rent for all service, and thereon he has the king's charter. So let him show his charter. To *judgement* upon William and John, let this be more fully discussed. Later Henry comes and proffers the king's charter, which testifies that the king gave the land to Adam Cok, father of Henry's wife, whose heir she is, paying to the bailiff of Clarendon for the time being 6d. a year for all service etc. The charter was made in the 31st year [of Henry III, 1246].[5] So Henry is quit. William and John cannot

---

1 A space left for about eight words.

2 *Tudeford* is clearly written but is probably a mistake for *Tudeword*, i.e. Tidworth.

3 For more about this case see note on **625** below.

4 William of Durnford was lord of the manors of Southend and Little Durnford, while John son of Aucher was lord of Normanton manor. *VCH Wiltshire* xv, 4.

5 The land held by Henry of Candover, a carucate in Figheldean, had been granted to Adam Cok on 4 December 1246. *CChR 1226–1257*, 309.

gainsay the said service, so it is decided that they should pay those arrears and be in *mercy* for unjustly withholding them.

20. Richard of Milston appeals Reynold of Bedford, Thomas of Bedford, Richard le Careter and Richard Daldry that with others they came at night on the Sunday next after the feast of the nativity of the Blessed Mary three years ago [12 Sept. 1265] to his house, broke his doors, entered it and set fire to it, so that it would have burnt down had not the fire been put out by rain coming down. And at dawn on the Monday following Reynold and the others, ordered and sent by Richard of Bedford, came to his house, and Reynold struck him with an axe on the left shoulder and broke the bone of it, and Thomas struck him with a hazel staff on his left arm and broke it in three places, and then with the same staff struck him on his right arm and broke it, and then with the same staff struck him on his left knee so that he broke his kneecap[1] and they gave him many other wounds and blows[2] all over his body so that he was maimed. And the said Richard [of Bedford] on the same day and year, wickedly and feloniously and against the king's peace, came to Richard of Milston's house and took away his corn found there and had it carried to his own house and still detains it. And that Reynold and the others, ordered and sent by Richard of Bedford, wickedly and feloniously have done him that trespass, and that Richard has in robbery taken away his corn, and ordered that the trespass and mayhem aforesaid be done to him, he asks that inquiry be made by the country, and that justice be done him as a maimed man.

Reynold of Bedford, Thomas of Bedford and Richard of Bedford come and deny all felony, robbery, mayhem, wounds and whatever is against the peace etc. And with regard to the ordering and sending, Richard of Bedford asks for judgement whether he should have[3] to answer for it until the deed is proved. As to the corn carried off, both he and Reynold and Thomas ask that it be allowed them that after this was allegedly done, Richard of Milston did not soon raise the hue, either himself or through another, and did not in his appeal mention the township in which this was said to have happened, nor offer to prove it against them either by the words of an appeal or as a maimed man. With those things allowed them, they agree that the king may inquire about the deed. And because it is proved that Richard of Milston does not sue against them by the words of an appeal and varies in his appeal, it is decided that his appeal is null whereby they should be put to law, and let the truth of the matter be inquired into by the country.

The twelve jurors of this hundred, with the jurors of the hundreds of Ellstub and Alderbury, come and say on their oath that Reynold and Thomas did him that trespass and felony, ordered and sent by Richard of Bedford,

---

1 *os rotundum in genu.*

2 *orbos ictus.*

3 *si debeat* is repeated.

and that Richard took away the corn as is alleged against him.[1] So let him
be taken into *custody*, and let Richard of Milston be taken into *custody* for his
false appeal. Later Richard of Bedford came and made a fine for his trespass
by *30 marks*,[2] by pledge of Walerand of Blunsdon and John Gugeon.

21. The same Richard [of Milston] appealed Richard Dalry, Richard le Careter
and William Hervest of that deed in the county court, so that William was
outlawed there by Richard's suit. Let his chattels and tithing be *inquired into of
Whorwellsdown hundred*. Richard [Dalry] and Richard [le Careter] previously
came to the fifth county court and found mainpernors for coming before
the present justices. They do not come now, so Walter Russel of Cheshunt
and James Mauger of Wilton, Richard Dalry's pledges, and master Henry
Tristram and Robert Isenbert of Wilton, Richard le Careter's pledges, are in
mercy. The jurors say that they [the parties] are not agreed, but that Richard
[Dalry] and Richard [le Careter] are guilty of the said trespass, so let them be
exacted and outlawed. They had no chattels, but they were in the mainpast of
Richard of Bedford's mainpast, so he is in mercy. They were received outside
a tithing in Brigmerston township, which is in *mercy*.

22. Richard son of Richard of Milston, who appealed Thomas of Bedford
and Richard Daldry in the county court of the deed and Richard of Bedford
of ordering it, in that Thomas and Richard came on that day and place and
assaulted his father Richard, and wounded him etc., does not now come. So
let him be *arrested*, and his pledges for prosecuting are in *mercy*, namely John
Gugeon of Amesbury and Geoffrey le Wyte of Bulford. Richard of Bedford
comes and the jurors say that they [the parties] are not agreed, but that Thomas
and Richard committed that trespass on Richard of Bedford's order, so let
him be taken into custody, and let Thomas, who comes, be likewise taken
into *custody*. Richard Daldry does not come, so let him be *exacted* as above.

23. Walter le Noreys of Tidworth, outlawed in the county court for the death
of Reynold, son of Robert of Tidworth, by the appeal of Isabel of Tidworth,[3]
comes and proffers the king's charter in these words: H[enry] by God's grace
to all his bailiffs and liegemen etc., greeting. Know that at the instance of
Beatrice our daughter we have pardoned Walter le Noreys of Tidworth the
suit for our peace pertaining to us for the death of Reynold, son of Robert of
Tidworth, of which he is accused, and also the outlawry proclaimed against
him for that death. And we grant to him thereon our firm peace, provided
that he stands to right in our court if anyone wishes to proceed against him

---

1 In the margin is a large *d*, with a stroke through it.

2 Richard of Bedford's acknowledgement of a debt of 6 marks to Richard of Milston,
   recorded among the civil pleas, may be connected with this case. JUST 1/998A m.
   9d.

3 For this case see also **10**, above.

for it. In witness whereof etc.[1] There is no-one who wishes to sue against him, so firm peace is granted him. Tidworth tithing has mainprised that henceforth he will behave lawfully.

24. Concerning persons indicted they say that Roger le Coruner, Alexander Tylye, Richard le Belde, Roger Brun of Winterslow, Thomas Roeld, William his brother, Adam le Waleys of Durrington, William Sparwe,[2] John Scvypere, Robert Bugwyn, William son of Geoffrey Buryman, Michael le Nethere, Thomas Lokeman, Simon Fytele, Peter Perungel, Peter son of Herbert, Geoffrey Aymiun, William Mynpe and John Solke have made off on suspicion of theft. All except Roger le Coruner and Alexander Tylie are suspected, so let them return if they wish, but their chattels are confiscated because of their flight. They had no chattels. And let Richard le Belde and all the others be *exacted and outlawed.* Richard le Belde's chattels *9s. 6d.*, the sheriff to answer, and he was in Newton tithing[3], which is in *mercy.* Roger Brun's chattels *20s.*, the sheriff to answer, and he was in the same tithing, which is in *mercy.* John le Suyppere's chattels *2s. 3d.*, and he was in Tidworth tithing, which is in *mercy.* The others had no chattels. Thomas Roelde was received outside a tithing in Knighton township, namely in the treasurer of Salisbury's fee, which is in *mercy.* Adam le Waleys was received outside a tithing in Durrington township, which is in *mercy.* Michael le Nyther was in Cholderton tithing, which is in *mercy.* Simon Fytele was in Allington tithing, which is in *mercy.* Peter son of Herbert was in West Amesbury tithing, which is in mercy. William Mynpe was received outside a tithing in the house of William le Fryth of Hindurrington, who is in *mercy.* The others were strangers. Later William Sparwe comes and is committed to gaol (*on Saturday*).

25. William le Deym and Roger le Coruner, arrested on suspicion of theft, come and deny theft etc., and for good and ill put themselves on the country. The jurors say etc. that Roger is not guilty, so he is quit. They also say that William is guilty, so etc. (*hanged*). He had no chattels.

26. William Sparwe, accused of burgling houses and associating with thieves, Martin le Wyllefulle[4] and his wife Maud, and Felice who was the wife of Serlo Chapman, arrested for the death of Geoffrey Chapman, come and deny all theft, burglary and all, and for good and ill put themselves on the country. The jurors of this hundred, together with the twelve jurors of Alderbury hundred, [say] that William, Maud and Felice are not guilty of any evildoing,

---

1 Walter's pardon was issued on 20 January 1264 at Amiens; Beatrice had married Jean de Dreux, later duke of Brittany, in 1260. *CPR 1258-1266*, 378.

2 The name is struck through, and *venit* (he came) written above it; see **26** below.

3 *tethinga* (also spelt *thethinga*) is used throughout this entry except in the three instances of the phrase 'outside a tithing' (*extra decennam*).

4 A small '*m*' for *malus* ('bad') written above Martin's name indicates that he was found guilty.

so they are quit. And they say that Martin is guilty. So etc. [hanged]. Inquiry is to be made of his chattels from New Salisbury.

27. Simon of Litlecot is in mercy for trespass.

[*At the foot of the membrane among several partly illegible words are* 'William le Deym' *and* 'Hugh of Amesbury to answer for abetting'.]

m. 25 (IMG 0357, 0358) *Continuing Amesbury hundred*

28. Concerning defaults, they say that Roger le Bigot, the earl marshal, Baldwin of Bassingbourne, William de St Omer (writ), Thomas Peverel, Nicholas de Vallibus (writ), John Renger, William le Broker (ill),[1] John de Brommere, William le Lunge of Alton (ill), John Pipar, Ralph Heringe of Amesbury, Adam le Neue, William de la Beche (ill) and Roger le Gras (ill) did not come on the first day, so they are in *mercy*.

29. Concerning serjeanties, they say that Matthew Turpin holds 100 shillings' worth of land in Winterslow of the king by the serjeanty of providing[2] a cask of claret wine at the king's summons So *let this be discussed*.

THE BOROUGH OF DEVIZES COMES BY TWELVE

30. Simon son of Robert le Careter and a stranger were lodged at the house of Agnes daughter of Nicholas, and in the night they got up and killed Agnes and fled immediately. They are suspected of the death, so let Simon be *exacted and outlawed*. Agnes's daughter Agnes, the first finder, comes and is not suspected. The four neighbours do not come, namely Ingelot Symund, John Wytlok, Gocelot and Thomas of the gate, so they are in mercy. Ingelot Symund, one of the neighbours, was attached by Sewy and Thomas Ascer; John Wytlok by Henry Wyllok and Walter le Radere, Gocelot by Thomas of the gate and Thomas Ernald, and Thomas of the gate by Thomas le Sage and Walter Holewey. So they are in *mercy*. William son of Robert le Tayllur, who was betrothed to Agnes, has made off and is suspected of the death, so let him be *exacted and outlawed*. He had no chattels.

31. The jurors present that Richard de la Rochelle has newly set up a market

---

1 A small '*b*' for *breve* written over two names shows that they had been granted writs of quittance; *lan*[*guidus*] is written above each of the names with '(ill)' appended.

2 *faciendi*. The serjeanty was described and valued in identical terms in 1249 and 1281. In the latter year Matthew's son Stephen was found to be in the custody of his mother Maud, who had paid the king 20 marks for the wardship. No doubt the serjeanty owed its existence to Winterslow's proximity to Clarendon palace. *Wiltshire crown pleas, 1249* no. 156; JUST 1/1005/2 m. 137d.

at [Market] Lavington,[1] to the loss to the king's free market of £10 a year, and they do not know by what warrant. So let this be *discussed*.

32. Concerning wines sold contrary to the assize, they say that John Isinbert, Nicholas of Mumham, William Gargate and William Kachepol have sold wines contrary to the assize, so they are in *mercy*.

33. Concerning churches, they say that there are two churches in Devizes township, namely the church of the Blessed Mary and the church of St. John the Baptist. They are in the king's gift, and John the chaplain of the king's chapel holds them by the king's gift, and they are worth 8 marks a year.

THE MANOR OF ROWDE COMES BY THREE FREE MEN AND FOUR MEN AND THE REEVE

34. John le Weete of Rowde struck Sibyl daughter of Emma with an iron-bound shovel so that she died instantly. John fled immediately after the deed and is suspected, so let him be *exacted and outlawed*. His chattels *15s. 2½d.*, the sheriff to answer, and he was in the tithing of Henry Uppehylle in Rowde, which is in *mercy*. Sibyl's mother Emma, the first finder, comes[2] and is not suspected. The township of Rowde did not come fully to the inquest before the coroner, so it is in *mercy*.

35. Unknown malefactors encountered Walter son of Aunger of Rowde as he was coming from Devizes township and killed him. His father Aunger, the first finder, comes and is not suspected. No Englishry is presented. Judgement *murder*, upon Rowde township.

36. Concerning churches, they say that Rowde church is in the king's gift and is worth 20 marks a year. Robert Fuke holds it by the king's gift.[3]

37. Concerning serjeanties, they say that Walter Snappe holds three and a half virgates of land of the king by serjeanty, and he should serve the king in wartime in Devizes castle at his own expense for 40 days. And he renders

---

1 Richard de la Rochelle in 1254 received from the king the grant of a market on Wednesday in Steeple Lavington (now Market Lavington). An order given in 1255 that it should be suppressed, as detrimental to the king's Thursday market at Devizes, was cancelled, and in 1268 Richard himself complained that his market was suffering from the competition of the abbess of Romsey's Wednesday market at Church (now Steeple) Ashton, 4 miles away; the abbess responded that she had no market at Church Ashton since she held no place of that name, and Richard withdrew his action. *VCH Wiltshire* viii, 210; x, 99; JUST 1/998A m. 10d.

2 *non* was written before *venit* but has been largely erased.

3 Rowde church was granted to Robert on 9 September 1257, *CPR 1247-1258*, 580.

3s. a year to the king.[1] Roger son of Henry le Oyselur holds one hide of land of the king, and he should go fowling and attend to catching birds from the feast of St. Michael [29 September] until the feast of the Purification [2 February], and when he does not perform the office of the serjeanty he shall give the king 8s. a year.[2]

THE HUNDRED OF ALDERBURY COMES BY TWELVE

38. Richard Cok of Alderbury fled to Alderbury church, admitted theft, and abjured the realm before the coroner. His chattels *8½d.*, the same sheriff to answer, and he was in the treasurer of Salisbury's portion of Alderbury tithing, which is in mercy.

39. An unknown man was found dead on the king's highway below Winterslow. Alexander Vyring, the first finder, does not come, and it is testified that he is dead. No Englishry is presented. Judgement *murder*, upon the hundred. Winterslow, Pitton, Idmiston and Porton townships did not come fully to the inquest before the coroner, so they are in *mercy*.

40. A stranger was found dead by a hedge near Middleton, having no wound. Tiffany[3] wife of William, the first finder, has died. It is not known who killed him. No Englishry is presented. Judgement *murder*, upon the hundred. Winterslow, Pitton, Farley and East Grimstead townships did not come fully to the inquest before the coroner, so they are in *mercy*.

41. One Roger le Ku fled to Porton church, admitted theft and *abjured* the realm before the coroner. He had no chattels, and was not in a tithing because he was a stranger. Porton township did not arrest him when this happened in daytime, so it is in *mercy*. The twelve jurors presented this case falsely, so they are in *mercy*. Later it was testified that he had chattels worth *12d.*, the sheriff to answer.

---

1 In 1249 the serjeanty, said to consist of three virgates of land, was held by Gillian of Rowde and Peter of Bulkington, by the service of attending the king for 40 days in wartime, and was valued at 15s. per annum. In 1255, however, it was held by Richard of Beanacre and his sister Gillian (probably identical with Gillian of Rowde) by the service of providing an armed serjeant for Devizes castle in wartime, and much of the land had been alienated to Peter of Bulkington and Nicholas de Barbeflet. Walter Snappe was still holding it in 1289, by the same service, but as he was paying 3s. per annum towards the keeping (*ad wardam*) of Devizes castle, this sum may have become a commutation. *Wiltshire crown pleas, 1249* no. 408: *Rot. Hund.* ii, 236; JUST 1/1011 m. 59.

2 Nothing was said of this serjeanty in 1249. By 1255 Roger was dead and his son Henry held it, valued at one mark per annum. If the king was in the county any birds caught were to be presented to him, otherwise they were to go to the constable of Devizes. *Rot. Hund.* ii, 236.

3 Thefania – an unusual name, but one found elsewhere.

42. Ranulf son of Emma of Alderbury, his brother John, Agnes daughter of Emma and Peter le Sawoner, arrested on suspicion of theft, come and deny theft and all, and for good and ill put themselves on the country. The jurors say on their oath that Ranulf and the others are not guilty of any theft, so they are quit. But they say that the crime was imputed to Ranulf, John and Agnes at the instigation of Peter, the treasurer of Salisbury's servant, so let him be taken into *custody*. Peter le Savoner was arrested out of hatred and at the instigation of John Strodde, so let him be *arrested* etc.

43. Thomas le Brazur was crushed by a cart with loppings, and Robert of Alderbury, attached because he was present, comes and is not suspected, nor is anyone else. Judgement *misadventure*. The value of the cart, the loppings and the horses (*deodand*) 17s. 5d., the sheriff to answer. Pitton, Whaddon, Farley and Alderbury townships valued the deodand falsely, so they are in *mercy*.

44. William Gurnard struck John son of Emelot with an arrow in the throat so that he died instantly. William fled immediately after the deed and is suspected, so let him be *exacted and outlawed*. He had no chattels, and was not in a tithing because he was a stranger.

45. Peter Hukel was crushed by a cart between Winterbourne and Pitton so that he died instantly. His daughter Alice, the first finder, comes and is not suspected, nor is anyone else. Judgement *misadventure*. The value of the cart and three stots (*deodand*) 10s., the sheriff to answer.

46. One Nicholas of Mathern from Netherwent got himself into Winterslow church, where he admitted theft and *abjured* the realm before the coroner. He had no chattels, and was not in a tithing because he was a stranger.

47. Walter Hereng got himself into Laverstock church and admitted that he had killed Stephen le Dosser of Salisbury and *abjured* the realm before the coroner. His chattels 23s. 6d., the sheriff to answer. He was in Laverstock tithing, which is in mercy.

Laverstock township did not arrest him when this happened in daytime, so it is in *mercy*. John Hareng, accused of that death, was previously arrested and imprisoned in Salisbury castle and later acquired a royal writ so that he could be released to pledges until now. He comes now, and likewise John le Sopere and Hugh Serle, accused of that death, come and deny the death and felony, and for good and ill put themselves on the country. The jurors say that they are not guilty. So they are quit, but because they earlier made off on suspicion of the said death, their chattels are to be be confiscated for their flight. Hugh's were valued at 28s. and John's chattels at 3s., the sheriff to answer.[1]

48. William son of John of Lincolnshire got himself into Winterbourne

---

1 For this case see also **614** below. No record of a grant of bail has been found.

Gunner church, where he admitted theft and *abjured* the realm. His chattels *15d.*, the sheriff to answer. Winterbourne Gunner township did not arrest him when this happened in daytime, so it is in *mercy*. The twelve jurors undervalued the chattels, so they are in *mercy*.

49. John le Hywe and Robert Hod quarrelled together, and John struck Robert with a staff on the head so that he died three days later. John fled immediately after the deed and is suspected, so let him be *exacted and outlawed*. He had no chattels, and was in Winterbourne Earls tithing, which is in *mercy*. And Gomeldon township did not come to the inquest, so it is in mercy.

50. William le Syur was crushed by a beam which he wanted to move from one place to another. Thomas of Alb[? . . .[1]], the first finder, comes and is not suspected, nor is anyone else. Judgement *misadventure*. The value of the beam (*deodand*) *12d.*, the sheriff to answer. Whaddon, Alderbury, West Grimstead and Pitton townships valued the beam falsely, so they are in *mercy*.

[*At the foot of the membrane is* Ricardus Perceval. *See below*, **74.**]

m. 25d (IMG 0438, 0439) *Continuing Alderbury hundred*

51. Unknown malefactors killed Ellis Bolte at the fold of Thomas of Canford. Alice Pul, the first finder, has died. It is not known who killed him. No Englishry is presented. Judgement *murder*, upon the hundred. Milford 'Pychard', Winterbourne Dauntsey and Milford 'Richard' townships did not come to the inquest before the coroner, so they are in *mercy*.

52. Concerning serjeanties, they say that Christian daughter of Ralph de Haraz holds three virgates of land in Alderbury township, rendering to the king 2s. a year, and the land is worth 2 marks a year. Christian is under age and in the custody of Walter of Heale, and she ought to be in the king's custody and to be given in marriage by the king.[2] They say also that Gilbert, the Lord Edward's chaplain, holds one carucate of land in Winterbourne Gunner by serjeanty, and it is assessed for a rent of 12s. a year and is worth 10 marks a year.[3] Reynold de Drumere holds one virgate of land by the serjeanty of

---

1 The edge of the membrane is worn, and the place-name partly illegible.

2 The serjeanty was held by the service of keeping the king's harriers, or hunting dogs (*canes hayerez*), hence the unusual surname of its holders. When held by Richard de Heyraz in 1236 it was said to consist of half a hide of land. In 1255, now only one virgate in extent, it had recently been held by another Richard, whose son and heir, presumably Christian's father William, was in the custody of his stepfather John Spruet. In 1281 Christian's husband Henry, who had taken his wife's surname, was holding two virgates by the service of providing the king with one harrier when he stayed at Clarendon. *Book of Fees* i, 587, ii, 1178; *Rot. Hund.* ii, 234; JUST 1/1005/2 m. 147.

3 Winterbourne Gunner took its suffix from Gunnora de la Mare, who died in

keeping the king's forest of Clarendon, and it is worth 9s. a year.[1] William of Pitton hold one virgate of land by the same serjeanty, and it is worth 8s. a year.[2] Jordan of Laverstock likewise holds one virgate of land in Laverstock by the same serjeanty, and it is worth 10s. a year.[3] Furthermore[4] they say that Maud de Baudehale with her parceners holds two carucates of land and 45s. of yearly rent in Porton by the serjeanty of providing one mounted man, armed with a breastplate, for the king's army, and they are worth 100s. a year.[5]

53. Concerning defaults, they say that the abbot of Glastonbury, Maud Lungespeye, Albreda de Boterel, Maud de Bondehale [struck through], John

---

possession of the serjeanty around the end of 1249. The service was variously described as acting as usher in the king's hall and providing the king's litter and firewood. Gunnora's heir was her cousin Henry de Tracy, who took the name of de la Mare. A minor in 1255, Henry forfeited his lands for felony sometime before 1272, and Winterbourne was given to the Lord Edward, who by 1274/5 had granted it to St Mark's hospital, Bristol. *Book of Fees* i, 587, ii, 1178-9; *Rot. Hund.* ii, 234, 242; *CIPM* i nos. 144, 185.

1 The serjeanty was held by successive members of the Milford family. It was held by Richard of Milford in 1236, when it was said to contain half a hide, but in 1255 its extent was assessed at one virgate. It had lately been taken into the king's hand, but Richard later recovered it, and in 1270 it was inherited by his nephew Edmund, whose under-age son, also Edmund, held it in 1281, when the service was said to be that of providing one man on foot to guard Clarendon forest. It was then valued at 20s. per annum. The interest in the serjeanty of Reynold de Drumere can only have been temporary. *Book of Fees* i, 587; *Rot. Hund.* ii, 234, 242; *CIPM* i no. 882; C 60/67 m. 11; JUST 1/1005/2 m. 146d. See also **60** below.

2 The serjeanty was assessed at half a hide in 1236, when it was held by James of Pitton. James was succeeded by his son William in 1255, when the serjeanty was reported to have been taken into the king's hand. William later recovered it, and still held it in 1281, when it was said to consist of two virgates in Plaitford, held by the service of providing two foresters on foot to keep Clarendon forest and 'Haywode', and valued at 20s. per annum. *Book of Fees* i, 587; *CIPM* i no. 330; *Rot. Hund.* ii, 234, 242; JUST 1/1005/2 m. 147.

3 Held by Robert of Laverstock in 1236, the serjeanty was inherited in 1250 by his son Jordan, who like his parceners recovered his share when it was taken into the king's hand in 1255. Jordan was still in possession in 1281, when the service was described as supplying a forester to guard the king's demesne wood in Clarendon forest, and the land was valued at 10s. per annum. *Book of Fees* i, 587; *CIPM* i no. 188; *Rot. Hund.* ii, 234, 242; JUST 1/1005/2 m. 147.

4 The sentence is added in the space before the next entry.

5 The serjeanty was that held by Hugh Burgenun in 1236, when he was described as holding land worth 100s. in Porton by the service of providing a serjeant equipped with a hauberk. The serjeanty was commuted to military service between 1268 and 1274/5, when Maud was reportedly holding holding half a knight's fee in Porton in chief of the king, and it was not presented with the other Alderbury serjeanties in 1281. *Book of Fees* i, 587; *Rot. Hund.* ii, 242.

de Insula, Ralph Rularye,[1] John le Taverner, Thomas de Posterna, Peter the
parson of Laverstock and John de Cherbourg did not come here on the first
day, so they are in *mercy*.

54. The jurors present that Maud Pesse was drowned in the river[2] by Hurdcott,
and she was later removed and carried onto the bishop of Salisbury's land by
men of Hurdcott 'Priors' township. So let them be arrested.

55. Concerning persons indicted, they say that Walter of Stratford, clerk,
Richard of East Dean, Richard of Oxenwood, Roger Kachepayn of Alderbury,
John son of John le Smeth, William Sparewe,[3] William le Hert,[4] Peter Scayl,
Richard of Rupington, John Runceval, Geoffrey Paucoke, Henry Hayne,
Christian of Oxenwood and Henry le Rok have made off on suspicion of
theft, and all are suspected except William Hert, Richard of Rupington
and Geoffrey Paucoke. So let Walter and the others be *exacted and outlawed*.
William, Richard and Geoffrey may return if they wish. They had no chattels.
Richard of East Dean's chattels *6d.*, the sheriff to answer, and he was in
Winterbourne Earls tithing, which is in *mercy*. Walter of Stratford had no
chattels, but he was in the same tithing. Henry Hayne's chattels *2s.*, the sheriff
to answer, and he was in West Grimstead tithing, which is in *mercy*. Richard
of Oxenwood, Roger Cachepain, John son of John Snez, John Runceval,
Christian of Oxenwood and Henry le Rok had no chattels, but John son of
John was in Porton tithing, and John Runceval was in 'la Forde' tithing, and
Henry le Rok was in Idmiston tithing, so they are in *mercy*.

THE HUNDRED OF UNDERDITCH COMES BY TWELVE

56. An unknown woman was found killed in the fields outside the cemetery
of St. Martin's, Salisbury. Nicholas Serle, the first finder, has died. It is not
known who killed her. No Englishry is presented. Judgement *murder*, upon the
hundred. Milford, Stratford-sub-Castle, Great Woodford and Heale townships
did not come to the inquest before the coroner, so they are in *mercy*. Later
it is testified that she was killed in New[5] Salisbury township, in the house
of Basile le Ro, and Basile and Alice le Ku were arrested and imprisoned
on suspicion of the death. Alice was hanged before justices assigned to gaol
delivery, she had no chattels, and Basile was delivered before the same. Let
there be a fuller inquiry of New Salisbury township (*of Salisbury*).

---

1 Above his name is *d. m.*, presumably meaning ½ mark.

2 The river Bourne.

3 Above the names William Sparewe and Peter Scayl is *in prisona*.

4 Above the names William le Hert, Richard of Rupington and Geoffrey Paucok is
  b, for *bonus* ('good'), indicating that they were acquitted.

5 *Novarum*, here and in the last line, evidently supposing that *Sarum* is a genitive
  plural.

57. Walter Cachebylle, Peter of Bulkington, Adam Brun and Thomas son of John, arrested and imprisoned in Salisbury castle, broke out of that gaol and killed Laurence, the keeper of the prison.[1] They escaped to the church of St. Cross at Stratford-sub-Castle, where they admitted theft and that deed, and *abjured* the realm before the coroner. They had no chattels. To judgement for the *escape* upon Robert, son and heir of John de Vernun, then sheriff, in whose keeping that prison was.

58. Roger le Ireys got himself into St. Martin's church, Salisbury, where he admitted theft and *abjured* the realm. His chattels 6d., the sheriff to answer, and he was received ouside a tithing in Wilcot township, which is in *mercy*.

59. William Page of Liddington got himself into the church of St. Cross at Stratford-sub-Castle, where he admitted theft and homicide and *abjured* the realm before the coroner. He had no chattels. He was received outside a tithing in Liddington township, which is in *mercy*.

60. Edmund son of John of Milford and Ralph Basile struggled together, and Reynold son of Reynold de Drumare and Robert son of the prior of Milford,[2] tried to separate them. Robert, who had an arrow in his hand, knocked Ralph to the ground so that he was wounded in the throat by the arrow, and died afterwards as a result, without Robert intending this. Robert fled immediately after the deed, so let him be exacted [and outlawed]. He had no chattels, but he was in Milford tithing, which is in *mercy*. Edmund and Reynold, attached because they were present, come and are not suspected, but because they did not arrest Robert they are in mercy. They are poor and are pardoned.

61. Richard Muchefoke of Boscombe[3] killed Richard son of Peter le Carver outside the city of Salisbury, and he was later arrested and imprisoned in Salisbury castle when Ralph de Aungers was sheriff. He escaped from the

---

1 Laurence the gaoler's wife Eve later took over the keeping of the gaol as an inherited fee but in 1269 was suspended by the sheriff after an approver's escape on the way to the county court. She appealed to the king, who on 10 May 1269 decided that the fault was not Eve's or her officers' but the sheriff's for not sending an adequate escort. Eve's men, who had been imprisoned, were to be released and Eve was to be provisionally restored to her office. *CR 1268-1272*, 46–7. On 12 December following she received a formal pardon, though this was left incomplete on the patent roll. *CPR 1266-1272*, 399.

2 *Robertus filius Prioris de Muleforde* – there was no priory at Milford, a manor of the bishop of Salisbury, so the title 'prior' must have been in some sense a nickname, perhaps for the leading man of the township. It is surprising to find Edmund and Reynold described as poor at the end of this case, since Reynold was the son of the holder of one of the Clarendon forest serjeanties, while Edmund inherited that same serjeanty in 1270 – see note on **52** above.

3 After the name 'and John his brother' has been crossed out and the plural form of 'killed' has been changed to the singular.

prison, so to judgement for the *escape* upon Ralph's son and heir John, Richard Muchefoke's brother John was present when this deed was done, and he has made off, but he is not suspected, so he may return if he wishes, but his chattels are confiscated for his flight. Let their chattels be inquired of in Amesbury hundred.

62. Savary of Woodford appealed Henry son of Andrew de Weteford[1] in the county court of robbery and breach of the king's peace. Savary does not come now, so let him be *arrested* and his pledges for prosecuting are in *mercy*, namely Bartholomew le Fysere of the city of Salisbury and Robert le Lung of the same. Henry does not come, and he was not attached because he [Savary] only sued against him at two county courts.

63. Concerning defaults, they say that William de Turbeville and Walter Pache did not come here on the first day, so they are in *mercy*.

THE HUNDRED OF FRUSTFIELD COMES BY TWELVE

64. Concerning serjeanties, they say that Henry Sturmy holds one hide of land in Cowesfield, by the service of keeping the king's forest of Savernake, and the land is worth 100s. a year.[2] They also say that William Spilleman holds one hide of land with appurtenances in the same township, by the service of providing one man for the king's army in wartime for forty days, and that land is worth 100s. a year.[3] They also say that Walter Loverace holds

---

1 This word is so heavily corrected as to make any reading conjectural. Present-day Woodford and Wilsford are both possibilities.

2 Cowesfield, which is a long way from Savernake, came to be a member of the manor of Burbage in Kinwardstone hundred, which was also held by the Sturmys. They seem to have had two serjeanties, seemingly linked only in the person of their holder. In 1236 William Sturmy held one hide in Burbage by the service of a serjeant with a hauberk, while in 1249 the Cowesfield serjeanty attached to Savernake forest, valued at 60s. per annum, was in the keeping of Richard Sturmy, acting on behalf of Henry, the heir of the recently-deceased Geoffrey Sturmy. In 1274/5 Henry was described as holding Burbage by the Cowesfield serjeanty, while in 1281 he was presented as holding two hides in Cowesfield, worth £5, by the serjeanty of keeping Savernake forest and for providing two serjeants for the king's army in Wales. This was largely repeated at Henry's death in 1295, albeit in an inquest focussed on Burbage. *Book of Fees* i, 586; *Wiltshire crown pleas 1249* no. 493 and note; *Rot. Hund.* ii, 259; JUST 1/1005/2 m. 150; *CIPM* iii no. 274.

3 William Spilleman was reported as holding a hide in Cowesfield, by the service described in 1268, in both 1236 and 1249. His serjeanty also included lands in Hampshire, and when presented in 1281 was associated with Brockenhurst in that county. The service was then said to be that of providing a serjeant for the king's army in Wales for forty days, and the land was still worth 100s. per annum. *Book of Fees* i, 587; *Wiltshire crown pleas 1249* no. 494B; JUST 1/1005/2 m. 150; *CIPM* iii no. 19.

one hide of land with appurtenances in the same township, by the service of hunting wolves,[1] and the land is worth 100s. a year.[2] So let this be *discussed*.

65. Concerning defaults, they say that Robert de Chartres, Walter Huskard, Harvey son of Aldeth, Richard Gorwy, Peter Yve, Richard le Tur, Aynolf of the wood, Robert Wythox and Peter of the wood from Highworth did not come on the first day, so they are in *mercy*.

66. The jurors present that Adam Bering, the servant of Robert of Glastonbury,[3] after peace was proclaimed in England seized the goods of Thomas, parson of Whiteparish,[4] and retained them in his possession until Adam de Chartres, the parson's servant, had made fine with him by 10s. and had paid the money. So let him answer for the 10s. and be in *mercy* for the trespass. They also say that Martin of Leigh, under-sheriff of Wiltshire at that time, took half a mark from Richard David, and half a mark from Robert David, and half a mark from William the charcoal-burner, alleging that they were harbourers of thieves, and he extorted the money from them to be left in peace. So let him answer etc. and be in mercy for the trespass etc. Later Adam [Bering] came and said that he took the money on Robert of Glastonbury's order and for his benefit. Robert is present and concurs with this, but says that he had the money with the good will of Adam de Chartres. So let this be discussed.

m. 26 (IMG 0359, 0360)

THE HUNDRED OF ELLSTUB COMES BY TWELVE

67. As Simon Cotele was drawing a cart at Fifield, he tried to climb into it and fell under its wheel, and was crushed by the cart so that he died instantly. His sister Margery, the first finder, comes and is not suspected, nor is anyone else. Judgement *misadventure*. The value of the horses and cart (*deodand*) 9s. 6d., the sheriff to answer.

68. John Alwrich and Richard his brother and William Suuel were coming

---

1 *fugandi ad lupum.*

2 The serjeanty's lands, later described as being in East Cowesfield, were held by Walter Loveraz in 1236. The service was then said to be that of keeping the king's wolfhounds (*loverez* – hence the family name), and this was repeated in 1281, when the estate was still valued at 100s. per annum. The family also held the keepership of Buckholt wood in Clarendon forest. *Book of Fees* i, 587; JUST 1/1005/2 m. 150; *CIPM* i no. 821, ii no. 303, iii no. 388.

3 Robert of Glastonbury was constable of Salisbury castle between 30 May 1266 and 17 December 1267, and perhaps also earlier, since he was directed to hand the castle over to an incoming sheriff on 28 April 1266. *CPR 1258-1266*, 587, 598; *CPR 1266-1272*, 174.

4 *de Albo Monasterio.*

from Collingbourne tavern below Everleigh park[1], and a quarrel having arisen between them, John attacked William, who in defending himself struck John with an axe on the head, so that he later died. William fled immediately after the deed and is suspected, so let him be *exacted and outlawed*. His chattels *20s.*, Chisenbury township to answer, and he was in Chisenbury tithing, which is in *mercy*. Richard was present and he does not come now, and is not suspected, but he was committed to the bail of Chisenbury tithing, which is in *mercy*. Chisenbury, Littlecott, Enford, and Netheravon townships did not come fully to the inquest before the coroner, so they are in *mercy*.

69. Philip Sueteblod wanted to fish in the river[2] at Netheravon, and Thomas Faukes came up and was angry because he fished there and struck him with a stone so that he died four days later. Thomas fled immediately after the deed and is suspected, so let him be *exacted and outlawed*. He had no chattels and was in Bulford 'Prioress' tithing, which is in *mercy*. Haxton, Fittleton, and Combe townships did not come fully to the inquest before the coroner, so they are in *mercy*.

70. Robert son of Martin of Haxton and Philip of Whaddon came from the house of Ralph Seman, where Robert was at the tavern, and a quarrel having arisen between them Philip struck Robert with his knife in the chest so that he died instantly. Philip was later arrested and hanged before justices assigned to gaol delivery. His chattels *12d.*, the sheriff to answer. William son of Gunilda, attached because he was present in the house where the quarrel arose, does not come, nor is he suspected. He was attached by William Turkyl and Roger Pakke, who are in *mercy*.

71. Richard of Westwood got himself into Fittleton church, pursued by William Pride, and was committed to the keeping of Fittleton township, from whose keeping he *escaped*. So to judgement for the *escape* upon Fittleton township. He fled to Netheravon church, where he admitted theft and *abjured* the realm before the coroner. He had no chattels, and was not in a tithing, but he was received outside a tithing in Corsham township in Chippenham hundred, which is in *mercy*. (*Elsewhere upon Chippenham*.) Netheravon township did not arrest him, so it is in *mercy*.

72. Concerning defaults, they say that William of Wick, Thomas Bacun, Maud of Kempsey (ill),[3] Nicholas of Fifield, priest, Nicholas Cloke, Philip of Grindham (he has a writ),[4] Richard Makerel, Nicholas son of Martin

---

1 Everleigh had been held by Simon de Montfort until shortly before his death in 1265, when he gave it to the king in exchange for lands elsewhere. By 1268 it was held by the king's second son Edmund, earl of Lancaster. *VCH Wiltshire* xi, 137.

2 The river Avon.

3 *languida* is written above the name.

4 *habet breve* is written above the name. In March 1269 Philip was granted a life-time

(writ),[1] Nicholas Trenchefoyl (writ), John de Cormaylle (writ), the prior of Carisbrooke and Walter Spigurnel did not come on the first day, so they are in *mercy*.

73. Concerning escheats, they say that Simon de Montfort, late earl of Leicester, held 40 marks' worth of land in Haxton and Netheravon which the lord Edmund, the king's son, has in custody until the coming of age of John son of Matthew. But the lord Edmund has the homages and fealties of John and of Amaury de St. Amand, and their service, by the king's gift through the escheat [of the estate] of the said Simon.[2]

74. William Hevede, William Dychewater and Mabel his wife, and Richard Perceval, arrested on suspicion of theft, come and deny felony and all, and for good and ill put themselves on the country. The jurors say that William Heved is not guilty of any evildoing, so he is *quit*. But they say that the crime was imputed to William at the instigation and procurement of Simon le Chamberleng and Richard son of John of Netheravon, so let them be taken into *custody*. They say also that William Dychewater and Mabel are in no way guilty of any evildoing, so they are quit. But they say that Richard is guilty of burglary, theft and harbouring thieves, so etc. (*hanged on Saturday*). He had no chattels. Later Simon came and made fine by *2½ marks* by the pledges of ( ). And Richard son of John made fine by 6 marks by the pledges of ( ).[3]

75. Roger Trenchefoylle, accused of associating with William Toc, who was hanged, and of other thefts, and Richard Tauncost,[4] likewise arrested on suspicion of robbery done in 'Chartus'[5] abbey and of other thefts,[6] come and deny theft, robbery and associating in theft, and for good and ill put themselves on the country. The jurors of Swanborough, Amesbury and Dole hundreds, together with the jurors of this hundred, say on their oath that Roger and Richard are in no way guilty of any evildoing, so they are *quit*.

76. Concerning indicted persons, they say that Robert Brangwayn, Maud

exemption. *CPR. 1266–1272*, 325.

1 *breve* is written above the name and the two following.

2 Simon de Montfort's estates in Haxton and Netheravon were part of his inheritance as earl of Leicester. Following his death in 1265 they were granted to Edmund along with the rest of Montfort's lands.

3 The last sentence was written after the rest of record and is squeezed into the space before the next entry. The names of the pledges are omitted.

4 The names Roger Trenchefoyle and Richard Tancost are noted at the foot of the membrane.

5 There was no Carthusian house in Wiltshire. The reference may be to Witham Friary, just across the Somerset border.

6 *aliorum latrocinium*, clearly a mistake for *latronum*.

Lynge, Ralph le Rut, Robert Stayn, Geoffrey Aygmin and William Tauncost have made off on suspicion of theft and all are suspected, so let them be exacted and outlawed. They had no chattels, but he[1] was in Netheravon tithing, which is in *mercy*. And William was in the tithing of Richard Tauncost, which is in *mercy*.

THE HUNDRED OF DOWNTON COMES BY TWELVE

77. John the shoemaker was drowned in the river[2] near Downton mill. Walter Boly, the first finder, has died. No one is suspected. Judgement *misadventure*. The twelve jurors falsely presented one Godfrey as finder, so they are in *mercy*.

78. Gillian the wife of Robert Richer was found killed in Downton township. Robert Richer, the first finder, comes and is not suspected. William of Bristol and his wife Amice,[3] who were lodged at Robert's house, are suspected of the death and has (*sic*) made off. So let him be exacted and outlawed, and let Amice be exacted and waived. They had no chattels, but they were received outside a tithing in Downton township for three weeks, so it is in *mercy*. No Englishry is presented. Judgement *murder*, upon Downton township, because it does not participate with the hundred. Pensworth, Wick and Charlton townships did not come fully to the inquest before the coroner, so they are in *mercy*.

79. Adam Cupping[4] fled to Bishopstone church, where he admitted theft and *abjured* the realm before the coroner. His chattels *4s.*, the bishop of Winchester[5] to answer.[6] Later it is testified that Adam was arrested by Bishopstone township and imprisoned there, and later he escaped to the church from the township's custody. So to judgement for the *escape* upon that township. And it is testified by the jurors that Nicholas of Hadlow, when he was keeper of the bishopric

---

1 The person concerned is not named.

2 The river Avon.

3 *et Amicia uxor ejus* is interlined.

4 The initial C has been expunged and a letter or sign (like an inverted Y with a vertical line between the arms) written above with a caret.

5 *episcopus Wynton* is interlined above *idem vic'*, which has been deleted.

6 The manor of Bishopstone, a detached part of Downton hundred, belonged, like the hundred, to the bishop. Aymer de Valence, the king's half-brother, had been elected bishop in 1250 when under age and unqualified. In 1258 the baronial regime forced him into exile, and on 24 December appointed Nicholas of Hadlow, an experienced administrator and justice, to be keeper of the now-vacant see, a position he held until 1261. A Harding (ed.), *The roll of the Shropshire eyre of 1256* (Selden Society 96, 1981 for 1980), xiv-xv. The vacancy ended on 10 September 1262, when John Gervase was consecrated bishop. An amercement of 100s. was the standard penalty for an escape from prison.

of Winchester during its vacancy, levied 100s. for the escape. So to *judgement* on Nicholas because he took those 100s. without warrant.

80. Gilbert le Blechere de Oddeston,[1] was drawing a cart through the middle of Bodenham township, and a dog was following the cart, so that one Roger Horn became enraged with Gilbert because that dog fought with his own dog. And a quarrel having arisen between them, Gilbert struck Roger with a staff on the forehead so that he died within a fortnight. Gilbert made off immediately after the deed, but in process of time he returned, and now he comes and that he is not guilty puts himself on the country for good and ill. And the jurors of this hundred, together with twelve from Cawdon hundred and twelve from Branch hundred, say on their oath that Roger did not die of any wound but of an illness coming upon him, wherefore they say that Gilbert is not guilty of the death. So he is quit, but because he made off his chattels are confiscated for his flight. He had no chattels. It is established by the jurors that he did not make off, but because he struck Roger as aforesaid, let him be taken into custody for trespass. He made fine by *20s.*, by pledge of Peter of Kingsmill and Ralph le Frye.

m. 26d (IMG 0440, 0441)[2] *Continuing Downton hundred*

81. Unknown malefactors burgled the house of John Polecoc and Jordan his brother and killed John and Jordan. It is not known who they were. Woodfalls township did not make pursuit, so it is in *mercy*. Downton, Hamptworth, Pensworth and Barford townships did not come fully to the inquest, so they are in *mercy*. Geoffrey Pokoc, the first finder, comes and is not suspected. No Englishry is presented. Judgement *murder*, upon the hundred. Later it is testified that Richard of Woodfalls and his sister Agnes (dead) made off on suspicion of the death. Richard comes, and it is testified that Agnes has died. Richard comes and denies the death and all, and for good and ill puts himself on the country. The jurors of this hundred, together with the jurors of Cawdon hundred, say etc. that Richard is not guilty of this, so he is quit. (*Upon Cawdon.*)

82. Adam the miller of Downton was arrested on suspicion of theft[3] and imprisoned in Downton township. And later he escaped from prison to the river Avon and drowned himself in it. His wife Amice, the first finder, comes and is not suspected. No one is suspected. Judgement *suicide*. His chattels *2 marks*, Downton tithing (bishop of Winchester[4]) to answer. Wick, Bodenham

---

1 Presumably a mistake for *Oddestok*, i.e. Odstock, a mile west of Bodenham.

2 At the foot of the membrane is written *Suaneberg'*; the entries for Swanborough hundred (**148–162**) are all on the lower part of of the face of m. 28.

3 *latronum*, in error either for *latrocinii*, theft, or [*receptu*] *latronum*, harbouring of thieves.

4 *episcopus Wynton* interlined.

and Charlton townships valued his chattels falsely, so they are in *mercy*. To judgement for the *escape* upon Downton township.

83. William Attewode was found killed in Privett wood. The first finder comes and is not suspected. It is not known who killed him. No Englishry is presented. Judgement *murder*, upon the hundred. Witherington, Standlynch, Barford and Pensworth townships did not come fully to the inquest before the coroner, so they are in *mercy*.

84. Robert Hayde struck his wife Agnes with an axe on the head so that she died instantly. Robert was later arrested and hanged. His chattels *19s.*, the parson of Downton's part of Downton tithing (bishop of Winchester[1]) to answer. It is testified that William of Zeals, parson of Downton, took the chattels without warrant, so he is in *mercy*.

85. Alwin de Wygeton was trying to cut a branch from an oak tree when the branch fell on his head, so that he died instantly. His wife Maud, the first finder, comes and is not suspected, nor is anyone else. Judgement *misadventure*. The value of the branch (*deodand*) *6d.*, the sheriff to answer.

86. The jurors present that the bishop of Winchester's bailiffs hold pleas of replevin,[2] but they do not know by what warrant.

87. Concerning defaults, they say that Geoffrey of Stowell (writ),[3] Humphrey of Dunster (writ), Roger of Stopham, Geoffrey of Burton, John Crasset and Brice of Bloxworth did not come here on the first day, so they are in *mercy*.

88. Concerning the escape of thieves, they say that Robert Corberand was arrested on suspicion of theft and imprisoned in Downton township, in the bishop of Winchester's courtyard. And he escaped from the custody of John of Chirton, then the bishop's bailiff, so to judgement of the *escape* upon Downton township. Because it is testified that while William of Wintershill was the bishop of Winchester's steward he had 100s. levied for the escape, let this be discussed.[4]

THE BOROUGH OF DOWNTON COMES BY TWELVE

---

1 *thethinga*. Above it *episcopus Wynton'* (the bishop of Winchester) is interlined.

2 The hearing of pleas *de vetito namio* was among the bishop's liberties listed in 1274/5: *Rot. Hund.* ii,. 235.

3 The first two names have *b* written above them, indicating that each had a writ (*breve*) of quittance.

4 No reference to this case has been noticed in the surviving pipe rolls of the bishop of Winchester, which show that William of Wintershill was episcopal steward by 1262/3, and that John of Chirton was 'serjeant' of Downton no later than 1265/6 (he may, however, have been the John the serjeant recorded there in earlier years). Hampshire Record Office MSS 11M59/81/30 m. 2, 11M59/81/31 m. 3d.

89. Concerning wines sold etc., they say that Simon le Vineter of Downton sold wines contrary to the assize, so he is in *mercy*.

THE HUNDRED OF DAMERHAM COMES BY TWELVE

90. Richard of Woodborough, one of the twelve jurors, has not come, nor did he wish to be with the twelve, so he is in *mercy*.

91. John Syward fell from a mare in the king's highway near Martin, so that he died instantly. His wife Ellen, the first finder, comes and is not suspected, nor is anyone else. Judgement misadventure. The value of the mare (*deodand*) 2s. 5d., the sheriff to answer.

92. Geoffrey of Dorchester, who was the servant of Roger Cusin, forester of Chettle, struck Martin of Dorchester with an arrow in the chest so that he died instantly. Geoffrey has made off and is suspected, so let him be *exacted and outlawed*. He had no chattels, and was not in a tithing because he was a stranger from another county. East Martin, West Martin, Damerham and Stapleton townships did not come fully to the inquest before the coroner, so they are in *mercy*.

93. Roger le Chapeleyn of Compton Chamberlayne, clerk, and William le Stywr of the same came to the house of Walter le Rus, killed Walter, and carried away the goods found there. They are suspected of the death, so let them be *exacted and outlawed*. Roger's chattels 20d., the sheriff to answer. William had no chattels, and was not in a tithing, but he was received outside a tithing in Compton Chamberlayne township, which is in *mercy*. Roger was not in a tithing because he was a clerk. Thomas Burgeys, attached because he was present, does not come. He was attached by John of the bishop of Salisbury's [portion of] Bishopstone and Thomas le Franceys of the same, so they are in *mercy*. Damerham, Compton Chamberlayne, Baverstock and Hurdcott townships did not come to the inquest, so they are in *mercy*.

94. Thomas Wypechump struck Gunnilda Ywayn with a rake on the head so that she later died. Thomas was later arrested for the deed and hanged before justices of gaol [delivery] etc. His chattels 12½d., the abbot of Glastonbury's tithing of Stapleton to answer.

95. A quarrel arose between Richard le Marchaunt of East Martin and his wife Clarice, so that Richard beat Clarice. And Peter Peytevin, Clarice's brother, hearing this, came up and entered Richard's house by force and arms, and attacked Richard in his house and tried to kill him and laid hands upon him, so that he could in no way escape except by defending himself, in that he was trapped in the house. And in defending himself and trying to save his own life he struck Peter with a knife so that he later died of it. Richard has made off, so let him be exacted and outlawed. His chattels 40s., W., bishop of Bath and Wells[1] to answer. He was in the frankpledge of Roger le Peytevin, which is in *mercy*. Tidpit township did not come to the inquest, so it is in *mercy*.

96. As William son of Adam of Compton Chamberlayne was riding on a mare at Cole Mill ford, he fell from the mare into the river[2] and drowned. William's sister Edith, the first finder, comes and is not suspected, nor is anyone else. Judgement *misadventure*. The value of the mare (*deodand*) 4s., the sheriff to answer.

97. Concerning defaults, they say that the abbot of Glastonbury (writ), Roger le Peytevin, William of Martin, William le Knyct de la Luvecote, Henry Pentecoste and John le Bor of Martin did not come here on the first day, so they are in *mercy*.

98. Richard son of John Scot, arrested on suspicion of theft, comes and denies theft and all, and for good and ill puts himself on the country. The jurors say that he is not guilty of any evildoing, so he is quit, and it is testified that Richard was arrested at the instigation and procurement of Thomas Upphylle, and that unjustly, so let him be taken into *custody*.

m. 27 (IMG 0361, 0362)

THE HUNDRED OF CHALKE COMES BY TWELVE

99. Henry son of Osbert of Chippenham got himself into Alvediston church, where he admitted theft and *abjured* the realm before the coroner. He had no chattels, and was not in a tithing because he was a stranger. Alvediston township did not arrest him, so it is in *mercy*.

100. Thomas the miller of Chalke came to the abbess of Wilton's mill, and Robert Curteys, this Roger's[3] man, came up, and a dispute arose between them because Robert was not in the mill, so that Thomas struck Robert with a stake on the head so that he later died. Immediately after the deed Thomas fled and is suspected, so let him be *exacted and outlawed*. He had no chattels, but he was in Chalke tithing, which is in *mercy*. And Chalke, Bower Chalke, Stoke and Fifield townships did not come fully to the inquest, so they are in *mercy*.

101. John le Templer[4] encountered William le Knyght outside Chalke township, and a quarrel having arisen between them, William struck John with

1 William (ii) of Bitton, 1267–1274.

2 The river Nadder.

3 Roger, who is not otherwise named, may be in error for Thomas.

4 John's surname may indicate that he was a servant of the Templars, who had a house at Rockley in Ogbourne St. Andrew.

a wooden fork on the neck so that he later died. William fled immediately and is suspected, so let him be *exacted and outlawed*. He had no chattels, but he was received outside a tithing in Chalke township, which is in *mercy*.

102. Andrew le Theyn got himself into Alvediston church, admitted to being a thief who had stolen corn, and *abjured* the realm before the coroner. His chattels *10d.*, the sheriff to answer. From the same sheriff (*4d.*).for the chattels of Walter Dyn, hanged before justices for gaol [delivery] etc.

103. Jordan son of Herbert of Shaftesbury was found killed in 'Whitemerse' marsh. John Frode, the first finder, comes and is not suspected. It is not known who killed him – he was apparently dragged to his death by a tether tied round his arm. No Englishry is presented. Judgement *murder*, upon the hundred. Semley, Berwick St John and Upton townships did not come fully to the inquest, so they are in *mercy*. The murder [fine] is to be *discussed*.

104. Concerning defaults, they say that the prior of Breamore (writ),[1] Walter of Bridmore, John Golde and Geoffrey of Trow did not come here on the first day, so they are in *mercy*.

105. Alexander of Trow appealed Richard de Bahuse of Standlynch in the county court of robbery and breach of the king's peace. Richard came to the fourth county court at Alexander's suit, and was mainprised by Peter the goldsmith of Wilton, who is in *mercy*.[2] At the fifth county court Alexander withdrew from his appeal, so he and his pledges for prosecuting are in *mercy*, namely John Maheu of Nippard and John le Blund of Wilton. The jurors say that they [the parties] are not agreed, but they say that after peace had been proclaimed in England, Richard, together with others whose names they do not know, came to Alexander's house and there in robbery took five horses and mares and 54 lambs and other goods, and now he does not come. So let this be *discussed*.

106. (*Dors'*.) The jurors present that after the battle of Lewes, and after peace was proclaimed, there came Walter of Letton and Ralph of the wood and others whose names they do not know, and they encountered brother Adam of St. Nicholas' hospital, Salisbury, and took a horse from him. So let this be *discussed*.

107. Robert Balle, arrested for stealing a wether, comes and denies theft and all, and for good and ill puts himself on the country. The jurors say that Robert is not guilty of this or of any other evildoing, so he is quit.

108. Concerning indicted persons, they say that Thomas le Thachere,

---

1 Above the name is written *b*, indicating that he had a writ (*breve*).

2 Peter evidently failed to produce Richard in court, but the fact is omitted from the roll.

later arrested and hanged for the deed. He had no chattels. William fled immediately and is suspected, so let him be *exacted and outlawed*. His chattels 5s., Ogbourne 'Prior's' township to answer. Ogbourne 'Prior's', Ogbourne Maizey and Draycot townships did not come fully to the inquest, so they are in *mercy*.

118. Maud the widow of Adam of Rockley appealed Thomas le Pestur of Marlborough, his son John, Ives of Crawley, John Purbygge, William the carter of Richard of Ospringe, William Unfrey, Walter le Tannur, Richard of Alton, John Moregan, Hugh Larke, William of Leicester, Walter Martin, William le Gras, John of Stanton and Richard of Ospringe in the county court of the death of her husband Adam. Maud does not come now, so let her be *arrested*, and her pledges for prosecuting, namely Ralph Hervy of Wilton and John Hervy of the same, are in mercy. (*Tuesday*.)[1]

m. 27d (IMG 0442, 0443) *Continuing Selkley hundred*

119. Geoffrey son of Walter the reeve got himself into Avebury church, where he admitted theft and *abjured* the realm before the coroner. He had no chattels, but he was in Avebury tithing, which is in *mercy*.

120. Walter le Priur and Adam Chubbe broke into the abbot of Stanley's grange in Richardson[2] at night. Bartholomew of Cherhill noticed this and cried out upon them, and he struck Walter on the head with an axe so that he later died. Bartholomew fled immediately after the deed and is suspected, so let him be *exacted and outlawed*. His chattels 13d., Richardson township to answer, and he was in Cherhill tithing, which is in mercy. Adam Chubbe has likewise made off and is suspected, so let him be *exacted and outlawed*. His chattels 3d., Richardson township to answer. Richardson township did not come fully to the inquest, so it is in *mercy*.

121. William le Schinnere, Adam son of the smith of Avebury, William Tryp, James Quintin, and Nicholas and Richard, brothers of James, came from a tavern in Fyfield and a quarrel having arisen between them William le Schinnere struck James on the knee[3] with an arrow, from which he died instantly. And Nicholas Quintin struck William le Schinnere on the back of the head with an arrow, from which he later died. Nicholas fled immediately after the deed and is suspected, so let him be *exacted and outlawed*. He had no chattels, and was received in 'Rokeruge' township, which is in mercy. Adam,

---

1 This case is recorded in full as **130**. The marginal annotation presumably indicates that the hearing was for some reason adjourned to another day.

2 Stanley Abbey, a Cistercian house, had several properties in Wootton Bassett parish, including at least three properties in Richardson. *VCH Wiltshire* xii, 188-9.

3 *in poplice*, perhaps the back of the thigh; it is strange that death was immediate, unless the arrow struck an artery.

William Tryppe and Richard Quintin[1] do not come and are not suspected, so nothing from them, but they are in mercy because they did not arrest Nicholas.

122. Roger Harding of Winterbourne struck John Balecoke, hayward of Matthew de Columbariis,[2] with a rake on the head, from which he later died. Roger fled immediately after the deed and is suspected, so let him be *exacted and outlawed*. He had no chattels, and was in Winterbourne Monkton tithing, which is in *mercy*. William of Stanmore was attached because he was present, and now he does not come, and he was attached by Winterbourne tithing, which does not have him now, so it is in *mercy*. It is testified that John Salewy and William Godefarhylle[3] were likewise present. They do not come now, and were not attached because they were not found at the inquest held before the coroner, nor are they suspected of the death. So nothing from them because they had no chattels, but they are in *mercy* because they did not arrest Roger. Beckhampton and Hinton townships did not come fully to the inquest, so they are in *mercy*.

123. Maud the wife of Walter de la Forde and her daughter Amice got themselves into Hinton church, where they admitted theft and *abjured* the realm before the coroner. Their chattels *10s.*, Hinton township to answer. Hinton township did not arrest them, so it is in *mercy*. Thomas Wybelin, accused of associating with Maud and Amice, comes and denies theft and all, and for good and ill puts himself on the country. The jurors say that Thomas is not guilty, so he is quit.

124. William Strut and Ralph le Wafe attacked Stephen Luve at night and killed him in Shaw township. William was later arrested and hanged before justices for gaol [delivery] etc. His chattels *22s. 4d.*, William Spileman's part of Shaw township to answer. Ralph fled immediately and is suspected, so let him be *exacted and outlawed*. He had no chattels, but he was in Alton Barnes tithing, so it is in *mercy*. West Overton and Clatford townships did not come to the inquest, so they are in *mercy*.

125. James le Cupere of Avebury and Nicholas the shepherd of the same quarrelled together in James's house. James killed Nicholas and fled immediately, and he is suspected, so let him be *exacted and outlawed*. His chattels *9d.*, Avebury township to answer, and he was in Avebury tithing, which is in *mercy*. East Kennett, West Kennett and Beckhamton townships did not come fully to the inquest, so they are in *mercy*. King's Barton, Poulton, Stitchcombe and Ogbourne townships did not come to an inquest held into the death of Hugh le Messer, so they are in *mercy*.

126. Richard Brodrybbe, Walter Bursy and John son of John of Rockley

---

1 Written above the three names is *pauperes*, 'poor'.

2 Lord of the manor of Beckhampton. *VCH Wiltshire* xii, 95.

3 Written above each name is *pp* for *pauper*, 'poor'.

killed John the chaplain of Preshute. Richard was later arrested and hanged at Marlborough. He had no chattels. Immediately after the deed Walter and John together with Richard carried away the chaplain's body so that it was never found afterwards. They fled immediately and are suspected, so let Walter and John be *exacted and outlawed*. They had no chattels and were not in a tithing, but they were in the mainpast of Roger de la Grene, archdeacon of Wiltshire,[1] so he is in *mercy*. Preshute township did pursue them, so it is in *mercy*. No Englishry is presented. Judgement *murder*, upon the hundred.

127. John of Rockley appealed John of Wanborough, William le Box of Seagry, William of Langley in the county court . . .[2]

128. Concerning defaults, they say that Alexander de Montford of Ogbourne (ill),[3] Ellis of the wood from the same (ill), William Walerand of the same, John of Downton of Kennett (ill), Thomas of Hendred and Robert de Hafford of Ogbourne did not come on the first day, so they are in *mercy*.

129. Concerning indicted persons, they say that Robert Edward of Snap, William le Noreys of Poulton and John the fisherman of the same have made off on suspicion of theft and are suspected, so let them be *exacted and outlawed*. Robert Edward's chattels *55s. 10d.*, Aldbourne township to answer, and he was in Aldbourne tithing, which is in *mercy*. William and John had no chattels, but they were in Poulton tithing, which is in *mercy*.

130.[4] Maud the widow of Adam of Rockley appealed Thomas le Pestur of Marlborough, his son John, Ives of Crawley, John Purbygge, William the carter of Richard of Ospringe, William Unfrey, Walter le Tanner, Richard of Alton, John Morgan, Hugh Larke, William of Leicester, Walter Martin, William le Gras, John of Stanton and Richard of Ospringe in the county court of the death of Adam of Rockley her husband. Maud does not come now, so let her be *arrested*, and her pledges for prosecuting are in *mercy*, namely Ralph Hervy of Wilton and John Hervy of the same. Thomas and all the others except William of Leicester and Walter Martin come. William and Walter[5] were not attached because she only sued against them at two county courts, so let them be arrested. Asked if they [the parties] are agreed, the jurors say no. For the preservation of the king's peace let the truth be inquired into by the country. The twelve jurors of this hundred and the five nearest townships,

---

1 Roger de la Grene had become archdeacon of Wiltshire by 27 December 1258, and still held that office in 1268. *Fasti Ecclesiae Anglicanae 1066-1300, iv: Diocese of Salisbury*, 36-7.

2 The record breaks off. There is a gap of about eight lines.

3 The first two names have *languid'* written above them and have been crossed through; John of Downton's name has *lan[guidus]* written above it.

4 In the margin is *Caret alibi* ('it is defective elsewhere'): see **118** above.

5 This sentence about William and Walter is interlined above a caret.

namely Ogbourne 'Priors', Okeburne Maizey, Poulton, Rockley and Clatford, say on their oath that Thomas and the others are in no way guilty of Adam's death and were not present or colluding in it, so they are quit. But they say that one David le Forester de March, Robert le Clerk who was in the service of William of Berkeley, and William le Porter who was in the service of the same are guilty of the death and are suspected, so let them be *exacted and outlawed*. They had no chattels and were not in a tithing because they were strangers, but they were in the mainpast of William of Berkeley, who is in *mercy*. The twelve jurors made no mention of this appeal, so they are in *mercy*.

131. The twelve jurors are in *mercy* because they withdrew without leave.

132. The jurors present that the abbess of Lacock holds one carucate of land in Upham by the gift of William Lungespeye the younger who died recently,[1] and she used to do suit to the hundred court every three weeks. That suit has been withdrawn for ten years to the king's loss of 2s. a year, and they do not know by what warrant. So let this be discussed.

133. Walter Hyon appeals[2] John Bundy that when he was in the king's peace on the Saturday next after the feast of St. Gregory in the 49th year [of Henry III, 14 March 1265] about midday on the king's highway, between Rockley township and Blackgrove wood on the east side of the road, John came in felony and premeditated assault, and with a Danish axe assaulted him and struck him with the axe on the left arm between the hand and the elbow and broke the arm so that he is maimed. And he appeals John le Careter that on the same day, hour, place and year in felony etc. he struck him on the chest with a stone, and gave him a wound two and a half inches long, one inch wide, and in depth to the bone. He also appeals John Cokke that on the same day etc. he struck him on the flank below the navel with a flint-stone, so that through that blow his bowels dropped to his testicles, so that he was ruptured. And he appeals Thomas le Hore, his wife Alice and Gillian daughter of Emma of ordering and sending [the attackers], that on that day etc. they ordered the said trespass to be done to him. And that John, John and John wickedly etc. did him this felony he offers to prove against John Bundy by his body as a maimed man, and when he has proved against him against each of the above in the same way.

The said John, John and John come and deny all felony etc. and whatever is against the peace. They ask that it be allowed them that when Walter appealed them in the county court he said that the trespass was done to him between Marlborough and Rockley, and now he says that it was done between

---

1 William (iii) Longespée died in 1257. The grant to Lacock was made sometime between 1232 and 1250. K. H. Rogers (ed.), *Lacock Abbey charters*, Wiltshire Record Society 34 (1979 for 1978) no. 305.

2 The appeal relates to an incident which was also the subject of the appeal of Henry Leggegode, **216** below. That appeal, however, did not name John Cokke as an assailant or the three who were alleged to have ordered the assault.

Rockley and Blackgrove. Wherefore they ask that it be allowed them that he varies in his appeal as aforesaid. And because it is established by the coroners' rolls that there is variation in the appeal in the manner aforesaid, it is decided that his appeal is null and that Walter be taken into custody for a false appeal and that John, John and John are quit as to the appeal. But asked how they wish to be acquitted with regard to the king they say that they willingly put themselves on the country. The twelve jurors of this hundred, together with the jurors of Thornhill and Blackgrove hundreds, say on their oath that Walter and Henry, coming from Marlborough, attacked John [Bundy] and others and knocked down John le Careter and made an attack on the others, but John Bundy struck Walter on his left arm and broke it, whereby he is maimed. And because it is established that Walter was maimed by John Bundy, and that John le Careter and others were present in his company, let them be taken into custody. Later Walter Ivon came and made fine by 1 mark by pledge of William de Merokes and Nicholas de Lyle.

m. 28 (IMG 0363, 0364)

THE CASTLE OF SALISBURY COMES BY TWELVE

134. The jurors present that the church of St. Peter in Old Salisbury township is in the king's advowson, and John the chaplain holds it by the king's gift, and it is worth 1 mark a year and the chaplain's service.

135. Concerning purprestures, they say that Walter Noswyche has diverted the course of a river towards his own mill and made it closer to the king's pond than it used to be, to the detriment of the king's mill. So let this be discussed.[1]

136. John Atteberton was arrested for the death of a child and imprisoned in the castle of Salisbury when Ralph Russel[2] was sheriff, and he escaped from that prison. So to judgement for the *escape* upon Ralph Russel. John fled and is suspected of the death, so let him be *exacted and outlawed*. He had no chattels, and he was not in a tithing because he was a stranger.

137. Concerning indicted persons, they say that Michael Feghin, a Jew of Old Salisbury, is a harbourer of thieves and is suspected of associating with and harbouring thieves, and has made off, so let him be *exacted and outlawed*. Let there be an inquiry into his chattels, which were taken to Wilton. Let this be *discussed*. The jurors say that he had chattels worth 20s., for which . . .[3]

---

1 This entry has been heavily corrected, and as it stands hardly makes sense. The mill was presumably the one which Walter was holding of the prior of St Denis, Southampton, in 1281, by when it had fallen into ruin. It stood on the river Avon. W. Illingworth (ed.), *Placita de Quo Warranto temporibus Edw. I, II, et III* (Record Commission, 1818), 797.

2 Russell was sheriff from July 1261 to Midsummer 1264.

3 The record breaks off. There is a narrow gap before the heading that follows.

THE HUNDRED OF CADWORTH COMES BY TWELVE

138. John Laggy and Robert Chubbe quarrelled together in Bishopstone fields. John struck Robert on the head with a hammer so that he later died, and immediately after the deed he fled and is suspected, so let him be *exacted and outlawed*. Let it be inquired of Downton[1] hundred about his chattels. He was in Bishopstone tithing, which is in *mercy*. Netherhampton, Burcombe, Hurdcott and Barford townships did not come fully to the inquest, so they are in *mercy*. Later it is testified by the jurors of Downton hundred that John had chattels worth *2s.*, Bishopstone township to answer.

139. John son of Roger Azelyn, intending to bathe in the river between Ugford and Wilton,[2] accidentally drowned. No one is suspected. Judgement *misadventure*. Ditchhampton, Burcombe 'Abbess' and Ugford 'St. James' townships did not come fully to the inquest, so they are in *mercy*.

140. Concerning serjeanties, they say that Maud de Karetem holds two virgates of land in Barford by the service of keeping half of Grovely forest, and she pays the king 10s. a year. The serjeanty is worth 1 mark a year.[3]

141. From W[illiam le Dun], sheriff, for the chattels of John Eve, hanged before justices for gaol [delivery] etc., *12d.*

142. The jurors present that the bailiffs of the king of Germany[4] do not allow the king's bailiff to enter his lands at Barford. And the bailiffs of Henry, the son of the king of Germany, do not allow the king's bailiff to enter Sutton

---

1 Bishopstone was a detached part of Downton hundred adjoining the southern boundary of Cadworth hundred, along which lay the four townships named below.

2 The river Nadder.

3 The half in question was the southern half. In 1243 William de Karentem was holding a virgate in Barford by this serjeanty, and paying 9s. 3d. per annum to Salisbury cathedral. He had acquired it by his marriage to Maud, the daughter of Roger the forester, and after William's death she held it until at least 1281, when it was said to contain two virgates. It 1274/5 the land was valued at 20s. per annum, of which she paid 9s. to the exchequer and 1s. to the cathedral. The Roger de Karentham who died possessed of the serjeanty in 1289 must have been Maud's son, named after her father. *Book of Fees* ii, 743; *Wiltshire crown pleas, 1249* no. 505; *Rot. Hund.* ii, 233; JUST 1/1005/2 m. 156d; *CIPM* ii no. 733. For the keeping of the northern half of Grovely see **335** below.

4 *Alemannie*. Richard of Cornwall, Henry III's younger brother, was crowned king of the Romans (with the expectation that he would become Holy Roman Emperor when he could be crowned by the pope) on 17 May 1257. Implicit in this title was the kingship of Germany – to the chronicler Matthew Paris he was crowned 'king of the Romans or of Germany' – explaining why here and elsewhere in the eyre roll Richard is referred to under that title (**143, 535, 544, 571**). Matthew Paris, *Chronica majora*, ed. H.R. Luard, 7 vols. (1872-3), v, 640.

manor to make distraints for what is owed to the king, and they do not know by what warrant.

143. Concerning suits, they say that the king of Germany holds Barford manor, which was William Avenel's, by the king's gift and that the manor used to do suit to the king's hundred court of Cadworth every three weeks, and the withdrawal has been made for fifteen years, to the king's loss of 10s. a year.[1]

And Henry, the son of the king of Germany, holds Sutton Mandeville manor by gift of the earl of Gloucester, and it used to do suit in the manner aforesaid, and that suit has been withdrawn for eleven years to the king's loss of 27s. 4d. a year.[2] They say that Henry's bailiffs at Sutton hold the plea of replevin, but they do not know by what warrant.

144. From W[illiam le Dun], sheriff, for the chattels of Richard Crubbe, hanged before justices for gaol [delivery] etc., *2s.*

145. From Sutton township, for the chattels of John of Stockbridge, hanged, *9s.*

146. Concerning indicted persons, they say that Robert le Ruter, Richard son of Hugh Payn, Richard Wranne, Gilbert le Pyg and Peter Warrok have made off on suspicion of theft and are suspected, so let them be *exacted and outlawed*. They had no chattels. Robert was in Fovant tithing, which is in *mercy*. Richard son of Hugh was in the same tithing, which is in *mercy*. Richard Wranne was in Hurdcott tithing, which is in *mercy*. Gilbert was in Barford tithing, which is in *mercy*. Peter was not in a tithing, but he was in the mainpast of Gillian of Bedford of Wilton, who is in *mercy*.

147. The jurors present that when Adam de Bukesyate was the earl of Gloucester's bailiff, he newly raised gallows at Sutton and hanged John of Stockbridge and executed judgement on him, and it is not known by what warrant.[3]

THE HUNDRED OF SWANBOROUGH COMES BY TWELVE

148. Unknown malefactors encountered Nicholas le Gros at Shaw outside Savernake, and beat and wounded him so that he died four days later. It is not known who they were. Alton Barnes, Draycott, Huish and Shaw townships did not come fully to the inquest, so they are in *mercy*.

---

1 The date of the withdrawal is confirmed by a presentment made in 1255, that it had been made two years earlier. *Rot. Hund.* ii, 233.

2 Also confirmed by a subsequent presentment. In 1274/5 the suit was said to have been withdrawn seventeen years ago, that is, in 1257/8, but the loss to the king was assessed at 37s. in all. *Rot. Hund.* ii, 245.

3 The earl of Gloucester's gallows at Sutton were still 'newly raised' in 1274/5, so their construction may have been very recent in 1268. *Rot. Hund.* ii, 245.

149. An unknown man was found killed on the hill outside Manningford. Bartholomew son of Henry, the first finder, has died. It is not known who killed him. No Englishry is presented. Judgement *murder*, upon the hundred. Manningford Bruce , Manningford Abbots, Upavon and Manningford Bruce townships did not come fully to the inquest, so they are in *mercy*.

150. Godelota de Stoke was found killed by unknown malefactors in her house in East Stoke. Roger le Cuper, the first finder, has died. William le Taylur was arrested on suspicion of the death and imprisoned in Salisbury castle and died there. It is not known who killed her. Woodborough, Newnton, Hillcot and Charlton townships did not come fully to the inquest, so they are in *mercy*.

151. Nicholas Mydewinter beat and wounded his wife Maud so that she later died. Nicholas fled immediately after the deed and is suspected, so let him be *exacted and outlawed*. His chattels *14s. 3d.*, the sheriff to answer, and he was in Woodborough tithing, which is in *mercy*. Manningford Bruce, Woodborough, Manningford Bohun and Beechingstoke townships did not come fully to the inquest, so they are in *mercy*.

152. Robert Norman struck William Cotyn with a sword on the head so that he died four days later. Robert fled immediately after the deed and is suspected, so let him be *exacted and outlawed*. His chattels *4d.*, the sheriff to answer, and he was not in a tithing because he was a stranger. Rushall and Charlton townships did not come fully to the inquest, so they are in *mercy*.

153. From W[illiam le Dun], sheriff, for the chattels of Richard Geky, hanged, *3s.* Likewise for the chattels of Thomas Pren, hanged, *22d.*

154. Unknown malefactors burgled the house of Robert Haselman in East Stoke township, killed Robert and carried off the goods found in the same. It is not known who they were. Beechingstoke township in which this happened did not pursue them, so it is in *mercy*. Stanton 'St Bernard', Aulton Priors and 'Estoke' townships did not come fully to the inquest, so they are in *mercy*.

155. Nicholas le Syur of Manningford got himself into Manningford church, admitted that he had killed William of Salisbury, clerk, and *abjured* the realm before the coroner. His chattels *6d.*, the sheriff to answer, and he was in Manningford Bruce tithing,[1] which is in *mercy*. Manningford Abbots township did not arrest him when this happened in daytime, so it is in *mercy*.

156. Unknown malefactors burgled the house of Walter le Pottere of Manningford Bruce, killed Walter and his wife Isabel, and carried away the

---

1 In 1268 Manningford 'of Reynold son of Peter'. It took its 'Bruce' suffix from Reynold's having conveyed it to William de Breuse in 1275. *VCH Wiltshire* x, 113-14.

goods there. It is not known who they were. Manningford 'Earl's' township did not come to the inquest etc., so it is in *mercy*.

157. Concerning serjeanties, they say that Silvester Dunel holds the township of Huish of the king, and it used to be held by the service of providing one man horsed for forty days in the army at the tenant's expense, and now it is assessed for a rent of 1 mark and renders that much to the king.[1]

158. Concerning defaults, they say that the abbot of Hyde (writ),[2] Reynold son of Peter (writ), Andrew Wake (writ), John Scilling (writ), the prior of Winchester (dead),[3] Michael of Hakenton and John Barnevile did not come here on the first day, so they are in *mercy*.

159. Concerning suits, they say that the manor of Manningford Abbots used to make suit to the hundred court, and that suit has been withdrawn for three years now to the king's loss of 2s. a year, and they do not know by what warrant.

160. Concerning indicted persons, they say that William son of Alice of Rushall who was the wife of Ellis Buttebryge, Robert Mydewynter, Walter le Grey, Simon Walkelyn of Charlton, Adam son of Robert le Juvene, Robert le Dober, John de Bacham of Stowell, Alice daughter of Robert de Pyla of Manningford and Walter Fys of Alton Priors have made off on suspicion of theft and they are all suspected, so let them be *exacted and outlawed*. The chattels of Walter le Fys *14s. 8d.*, Alton Priors township to answer, and he was in Alton Priors tithing, which is in *mercy*. The others had no chattels, and they were not in tithings because they were strangers.

161. From W[illiam le Dun], sheriff, for the chattels of Roger Borolde, hanged before justices for gaol [delivery] etc., *18d.*

1 In 1243 the serjeanty was held by Robert Dunel or Doinel, by the service recorded in 1268. At his death in 1247 custody of his heir was granted to Silvester of Everdon, bishop of Carlisle, for a payment of fifty marks. The property was then valued at nearly £4 per annum. Three years later a number of alienations were detected, valued at a total of one mark, which became payable to the exchequer, but what was left was still reckoned to be worth £5 per annum in 1255. Silvester was said to still owe the service, as well as the money, in 1281, but nothing was said of the serjeanty at his death in 1293. *Book of Fees* ii, 741, 1179; *Wiltshire crown pleas, 1249* no. 427 and note; *Rot. Hund.* ii, 234; JUST 1/1005/2 m. 142d; *CIPM* iii no. 47.

2 Above each of the first four names is written *b* (for *breve*), indicating that he had a writ of quittance.

3 Prior Valentine was not in fact dead, but had resigned on 7 August 1267, and the priorate was vacant at the time of the eyre. Valentine was reinstated on 3 July 1268, but resigned a second time in 1276. Restored again later that year, he was finally deprived by the bishop. Of all this the jurors were seemingly ignorant. D.M. Smith and V.C.M. London, *The heads of religious houses: England and Wales, ii: 1216-1377* (Cambridge, 2001), 83-4.

162. Henry of Berwick and William le Sopere of Alton and John Aume, arrested on suspicion of theft, come and deny theft and all, and for good and ill put themselves on the country. The jurors say that Henry and the others are not guilty etc., so they are *quit*.

m. 28d (IMG, 0444, 0445)

THE HUNDRED OF BRADFORD COMES BY TWELVE

163. Reynold de la Sale fell from a boat on the river Avon and drowned. Thomas Patelot and Walter Basset, attached because they were present, come and are not suspected, nor is anyone else. Judgement *misadventure*. The value of the boat (*deodand*) 6d., the sheriff answer. Bradford, Winsley, Wraxall and Atworth townships did not come fully to the inquest, so they are in *mercy*.

164. Walter Peree, trying to draw back the sluice-gate of the mill of Bradford, fell in the river[1] and drowned. Henry Peree, the first finder, has died. No one is suspected. Judgement *misadventure*. The value of the sluice-gate (*deodand*) 3d., the sheriff to answer. Leigh, Atworth and Bradford townships concealed the deodand, so they are in *mercy*.

165. Unknown malefactors encountered Nicholas Spyrewyt at night outside Bradford township and killed him. William Spirewyt, the first finder, comes and is not suspected. It is not known who killed him. No Englishry is presented. Judgement *murder*, upon the hundred. Westwood, Trowle and Leigh townships did not come fully to the inquest, so they are in *mercy*.

166. Geoffrey Espygurnel and John Espigurnel were together in a mill at Farleigh in Somersetshire, and a dispute having arisen between them John killed Geoffrey. John's brother Hamon aided him in doing the deed, and after it they carried Geoffrey's body into Wiltshire and placed the body in the river Avon near 'Wittenham' and immediately afterwards made off and are suspected. So let them be *exacted and outlawed*. Their chattels and tithings are unknown because they were strangers from Somersetshire.[2] Chalfield township did not come to the inquest etc., so it is in *mercy*.

167. Robert le Franceys, Hugh le Charpenter of Woodhill, John Oyselur and John the smith of Avebury appealed master Walter Escamel,[3] master

---

1 The river Avon.

2 Farleigh Hungerford lies immediately to the west of the river Frome, which here forms the county boundary. 'Wittenham' (now lost) was formerly a separate parish within what is now the parish of Wingfield. *VCH Wiltshire* vii, 70.

3 It is unfortunate that there is no date to indicate when the dispute behind this appeal occurred – it does not seem to be recorded elsewhere. It is possible that the appellors were parish officers of some kind. Walter Scammel, who became bishop of

Stephen, the parson of 'Icherygge', Henry his chaplain, Roger, the parson of Shipton, Ralph his servant, David the parson of Manton, Michael le Clerk, Philip le Clerk, kinsman of the wife of Roger of the hall, Robert of Mene, chaplain of Kington, John the parson of 'Rutelyge', Roger the almoner of St. Edward, William of Oaksey, Walter the marshal of Trowbridge, William le Warener, Geoffrey the baker, Henry the baker, Adam the baker, Robert Herding de Bradelige Tredgold, William Basset, Thomas le Porter, Roger Turgys, John Bulebek, Richard Patelot, Richard Wage, Cecily Myke, Richard of Motcombe, William le Engleys of Gussage, William le Orfevere, Roger le Ku of St. Edward, Roger of Midford, Thomas son of Thomas of Perham, Richard of Devon, William fiz le Mestre, Dycun Petitot, William Chauflur, John nephew of master Walter, William son of Katherine, Walter Nol, Henry de la Hole, Michael Pers, Clement Haym, William Bardolf of Bath, Richard the chaplain of Calstone, Adam son of Hamon of Calstone, John the marshal of Bath, William Burgeys, Henry Peytevyn, Gilbert the tailor, Henry Burgeys and Gilbert Grasaloyl in the county court of the robbery of £200 in money and of breach of the king's peace. Robert le Franceys and the other appellors do not come, so let them be *arrested* and their pledges for prosecuting are in mercy, namely William Quintyn of Clyffe Pypard and Henry de Burle. Walter the marshal who was appealed comes. The jurors, asked if Walter [the marshal] is agreed with Robert and the others, say no, and that he is not guilty of any robbery, but because he came with the said [master] Walter and the others and stayed with them, let him be taken into *custody*.

(*Let it be discussed whether it has been concluded.*) Master Walter and the other appellees do not now come. Master Walter was attached by Godfrey Russel of Bradley and William Hardinge of the same, David the parson of Manton by Richard Acheford of Bradley and Robert son of Walter of the same (*in mercy*). Master Stephen and the others were not attached because Robert and the others only sued against them at three county courts. The jurors say that they [the parties] are agreed, and for the preservation of the king's peace let the truth, and the facts, of the matter be inquired into by the country. The jurors say on their oath that there was a quarrel between Ralph de Englescheville and master Walter about Bradford church, and that master Walter and the others came to that church, intending to seize it on master Walter's behalf, and master Stephen and the others on master Walter's order took possession of the church and broke open a chest found there and took £20 sterling from it. So let them be *arrested*. Later it is testified by some that the appeal was concluded before the king, so let this be *inquired into and discussed*.[1]

Salisbury in 1284, was made archdeacon of Berkshire in 1265 and became treasurer of Salisbury cathedral around the time of the 1268 eyre. He was also a royal clerk, who in December 1267 was appointed a collector of the papal tenth granted to Henry III in the previous year. B.R. Kemp, 'Scammel, Walter (d. 1286)' [http://www.oxforddnb.com/view/95177, accessed 1 July 2012].

1 There is a gap of about eight lines between this entry and the next.

168. Henry de Seymor appealed Eve the wife of Robert Waspre, Robert Waspre, Hugh of Ashgoe, Henry le Wodewarde [repeated], Adam le Parker, Philip le Quyle, Hugh Svynghedeu and William of Westwood in the county court of wounds, robbery and breach of the king's peace. Henry does not come now, so let him be *arrested* and his pledges for prosecuting are in *mercy*, namely Robert de Wancy and William Munte from Warminster hundred. Eve and the other appellees come, and the jurors say that they [the parties] are not agreed and [Eve and the others] are not guilty, so they are quit.

169. William son of Richard Seman got himself into Farleigh church, admitted that he had killed Benedict of Morton and *abjured* the realm before the coroner. He had no chattels and was received outside a tithing in the township of Sopworth, which is in *mercy*. Monkton Farleigh township did not arrest him, so it is in *mercy*.

170. Thomas Tartarin and John le Crispe jousted together, and they coursed once and then again, when Thomas struck John in the eye with his lance, so that he died instantly. Thomas Above Wode, the first finder, comes and is not suspected. It is testified that Robert of Broughton Giffard held[1] Thomas's rein in riding with him and master Walter of Lucknam held John's rein, and they are not suspected of the death, but because they were present and did not arrest him they are in *mercy*. To judgement upon Sampson of Boxe, then coroner, because he did not order the attachment of Robert and master Walter. Chalfield, Broughton and Atworth townships were present and did not arrest Thomas, so they are in *mercy*. Thomas fled immediately after the deed and is suspected of the death, so let him be *exacted and outlawed*. He had no chattels, and he was not in a tithing, but he was in the mainpast of John Gyffarde, who is in *mercy*.[2] Afterwards Robert of Broughton Giffard came and made fine by ½ *mark* (*the sheriff to answer*) by pledge of John of Durnford.

171. Richard le Wode and Richard le Eremite quarrelled together, and Richard le Wode struck Richard le Eremite with a knife in the stomach so that he later died. Richard le Wode fled immediately after the deed and is suspected, so let him be *exacted and outlawed*. He had no chattels, but he was received outside a tithing in Winkfield township, which is in *mercy*.[3] Trowle township did not come to the inquest etc., so it is in *mercy*.

---

1 *duxit* in each instance.

2 John Giffard formally acquired Broughton Giffard from Walter de Dunstanville in November 1268, but this case suggests that he had come into possession of it somewhat earlier. CP 25/1/252/22 no. 12.

3 Presumably the amercement of 6s. 8d. which the king's officers were subsequently unable to collect at Wingfield after the eyre, owing to the resistance of the earl of Gloucester's bailiffs. JUST 1/1005/2 m. 125.

172. Concerning defaults, they say that the abbot of Keynesham (writ)[1], Richard Cotel, William le Bret, Robert de Chaundos, Reynold de Clyve, Richard Purewlle, John the cook, Walter Wayrchylde, Roger Bovewode, Hugh of Atworth. Adam Trudebus and Warin of Iford did not come here on the first day, so they are in *mercy*.

173. Concerning suits withdrawn, they say that the abbot of Keynesham and his men of Wingfield, and likewise John de St Lô and his men of Wittenham, the prior of St. Swithun, Winchester, and his tithing of Westwood, and Richard of Wick have withdrawn the suit which they used to do to the hundred every three weeks. Concerning this they say that the abbot and John owe the king 7s. a year for the sheriff's tourn and ½ mark a year for sheriff's aid, and that the withdrawal has been made for eight years now. Richard of Wick owes suit to the view of frankpledge twice a year [and has withdrawn it] to the king's loss of 2s. a year.[2]

THE BOROUGH OF CALNE COMES BY TWELVE

174. John Grym of Westwood got himself into Calne church, where he admitted theft and *abjured* the realm before the coroner. His chattels *3d.*, the sheriff to answer. His tithing is unknown because he was a stranger.

175. Concerning indicted persons, they say that Walter Bovy has made off on suspicion of theft and is suspected, so let him be *exacted and outlawed*. His chattels ½ *mark*, the treasurer of Salisbury's tithing in Calne to answer.[3] He was in the same tithing, which is in *mercy*.They also say that Adam the treasurer of Salisbury's porter[4] has likewise made off on suspicion of theft and is suspected, so let him be *exacted and outlawed*. His chattels 5s., that tithing to answer. He was in the same tithing, which is in mercy.

m. 29 (IMG 0365, 0366)[5]

THE HUNDRED OF CALNE COMES BY TWELVE

176. John son of Adam of Bulkington was struck by a mare[6] so that he

---

1 Above his name is written *b* (for *breve*), indicating that he had a writ of quittance.

2 After this entry is a space of about five lines.

3 The manor known as Eastman Street in Calne itself, together with tithes there and in other parishes in Calne hundred, constituted a prebend in Salisbury cathedral, which from the 1220s was annexed to its treasurership. *VCH Wiltshire* xvii, 13, 65, 129, 140, 154.

4 *portarius*, but perhaps *porcarius*, swineherd.

5 Written above the stitching at the head of the membrane is *primus post villam de Kalne* ('first after the township of Calne').

6 *jumento*, but where its value is given it is *eque*.

died instantly. The first finder has died. No one is suspected. Judgement *misadventure*. The value of the mare (*deodand*) 3s., the sheriff to answer.

177. William Heymor shot an unknown man with an arrow in Pewsham forest so that he later died. Robert son of William, the first finder, has died. William fled immediately after the deed and is suspected, so let him be *exacted and outlawed*. He had no chattels, and was not in a tithing because he was a stranger. No Englishry is presented. Judgement *murder*, upon the hundred. Studley, Whitley, Blackland and Heddington townships did not come fully to the inquest, so they are in *mercy*.

178. An unknown man was found dead in Chippenham forest below Calstone Wellington. Pain le Forester, the first finder, comes and is not suspected. It is not known who killed him. No Englishry [is presented]. Judgement *murder*, upon the hundred. Bromham and Calstone Wellington townships did not come fully to the inquest, so they are in *mercy*.

179. John le Messor of Compton wanted to take a pledge from Robert Palling, and a quarrel having arisen between them, Robert struck John on the head with a staff and gave him many wounds from which he later died. Robert fled immediately after the deed and is suspected, so let him be *exacted and outlawed*. He had no chattels, and was not in a tithing because he was a stranger. William Cubebat was present when this was done and has made off, but is not suspected of the death, so let him return if he wishes, but his chattels are confiscated for his flight. William's chattels 8d., the sheriff to answer. Yatesbury, Cherhill and Blackland townships did not come fully to the inquest, so they are in *mercy*. The twelve jurors made no mention of the chattels and did not present any finder [of the body], so they are in *mercy*.

180. John the dyer fled to Yatesbury church, where he admitted theft and *abjured* the realm before the coroner. His chattels 3d., the sheriff to answer. The township of Yatesbury did not arrest him, so it is in *mercy*.

181. Unknown malefactors came to the house of Christian la Bere in Blackland, killed Alice her daughter and carried away the goods found there. It is not known who they were. Christian's son William, attached because he was present, comes and is not suspected, nor could he have arrested them because he was badly wounded, so he is quit. Calstone Wellington and Heddington townships did not come to the inquest, so they are in *mercy*.

182. Walter son of Roger Avenel and William son of Walter Pede quarrelled together in Heddington fields. Walter killed William and fled immediately after the deed. He is suspected, so let him be exacted and outlawed. He had no chattels, and was in Tasworth tithing, so it is in mercy. Roger Avenel, the first finder, and four neighbours come and are not suspected.

183. From W[illiam le Dun], sheriff, for the chattels of Simon of Ewyas, hanged before justices for gaol [delivery] etc., *2s. 6d.*

184. Henry son of Walter fell from an oak tree in Chippenham forest so that he died instantly. The first finder has died. No one is suspected. Judgement *misadventure*. The value of the oak tree (*deodand*) *12d.*, the sheriff to answer.

185. Roger le Wodeward struck Walter le Clerk of Calstone Wellington with a knife to the heart so that he died instantly. Roger fled immediately after the deed and is suspected, so let him be *exacted and outlawed*. He had no chattels, but he had land from which the king's year and waste [are worth] *3s.*, the sheriff to answer. Roger was in Calstone Wellington tithing, so it is in *mercy*. John le Careter and Walter Elys, attached because they were present when this was done, come and for good and ill put themselves on the country. The jurors say on their oath that they are not guilty, so they are quit of that, but because they did not arrest Roger they are in *mercy*. They have made fine by ½ mark, pledge Walter Rawe.

186. Concerning defaults, they say that the abbot of Battle and Robert de Cantulupo did not come here on the first day, so they are in *mercy*.

THE HUNDRED OF BLACKGROVE COMES BY TWELVE

187. An unknown man was found dead in the fields towards[1] Uffcott. John of Elcombe, the first finder, does not come, and he was attached by Thomas of Elcombe and Hugh le Duk of the same, who are in *mercy*. No one is suspected because he died of hunger and cold. Judgement *misadventure*. Elcombe, Wroughton, Westlecott and Salthrop townships did not come to the inquest, so they are in *mercy*.

188. Adam de la Troye was found killed[2] in Wootton township. Hugh le Carpenter, the first finder, and four neighbours come and are not suspected. John son of the hayward of Wootton, John son of Emma and John Blakhod have made off on suspicion of the death and are suspected, so let them be *exacted and outlawed*. They had no chattels and they were not in a tithing because they were strangers. Tockenham, Thornhill, Chaddington and Midgehall townships did not come to the inquest, so they are in *mercy*.

189. Margery of Uffcott appeals Adam le Burler and John Russel that when she was in the king's peace in her house in Uffcott on the Friday next before the middle of Lent around the third hour in the 47th year of King Henry's reign [9 March 1263], Adam and John came wickedly and in felony and in premeditated assault to Margery's house, broke down its doors, and carried them to the township's common pasture. And in the same house they took

---

1 *versus* is written very clearly above *de*, which is struck through.

2 Adam's death is recorded again at **213**, below.

in robbery eight oxen of Margery's worth 41s., a cow and two bullocks worth 14s., nine ewes worth 1 mark, twenty-one yearlings[1] worth 14s., two gold rings worth 3s., two gold brooches worth 3s., 15 marks of silver, vessels and other small things to the value of 100s., and they took and carried them off. And they demolished the building called the hall together with an adjoining chamber. And that they did this wickedly and in felony and against the king's peace she offers to prove against them as the court shall decide, as a woman etc.

The same Margery appeals master Ralph of Heigham, chancellor of Salisbury,[2] of ordering and sending [them].

Adam, John and master Ralph come and deny all felony, robbery and whatever is against the king's peace. Master Ralph asks for judgement as to whether he should answer concerning the ordering and sending until the deed is established.

Adam and John ask that it be allowed them that a woman has no appeal for which anyone ought to be put to law except for rape of her virginity or for her husband killed in her arms or for a child miscarried in her womb. They also ask that it be allowed them that when this deed was supposedly done Margery did not promptly raise the hue or promptly pursue [the matter] to any bailiff or coroner. Because it is established by the coroners' rolls and by the twelve jurors that she did not promptly raise the hue and that she cannot have an appeal except in the manner aforesaid, it is decided that her appeal is null whereby they ought to be put to law, and that Adam and John may go quit as to the appeal, and let Margery be taken into custody for a false appeal. Asked how they wish to be acquitted themselves with regard to the king's suit, Adam and John say that they willingly put themselves on the country that they took nothing and carried nothing off in robbery etc. The twelve jurors of this hundred, together with twelve jurors of Kingsbridge hundred, come and say on their oath that master Ralph, from whom Margery held her tenement at Uffcott, †came to his manor of Uffcott and there held his court, to which†[3] Margery owed suit. And because she refused to come to the court he ordered that she be distrained to attend. And master Ralph's bailiffs had twice come to the tenement to make distraints, and as far as she could she resisted with force and arms their efforts to make a distraint, so that on a third occasion †Adam† came †armed in a breastplate, iron helmet and gorget, and many others with him, [sent] by the said master,† and they entered the house and demolished it and removed oxen and cows †from the stalls and drove off sheep found there and carried off corn and other goods† found there and ejected her from the house. Because of this she brought

1 *hoggastri* – young sheep.

2 Ralph of Heigham became chancellor around the end of 1240, and was still in office at the time of the 1268 eyre. *Fasti Ecclesiae Anglicanae 1066-1300, iv: diocese of Salisbury*, 19.

3 The words between daggers here and later in the entry were added over erasures, in some instances being crammed into spaces too small, requiring cramped writing and interlineations with carets. Before the first erasure the word *ven*[it] was not deleted from *ten*[ementum] *suu*[m] *ven*[it] *apud Ofcote*.

an assize of novel disseisin against the said master and others, whereby
it was established that they had disseised her, so that by that assize she recovered
her seisin against them, and damages, namely 36 marks for †that disseisin,
which were awarded to her in the same court, viz. before† W. of Englefield,
the justice then assigned to this. And because she then recovered †the value of
the things that were taken from her they are quit on this point. Asked if Adam,
John and others made that superfluous distraint and trespass in the manner
aforesaid on the order and at the sending of the said master, the jurors say
yes. So let Adam and John, and likewise master Ralph, be taken into *custody*.†

190. The same [Margery] appealed William of Rowde, Walter his son, Walter
le Traventer and Roger Woderove in the county court of that robbery and
that deed, and of breach of the king's peace. William of Rowde and the
other appellees do not come. William of Rowde was attached by Richard
Purchaz of Beanacre and William of Beanacre; Walter by William of Shaw
and Thomas of Melksham; Walter le Traventer by Hugh le Clerk of Uffcott
and John de la Lane of the same; and Roger by John Silvester of Corton and
William son of John de la Forde. So they are in *mercy*.

191. Walter le Traventer appealed Margery of Uffcott, Henry, John and
Stephen her sons and Roger de la Penne in the county court of robbery and
breach of the king's peace. Walter does not now come, so let him be arrested
and his pledges for prosecuting are in mercy, namely Hugh le Clerk of Uffcott
and John de la Lane of the same. Margery, Henry and John come. The jurors
say that they [the parties] are not agreed, but they say that Margery and
the others who are appealed broke into Walter's houses, and took away the
timber of his house along with the corn from two acres of land, against the
peace etc. So let them be taken into *custody*. Stephen and Roger do not come
now, so let them be *arrested*. Stephen was attached by Richard le Chareter of
Chiseldon and Richard Isac of the same, and Roger by William le Paumer
of Wroughton and Thomas Curteys of the same, so they are in *mercy*.[1]

m. 29d (IMG, 0446, 0447) *Continuing Blackgrove hundred*

192. As Robert Eteneue was leading a cart on the king's highway near Little
Town he fell under the cartwheel and was crushed by it, so that he died
instantly. Robert Kempe, attached because he was present, has died. No one
is suspected. Judgement *misadventure*. The value of the horse and cart (*deodand*)
8s., the sheriff to answer. Thornhill, Salthrop, Bincknoll and Broad Town
townships valued the deodand falsely, so they are in *mercy*.

193. Peter de Salingford and his brother Thomas killed William of Appelby,
and pursued by William's wife Agnes they fled to Wootton church, admitted

---

1 At the foot of the membrane is written *ff Ricardus le Careter et Ricardus Isac de eadem*,
apparently meaning that Richard and Richard made a fine (*finem fecerunt*), and *Q
Willelmus le Paumer of Wroughton et Thomas Curtys*, apparently meaning that William
and Thomas were quit.

the deed and *abjured* the realm. Peter's chattels *6d.*, the sheriff to answer. Lydiard Tregoze and Tockenham townships did not come fully to the inquest, so they are in *mercy*. Peter and Thomas were not in a tithing because they were strangers.

194. Agnes of Barbury was found dead in the house of Azo le Taverner. Maud of Barbury, attached because she was present, does not come, and she was attached by William Snou of Barbury and Thomas Such of the same, who are in *mercy*. Elcombe, Bincknoll and Westlecott townships did not come fully to the inquest, so they are in *mercy*. No one is suspected. Judgement *misadventure*.

195. An unknown man was found killed in the grange of the recluse of 'Elindon'.[1] Simon Cutel, the first finder, and four neighbours come and are not suspected. It is not known who killed him. No Englishry is presented. Judgement *murder*, upon the hundred. 'Elendon', Wroughton 'Prior's', Wroughton 'Tony' and Salthrop townships did not come to the inquest, so they are in *mercy*.

196. Hugh le Lung and William Pryde quarrelled together, and Hugh struck William with a knife in the stomach from which he later died. Hugh fled immediately after the deed and is suspected, so let him be *exacted and outlawed*. He had no chattels and was not in a tithing, but he was in the mainpast of Robert Tregoz, who is in *mercy*. Swindon 'Valence' and Midgehall townships did not come to the inquest, so they are in *mercy*.

197. Unknown malefactors came to Philip Basset's mill at Wootton Bassett, killed Solomon the miller who was in it, and fled immediately. It is not known who they were, but they left behind them chattels worth *3s.*, the sheriff to answer. Mannington township did not come to the inquest, so it is in *mercy*.

198. Walter Dru was run over by a cart in Purton fields so that he later died. No one is suspected. Judgement misadventure. The value of the mare and cart (*deodand*) *5s.*, the sheriff to answer. Lydiard Millicent and Purton townships did not come fully to the inquest, so they are in *mercy*.

199. Robert son of Ranulf of Swindon killed Robert Golding in Swindon fields. William son of Roger, the first finder, comes and is not suspected. Robert fled immediately after the deed and is suspected, so let him be *exacted and outlawed*. He had no chattels and was not in a tithing because he was under age. Midgehall township did not come fully to the inquest, so it is in *mercy*.

200. Concerning defaults, they say that Robert Tregoz (writ)[2], John Tregoz

---

1 'Elindon' was the original name of Wroughton, *PNS* 278. For other recluses in thirteenth-century Wiltshire see *VCH Wiltshire* iii, 152

2 The six names followed here by '(writ)' have *b* (for *breve*) written above them,

(writ), the abbot of Stanley (writ), Robert Bluet (writ), Hugh son of John (writ), Henry Bluet, the abbess of Lacock (writ), Robert Abraham of Mannington, Stephen the clerk of Swindon, Robert Randolf of the same, John Ruherd of the same, William de la Grene of the same, Roger the clerk of the same, John Mauger of Eastcott, William Engleys of Elcombe, Walter the Frenchman[1] of Uffcott, Walter of Ogbourne of the same, John his son of the same (poor),[2] Walter the servant of Uffcott, Osbert le Cupere of Swindon and Hugh Croke (poor) did not come here on the first day, so they are in *mercy*.

201. Thomas le Chamberleng of Wroughton, Walter le Porker, Henry le Pypere and Cecily Atteworde, arrested on suspicion of theft and harbouring thieves, come and deny all felony and all, and for good and ill put themselves on the country. The jurors say on their oath that Thomas and the others are not guilty of any evildoing, so they are quit.

202. William Scut, accused of harbouring William his son and his theft, comes and denies harbouring and all, and for good and ill puts himself on the country. The jurors of this hundred, together with Heytesbury and Deverill hundred, say on their oath that he is not guilty of any evildoing, so he is *quit*. But they say that this crime was imputed to him out of hatred and at the instigation of Thomas de Kardeville, so let him be taken into *custody*. He is pardoned.

203. Concerning indicted persons, they say that Richard of Inkberrow and Robert son of Adam Preueshe of Swindon have made off on suspicion of theft. They are suspected, so let them be *exacted and outlawed*. They had no chattels, and were not in a tithing because they were strangers.

THE HUNDRED OF KINGSBRIDGE COMES BY TWELVE

204. Unknown malefactors burgled the house of Margery of Lyneham in Lyneham, killed her and carried off the goods found there. It is not known who they were. Richard Halbard, the first finder, and four neighbours come and are not suspected. Lyneham township did not pursue them, so it is in *mercy*. West Tockenham, Littlecott and Witcomb townships did not come fully to the inquest, so they are in *mercy*.

205. Nicholas de Kyngebure struck himself in the stomach with a knife so that he later died. Four neighbours come and are not suspected, nor is anyone else. Judgement *suicide*. He had no chattels. Hilmarton, Witcomb and East Tockenham townships did not come fully to the inquest, so they are in *mercy*.

206. An unknown man was found killed in Broad Town fields. Philip de la Dune, the first finder, has died. It is not known who killed him. No Englishry,

---

indicating that they had writs of quittance.

1 *franciscus*.

2 Written above each of the names followed by '(poor)' is *pp*, for *pauper*.

judgement *murder*, upon the hundred. Bincknoll, Thornhill, Hilmarton and Witcomb townships did not come fully to the inquest, so they are in *mercy*.

207. As John le Kyng of Catcomb and Robert his brother were going in Lyneham fields they quarrelled together, and John struck Robert with an axe on the head so that he died instantly. He fled immediately after the deed and is suspected, so let him be *exacted and outlawed*. He had no chattels, but he was in Catcomb tithing, which is in *mercy*. Bushton township did not come fully to the inquest, so it is in *mercy*.

208. Nicholas de la Holeweye and Ralph Fesant came from a tavern in Clyffe Pypard quarrelling together, and Ralph struck Nicholas with a staff on the head so that he died instantly. He fled immediately after the deed and is suspected, so let him be *exacted and outlawed*. His chattels *16d.*, the sheriff to answer, and was not in a tithing because he was a stranger. Clyffe Pypard and Bushton townships did not come to the inquest, so they are in *mercy*.

209. Ellis le Messer of Tockenham and John de Chastelle were at a tavern at the house of Richard Sterre in East Tockenham, and after a dispute had arisen between them Ellis struck John with a knife in the stomach so that he died instantly. He fled immediately and is suspected, so let him be *exacted and outlawed*. He had no chattels and was not in a tithing because he was a stranger. East Tockenham township did not come fully to the inquest, so it is in *mercy*.

210. Walter le Bercher and William son of Reynold of East Tockenham quarrelled together, and William struck Walter with a staff on the head so that he died two days later. William fled immediately after the deed and is suspected, so let him be exacted and outlawed. He had no chattels, but he was in East Tockenham tithing, which is in *mercy*.

211. Concerning defaults, they say that Walter Maudut and Ralph Gorgeville did not come here on the first day, so they are in *mercy*.

212. Concerning purprestures, they say that the prior of St. Swithun, Winchester, has made a purpresture at Bushton to the extent of half an acre, in that he has occupied a site called Kingsbridge which used to answer to the king for 6d. a year, and the sheriffs were accustomed to hold their hundred courts there. So *let this be discussed*.[1]

213. The jurors present that while John le Pek was bailiff of Kingbridge, he took 10s. from Robert le Hunymongher, Robert his son and Denis of

---

1 What seems to have been the same purpresture was recorded nineteen years earlier. In 1281 it was presented that the king's gallows also stood at the place in question, and that the prior of St Swithun's had made the purpresture twenty years ago. The date may have been wrong, but it is also possible that the encroachment was rectified after the 1249 eyre, only to be repeated around 1261. *Wiltshire crown pleas, 1249*, no. 267; JUST 1/1005/2 m. 139d.

Tockenham, who were accused of the death of Adam of la Trowe,[1] so that they should be released to pledges for ten days, and nevertheless he kept them in prison until they were delivered by the country before justices for gaol [delivery] etc. So let him answer for the 10s., and to *judgement* on John, let him be *arrested*. Later John came and made fine by ½ mark, pledges John de Berners and Robert de Wanci.

214. The jurors present that Alice the widow of William de Englescheville, who held the manor of Woodhill in chief of the king, was granted dower in it by the king and is now married to one John de Sokerville, but they do not know by what warrant. Her land is worth £5 a year. So let this be discussed.[2]

215. Walter of Wick,[3] arrested on suspicion of theft, comes and denies theft and all, and for good and ill puts himself on the country. The jurors say that he is not guilty, so he is quit, but the jurors say that this crime was imputed to him out of hatred and at the instigation of John of the wood and the tithingman of Clyffe Pypard. So let them be taken into *custody*. Later Walter de la Stret, the tithingman of Clyffe, came and made fine by ½ *mark*, pledge Roger Pipard.

m. 30 (IMG 0367, 0368) *Continuing Kingbridge hundred*[4]

216. [Selkley Hundred] Henry Leggegode appealed[5] John Bundy and John le Carreter that when he was in the king's peace on the king's highway between Rockley and Blackgrove wood, on the east side of the road, on the Saturday next after the feast of St. Gregory in the 49th year [14 March 1265], John and John came, and John Bondy atttacked Henry and with a Danish axe dealt him a blow on the top of his head, one inch and a half long and in depth to the

---

1 Evidently the same as the man whose death is the subject of **188**, above.

2 William was the son of the courtier Theobald de Englescheville, to whom Woodhill was granted in 1248. In 1262 Theobald was said to have conveyed the manor ten years ago to his son, who held it until his father's death – possibly inaccurately, since a year later Theobald was said to have died without an heir. Alice was holding a third of the manor as her dower in 1268, when no mention was made of her husband. *CChR 1226-1257*, 331; *CIPM* i nos. 509, 548, 718.

3 Written at the foot of the membrane is *J. de Wyk.*

4 The heading of the membrane shows that the clerk prepared it for a continuation of the Kingsbridge pleas, before it was realised that a Selkley case had been overlooked which should have been placed at the head of m. 28. It is probably significant that the hand which wrote this entry was not the one responsible for the cases surrounding it, but occurs elsewhere only in **370** and **426-31**, at other points at which the principal clerk for some reason broke off. It was probably this substitute who noticed the omission and therefore remedied it, albeit without providing any indication that the new entry was out of place.

5 The appeal relates to an incident which was also the subject of the appeal of Walter Hyon, above, **133**. Walter's surname is here given as Iwon.

bone. And that John le Caretter on the same day, hour[1] and year dealt him
a blow with a Danish axe above the right eye, one inch long and in depth
to the bone. And that they did this in felony and against the peace etc. he
offers to prove by his body against John Bondy as the court shall decide, and
against John le Caretter in the same way. John and John now come and deny
all felony, the wounds and whatever is against the peace etc., and they ask
that it be allowed them that when Henry appealed them in the county court
he said in his appeal that the trespass was done between Marlborough and
Rockley, and moreover they say that after this was supposedly done he did not
promptly raise the hue. These things allowed them, they put themselves on
the country. Because it is established that he [Henry] varies his appeal in his
charges, it is decided that his appeal is null whereby etc., let Henry be taken
into custody for a false appeal, and let the truth of the matter be inquired
into by the country. The twelve jurors of this hundred, together with twelve
jurors of the hundreds of [Blackgrove][2] and Thornhill, say on their oath
that as Henry was coming from Marlborough along with Walter Iwon, they
assaulted John and others, and John Bondy struck Henry on the top of the
head with a Danish axe and John le Caretter gave him a wound above the
right eye. So let John and John be taken into custody for the trespass. Later
Henry came and made fine by ½ mark, pledge . . .[3]

THE BOROUGH OF MALMESBURY COMES BY TWELVE

217. From W[illiam le Dun], sheriff, for the chattels of William le Waleys,
hanged before justices for gaol [delivery], *21d.*

218. Thomas Levelance from Gloucestershire fled to St. Aldhelm's church in
Malmesbury, where he admitted theft and *abjured* the realm before the coroner.
His chattels *12d.*, the sheriff to answer. He was not in a tithing because he
was a stranger from Gloucestershire. Malmesbury township did not arrest
him when this happened in daytime, so it is in *mercy*.

219. Henry le Wlf of Huntingford got himself into St. Aldhelm's church
in Malmesbury, where he admitted theft and *abjured* the realm before the
coroner. His chattels *12d.*, the sheriff to answer. He was not in a tithing
because he was a stranger.

220. Robert le Bulur killed Robert of Dursley in Malmesbury township, and
immediately after the deed fled to St. Mary's church in Malmesbury, admitted
the deed and *abjured* the realm before the coroner. He had no chattels, and
was not in a tithing because he was a pauper wandering through the country.
Malmesbury township did not come fully to the inquest, so it is in *mercy*.

1 The hour has not been mentioned earlier in the entry. It is given as about midday
  in **133**, above.

2 The name of the hundred is accidentally omitted.

3 The entry breaks off and is followed by a space.

221. Ralph le Taylur of Marlborough wounded Roger the servant of master John, vicar of St. Mary's church, so that he later died. Ralph fled immediately after the deed and is suspected, so let him be *exacted and outlawed*. He had no chattels and was not in a tithing because he was a stranger, but he was in the mainpast of Robert Tregoz, who is in *mercy*.

222. Concerning wines sold, they say that John Wyssy of Bristol and William the cook of Malmesbury have sold wines contrary to the assize, so they are in *mercy*.

223. Gillian, daughter of Clarice of Malmesbury, appealed Henry, a man of St. Cross,[1] Gillian daughter of Margery Thoughe, Nicholas le Porter, Isabel sister of Nicholas's wife Agnes and Edith Basily in the county court of robbery, beating and breach of the king's peace. Gillian [daughter of Margery] and Isabel do not come now. Gillian was attached by John Michel and Walter de la Cote, and Isabel by Ralph le Mazecref and William le Porter, who are in *mercy*. Gillian daughter of Clarice, the appellor, does not come now, so let her be arrested, and her pledges for prosecuting are in *mercy*, namely Robert le Clerk of Malmesbury and William Godard of Chisenbury, who are in *mercy*. Henry, Nicholas and Edith come, and it is testified by the jurors that they [the parties] are not agreed, and that they [Henry and the others] are not guilty of that trespass, so they are quit.

THE HUNDRED OF STARTLEY COMES BY TWELVE

224. Unknown malefactors met John Gorwy of Brinkworth outside Brinkworth township and killed him. It is not known who they were. William Gorwy, the first finder, comes and is not suspected. Brinkworth, Little Somerford, Great Somerford and Lea townships did not come fully to the inquest, so they are in *mercy*.

225. John Jace got himself into Seagry church, admitted that he had killed his wife and *abjured* the realm. His chattels *12d.*, the sheriff to answer, and he was in Great Somerford tithing, which is in mercy. Seagry township valued the chattels falsely before the coroner, so it is in *mercy*.

226. Simon le Porker burgled the house of Philip le Wodeward in Grittenham, killed Philip's daughter Isabel in it, carried off the goods found there and fled. Grittenham township is in mercy for not arresting him. It is testified that Simon was later arrested at Marlborough for that deed and hanged. He had no chattels.

227. The jurors present that Henry le Crok, the earl of Gloucester's bailiff,

---

1 Perhaps the hospital of St. Cross at Winchester, although its leger book records no property in or near Malmesbury. British Library, MS Harley 1616.

arrested William de Chyselemp and imprisoned him in Stanton St. Quintin township, keeping him in that prison until he died there. Later he took the dead man's body and carried it to the gallows at Stanton which he had newly erected, and had it buried there without a coroner's view. So let him be arrested if he is found. The sheriff and Richard Pypard, then coroner, came to hold an inquest on the dead man, and Stanton township would not come before the coroner, so it is in *mercy*.

228. William Beket fell from a horse into the river Avon and drowned in it. John de Husseburne, the first finder, has died.[1] No one is suspected. Judgement *misadventure*. The value of the horse (*deodand*) 10s., the sheriff to answer.

229. Roger son of Agnes la Blake of Malmesbury, Robert Munford of Little Somerford and John le Kenysse of the same burgled the house of Bernard the reeve, killed Bernard and carried off the goods found there. They fled immediately and are suspected, so let them be *exacted and outlawed*. They had no chattels. Robert and John were in Little Somerford tithing, which is in *mercy*. Roger was not in a tithing because he was a clerk. Golda his [Bernard's] wife, the first finder, had died. Brokenborough township did not come to the inquest before the coroner, so it is in *mercy*.

230. William Langheye was crushed by a cart outside Somerford township, so that he died instantly. William Hamund, attached because he was present, comes and is not suspected, nor is anyone else. Judgement *misadventure*. The value of the horse and cart (*deodand*) 4s. 6d., the sheriff to answer.

231. Roger le Fader encountered Richard le Thunt on Christian Malford bridge, and a dispute having arisen between them, Roger struck Richard with an axe on the back so that he died four days later. Roger le Fader fled immediately after the deed and is suspected, so let him be *exacted and outlawed*. He had no chattels, but he was in Christian Malford tithing, which is in *mercy*. Seagry township did not come to the inquest before the coroner, so it is in *mercy*.

232. William Wynter and Walter Schay quarrelled together in Norton township, and Walter struck William with a knife in the stomach so that he later died. Walter fled immediately after the deed and is suspected, so let him be *exacted and outlawed*. He had no chattels, and was not in a tithing, but he was received outside a tithing in Norton township, so it is in *mercy*. Norton, Hullavington, Brokenborough and Foxley townships did not come fully to the inquest, so they are in *mercy*.

233. Richard of Essex and Roger Fresel quarrelled together in Brinkworth township, and Richard struck Roger with a knife in the stomach from which

---

1 John was recorded in 1249 as holding land in Purton, in Staple hundred. *Wiltshire civil pleas, 1249* no. 549.

he died instantly. William Wraggy, attached because he was present, comes and is not suspected. Richard was later arrested for that deed and hanged before justices for gaol [delivery] etc. He had no chattels. Dauntsey township did not come fully to the inquest, so it is in *mercy*.

234. Simon le Hund, Thomas le Rus of Minety, Henry Cotewyne and Walter his brother of the same killed an unknown man in Hankerton fields. Robert son of John, the first finder, comes and is not suspected. No Englishry [is presented]. Judgement *murder*, upon the hundred. Hankerton, Crudwell, Charlton and Cloatley townships did not come fully to the inquest, so they are in *mercy*. Later it was testified that Simon and the others were arrested in Gloucestershire for stealing pigs and hanged there. Their chattels are unknown because they were strangers.

m. 30d (IMG 0448, 0449) *Continuing Startley hundred*

235. Unknown malefactors came to Foxley church to break into it. Nicholas, the son of its parson, noticed this and raised the hue, and the malefactors attacked and maltreated him so that he later died. Robert le Cornewaleys, the first finder, has died. It is not known who they were. Draycot township did not come fully to the inquest before the coroner, so it is in *mercy*.

236. William Jace, John le Scut and Geoffrey Tormauntel, arrested on suspicion of theft, come and deny theft and all, and William and John put themselves on this hundred for good and ill. The jurors say that they are not guilty, so they are quit. Geoffrey puts himself on the verdict of Selkley, and the jurors say that he is guilty of many thefts, so etc. (*hanged*). Let his chattels be inquired into of *Cannings*.

THE HUNDRED OF CHEDGLOW COMES BY TWELVE

237. John of Brinkworth, the shepherd of Geoffrey Cuf,[1] drove Geoffrey's sheep in West Crudwell fields. Henry son of Thomas de Smalcumbe came up wanting to impound them, and John would not allow this, but struck Henry with a stone on the head so that he later died. Geoffrey Cuf, attached because he was present, does not come now, and he was attached by Geoffrey Brun of West Crudwell, who is in mercy. John fled immediately after the deed and is suspected, so let him be *exacted and outlawed*. He had no chattels, and was not in a tithing because he was under age. Crudwell, Newnton, Brokenborough and Ashley townships did not come fully to the inquest, so they are in *mercy*.

238. Robert son of Henry fell from a horse so that he died instantly. His brother John, the first finder, comes and is not suspected, nor is anyone else.

---

1 Geoffrey was recorded around 1284 as a tenant of Malmesbury Abbey at West Crudwell. J.S. Brewer and C.T. Martin (eds.), *Registrum Malmesburiense: the register of Malmesbury Abbey*, 2 vols. (Rolls Series, 1879-80), i, 144-5.

Judgement *misadventure*. The value of the horse (*deodand*) *3s.*, the sheriff to answer.

239. William le Boltere of the forest of Dean came to Nabals mill, where he found Richard Smetheheved, the miller's servant. He killed Richard and carried off the goods found in the mill, and fled immediately after the deed. He is suspected, so let him be *exacted and outlawed*. His chattels *2d.*, the sheriff to answer, and he was not in a tithing because he was a stranger. Charlton township did not come fully to the inquest, so it is in *mercy*.

240. William Pertryke struck Henry Brun with an axe on the head so that by that blow he fell in the river Avon and drowned. Henry's sister Sibyl, the first finder, comes and is not suspected. William fled immediately after the deed and is suspected, so let him be *exacted and outlawed*. His chattels *8s.*, the sheriff to answer, and he was not in a tithing because he was a stranger. Adam le Wyse was arrested because he was present, and he was handed over to John de Vernun, then sheriff, and was later delivered before the justices for gaol [delivery] etc.

241. An unknown man was found killed on the king's highway of the Fosse.[1] It is not known who killed him. Henry Eskyrmur, the first finder, comes and is not suspected. No Englishry is presented. Judgement *murder*, upon the hundred. Ashley and Oaksey townships did not come fully to the inquest, so they are in *mercy*.

242. Maud of Minety and her son Richard were found killed in 'Moburne' township. Adam of the wood, the first finder, and four neighbours come and are not suspected. William Randolf was arrested for the death and handed over to John de Vernun, then sheriff, and later hanged before justices for gaol [delivery] etc. His chattels *7s.*, the sheriff to answer. William's daughter Alice and Miles son of Adam,[2] accused of the death, have made off and are suspected, so let Miles be *exacted and outlawed* and let Alice be *waived*. Miles had no chattels and was not in a tithing because he was a stranger. Poole Keynes township did not come fully [to the inquest] etc., so it is in *mercy*.

243. John le Frege struck Ralph Charbe with a knife in the stomach in Richard of Wick's house in Oaksey so that he died instantly. Richard of Wick, the first finder, comes and is not suspected. John fled immediately after the deed and is suspected, so let him be *exacted and outlawed*. He had no chattels and was in Poole Keynes tithing, which is in *mercy*. Oaksey township did not arrest him, so it is in *mercy*. Kemble and Garsdon townships did not

---

1 The Fosse Way, the Roman road from Exeter to Lincoln, ran along the western edge of the parishes of Brokenborough, Foxley, Norton and Crudwell, and constituted part of Wiltshire's border with Gloucestershire.

2 Presumably not Adam of the wood, since unlike Alice's father, Miles's father is not described as 'aforesaid', to link him to someone already mentioned.

come fully to the inquest etc., so they are in *mercy*. The twelve jurors are in *mercy* for concealment.

244. As William son of William of Chedglow and Reynold son of John le Paumer of the same were coming from a tavern they quarrelled together, and Reynold struck William with an axe on the head so that he later died. Reynold fled immediately after the deed and is suspected, so let him be *exacted and outlawed*. He had no chattels and was in Chedglow tithing, which is in *mercy*. John son of Walter, accused of the death, comes and denies the death and all, and for good and ill puts himself on the country. The jurors say that John is not guilty, so he is quit. Leigh township did not come fully [to the inquest] etc., so it is in *mercy*.

245. William son of William the miller of Somerford killed John le Sumenur in Great Somerford township. William was later arrested and hanged in Gloucestershire. His chattels *8d.*, the sheriff to answer. Great Somerford township did not come fully [to the inquest] etc., so it is in *mercy*.

246. Unknown malefactors encountered Thomas Trepas and his wife Emma in Braydon forest, and they killed Thomas, wounded Emma and carried off their clothes. It is not known who they were. Emma his wife, attached because she was present, does not now come, and she was attached by Adam Tredegold and William le Parker of Brinkworth, who are in *mercy*. Brinkworth, Little Somerford and Grittenham townships did not come fully to the inquest, so they are in *mercy*.

247. William son of Roger of Eastcourt and Thomas of Kemble quarrelled together, and Thomas struck William with a staff on the head so that he died instantly. Thomas fled immediately after the deed and is suspected, so let him be *exacted and outlawed*. His chattels *4s.*, the sheriff to answer, and he was not in a tithing because he was a stranger. Adam Halfmare, attached because Thomas and William went out of his house when this was done, does not come now, and he was attached by Jordan of Hulle of Hankerton and Henry Bernard of the same, who are in *mercy*.

248. Concerning defaults, they say that Humphrey de Bohun, earl of Hereford, Robert son of Pain, Walter Scut, William Silvester, Richard de Stroda and Walter de Cotes did not come here on the first day, so they are in *mercy*.

249. The jurors present that Stanton St. Quintin township used to do suit to the hundred every three weeks, and that suit was first withdrawn through the might of Richard late earl of Gloucester ten years ago now, to the king's loss of 2s. a year. Moreover it has withdrawn the sheriff's tourn, 8s. 4d. They also say that Hullavington township has withdrawn 66s. from the sheriff's tourn for Startley and Chedglow hundreds, and that withdrawal has been made for four years now. Foxley township has likewise withdrawn 9s. a year and Great Somerford[1] township 16s. 8d., and those two withdrawals have been made for two years now. Seagry township has withdrawn 16s. a year, and this has been done for four years. Draycot township has withdrawn 12s. 4d. a year and this has been done for two years. They also say that while Malmesbury castle was in the king's hand they held no sheriff's tourn. They also say that Hullavington has withdrawn 13s. 4d. from sheriff's aid, and they are in arrears for three years, and for 3s. 4d. for a fourth year. Bradfield township [has withdrawn] 2s. of sheriff's aid and they are three years in arrears. Great Somerford [has withdrawn] 18d. from sheriff's aid, and they are two years in arrears. Seagry [has withdrawn] 2s. from sheriff's aid, and they are three years in arrears. Draycot [has withdrawn] 2s. from sheriff's aid, and they are three years in arrears. Ashton 2s. likewise for two years. The fee of Nabals [has withdrawn] 2s. from sheriff's aid, and is three years in arrears. So the sheriff was ordered to distrain them to be [here] on Sunday etc. And those men with force and arms hindered the king's bailiffs from distraining them, and took their animals from them, so let them be arrested. Later all the men of Hullavington township came and made fine for that township by *10 marks*, pledge the prior of Hullavington.[2] And all the other townships came and conceded that they owed that revenue, and because they had not paid it before they are in mercy. The sheriff is ordered to distrain etc.[3]

m. 31 (IMG 0369, 0370)

THE HUNDRED OF CAWDON COMES BY TWELVE

250. William son of Richard Trot, a five-year-old boy, was found drowned in the river Wylye between Harnham and Bemerton. Richard Trot[4] his father, the first finder, does not come, and he was attached by Thomas Knoteling and John Coppere, who are in *mercy*. No one is suspected. Judgement *misadventure*.

251. Nicholas Russel and one Roger, two strangers, came to a tavern at John Bonhaye's house. A quarrel arose between them and John, whose brother Matthew came up and tried to help him, and Roger struck Matthew with a knife in the chest so that he died instantly. Roger and Nicholas fled immediately after the deed and are suspected of the death, so let them be *exacted and outlawed*. They had no chattels and were[5] not in a tithing because they were strangers. John Bonaye, the first finder, and four neighbours come and are not suspected. John's wife Ellen, attached because she was present,

---

1 Followed by *Draycote*, which has been deleted..

2 The alien priory of Hullavington or Clatford was the very small cell of the Norman Benedictine abbey of St Victor-en-Caux. *VCH Wiltshire* iii, 393-4.

3 The last two sentences are in a different, less tidy hand with a shaky cross in the margin.

4 Written above the name is *pp*, for *pauper*.

5 *fuit* ('was'), in error for *fuerunt*.

does not come, and she was attached by Robert le Jovene of Homington and Thomas le Rus of the same, who are in *mercy*. Coombe, Homington, Stratford and Odstock townships did not come to the inquest etc., so they are in *mercy*.

252. Stephen de Wynterburneforde[1] stole a mare and a cart and was pursued by Nicholas Royrun, whose cart it was, to Coombe township, where Stephen fled to Coombe church, admitted the theft and *abjured* the realm before the coroner. His chattels 7s. 5d., the sheriff to answer. Coombe township did not arrest him and does not answer for those chattels, so it is in *mercy*.

253. Serlo de Bernake struck himself with a knife in the stomach so that he later died. No one is suspected. Judgement *suicide*. He had no chattels. Britford township did not come to the inquest, so it is in *mercy*.

254. Adam Gerveyse got himself into Britford church, where he admitted theft and *abjured* the realm before the coroner. He had no chattels and he was not in a tithing because he was a stranger.

255. An unknown man was killed on the king's highway outside Harnham. John le Esquier of Coombe, the first finder, comes and is not suspected. It is not known who killed him. No Englishry is presented. Judgement *murder*, upon the hundred. Netherhampton and East Harnham townships did not come to the inquest, so they are in *mercy*. Later it was testified by the jurors that one Philip le Messer made off on account of the death and is suspected, so let him be *exacted and outlawed*. He had no chattels and was not in a tithing, but he was in the mainpast of John of Holtby,[2] who is in *mercy*.

256. From W[illiam le Dun], sheriff, for the chattels of Andrew le Mouner of Homington, hanged before justices for gaol [delivery] etc., *8s. 6d.*

257. Concerning defaults, they say that John of Baddesley, Alexander Dun, Walter the butcher, Roger le Presser, Herbert de Wydenhale and Wybert Russel of Homington did not come here on the first day, so they are in *mercy*.

258. Concerning serjeanties, they say that Robert Walerand holds Longford manor by the serjeanty of providing the king with one serjeant for the army at the king's command for forty days at Robert's expense, and it is worth £10 a year.[3]

----

1 A place-name associated with the river Till, originally 'Winterbourne Water'. *PNS*, 10.

2 A leading official of Bishop Bridport, recorded as his steward in 1257. In 1268 he sued as warden of the newly founded Vaux College in Salisbury. *EEA, Salisbury*, xliii; JUST 1/998A m. 11.

3 The manor of Longford, together with lands in Hampshire, was held by Walter of Longford in 1236 and Roger of Longford in 1249, by the same service as in 1268.

259. Henry Heleman, reeve of Coombe Bissett, appealed Thomas Basset, a monk [of…],[1] Peter de Moles, John de Chaundos, Ralph le Sumeter and Thomas Russel in the county court of robbery, burning houses and breach of the king's peace. And he appealed Hugh de Plessetis and Walter Nultel of abetting and ordering [the deeds].[2] Henry now comes and has withdrawn from his appeal, so let him be taken into *custody* and his pledges for prosecuting are in *mercy*, namely Thomas le Rus of Coombe and Thomas Kute of the same. Thomas [Basset] and the others appealed of the deed do not come, and they were not attached because Henry only sued against them at two county courts. Walter Nultel, who was appealed of abetting and ordering, comes. The jurors say that they [Henry and Walter] are not agreed and that Walter is not guilty of ordering, but they say that a quarrel arose between Hugh de Plessetis and John of Wootton, whose reeve Henry was, and because of that quarrel Thomas Byset and others came to Henry's house and made severe threats to him and tried to beat him, but he fled out of fear. An agreement was later made between Hugh and John, as a result of which Henry did not dare to prosecute his appeal. They also say that Thomas and the others, coming from Hugh's house after the deed, returned later to it, so let this be *discussed*. They also say that all the persons aforesaid were in Hugh's mainpast, so he is in *mercy*. Ralph le Frye, one of the jurors, is in *mercy* for trespass, let him be taken into *custody*. Later he made fine by *1 mark*, pledges Thomas le Rus of Coombe and John le Dekne of the same. Later Henry Heleman came and made fine by *1 mark*, the same pledges.

260. Edward Trat is in *mercy* for trespass, pledge Thomas of Coombe.

261. Roger Andreu stole 40 ells of linen cloth belonging to his master William Suetof, who held Roger in suspicion for it and complained about him in the court of William de St Omer, his own lord,[3] with the result that Roger made

---

Roger granted the manor to Robert Walerand, a powerful royal servant, who in January 1252 secured the king's ratification of Roger's gift of land held in dower in Longford, 'which land is the king's serjeanty'. In 1255 the estate was still worth £10 per annum, but the serjeant did only fifteen days's service. Longford was listed among Walerand's possessions at his death in 1273, but nothing was said about the serjeanty, then or in 1281, so it was probably extinguished or commuted. *Book of Fees* i, 587, ii, 741, 1177; *Wiltshire crown pleas, 1249* no. 534; *CChR 1226-1257*, 375; *Rot. Hund.* ii, 232; *CIPM* ii no. 6.

1 *de* is written above Thomas's name but the name of his house was not added.

2 Hugh de Plessetis, or de Plessis, was the son of John de Plessis, who died in 1263 as earl of Warwick. Hugh was lord of Coombe Bissett through his marriage to Isabel Biset. M. Ray, 'Living with father's reputation; the careers of two thirteenth-century Oxfordshire knights of alien origins, Thomas de Bréauté and Hugh de Plessis', J. Burton, P. Schofield and J. Burton (eds.), *Thirteenth Century England xii* (Woodbridge, 2009), 167-181, at 172.

3 William's court was probably in Stratford Tony, where in 1274/5 he claimed the right

fine with William his master by 9s. and William took the 9s. for the cloth by judgement of that court. But because Roger made off after the deed, and the jurors now testify on their oath that Roger is guilty of that and other thefts, let him be *exacted and outlawed*. He had no chattels and was in Stratford tithing, which is in mercy. To judgement on the said William Suetof. Later William came and made fine by *20s.*, pledges Robert of Piddle and Ralph of Mere.[1]

262. Nicholas Squal, arrested on suspicion of theft, and his brother Roger the miller, likewise arrested for the same, and Nicholas Forst, arrested on suspicion of theft, come and deny theft and all, and for good and ill put themselves on the country. The jurors say that Roger and Nicholas Forst are not guilty of any evildoing, so they are quit. They also say that Nicholas Squal is guilty etc., so etc. (*hanged*). His chattels *8d.*, the sheriff to answer.

263. Concerning indicted persons, they say that Walter Warroke, Adam Pacok, Thomas Brod, Stephen son of William le Frankeleyn, Geoffrey Sumer, John Redhod and Gilbert le Hopere of Britford have made off on suspicion of theft and are all suspected, so let them be *exacted and outlawed*. Walter Warrok's chattels *2s.*, the sheriff to answer, and he was in Britford tithing, which is in *mercy*. Adam's chattels *1 mark*, the sheriff to answer, and he was in Odstock tithing, which is in *mercy*. Thomas Brod's chattels *12d.*, the bishop of Salisbury to answer, and he was in Coombe tithing, which is in *mercy*. Geoffrey Sumer had no chattels, but he was in Homington tithing, which is in mercy. Later Gilbert le Cupere comes and denies theft and all, and for good and ill puts himself on the country. The jurors and four neighbouring townships say on their oath that Gilbert is not guilty, so he is quit. Later Thomas Brod comes and denies theft and all, and for good and ill puts himself on the country. The jurors of this hundred, together with the jurors of Branch hundred and the neighbouring townships, say on their oath that he is not guilty of any evildoing, so he is *quit*, but the crime was maliciously imputed to him by Whitsbury tithing, which is in *mercy*.[2]

264. Maud of Hungerford appealed John Balriche in the county court of rape, robbery and breach of the king's peace. Maud does not come now, so let her be *arrested*, and her pledges for prosecuting are in *mercy*, namely John de Duna in Coombe and Jordan of Wilton. John now comes and the jurors say that they [the parties] are not agreed, but they say that John threw her to the ground against her will, but did her no other trespass, neither rape nor robbery. So he is quit as to that, but because he threw her to the ground he is in *mercy* for trespass.

---

to gallows and the assizes of bread and ale. Nearby Britford is another possibility. *Rot. Hund.* ii, 248.

1 Above Ralph's name what appears to be 'Ranulf' is written, perhaps a correction.

2 The line ends *decennam de Whi*'; interlined in the middle between that line and the next entry is *chebyr*'. *Ideo in mis*'.

m. 31d (IMG 0450, 0451)

THE HUNDRED OF MELKSHAM COMES BY TWELVE

265. William Marmyun and his brother Philip, who have died, appealed Robert son of Gilbert of Trowbridge, William the hayward of the same, Rocelin of Staverton, Robert Mogge, William the smith, William Horn of Kingston Deverill, Robert Nyctegale of Trowbridge, William Harolde of the same and Adam the clerk of Colerne in the county court of the death of their brother Nicholas Marmyun, so that Robert son of Gilbert, Richard Tyler and Rocelin were outlawed in the county court by their suit. Richard Tyler's chattels 5*s.*, the sheriff to answer. The others had no chattels. Rocelin was in Staverton tithing, which is in mercy. Robert son of Gilbert was received outside a tithing in Trowbridge township, which is in mercy. Robert Mogge and Robert Nyctegale, who were appealed, do not come now, and it is testified that they came to the fourth county court, where each of them found twelve mainpernors for being here today, when Ralph Russel was sheriff, through a royal writ which came to him about it.[1] So to *judgement* upon Ralph Russel, as he does not answer for the mainprise. Robert Mogge and Robert Nictegale have made off for that death and are suspected, so let them be *exacted and outlawed*. They had no chattels and were received outside a tithing in Trowbridge township, which is in *mercy*. William the hayward, William Horn, William le Fevere, William Harold and Adam le Clerk come, and Adam says he is a clerk and does not wish to answer. The bishop of Salisbury's official comes and claims him as a clerk, and that it may be known what sort of man is to be handed over to him, let the truth of the matter be inquired into by the country. The others come and deny the death, felony and all, and for good and ill put themselves on the country. The twelve jurors of this hundred, together with the jurors of Whorwellsdown hundred, say on their oath that William and the others, and also Adam le Clerk, are not guilty of the death, so they are quit, and it is unnecessary for Adam to be handed over to the bishop.

266. Roger le Schyreve was found killed in Poulshot. His sister Emma, the first finder, comes and is not suspected. William Enok and Peter Enok, accused of the death, made off immediately after the deed and are suspected of the death. It is testified that William has died, so nothing concerning him.[2] Let

---

1   A largely illegible inquest held under a writ of 18 October 1262 found that Adam of Colerne, William Harold of Trowbridge and William the hayward had been maliciously appealed of the death of Nicholas, and order was given around 13 November following that they be released to bail. C 144/5 no. 34; *CR 1261-1264*, 187.

2   Roger's death probably took place in 1259. At an inquest held before William of Englefield and Peter of Membury on 6 December 1260, the jurors, who were headed by Sir Ralph of Poulshot, described a free-for-all involving Roger and Peter and William Enok, in which both the Enoks had struck Roger but the fatal blows were dealt him by Peter,. The writ ordering the inquest, issued around 24 July 1260,

Peter be *exacted and outlawed*. His chattels £6 Os 7d., the sheriff to answer. Ralph of Poulshot[1] took the chattels without warrant, so let him answer to the sheriff and be in mercy because he did this without warrant. He [Peter] had lands in this hundred from which the [king's] year and waste are worth 20s.[2] Let his chattels and land be more fully inquired into in *Whorwellsdown* hundred. It is testified that Richard de Roscruk[3] entered the land after the deed and has held it for two years now without warrant, and the land is worth 1 mark a year (*2 marks*). So let him answer for the issues during that term, and because he took the land without warrant he is in mercy. The same Peter had chattels in *Whorwellsdown* hundred worth 11s. 4d., the sheriff to answer. Later Peter came and denied the death, felony and all, and for good and ill put himself on the country. The twelve jurors of this hundred, together with the jurors of Whorwellsdown hundred, say on their oath that Peter is not guilty, so he is quit. But they say that this crime was maliciously imputed to him by Ralph of Poulshot, his lord, so that he might have the land which he holds of him. So to judgement on him and let him be taken into *custody*. He is amerced at 10 marks, and let him answer for *5 marks*, the issues of the land over five years.

267. Henry son of Hamon of Rowde appealed Nicholas le Jeu, clerk, in the county court of the death of John le Heyward his brother, so that he was outlawed by his suit in the county court. He had no chattels, and he was not in a tithing because he was a clerk, but he was received in Bradford township, which is in *mercy*.

268. Agnes of Hilperton and her daughter Alice complain of Maynard le Mouner of Melksham and Richard Blundel, clerk, that on the night of Wednesday next after the [feast of the] translation of St. Thomas the martyr in the 41st year [11 July 1257] they came to Agnes's house in Melksham and robbed her of a tunic of green worth 5s., and beat and maltreated them against the peace etc.

Maynard and Richard come and deny felony, robbery and whatever is against the peace etc. Richard says that he is a clerk and cannot and should not answer here. Whereupon the bishop of Salisbury's official comes and claims

---

stated that there were rumours that the charge against William was malicious, and that he already been released to bail – the order to that effect was given around 10 September 1259. C 144/2 no. 4; *CPR 1258-1266*, 102; *CR 1256-1259*, 436.

1 Lord of the manor of Poulshot in this hundred. *VCH Wiltshire* vii, 122.

2 The sum is struck through and is followed by *unde idem vicecomes respondeat*, which is also struck through.

3 Richard was styled steward of Melksham, presumably in the employment of the countess of Devon, in three undated grants to Lacock Abbey. At this eyre, he was the defendant, along with three others, in an action over land in Poulshot brought by John Shirreve, probably a kinsman of Roger's. K.H. Rogers (ed.), *Lacock Abbey charters* (Wiltshire Record Society 34 (1979 for 1978), nos. 98-100. JUST 1/998A m. 1.

him as a clerk and he is handed over to him, but so that it may be known what sort of man is to be handed over to him, let the truth of the matter be inquired into by the country. Maynard comes and for good and ill puts himself on the country. The twelve jurors say on their oath that Maynard and Richard are not guilty of that trespass. So they are quit. Let Agnes and Alice be taken into *custody* for a false complaint. They are poor and are pardoned by H[enry] de Montfort.[1]

269. Agnes daughter of Robert, a five-year-old child[2], was found drowned at Seend Head. Her mother Agnes, the first finder, comes and is not suspected, nor is anyone else. Judgement *misadventure*. The four townships of Melksham, Poulshot, Bulkington and Seend buried her without a coroner's view, so they are in *mercy*.

270. Henry of Rodden got himself into Poulshot church, admitted theft and *abjured* the realm before the coroner. He had no chattels and he was not in a tithing because he was a stranger. Poulshot township did not arrest him, so it is in *mercy*.

271. William son of Richard and his sister Aldith were found killed in Aldith's house in Erlestoke township. Eve Cok, the first finder, and four neighbours come and are not suspected. It is testified that Robert le Peleter of Bishopstrow and John Balun of Bulbridge were arrested for the deaths and hanged before justices for gaol [delivery] etc. They had no chattels. Stoke and Hilperton townships did not come fully to the inquest etc., so they are in *mercy*.

272. Agnes of Gloucester got herself into Shaw church, where she admitted theft and *abjured* the realm before the coroner. She had no chattels. Shaw township did not arrest her, so it is in *mercy*.

273. Unknown malefactors came to the house of the widow Aldith in Seend and killed John the weaver there. His brother Robert, the first finder, and four neighbours come and are not suspected. It is not known who they were. No Englishry [is presented]. Judgement *murder*. Woolmore, Seend Row, Beanacre and Stanley townships did not come fully to the inquest, so they are in *mercy*.

274. Concerning defaults, they say that Richard Purcaz,[3] Nicholas son

---

1 A paraphrase of the writ appointing Henry as one of the justices in eyre, replacing Robert de Briwes, constitutes the first item on this roll, JUST 1/998A m. 1. Montfort's estate of Farleigh Hungerford, earlier called Farleigh Montfort, was 8 miles south west of Melksham, just inside Somerset.

2 *puer*, presumably used as a noun of common gender, even though it is followed by *inventus* and *submersus*.

3 The name is struck through.

of Martin (writ),[1] Alfred de Chynon (poor),[2] John Auvrey (poor), Ellis de Rabayne (writ), Thomas of Atworth, Gilbert son of Edmund, Adam le Botiller, John the clerk of Poulshot, Nicholas the long (poor), William Harolde, Robert Gent and John of Blackmore did not come here on the first day, so they are in *mercy*.

275. Walter of Wiltshire appealed John le Knyct of Seend Row in the county court of mayhem and breach of the king's peace. Walter does not come now, so let him be *arrested*, and his pledges for prosecuting are in *mercy*, namely Robert Mauclerk of Melksham and William atte Stubbe. John does not come, and he was attached by Peter of Baldham and William le Ruter of Seend Ridge, who are in *mercy*. Later Walter came and made fine for himself by ½ mark, pledge Peter of Baldham. John le Knyght had no goods.

276. Alice daughter of Philip Scheue appealed Richard le Fox of Bulkington in the county court of burning houses and breach of the king's peace. Richard does not come now, and he was attached by the tithingman of Bulkington with his tithing, who are in *mercy*. It is testified by the jurors that they [the parties] are not agreed and that Richard is not guilty in any way. So he is quit. The twelve jurors concealed these appeals,[3] so they are in *mercy*.

277. Robert Sconing and Robert le Ster, arrested for the death of Stephen of Whaddon, and William at the gate, arrested for the death of Jordan son of Hugh, and Nicholas le Duk (acquitted),[4] Geoffrey Maynard (acquitted) and John Walweyn (acquitted), arrested on suspicion of theft, come and deny felony and all, and for good and ill put themselves on the country. The jurors say on their oath that Robert and the others are not guilty, so they are quit. But they say . . .[5]

278. Concerning serjeanties, they say that John de Cherbourg holds a grove in Seend of the king, and it is assessed for a rent of 12d. and is worth that much.[6]

---

1 Written above the two names followed by '(writ)' is *b*, for *breve*, indicating that each had a writ.

2 Written above the three names followed by '(poor)' is *pp*, for *pauper*.

3 The use of the plural presumably relates also to the preceding entry.

4 The names of Nicholas, Geoffrey and John have *b* for *bonus* written above each of them, meaning that they were acquitted.

5 The entry breaks off and is followed by a space of about four lines.

6 The serjeanty in question was not John's own but that of the Rous family of Imber, in Heytesbury hundred, which had a hereditary chamberlaincy. The grove at Seend, fourteen acres in extent, had been alienated to John by 1250, when it was ordered that the rent of 12d. be commuted to a fortieth part of a knight's fee. This does not seem to have taken effect, at his death in 1269 John was still paying the rent and holding in serjeanty. *Book of Fees* ii, 1177; *CIPM* i no. 721; E.G. Kimball, *Serjeanty*

279. Concerning purprestures, they say that Amice countess of Devon, who holds the manor of Melksham at farm from the king,[1] has raised a bank in Melksham township upon the king's highway, and in length and breadth it contains 1 perch of land. Again, the abbess of Lacock has made a purpresture in Melksham forest by enclosing 40 acres within the king's forest, to the detriment of the whole liberty of Melksham, and they do not know by what warrant. Later the abbess's attorney comes and shows the king's charter whereby the king granted to the abbess and her nuns etc., and to their successors, [the right] at their will to enclose that place with a bank and hedge.[2]

280. Concerning wines sold, they say that Henry le Petyt (poor)[3] of Trowbridge has sold wine contrary to the assize,[4] so he is in *mercy*.

281. Concerning squires,[5] they say that Humphrey of Whaddon holds a whole knight's fee, is of full age and is not yet a knight.[6] So let this be *discussed*.

282. The jurors present that Walter the fisherman of Beanacre, John Calker, William Pykok, William Sprot, Hugh Wytyng, Adam Pope, Philip Cregel, John of Whaddon, Gilbert Hereward, Walter Arnold and Adam de la Splote have fished in the river Avon with kiddle-nets, so they are in *mercy*.

283. Concerning indicted persons, they say that Adam of Asthall, Richard Cotun, Edmund son[7] of Mary, Gilbert le Sukere and Richard Tutprest have made off on suspicion of theft and are suspected, so let them be *exacted and outlawed*. Adam of Asthall's chattels 6d., the sheriff [to answer], and he was in the tithing of Melksham, which is in *mercy*. Gilbert's chattels 6s. 3d., the sheriff to answer, and he was in Erlestoke tithing, which is in *mercy*. The others had no chattels, but Edmund was in the same tithing, which is in *mercy*. Richard [Cotun] was in Melksham tithing. Edmund was in Erlestoke tithing. Richard Tutprest was in Melksham tithing, so all those tithings are in *mercy*. They also say that Roger Russel and Adam Pak have made off on suspicion of theft and

---

tenure in medieval England (Yale Historical Publications 30, New Haven, 1936), 38.

1 In 1257 Henry III granted the manor of Melksham to Amice, dowager-countess of Devon, for an annual fee-farm of £48. Shortly after the eyre, on 9 July 1268, he gave the fee-farm and the reversion of the manor to Amesbury Priory. *VCH Wiltshire* vii, 95.

2 The royal charter was granted on 3 June 1260. K.H. Rogers (ed.), *Lacock Abbey charters* (Wiltshire Record Society 34, 1979 for 1978) no. 22.

3 Written above the name is *pp*, for *pauper*.

4 Repeated below, **286**.

5 *De valettis*.

6 Humphrey was lord of the manor of Whaddon. *VCH Wiltshire* vii, 172.

7 Above this word *Stok'* is interlined, presumably meaning 'of Erlestoke'.

are suspected, so let them be *exacted and outlawed*. Roger Russel's chattels *2 marks and 6d.*, the sheriff to answer, and Adam Pak had no chattels, but they were in Melksham tithing, which is in *mercy*.

[*At the foot of the membrane* Ricardus Tutprest *is written very faintly, and afterwards seven words, hardly less faint, which appear to read* 'Walterus Cotele quare retinuit Clementem del Ewe'[1].]

m. 32 (IMG 0371, 0372) *Continuing Melksham hundred*

284. The jurors present that Maud Bareleg was arrested and imprisoned in the prison of Melksham manor, and she escaped from that township's custody. So to judgement for the *escape* upon Melksham township. She has made off and is suspected, so let her be *exacted and waived*. Her chattels *11d.*, the sheriff to answer.

285. The jurors present that, whereas of old each tithingman with his tithing used to give 2s. on every lawday [*qualibet die de Laghedayes*] not to be challenged over the articles and other pleas, Amice countess of Devon and her bailiffs arbitrarily[2] amerce all the tithingmen and the tithings if they do not answer to all and each of the articles put to them.

286. Concerning wines sold, they say that Henry le Petit has sold wine at Trowbridge contrary to the assize,[3] so he is in *mercy*.

287. The jurors present that Robert de Vernun, the son and heir of John de Vernun, sometime sheriff, after the death of his father took 5 marks from Humphrey of Whaddon[4] against his will for postponing his becoming a knight.[5] Let this be *discussed*. Later it was testified that Robert had the 5 marks levied towards his father John de Vernun's arrears, so nothing concerning this.

THE HUNDRED OF WHORWELLSDOWN COMES BY TWELVE

288. Unknown malefactors encountered Roger Selegor, who has died, and William the shepherd of Edington, and they killed William. It is not known who they were. Roger Selgor, attached because he was present, has died. Tinhead, Coulston and Edington townships did not come fully [to the inquest] etc., so they are in *mercy*.

---

1 Presumably the Clement de Aqua whose unjust outlawry cost the county 60 marks at the 1256 eyre. E 372/102 m. 9.

2 *ad voluntatem suam.*

3 Apparently a repetition of **280**, above.

4 See also **281** above.

5 *pro respectu milicie habendo ne fieret miles.* The phrasing is tautological.

289. Gilbert Pykeman and John the marshal quarrelled together on the border between Somersetshire and this county, as they were coming from the house of John de la Frythe, and John struck Gilbert on the head with his sword so that he later died. John fled immediately and is suspected, so let him be *exacted and outlawed*. He had no chattels and he was not in a tithing because he was a stranger from Somerset.[1] Southwick, Bradley, West Ashton and Cutteridge townships did not come fully [to the inquest] etc., so they are in *mercy*.

290. Alice daughter of John Sot of Ashton got herself into Ashton church and admitted theft and *abjured* the realm before the coroner. She had no chattels. West Ashton township did not arrest her, so it is in *mercy*.

291. William, the servant of Simon Trenchefoyle, struck Peter the hayward of Coulston with a knife in the stomach in Coulston fields so that he died four days later. He fled immediately after the deed and is suspected, so let him be *exacted and outlawed*. He had no chattels and was not in a tithing, but he was in the mainpast of Simon Trenchefoyle, who in *mercy*. Coulston, Erlestoke, Bulkington and Poulshot townships did not come fully [to the inquest] etc., so they are in *mercy*.

292. Robert, the servant of the parson of Keevil, and John son of Eve quarrelled together at the house of Henry the smith of Keevil, and Robert struck John with his knife in the stomach so that he died instantly. Eve his mother, the first finder, and four neighbours come and are not suspected. Robert was later arrested and handed over to the bishop. It is not known as what he was handed over, so let this be discussed. Keevil, Ashton, Semington and Hinton townships did not come fully [to the inquest] etc., so they are in *mercy*. Asked to which bishop he was handed over, they say that it was to Bishop Giles.[2]

293. Richard Fryday and Alexander Suyn quarrelled together in the house of Richard Friday's father, and Richard struck Alexander with a knife in the stomach so that he died instantly. Richard fled immediately after the deed and is suspected, so let him be *exacted and outlawed*. His chattels 6d., the sheriff to answer, and he was in Steeple Ashton tithing, which is in *mercy*. Richard's father Richard, attached because he was present, comes and is not suspected. West Ashton township did not come fully [to the inquest] etc., so it is in *mercy*.

294. An unknown man was found killed in West Aston township. Bartholomew Makerel, the first finder, comes and is not suspected. It is not known who killed him. No Englishry is presented. Judgement *murder*, upon

---

1 Although it is not mentioned in the eyre roll, John was granted a pardon for Gilbert's death on 27 March 1261, on the grounds that he had killed him by misadventure. *CPR 1258-1266*, 147. The four townships listed are all close to the Wiltshire-Somerset border, especially Southwick.

2 i.e. Giles of Bridport, bishop of Salisbury between 1257 and 1262.

the hundred. Steeple Ashton township did not come fully [to the inquest] etc., so it is in *mercy*.

295. As Robert Cleremund, servant of Alice, the widow of Robert de Beauchamp,[1] was trying to cross the ford in Semington Brook, he fell from his horse into the river and was drowned in it. Simon of Erlestoke, the first finder, has died. No one is suspected. Judgement *misadventure*. The value of the horse (*deodand*)[2] 100s., Alice de Beauchamp to answer. Because she took the horse and led it away before it was presented before the coroner she is in mercy, and let her answer for the money. (*On Middlesex*.)[3]

296. Thomas le Chyld and Nicholas Nel quarrelled together in Hinton township, and Nicholas struck Thomas with an axe on the head so that he died instantly. Nicholas fled Hinton and is suspected, so let him be *exacted and outlawed*. His chattels 2s. 6d., the sheriff to answer, and he was in Hinton tithing, which is in *mercy*. Littleton township did not come fully [to the inquest] etc., so it is in mercy.

297. Concerning wines sold, they say that William Sturdy and Walter Copel have sold wine contrary to the assize, so they are in *mercy*.

298. Concerning defaults, they say that the abbess of Romsey (writ),[4] Richard of Worcester,[5] Richard of Wallop and Brian of Southwick[6] did not come here on the first day, so they are in *mercy*.

299. The jurors present that Keevil township used to do suit to this hunded every three weeks, and the suit has been withdrawn for seven and a half years now, to the king's loss of 1 mark a year.[7] So let this be discussed.

THE HUNDRED OF WESTBURY COMES BY TWELVE

300. Geoffrey Motun was struck by a horse in Penleigh township so that he

---

1 Alice de Mohun married Robert (v) de Beauchamp, lord of the Somerset barony of Hatch Beauchamp, who died in 1264. I.J. Sanders, *English baronies: a study of their origin and descent, 1066-1327* (Oxford, 1960), 51 and note 5.

2 *dd*, for *deodandum* is in the margin on each side of the sum of money.

3 *Super Midd.* in the margin indicates the county in whose pleas the debt to the crown might be dealt with. No reference to this debt has been noticed in Middlesex entries on the pipe rolls of the rest of Henry III's reign.

4 Above the name is written *b* for *breve*.

5 The name is struck through.

6 Above the name, which is struck through, is written *b* for *breve*.

7 In 1274/5 the suit was said to have been withdrawn by John FitzAlan, lord of the manor of Keevil, presumably John (ii), who died in 1267. *Rot. Hund.* ii, 278.

died three days later. No one is suspected. Judgement *misadventure*. Value of the horse (*deodand*) 10s., the sheriff to answer. Westbury, Bratton, Leigh and Dilton townships did not come fully [to the inquest] etc., so they are in *mercy*.

301. Maud, daughter of Simon le Brewere, drove the oxen of Walter the baker in 'la Brodecrofte' fields, and unknown malefactors came up and killed her. It is not known who they were. The first finder has died. Penleigh and Brook townships did not come fully [to the inquest] etc., so they are in *mercy*.

302. Philip Marmyun was at the house of Reynold Crey in 'Hurste' township, and a dispute having arisen between them Philip struck Reynold with a knife in the stomach so that he died instantly. Philip fled immediately after the deed. His chattels 4s. 4d., the sheriff to answer. It is testified that he has died,[1] so nothing from his tithing. Chalcot township did not come [to the inquest] etc., so it is in *mercy*. Hawkeridge township did not come to the inquest held on the death of Christian wife of William Everard, so it is in mercy.

303. Unknown malefactors encountered brother Richard, a lay brother of Stanley, in the fields between Chalcot and Westbury Leigh, and wounded him so that he later died. It is not known who they were. Chapmanslade, Little Corsley and Great Corsley townships did not come fully [to the inquest] etc., so they are in *mercy*.

304. Concerning serjeanties, they say that William de Aete, who has custody of Giles, the son and heir of Richard Danesy, holds three carucates of land in Dilton and Bratton by the serjeanty of finding one mounted serjeant to serve for forty days at his expense in the king's army, and he renders 10 marks a year to the king.[2]

---

1 Philip's death is also recorded at **265** above. In 1281 a lawsuit over property in five townships turned in part on the issue of whether he had been convicted of homicide. The jury found that he had not been. It is possible that he was the Philip son of Philip Marmiun convicted of rape in 1249. JUST 1/1005/1 m. 9; *Wiltshire crown pleas, 1249*, no. 296.

2 The serjeanty was originally held by the service of keeping the royal larder. By 1242/3 Richard Danesy, Giles's grandfather, had on his own initiative changed this to the military service recorded in 1268. In 1250 numerous alienations from the estate were discovered, and it was therefore decided that Richard should account to the exchequer for the rents from these, valued at ten marks per annum, and also perform the service of half a knight's fee. This last stipulation took only partial effect. Richard died later in 1250, his son, another Richard, in 1266, when Giles's wardship was granted to the king's steward William de Aete. The alienations were at first reassessed, at £7. 1s. 8d. per annum, but later brought back to ten marks. Giles probably died young, since in 1274/5 the serjeanty was held by another Richard, probably his brother, then a minor but of age by 1281, when the serjeanty was worth £25 per annum. Confusingly, he was said to be holding half a knight's fee by the serjeanty prescribed in 1268. *Book of Fees* i, 341, ii, 740, 1178, 1225–6; *CIPM* i no. 197; *CPR. 1266–72*, 8, 56, 86; *Rot. Hund.* ii, 204–5; JUST 1/1005/2 m. 133; E.G. Kimball, *Serjeanty tenure in medieval England* (Yale Historical Publications 30, New

305. Concerning defaults, they say that the abbot of Stanley, Walter Balun, Walter Sewale and Nicholas of Littleton did not come here on the first day, so they are in *mercy*.

[*At the foot of the membrane is written, below a space*, Willelmus le Hopere, W. le Penant, Ricardus le Chapman.]

m. 32d (IMG 0452, 0453) *Continuing Westbury*

306. Roger of Horsington appealed John Alvysse[1] of Westbury in the county court of wounding and breach of the king's peace. Roger does not come now, so let him be *arrested*, and his pledges for prosecuting, namely William of Horsington and Hugh Roed of the same, are in *mercy*. John does not come and he was not attached because he [Roger] only sued against him at two county courts. The twelve jurors made no mention of this appeal, so they are in *mercy*.

THE HUNDRED OF CANNINGS COMES BY TWELVE

307. Nicholas de la Wyche appealed Alan of Reading, the servant of Pain, a monk of Reading, and John le Sumeter, the servant of master Osmund of Idmiston,[2] in the county court of robbery, battery and breach of the king's peace. Nicholas de la Wyche does not come now, so let him be *arrested*, and his pledges for prosecuting, namely Reynold Rumeye of Bishop's Cannings and Osmund de la Wyche of the same, are in *mercy*. He also appealed master Osmund of Idmiston, master Daniel of the same, Pain of Leominster, a monk of Reading, Peter of Bucklebury, and William, the squire of the prior of Reading, of ordering and abetting [the attack]. Master Osmund, master Daniel and John le Sumeter come, and the others have not come. Alan was attached by William Turburne of Whitsbury and Seman of the same, and Pain by Roger le Jovene of Whitsbury and Richard the long of the same. Peter was attached by Wakeman of Whitsbury and Geoffrey le Notte of the same, and William the squire by John le Champyon of Whitsbury and Ralph le Ireys of the same. So they are in mercy. The jurors say on their oath that they [the parties] are not agreed, but they say that Alan and John le Sumeter beat Nicholas but took nothing from him in robbery. So they are quit with regard to that, but let John be taken into *custody* for the trespass and let Alan be *arrested* if he is found. They say that neither masters Osmund and Daniel nor anyone else who was appealed of abetting and ordering are in any way

_____

Haven, 1936), 47-8.

1 Written above *Adwysse*, which it corrects.

2 In July 1259 a petitioner to Henry III on behalf of Oxford University concerning the disregard of its privileges by the town of Oxford. A.B. Emden, *A biographical register of the University of Oxford to A.D. 1500* ii (1958), 997.

guilty either of the deed or of ordering it, so they are quit. Let Pain, Peter and William be *arrested*. John is poor.

308. John de Herteshorne of Derbyshire fled to Cannings church, admitted theft and abjured the realm before the coroner. His chattels *8½d.*, Cannings township to answer. Cannings township did not arrest him when this happened in daytime, so it is in *mercy*.

309. Roger Tyremys fell from a mare in the fields outside Devizes and died instantly. His sister Ellen, the first finder, comes and is not suspected, nor is anyone else. Judgement *misadventure*. The value of the mare (*deodand*) *2s.*, the sheriff to answer.

310. From the same sheriff for a press which crushed William Suengelok (*deodand*) *2s.*

311. Adam Hachewlf of Horton wounded his wife's sister Christian, so that she died three days later. Adam's wife Maud, attached because she was present, comes and is not suspected. Adam fled immediately after the deed and is suspected, so let him be *exacted and outlawed*. His chattels *2s.*, Horton township to answer, and he was in Horton tithing, which is in *mercy*.

312. Concerning defaults, they say that Robert the cook,[1] William Mautravers,[2] Ellis Makerel and Richard le Breton did not come here on the first day, so they are in *mercy*.

313. Stephen of Brockley was arrested with a stolen ox and imprisoned at Southbroom. He escaped from the custody of Bedborough township, so to judgement for the *escape* upon that township. Stephen has fled and is suspected, so let him be *exacted and outlawed*. He had no chattels and his tithing is unknown because he was a stranger.

THE HUNDRED OF STUDFOLD COMES BY TWELVE

314. Walter Jagard and John son of Aldith fought in Cannings township, and John struck Walter with a flail on the head so that he died eight days later. John fled immediately after the deed and is suspected, so let him be *exacted and outlawed*. His chattels *2s.*, the sheriff to answer, and he was in a tithing in All Cannings, which is in *mercy*. Stert, Etchilhampton, Allington and All Cannings townships did not come fully [to the inquest] etc., so they are in *mercy*.

315. Unknown malefactors wounded Walter le Cok as he came from Heytesbury fair[3] so that he died eight days later. It is not known who they

---

1 Above his name, which is struck through, is written *pp*, for *pauper*.

2 His name is struck through.

3 Heytesbury fair was held on 3 May.

were. No Englishry [is presented]. Judgement *murder*, upon the hundred. Conock, Patney, Wedhampton and Chirton townships did not come fully [to the inquest] etc., so they are in *mercy*.

316. William le Dossere came to the house of Richard Kuman in Urchfont, and a dispute having arisen between William and Parnel Bacheler, William struck Parnel with an axe on the head so that she died instantly. William fled immediately and is suspected, so let him be *exacted and outlawed*. His chattels *3s.*, the sheriff answer, and he was in Urchfont tithing, which is in *mercy*. Patney township did not come fully [to the inquest] etc., so it is in *mercy*.

317. Concerning defaults, they say that Reynold son of Peter, Robert Tregoz (ill),[1] Alan of Cannings, Howell of Stert, Clement Pateny, the prior of St Swithun, the abbot of Grestain (writ),[2] Ralph Roel and Nicholas the chaplain of Chirton did not come here on the first day, so they are in *mercy*.

318. From W[illiam le Dun], sheriff, for the chattels of Thomas le Bete, hanged, *13s. 5d.* Likewise for the chattels of Richard Waldof and John le Trug, hanged, *9s.*

319. Concerning indicted persons, that say that John Baldewyne of Eastcott has made off on suspicion of theft and is suspected, so let him be *exacted and outlawed*. He had no chattels, but he was in Eastcott tithing, which is in *mercy*.

320. Concerning suits withdrawn, they say that the prior of Bradenstock has withdrawn 2s. a year of sheriff's aid owed for one hide of land in Etchilhampton.[3] So let this be *discussed*.

m. 33 (IMG 0373, 0374)

THE HUNDRED OF RAMSBURY COMES BY TWELVE

321. Robert son of Richard was found killed in Ramsbury township. Richard his father, the first finder, has died. William son of Robert the miller and Christian the wife of Walter le Hethen, accused of the death, were previously

---

1 Above his name is written *lang*[*uidus*].

2 The Norman abbey of Grestain, a few miles east of Honfleur on the south side of the Seine estuary, held the manor of Conock in Chirton parish. *VCH Wiltshire* x, 63. Written above the abbot's name is *b*, for *breve*, indicating that he had a writ of quittance.

3 Bradenstoke Priory had acquired a hide of land in Etchilhampton no later than 1179. In 1255 the suit was said to have been withdrawn by the prior's men, rather than by the prior himself, seventeen years ago, that is, around 1238. V.C.M. London (ed.), *The cartulary of Bradenstoke Priory* (Wiltshire Record Society 35, 1979), nos. 5, 329-34, 549; *Rot. Hund.* ii, 235.

arrested and imprisoned and later released until now by royal writ,[1] and now they come and deny the death and put themselves on the country. The jurors of this hundred and four neighbouring townships say on their oath that William and Christian are not guilty, so they are quit. Ramsbury, Eastridge, Axford and Whittonditch townships did not come fully to the inquest before the coroner, so they are in *mercy*. Asked who was guilty of that death, the jurors say that William son of Adam le Parker, William Hetheryge and Edmund Fareman have made off because of it and are suspected, so let them be *exacted and outlawed*. They had no chattels and were not in a tithing, but they were received in Ramsbury township outside a tithing, so it is in *mercy*.

322. William le Bercher de Kyngeston and John son of Richard de Benham assaulted John le Boltere in a meadow outside Ramsbury, and William struck John on the head with a pickaxe and John [son of Richard] struck him on the neck with a staff so that he later died. They fled immediately after the deed and are suspected, so let them be *exacted and outlawed*. William's chattels *6s.*, Ramsbury township to answer, and he was in Eastridge tithing, which is in *mercy*. John's chattels *24s. 5d.*, the same township to answer, and he was in Eastridge tithing, which is in *mercy*.

323. Peter son of Hugh le Rus struck Nicholas of Preston with a stone on the head so that he later died. Peter fled immediately and is suspected, so let him be *exacted and outlawed*. His chattels *6d.*, Ramsbury township to answer, and he was in Whittonditch tithing, which is in *mercy*.

324. Concerning defaults, they say that Walter Lof did not come here on the first day, so he is in *mercy*.

THE HUNDRED OF BRANCH COMES BY TWELVE

325. Ellis Godrych and Ellis Hardeche encountered Geoffrey Parche in Sherrington fields, and Geoffrey wanted to take a pledge from Ellis and Ellis. A quarrel having arisen between them, Ellis Hardeche struck Geoffrey with a staff on the head so that he later died. Ellis and Ellis fled immediately after the deed and are suspected, so let them be *exacted and outlawed*. They had no chattels and were in Stockton tithing, which is in *mercy*. Sherrington, Wylye, Langford and Steeple Langford townships did not come fully to the inquest, so they are in *mercy*.

326. William Wlgeon fell in the river Wylye near Bemerton[2] and drowned in it. Peter son of William,[3] the first finder, comes and is not suspected, nor

---

1 Order was given around 4 September 1259 that William and Christian, along with Henry le Taylur, should be released to bail. *CR 1256-1259*, 433.

2 Written as 'Wymerton', clearly in error.

3 It is not clear whether Peter was the son of the drowned man, but since his wife and daughter were present it seems highly likely.

is anyone else. Judgement *misadventure*. William's wife Maud and his daughter Edith, attached because they were present, do not come now. It is testified that Edith has died. The tithingman of Bemerton with his whole tithing mainprised Maud, so they are in *mercy*.

327. Richard de Cumbe appealed Edmund Falke, William le Careter, William Everad, Nicholas Everad, Robert Everard, Richard Everard, Ralph Pentecoste, Richard Dudding, Robert Bygge, Robert le Fox, Ralph Tyberd, Thomas Croke, Robert Stoyle, Rycheman le Berker, Henry le Berker, Ralph le Berker, Reynold le Berker, William Storcheval, Gilbert the fisherman, Richard Bule, William Baldewyn, Gilbert Vring, William le Potter, Henry Wynter, Ralph Soule, Nicholas of Downton, Ellis de la Lane, William le Rede, William son of William le Rede, William Heyne, Jordan le Fox, John Tukeman, Richard the shepherd, Jordan the cook, Nicholas the cook, Walter le Careter, Roger le Careter, Walter le Mouner, Savary le Clerk, Alice wife of Henry Wynter, Maud Halfdevel, Maud wife of Nicholas Everard, Alice wife of Jordan the cook, Gunnilda Saklof and Agnes Wegge of the death of his brother John de Cumbe.[1] Wherefore he says that when John was in the king's peace on the Thursday next after the feast of St. John before the Latin Gate in the 45th year [12 May 1261], in the curtilage of Edmund Falke in Quidhampton township, in the north corner of the curtilage at the evening hour before sunset, as he was coming from Wilton and going towards Salisbury, there came the said Edmund, William le Careter and Edmund's servant Gilbert, who was outlawed in the county court by Richard's suit, and Edmund, with a Cologne[2] sword drawn in his right hand and a horn in his left hand, raised the hue with both horn and mouth. Gilbert struck John on the shoulder with an ash staff which he held in his hand, so that he fell to the ground, but he got up and fled to Quidhampton field, on the land of Henry le Bercher. There they caught up with him again, and Edmund struck John with the sword on the left side of the head, between the crown and the ear, giving him a mortal wound ten inches long and in depth to the brain, and William le Careter struck him on the back with an iron fork, giving him a wound six inches long and in depth to his bowels. And afterwards they took him and

---

1 Arrests must have followed soon after John de Cumbe's death, since on 30 June 1261 order was given for the release to bail of 28 men accused of it, all but three of them among the men appealed by Richard at the eyre. Two further writs secured the release of five more suspects. At this stage they do not seem to have been appealed, but in Michaelmas term 1261 Richard de Cumbe, with his brother and sister and Giles of Fittleton, appealed in the Bench all but one of the men and women whom Richard appealed of John's death at the eyre. Only the prior of Ivychurch and John of Langport then appeared in court, and as clerks were handed over to the bishop. The case was clearly referred back to the county court, where all the other appellees except the three men outlawed were presumably able to find pledges for their appearance at the next eyre, perhaps by reference to the order for their release on bail of which they had recently been beneficiaries. *CR 1259-1261*, 402, 405-6, 444; KB 26/171 mm. 13, 45.

2 *de Colonia*.

placed him on William le Careter's horse, and brought him to a place called
[blank], and in robbery they took his purse, worth 3d., and took 6s. 10½d.
in cash from it. William Everard, Nicholas, Robert and the others held him
while that felony was done to him, as many as could lay hands on him, with
all of them involved in the attack on him, so that he might somehow have
escaped from the hands of Edmund and William had he not been held by
William Everard, Nicholas and the others. And that they did this wickedly
and in felony and in premeditated assault he offers to prove by his body against
Edmund as his [Edmund's] own deed as the court shall consider. And when
by God's grace he shall have obtained victory over Edmund, he is ready to
prove it against William le Careter by the same words and in just the same
way as against Edmund, and so against each of the aforesaid by his body as
the court shall consider etc.

The same Richard also appeals Henry, prior of Ivychurch, and John of
Langport of harbouring the aforesaid Robert Falke,[1] who was outlawed in
the county court by the suit of the same Richard de Cumbe.

The prior and John of Langport, who are appealed of harbouring,
come and deny harbouring and whatever is against the peace etc., and ask
for judgement whether they should answer for harbouring before the deed
is established.

Edmund and William and all the others appealed of the deed come and
deny the death, robbery and whatever is against the peace, and ask that it
be allowed them that when he sued his appeal in the county court he made
no mention in it of the length, breadth or depth of any wound given him[2].
They also ask that it be allowed them that after the deed was supposedly
done Richard de Cumbe did not promptly raise the hue and also that he
varies his appeal, in that whereas he appealed them[3] in the county court of
having placed him [John] on a white mare after the deed, in his appeal now
he says that they placed him on a roan horse. Asked how they intend to
defend themselves with regard to the king's suit, if it can be established by
the coroners' rolls or by the twelve jurors that he varied in his appeal, they
say that they willingly put themselves on the country. Because it is established
by the coroners' rolls that he varies in his appeal, as in those challenges, it is
decided that his appeal is null by which they should be put to law, and let
Richard be taken into *custody* for his false appeal. And for the preservation of
the king's peace let the truth of the matter be inquired into by the country.
The prior and John of Langport who were appealed of harbouring come and
say that they are clerks and cannot and should not answer here. Whereupon
the bishop of Salisbury's official comes with the bishop's letters patent and
claims them as clerks, and they are handed over to him, and let it be inquired
into by the country what sort of men are to be be handed over to him. The
twelve jurors of the hundred of Cawdon, with eight of Cadworth hundred

---

1 Robert Falke has not in fact been previously named, but he is referred to at the
  end of this entry, and in its successor, as having been outlawed for John's death.

2 *sibi*, in error, as though the alleged assault was on Richard.

3 *eum*, i.e. Edmund Falke, but *eos* is required.

and eight of Dole hundred, together with the jurors of this hundred and four neighbouring townships, namely Fisherton, Bemerton, Ditchampton and Harnham [come], with each township being carefully examined by itself. And all and each of both the hundreds and the townships agree as one to say on their oath that neither Edmund nor any of those persons now appealed, except for Gilbert le Careter, Robert Falke and Thomas le Fox, who were outlawed in the county court by Richard's suit, are in any way guilty of that death either in deed or in abetting it, so they are quit. Let the chattels of Gilbert, Robert and Thomas be inquired into. They also say that the prior and John are not guilty of collusion or of harbouring the said [outlaws]. So they are quit, and it is unnecessary for them to be handed over to the bishop.

m. 33d (IMG 0454, 0455) *Continuing Branch*

328. Richard de Cumbe appealed Gilbert, the servant of Edmund Falke, Thomas Fox and Robert Falke in the county court of the death of his brother John de Cumbe, so that they were *outlawed* there by Richard's suit. They had no chattels. Gilbert and Thomas were in Quidhampton tithing, which is in *mercy*. Robert was not in a tithing because he was a clerk. Later it was testified that Thomas had chattels worth *22d.*, the sheriff to answer.

Giles of Fittleton, Richard Solke, Robert Kene, Hugh Funteyn le Bedel, Peter Kyng and Richard son of Emelot likewise appealed Edmund and the others in the county court of John's death in exactly the same way as Richard appealed them. Giles and Hugh now come and do not wish to pursue their appeal, so let them be taken into *custody*, and their pledges for prosecuting are in *mercy*, namely John de Cormayles, John of Fifield, Richard Tancost and Richard son of John of Netheravon. Richard Solk, Robert, Peter and Richard son of Emelot do not come, so let them be *arrested*, and their pledges for prosecuting are in *mercy*, namely the said John, John, Richard and Richard.

329. Richard Burdone fell from a horse in Chilhampton Slade fields and was crushed by the horse's falling on him, so that he died instantly. Richard le Mayster, the first finder, comes and is not suspected, nor is anyone else. Judgement *misadventure*. The value of the horse (*deodand*) *6s. 6d.*, the sheriff to answer. Great Wishford, Stoford, South Newton and Little Wishford townships did not come fully to the inquest, so they are in *mercy*.

330. Godfrey Tivychedou fell from a stot in Quidhampton township and was crushed by it so that he died instantly. William Lupus, the first finder, comes and is not suspected. Judgement *misadventure*. The value of the stot (*deodand*) *4s.*, the sheriff to answer. Bemerton, Quidhampton, Fisherton and Fugglestone townships did not come fully to the inquest, so they are in *mercy*.

331. Thomas, the son of the priest of Little Durnford, and his brother Thomas came from Wilton towards Durnford and encountered John le Gardiner of Wilton. A dispute having arisen between them, John struck the younger Thomas almost in the middle of the neck with a knife and struck his elder brother Thomas to the heart with the same knife, so that the latter Thomas died immediately.[1] John fled immediately after the deed and is suspected, so let him be *exacted and outlawed*. He had no chattels and was not in a tithing, but he was received in Wilton township, which is in *mercy*. Chilhampton township did not come fully [to the inquest] etc., so it is in *mercy*.

332. Unknown malefactors came to the mill of Chadwell and killed William its miller, tied up Alice daughter of Gillian de Furno and Nicholas son of Juetta and carried off the goods found there. It is not known who they were. No Englishry is presented. Judgement *murder*, upon the hundred. Alice and Nicholas, attached because they were in the mill, do not come now. They were attached by Nicholas le Jovene of Ugford, Gilbert of the water from the same township, Walter Dawe [of] Ditchampton and John le Nywe, who are in *mercy*. Burcombe 'Salvage' and Ugford 'St. John' townships did not come fully [to the inquest] etc., so they are in *mercy*.

333. Henry le Gos struck Edward le Torre with a knife to the heart on Stapleford hill, so that he died instantly. Henry fled immediately after the deed and is suspected, so let him be *exacted and outlawed*. His chattels *23s. 6d.*, the sheriff to answer, and was in Winterbourne Stoke tithing, which is in *mercy*. Stapleford, Berwick St. James and 'Little' Winterbourne townships did not come fully [to the inquest] etc., so they are in *mercy*.

334. Cecily the widow of Richard le Frankeleyn appealed Walter son of Roger of Charlton in the county court of rape and breach of the king's peace. Cecily does not come now, so let her be arrested, and her pledges for prosecuting are in *mercy*, namely Edmund Falk and Peter le Orfevre of Wilton. Walter now comes. The jurors say that they [the parties] are not agreed and that Walter is not guilty in anything, so he is quit. The twelve jurors made no mention of the appeal, so they are in *mercy*.

And to judgement[2] upon John of Langford and Peter Crey, the two electors who chose Adam de Knolle who was appealed of robbery [as a juror].

335. The jurors present that Edith of Wishford holds one hide of land in Wishford of the king by the service of keeping Grovely forest, and the land is worth 4s. a year.[3]

---

1 Despite the apparent severity of his wound, the younger Thomas does not seem to have been killed in this affray.

2 The sentence may have been added later. That it begins with a conjunction suggests that it was seen as closely connected with the foregoing entry, the connection being that it concerned the shortcomings of jurors.

3 The serjeanty was that of keeping the northern half of Grovely forest. In 1255 Edith, described as the daughter of John Humphrey of Wishford and as married to John Truer by the king, shared the serjeanty with her sister Agnes, who had either died

336. Concerning defaults, they say that John Peytevin, Robert of Blackford and the prior of Bath[1] did not come on the first day, so they are in *mercy*.

337. Concerning indicted persons, they say that Robert Sumeler, Hake son of Deulecresse of Wilton[2] and Walter the smith of Fonthill Bishop have made off on suspicion of theft, and except for Walter they are suspected. So let them be *exacted and outlawed*. Walter may return if he wishes. Hake's chattels are unknown, but let them be inquired into of Wilton. Walter's chattels *6s. 8d.*, Stockton township to answer. Robert had no chattels, but he was in South Newton tithing, which is in *mercy*.

338. Reynold de Pavely and Geoffrey Hosee are in *mercy* for a false claim against John de Quarenteyne and Richard the chaplain of Burcombe.

339. John the smith and Thomas le Pechur, arrested on suspicion of theft, come and deny theft and all, and for good and ill put themselves on the country. The twelve jurors come and say that they are not guilty, so they are quit.

THE HUNDRED OF DOLE COMES BY TWELVE

340. From W[illiam le Dun], sheriff, for the chattels of Richard le Bedel, hanged at Stockbridge, *3s.*

341. Simon son of John the cook was found killed in his father's house in Orcheston. The first finder and four neighbours come and are not suspected. Robert le Resere and John son of John of Homanton, accused of the death, have made off and are suspected, so let them be *exacted and outlawed*. John's chattels *6d.*, the sheriff to answer, and he was in Homanton tithing, which is in *mercy*. Let Robert's chattels be inquired of in Heytesbury. Elston, Orcheston St George, Tilshead and Gore townships did not come fully to the inquest etc., so they are in *mercy*. William de Bakham, clerk, intruded himself among

---

by 1268 or had forfeited her portion for marrying without royal consent. The land was then valued at 20s. per annum. At Edith's death in 1281 her heir was her son Henry Quintyn, who at that year's eyre was said to be holding two virgates in Wishford, worth 40s. per annum. *Rot. Hund.* ii, 232; JUST 1/1005/? m. 153d; *CIPM* ii no. 402. For the keeping of the southern half of the forest see **140** above.

1   Literally *Buton'*, presumably in error for *Bathon'*. The prior of Bath had land in Stapleford, in Branch hundred, in 1291. T. Astle, S. Ayscough and J. Caley (eds.), *Taxatio ecclesiastica Angliae et Walliae auctoritate P. Nicholai IV, circa A.D. 1291* (Record Commission, 1802), 186.

2   A member of the Jewish community in Wilton – his father makes several appearances in records of the Jewish exchequer of the late 1260s and early 1270s. J.M. Rigg (ed.), *Calendar of the plea rolls of the exchequer of the Jews i: Henry III, A.D. 1218-1272* (Jewish Historical Society of England, 1905), 177, 205, 209, 246, 271; *ii: Edward I, A.D. 1272-1275* (Jewish Historical Society of England, 1910), 228, 257-8.

the [other] eleven jurors for their deliberations and did not take the oath, so let him be taken into custody for trespass. He made fine by *1 mark*, pledges Nicholas of Rolleston and John de Bakham.

342. Concerning defaults, they say that William of Maddington, William Walerand, Hervey de Chauz and the abbot of Hyde did not come here on the first day, so they are in *mercy*.

343. The jurors present that the church of Tilshead is in the king's advowson, and John le Fauconer holds it by gift of the king, and it is worth 15 marks a year.[1]

344. Concerning serjeanties, they say that William le Moyne holds £10 worth of land in Maddington by serjeanty of the king, by the service of keeping the king's larder.[2]

345. Cecily the widow of Adam Wysdom appealed Simon Edeline that wickedly and in felony he assaulted her on the king's highway outside Tilshead township and struck her on the shoulder with a staff so that she fell to the ground, and then broke her left arm with the staff, ill-treated her, and in robbery took from her a purse containing 7s. and a brooch worth 2s. And that he did this wickedly etc. she offers to prove against him as a woman, as the court [shall decide] etc.

Simon comes and denies the felony and all, and asks that it be allowed him that she cannot have any appeal against anyone except in three cases, namely for the rape of her virginity, her husband killed in her arms and a miscarried child, and moreover that she does not now mention in her appeal what kind of wood the staff was made of. With these things allowed him he puts himself on the country. Because it is sufficiently established that she varies in her appeal it is decided that her appeal is null and that she be taken into custody, and Simon is quit as to the appeal. But for the preservation of the king's peace let the truth of the matter be inquired into by the country. The jurors of this hundred, together with those of Branch, say on their oath that Simon beat Cecily and ill-treated her, but took nothing from her in robbery. So let him be taken into *custody* for trespass. Cecily is poor, so she

---

1 John le Fauconer, a royal clerk, was presented to Tilshead church on 7 November 1262. *CPR 1266-1272*, 738.

2 The service was also described – for instance in 1249 – as that of making purchases for the king's larder. The Moyne family had held the manor of Winterbourne Maddington since the twelfth century. By 1250 half the lands had been alienated to three tenants, and it was arranged that these should henceforth pay William 50s. per annum in equal portions, for which he was to answer to the king, along with the remaining 50s. owed for his own share. In 1281 the serjeanty was valued at £5 per annum, and William was said to be performing the service of purchaser. *Book of Fees* ii, 742, 1178, 1227-8; *Wiltshire crown pleas, 1249* no. 468; *Rot. Hund.* ii, 234; JUST 1/1005/2 m. 150d; *VCH Wiltshire* xv, 205.

is pardoned the amercement. Later Simon came and made fine by ½ *mark*, pledge Walter of Tilshead.

346. The jurors present that 'Little' Winterbourne manor used to do suit to the hundred court every three weeks, and the suit has been withdrawn by William Waleraund for seven years now, to the king's loss of 2s. a year.

347. They also say that Robert of Gore and Matthew de Bovile hold whole knights' fees and are of full age but are not yet knights, so they are in *mercy*.

348. Concerning indicted persons, they say that William Mauger has made off on suspicion of theft and is suspected, so let him be exacted and outlawed. He had no chattels, but he was in Sherrington tithing, which is in *mercy*. The twelve jurors are in *mercy* for trespass, in that they allowed William de Bacham, clerk, to be present at their deliberations and to answer before the justices when he had not taken the oath. Let William be taken into *custody* for this reason. He made fine as appears above.[1]

m. 34 (IMG 0375, 0376)

THE HUNDRED OF THORNHILL COMES BY TWELVE

349. David of Medbourne was killed on Wanborough hill. Christian his wife, the first finder, was arrested and imprisoned for the death, and was later burnt before justices for gaol [delivery] etc. Walter of the bridge from Liddington and Thomas son of Everard were likewise arrested for the death and imprisoned in Salisbury castle when John de Vernun was sheriff, and they escaped from that prison. So to judgement of the *escape* upon Robert, the son and heir of John de Vernun. Walter of the bridge fled and is suspected, so let him be *exacted and outlawed*. His chattels *11s. 6d.*, the sheriff to answer, and he was in Liddington tithing, which is in *mercy*. Thomas had no chattels and was in the same tithing. Later Thomas comes and proffers the king's charter,[2] which testifies that the king has pardoned him his suit for his peace for the death and likewise for the escape and [has granted him] firm peace etc. There is no-one who wishes to sue against him, so firm peace is granted him. Wanborough, Medbourne, Chiseldon and Badbury townships did not come to the inquest etc., so they are in *mercy*.

350. Adam the thresher of Wanborough fled to Wanborough church, where he admitted theft, and likewise William Edmund and Emma his wife fled to Liddington church, where they admitted theft and *abjured* the realm before the coroner. Adam's chattels *6d.*, the sheriff to answer, and he was in Wanborough

---

1 See **341** above.

2 *CPR 1266–1272*, 82. John de Vernun was replaced as sheriff in July 1261. The pardon was granted on 3 or 4 July 1267, at the instance of John Giffard.

tithing, which is in *mercy*. William Edmund's chattels *16d.*, the sheriff to answer, and he was in Liddington tithing, which is in *mercy*.

351. Unknown malefactors burgled the house of Thomas of Stert, killed Thomas's brother Walter and wounded Thomas, who has died, and carried off the goods found there. It is not known who they were. Swindon township did not come to the inquest before the coroner, so it is in *mercy*.

352. As Adam Aylwyn was trying to grease the axle of a mill, he was struck by the mill's sail-yard so that he died. His brother Walter, attached because he was present, comes and is not suspected, nor is anyone else. Judgement misadventure. The value of the sail-yard (*deodand*) *12d.*, the sheriff to answer. Wroughton and Broom townships did not come fully to the inquest etc., so they are in *mercy*.

353. Maud the widow of John the tithingman of Wanborough appealed John le Bole and William Page in the county court of the death of her son Robert. Maud does not come now, so let her be *arrested*, and her pledges for prosecuting are in *mercy*, namely Thomas of the bridge from Wanborough and Roger le Grant from the same. So they are in *mercy*.[1] John and William come. The jurors testify that they [the parties] are not agreed, and that they are not guilty, so they are quit.

354. John le Waleys got himself into Wanborough church, admitted theft and *abjured* the realm before the coroner. His chattels *6d.*, the sheriff to answer, and was in Wanborough tithing, which is in *mercy*.

355. Adam son of Robert the merchant, a ten year old boy, was crushed by a hurdle which fell on him in a storm of wind so that he died instantly. Agnes daughter of William, the first finder, does not come, and she was attached by John le Cuberge of Hinton and John le Notte of the same, who are in *mercy*. No one is suspected. Judgement *misadventure*. The value of the hurdle (*deodand*) *three halfpence*, the sheriff[2] to answer. Hinton township did not come before the justices with the deodand or to answer before them. 'Westrop' township did not come [to the inquest] etc., so it is in *mercy*.

356. John de Gofy and John son of John le Boys were together at a tavern in the house of Robert of Earl's Court, and a dispute having arisen between them as they went out of the house into the fields outside Earlscourt, John Gofy from Berkshire struck [the other] John on the head with a club so that he later died. John Gofy fled immediately after the deed and is suspected, so let him be *exacted and outlawed*. He had no chattels and was not in a tithing

---

1 A careless repetition.

2 *vic*[*ecomes*] is interlined above *vill' de Hyninton*, which has been struck through; apparently the clerk had anticipated the next sentence.

because he was a stranger from Berkshire. Earlscourt township did not come to the inquest etc., so it is in *mercy*.

357. A stranger was found killed in Liddington pasture. Laurence le Pyper, the first finder, comes and is not suspected. It is not known who killed him. No Englishry is presented. Judgement *murder*, upon the hundred.

358. Simon le Carpenter of Hinton killed his brother William, fled to Liddington church, admitted the deed and *abjured* the realm before the coroner. His chattels *50s. 2d.*, Hinton township to answer. The twelve jurors concealed those chattels, so they are in *mercy*.

359. Alice daughter of Richard le Frye appealed John de la Punde in the county court of rape and breach of the king's peace. Alice does not come now, so let her be arrested, and her pledges for prosecuting are in mercy, namely William de la Were of Liddington and William of Medbourne. John does not come now, and he was attached by Michael le Akerman of Badbury and Nicholas son of Henry of Chiseldon, who are in mercy. The jurors say that they [the parties] are not agreed, but they say that John forcibly lay with her, so let him be taken into *custody*.[1]

360. The jurors present that Adam of Codford, formerly John de Vernun's clerk, took 40s. from Everard de la Wyke, charging him with having killed Walter le Torp, and he kept him in prison until he had paid those 40s., against his will, even though Everard sought out Walter and brought him alive before the country. Later Adam likewise took 20s.from William of Medbourne and John le Varl, charging them with having harboured Walter. So let him be taken into *custody* and let him answer for the money. Later he came and made fine by *1 mark*, and he has satisfied Everard for 2 marks, pledges William Luddog of Heytesbury, William Selyman and Roger de la Sale of Winterbourne, and let him pay those *20s.*[2] to the king. He has satisfied the injured party, so nothing concerning the 20s.

361. Concerning defaults, they say that Sampson Folyot, the abbot of Hyde (he has a warrant), the abbess of Marcigny[3] and Emelina countess of Ulster (she has a warrant) did not come here on the first day, so they are in *mercy*.

---

1 Since John was not present the order was presumably a mistake, and he was to be arrested. At the end of the entry a sentence, *Et respondeat de predictis denariis* ('Let him answer for that money') appears to have been squeezed in erroneously; it is repeated in the next entry, where it belongs.

2 The sum has been struck through in the body of the entry.

3 The monastery of Marcigny-sur-Loire, which held the manor of Broom, was in fact a priory, a Cluniac double house which was founded as a nunnery, headed by a prioress, but came to have a small community of monks, with a prior at their head, attached to it. Nuns and monks held the priory's property in common. J.Richard (ed.), *Le cartulaire de Marcigny-sur-Loire (1045-1144): essai de reconstitution*

362. William Wykeman was found killed in Hinton township. William's son John, the first finder, does not come, and he was attached by the tithingman and his whole tithing of Hinton, who are in *mercy*. The four neighbours do not come and were attached by the same tithingman and his tithing, so they are in *mercy*. Robert of Earl's Court, accused of the death, comes and denies the death, felony and all and for good and ill puts himself on the country. The jurors and four neighbouring townships say on their oath that Robert is not guilty of it, either of the deed or of colluding in it, so he is quit.[1]

363. Adam of Codford has acknowledged that he owes Everard de la Wyke 2 marks to be paid at mid Lent, and if he has not done it he agrees that the sheriff should cause it [to be raised] from his lands etc.[2]

364. Edith daughter of William de la Cote appealed Philip de Wyxsy that when she was in the king's peace at 'la Blakethorne' between Badbury and Stert on the Sunday next after the feast of St. Peter in Chains in the 45th year [7 August 1261], at the first hour, Philip came wickedly and in felony and in premeditated assault and took her by the throat and threw her to the ground and squeezed her so that she bled from her mouth and nostrils, and then raped her of her virginity. That he did this wickedly and in felony she offers to prove against him as a woman as the court shall consider etc.

Philip de Wyxsy comes and denies the felony, rape and all and whatever etc. He asks that it be allowed him that when she appealed him in the county court she said that the deed was done on the Sunday next after the feast of the translation of St. Thomas the Martyr [10 July] and now varies in her appeal in this, and this being allowed him he asks that the truth of the matter be inquired into by the country. And because it is established by the coroners' rolls that she varies in her appeal it is decided that her appeal is null whereby etc., and that Edith be taken into *custody* for a false appeal. She is poor. The jurors say on their oath that Philip threw her to the ground when playing, so that blood came from her nose, but he did her no other trespass. So let him be taken into custody for trespass. He made fine by ½ *mark*, pledge William Wyxi.

---

d'un manuscrit disparu (Analecta Burgundica, Dijon, 1957), 102 n. 2. R. Graham, *English ecclesiastical studies* (1929), 19. See also **571** below.

1 An undated inquest, held under a writ issued on 19 September 1262, found that Robert had been maliciously indicted for killing William le Wicman and also one John Harevost. C 144/5 no. 32. On that occasion he was called Robert of Oaksey, and it may be significant that in 1281 the Thornhill jurors presented that a man of that name had been arrested for theft sometime between 1270 and 1272; he escaped from Salisbury castle prison, but was eventually re-arrested and hanged before justices for gaol delivery. JUST 1/1005/2 m. 132d.

2 This entry is in effect a continuation of **360** above. It is followed by a space of several lines.

[*At the foot of the membrane below a large space is written, in two columns*, Nicholas le Duk for associating with thieves, Geoffrey Maynard, William at the gate, for the death of a man, and William le Penaund, Roger le Chapman, John Walewayn.][1]

m. 34d (IMG 0456, 0457)

THE HUNDRED OF KINWARDSTONE COMES BY TWELVE

365. Adam the smith of Collingbourne, taken with madness, was lodged at the house of Thomas Avenel in Collingbourne, and as they sat together by the fire Adam struck Thomas with a knife in the stomach so that he later died. Alice Avenel, attached because she was present, comes and is not suspected. Adam was arrested after the deed and imprisoned at Salisbury, and he died in prison when John de Vernun was sheriff. Collingbourne 'Valence', Collingbourne 'Abbot's', Easton 'Prior's' and West Grafton townships did not come fully to the inquest etc., so they are in *mercy*.

366. Robert of Battle and his wife Sarah were lodged at the house of Emma of Eastridge in Chute, and they got up in the night and killed Emma and carried off her goods found there. They have fled and are suspected, so let Robert be *exacted and outlawed* and let Sarah be (*exacted and*) *waived*. They had no chattels and were not in a tithing because they were strangers. Chute, Fosbury, Conholt and Tidcombe townships did not come fully to the inquest etc., so they are in *mercy*.

367. Walter Shulder was arrested on suspicion of theft and imprisoned in Everleigh prison, and he escaped from it to Everleigh church, where he admitted theft and *abjured* the realm before the coroner. He had no chattels, but he was in Everleigh tithing, which is in *mercy*. To judgement for the *escape* upon Everleigh township because he escaped from its keeping.

368. William Semek got himself into Collingbourne 'Abbot's' church, where he admitted theft and abjured the realm before the coroner. He had no chattels, but he was in Wootton Rivers tithing, which is in *mercy*. And John le Batur, a malefactor and stranger, got himself into Easton church, admitted that he was a thief and *abjured* the realm before the coroner. He had no chattels and was not in a tithing because he was a stranger wandering through the country. Collingbourne and Easton townships did not arrest them, so they are in *mercy*.

369. Walter Wavel and John of Lyme got themselves into Collingbourne church, where they admitted theft and *abjured* the realm before the coroner. They had no chattels and were not in a tithing because they were strangers.

---

1 Nicholas, Geoffrey, William ad portam and John are named in **277**, above, and W. le Penant and Richard (not Roger) le Chapman at the foot of m. 32.

370. Two men, strangers, were found killed in Collingbourne 'Valence' field. Michael Selk, the first finder, comes and is not suspected. It is not known who killed them. No Englishry is presented. Judgement *murder*, upon the hundred. Haxton township did not come fully to the inquest, so it is in *mercy*. And Walter the long of Ludgershall and Edith his wife, Bernard le Lung, Geoffrey Lung, Nicholas Heyman and Thomas Lung were previously arrested on suspicion of the deaths and imprisoned at Salisbury, and later they were released by royal writ until now.[1] Edith, Bernard and the others come and deny the deaths, collusion, abetting and all, and for good and ill put themselves on the country. The twelve jurors of Amesbury hundred and the twelve jurors of Ellstub hundred, together with the four neighbouring townships, say on their oath that Walter the long and Edith and the others are not guilty of the deaths, so they are quit. But they say that Robert le Webbe of Wootton Rivers and John le Tayllor of the same were guilty of the deaths and were later arrested and admitted the deed and were hanged for it. Their chattels are unknown, but let those of John le Tayllor be inquired of in Dunworth (*Dunewirth'*) hundred. It is testified that Robert was arrested on suspicion of the deaths and on suspicion of theft, but he was not arrested with stolen goods and nor did anyone sue against him. The bailiffs of Ludgershall, questioned about this, acknowledge the same, (*to judgement*) so the liberty of that township is taken into the king's hand and the whole township is in *mercy*.

371. Thomas Tosh was found killed in Savernake forest. His daughter Gillian, the first finder, comes and is not suspected. It is not known who killed him. Wootton Rivers, Burbage, Wick and Oare townships did not come fully to the inquest etc., so they are in *mercy*.

372. John of Oxford, a malefactor and stranger, entered Easton church and admitted that he was a thief and *abjured* the realm before the coroner. His chattels 2s. 5d., the sheriff to answer. His tithing is unknown because he was a stranger.

373. John son of John of the wood was found hanged by his own belt on a hazel tree in Stype Wood. William his son, the first finder, comes and is not suspected. The jurors say that Thomas de la Slade killed John in the wood, and later hung him up and made off immediately after the deed. He is suspected, so let him be *exacted and outlawed*. His chattels 13s., the sheriff to answer, and he was in Standen tithing, which is in *mercy*. North Standen,

---

1 A writ dated 19 July 1260 ordered an inquest into the indictment of Walter le Lung and his wife, imprisoned at Ludgershall for killing unknown men. The resulting inquest does not survive, but its findings must have been favourable, for on 2 September following order was given that Walter and Edith, and also Nicholas le Hayman, should be released to bail. A similar order on behalf of Thomas le Lung, Bernard le Lung and the latter's brother Geoffrey was issued around 1 October. C 144/5 no.9; *CR 1259-1261*, 108, 124. The second half of this entry is written in a different hand, more spacious than that of the first half.

Charlton, Little Bedwyn and Shalbourne townships did not come fully [to the inquest] etc., so they are in *mercy*.

374. As Walter de Berlee was leading a cart between Chisbury and Bedwyn he was crushed by it so that he died instantly. John le Butiller, the first finder, has died. No one is suspected. Judgement *misadventure*. The value of the mare and cart (*deodand*) 6s., the sheriff to answer. Chisbury, Froxfield and Crofton townships valued the deodand falsely, so they are in *mercy*.

375. Benedict of Soley killed Geoffrey son of Agnes in Chilton Foliat wood and later carried the dead man's body into Chilton Foliat field. Benedict fled immediately after the deed and is suspected, so let him be exacted and outlawed. His chattels 20s. 8d., the sheriff to answer. Later it is testified that Benedict was arrested, but he was delivered by the country before justices for gaol [delivery] etc. and had his chattels back and later died. So nothing from his chattels. Chilton Foliat and Haxton townships did not come [to the inquest] etc., so they are in *mercy*.

376. Geoffrey Tony fell from an oak tree in Savernake forest so that he died instantly. The first finder has died. No one is suspected. Judgement *misadventure*. The value of the branch (*deodand*) 4d., the sheriff to answer. Burbage and Wolf Hall townships did not come fully to [the inquest] etc., so they are in *mercy*. From the same sheriff, for a cart from which Simon Pyk fell (*deodand*), *22d.*

377. Robert son of Thomas the smith of Minsterworth was arrested on suspicion of theft and imprisoned in Ham township. He later escaped from that prison to Ham church, where he admitted theft and abjured the realm before the coroner. He had no chattels, and he was not in a tithing because he was a stranger. Because he escaped from that prison, to judgement for the *escape* upon Ham township. The jurors testify that the prior of St. Swithun, Winchester, levied 100s. from the township for the escape, and did so without warrant, so he is in *mercy*.

378. Miles of Hartfield got himself into Buttermere church, where he admitted theft and *abjured* the realm etc. He had no chattels and was not in a tithing because he was a stranger from Gloucestershire. Buttermere township did not arrest him, so it is in *mercy*.

379. An unknown man was found killed in Froxfield fields. Ingold le Vacher, the first finder, comes and is not suspected. It is not known who killed him. No Englishry [is presented]. Judgement *murder*, upon the hundred. Froxfield township did not come fully to the inquest etc., so it is in *mercy*.

380. Thomas Blaunchard quarrelled with his wife Gillian and struck her with an axe on the head so that she died instantly. Gillian's daughter Agnes, the first finder, comes and is not suspected. Thomas fled immediately after the deed and is suspected, so let him be *exacted and outlawed*. His chattels *6s. 3d.*, the sheriff to answer, and he was in Collingbourne 'Abbot's' tithing, which is in *mercy*. It is testified that Thomas's mother Agnes was in the house when the deed was done, and she was not attached, so let her be arrested. 'Bokland' township did not come fully to the inquest, so it is in *mercy*. Later Agnes comes and, asked how she wishes to be acquitted of this, says that she willingly puts herself on the country. The twelve jurors say that Agnes is not guilty, so she is quit. But they say that this crime was imputed to her by Edmund le Lad of Collingbourne, so let him be *arrested*.

381. Stephen of Stert tried to bring down a branch of an oak tree, and because of the branch he fell and died instantly. His daughter Isabel, the first finder, comes and is not suspected, nor is anyone else. Judgement *misadventure*. The value of the branch (*deodand*) *5d.*, the sheriff to answer. Tidcombe township did not come fully to the inquest, so it is in *mercy*.

382. Concerning ladies, they say that Gillian Boveclyve holds her land in Wick of the king in chief and is in the king's gift, and she has married without the king['s consent]. The land is worth £4 a year and renders 35s. a year to the king at Marlborough castle. So let this be *discussed*, namely concerning Gillian who has married without the king['s consent].[1]

383. Concerning defaults, they say that James le Sauvage, the prior of St. Swithun, the abbot of Cirencester, Geoffrey the cook, John le Franceys the younger, William le Cornewaleys and Alan de Wauton did not come on the first day, so they are in *mercy*.

384. Concerning serjeanties, they say that Hawise Kernet of Shalbourne [holds] 1 carucate in Shalbourne by the serjeanty of providing one serjeant for the king's army for 40 days. The land is worth [*blank*] a year.[2] John Baxman holds 1 carucate of land in Grafton by the service of transporting the king's wine butts, and the land is worth 40s. a year.[3] William Michele

---

1 Presumably Gillian was the heir of the William de Bouclive recorded around 1220 as a forester. The estate was at East Wick. *Book of Fees* i, 342; *VCH Wiltshire* xvi, 233.

2 The manor of Shalbourne Dormer, or Westcourt, is now in Berkshire. It had been held by Walter Sturmy, who died in 1243 and was succeeded by his sisters Alice and Letuaria. Alice married Robert Kernet, and Hawise (also recorded as Alice) who held half the serjeanty in 1268 was probably their daughter. In 1289 the entire estate was said to have been worth 40s. at Walter's death, so Hawise's share should have been valued at 20s. *VCH Berkshire* iv, 231; JUST 1/1011 m. 52.

3 *servicium ducendi buttella domini regis*. In 1236 Richard Baxman held half a hide by the serjeanty of being in the king's buttery. In 1274/5 Stephen Baxman held one carucate in East Grafton, and the service was defined as carrying the king's wine in bottles – with a single packhorse, it was said in 1281. In the latter year Stephen was presented as holding the serjeanty, which had been assessed for a rent of *6d.* per annum, *as* the inheritance of his wife Joan, so he may have taken her name. In

holds 1 virgate of land in Milton Lilbourne by serjeanty, and it is assessed for a rent of 13d. a year.[1]

385. Concerning indicted persons, they say that Adam Spronke, Robert Piper and Henry Smikering have made off on suspicion of theft and are all suspected, so let them be *exacted and outlawed*. They had no chattels, but Adam was in Pewsey tithing, Robert in Everleigh tithing, and Henry in Chilton tithing, so all the tithings are in *mercy*. They also say that Richard le Fuotere of Crofton, William le Cok of Ham and Geoffrey Blundel of Ham have made off on suspicion of theft and are suspected, so let them be *exacted and outlawed*.

m. 35 (IMG 0377, 0378) *Continuing Kinwardstone*

386. John Ingolf and Hugh his son, arrested on suspicion of burning Sampson Folyot's houses, and John the smith (good),[2] Adam Aylwyne (bad), Thomas le Gul, John the weaver (good), William Sturdy (good), Nicholas Attehulle (good), William Wyte (good), Henry le Hyrde (good) and Thomas le Scut (bad), arrested on suspicion of theft, come and deny felony and all, and for good and ill put themselves on the country. The jurors say on their oath that John [Ingolf] and all the others except Adam Aylwine and Thomas Scut are not guilty of any evildoing, so they are quit. And Adam and Thomas are guilty etc., so etc. (*hanged*). Adam Aylwine's chattels 3s., the sheriff to answer. Thomas le Scut's chattels 5s., the sheriff to answer. They also say that the crime was imputed to Thomas Gule by Robert the tithingman of Buttermere, so let him be arrested. The crime was imputed to John Ingolf and his son by Gilbert Norcyn of Chilton, so let him be arrested.

387. John of the park from Marlborough appealed William Tutlemund and John le Provost of Burbage in the county court of robbery, mayhem and breach of the king's peace. John of the park does not come now, so let him be *arrested*, and his pledges for prosecuting are in *mercy*, namely Henry of

---

1289 their son William claimed nothing in the serjeanty except through his mother, who claimed to be paying the 6d. to the earl of Gloucester's bailiffs. They denied this, saying that the money they received was 'hundred-penny', and that the rent should go towards the county farm. Consequently the serjeanty was taken into the king's hand, as Joan was neither paying a rent nor performing a service for it. *Book of Fees* i, 586; *Rot. Hund.* ii, 260; JUST 1/1005/2 m. 127; JUST1/1011 m. 52.

1 In 1236 Richard Michel held a cotland in Milton by the service of keeping two wolfhounds at the king's expense. In 1250 Michael of Milton – Michael may be in error for Michel, with a given name accidentally omitted – held the serjeanty, part of which had been alienated. For the alienation its tenant was to pay 13d. per annum to Michael, who was to account for the money to the crown and also to perform the accustomed service. In 1281 John Michel was holding two virgates by that service and paying 13d. yearly to Salisbury castle. *Book of Fees* i, 586, ii, 1179, 1228; JUST 1/1005/2 m. 127.

2 Most of the names have written above them *b* (for *bonus*, good) or *m* (for *malus*, bad), indicating that the men were respectively acquitted or condemned.

Axford and William Meysy. William and John come now. The jurors, asked if they [the parties] are agreed and if William and John are guilty or not, say on their oath that they are not agreed, but they say that William and John killed John of the park's horse, worth 20s. So they are quit as to the appeal, but let them be taken into *custody* for trespass. Later William and John came and made fine by ½ *mark*, pledges Henry Chiche and William Malewayn.

388. Agnes the widow of John son of Philip of Chilton appealed William le Sauvage of Chilton in the county court of the death of her husband John. William does not come now, and he was mainprised by Walter de Hune of Garsdon, William Alweyn, Hugh son of John of Chilton and John of Bridzor, who are in *mercy*. The jurors, asked if he is guilty of that death, say no, because they say that John died of a natural disease and not through William's agency, but they say that William beat John. So let him be *arrested* for trespass.

389. Wymark the widow of Henry Sauvage of Crofton appealed Nicholas son of Alan son of Warin, Peter son of Alan, Alan son of Warin, and Giles of Ashby in Northamptonshire in the county court of the death of her husband Henry, so that Nicholas and Giles were outlawed at her suit in the county court. They had no chattels and were not in a tithing, but they were in the mainpast of Alan son of Warin, who has died. Wymark does not come now, so let her be arrested, and her pledges for prosecuting are in *mercy*, namely John Maunsel of Wilton and Gervase Attekychene of Crofton. It is testified that Alan has died. Peter does not come now. He was attached by William Russel, Ralph Parele, Henry Chyche and John le Seler, who are in *mercy*.

THE TOWNSHIP OF BEDWYN COMES BY TWELVE

390. The jurors present that whereas the market of Ramsbury used to be on Tuesday it now takes place and is held on Sunday.[1] So let this be discussed.

THE HUNDRED OF ROWBOROUGH COMES BY TWELVE

391. Clarice de Walle, a malefactor and a stranger, got herself into Potterne church and admitted theft and *abjured* the realm before the coroner. She had no chattels. Potterne township did not arrest her, so it is in *mercy*.

392. Richard Attehorne, Edmund Maresone and Gilbert le Sukere were together at a tavern in Littleton township, and as they came away from it a quarrel arose between them, and Gilbert struck Richard with an axe on the head so that he later died. Gilbert fled immediately after the deed, as did Edmund, and they are suspected, so let them be *exacted and outlawed*. Gilbert's

---

1 Bishop Poor was granted a Tuesday market in 1227, but a year later the sheriff was ordered to suppress it, as prejudicial to neighbouring markets. It must have continued, however, for in 1240 Bishop Bingham agreed to give up the market in return for a grant of fairs at Ramsbury itself and at Sherborne. The exchange evidently took only partial effect. See also **502** below. *VCH Wiltshire* xii, 40, 210.

chattels *6s. 3d.*, the sheriff to answer, as appears in Melksham hundred. Edmund's chattels *2s. 5½d.*, the sheriff to answer. Edmund and the others were in Erlestoke tithing, which is in *mercy*.

393. Ralph Ful killed his wife Clarice and his daughter Christian in Market Lavington township. Christian la Veysine, the first finder, and four neighbours come and are not suspected. Ralph fled immediately after the deed and is suspected, so let him be *exacted and outlawed*. His chattels *26s. 0½d.*, the sheriff to answer, and he was in Robert de la Mare's portion of Market Lavington tithing, which is in *mercy*. Littleton, Lavington, Eastcott and Great Cheverell townships did not come fully to the inquest, so they are in *mercy*.

394. John le Wyse and an unknown man were found killed beside the bishop of Salisbury's sheepcote.[1] Peter Doryval, the first finder, and four neighbours come and are not suspected. It is not known who killed them. No Englishry is presented. Judgement *murder*, upon the bishop of Salisbury's liberty, in which this happened, because it does not participate with the hundred.[2] West Lavington, Marston, Potterne and Little Cheverell townships did not come fully to the inquest etc., so they are in *mercy*.

395. Maud of Hereford got herself into Potterne church, admitted theft and *abjured* the realm before the coroner. She had no chattels. Potterne township did not arrest her, so it is in *mercy*.

396. Concerning indicted persons, they say that William le Potter,[3] John Thurbern, Walter le Hyrde, Aylward Fresel and Roger de Clere have made off on suspicion of theft. They are all suspected, so let them be *exacted and outlawed*. William le Potter's chattels *4s.*, the sheriff to answer. John's chattels *10s.*, the sheriff to answer. They were in Littleton tithing, which is in *mercy*. Walter had no chattels, but he was in Potterne tithing, which is in *mercy*. Aylward's chattels *26s.0½d.*, the sheriff to answer, and he was in Lavington 'Hawys' tithing, which is in *mercy*. Roger had no chattels, but he was in Market Lavington tithing, which is in *mercy*. William Paynel[4] took John's chattels without warrant, so he is in *mercy*.

---

1 Possibly the killing which Martin of Littlebury was ordered to investigate on 24 January 1262. The bishop of Salisbury's shepherds had been attacked at Lavington, and one of the assailants, John le Chapelein of Littleton, was killed in the resulting affray. *CPR 1258-1266*, 230.

2 Rowborough hundred was divided between the king and the bishop of Salisbury. Of the townships named, Little Cheverell lay within the king's portion, and would therefore not have had to contribute to the murder fine levied upon the bishop's half.

3 Above the names of William and John is written the amount of their chattels.

4 In 1249 William Paynel and his wife were sued over a rent in Littleton. *Wiltshire civil pleas, 1249* no. 405.

397. Concerning defaults, they say that Richard de la Rochelle, Maud of Whitchurch[1] and Hawise of London did not come here on the first day, so they are in *mercy*.

398. From W[illiam le Dun] the sheriff for the chattels of Geoffrey Cuterygge, hanged before justices for gaol [delivery] etc., *6s.*

399. William le Royt, arrested on suspicion of theft, comes and denies theft and all, and for good and ill puts himself on the country. The twelve jurors of this hundred together with the jurors of Studfold hundred say on their oath that William is not guilty, so he is quit.

400. Concerning indicted persons, they say that Ralph Gofayre has made off on suspicion of theft and is suspected, so let him be *exacted and outlawed*. He had no chattels, but he was in Market Lavington tithing, which is in *mercy*.

401. Emma the widow of Walter le Rublere appealed William son of William Paynel and his brother Thomas in the county court of the death of her husband Walter. Emma does not come now, so let her be *arrested*, and her pledges for prosecuting are in *mercy*, namely Humphrey of Market Lavington and Robert le Hopere of the same. Thomas comes and the jurors testify that they [the parties] are not agreed and that Thomas is not guilty, nor is William, so they are quit. But they say that William le Waleys was guilty of that death and has made off, and it is testified that he has died.

m. 35d (IMG 0458, 0459)

THE HUNDRED OF HIGHWORTH COMES BY TWELVE

402. William son of Philip of Leintwardine and his wife Parnel got themselves into Stratton church, where they admitted theft and *abjured* the realm before the coroner. They had no chattels, and he [William] was not in a tithing because he was a stranger. Stratton township did not arrest them, so it is in *mercy*.

403. Hugh of Lambourne got himself into Hannington church, admitted theft and *abjured* the realm before the coroner. He had no chattels and was not in a tithing because he was a stranger. Hannington township did not arrest him, so it is in *mercy*.

404. Walter the weaver of Lydiard struck John the hayward of Blunsdon with a knife in the stomach so that he later died. He [Walter] fled immediately after the deed and is suspected, so let him be exacted and outlawed.[2] His chattels *18d.*, the sheriff to answer, and he was in Lydiard Tregoze tithing, which is

---

1 *de albo monasterio.*

2 *abjur*[*et*] is written in the margin in error for *exigatur et utlagetur.*

in *mercy*. Eaton, Lus Hill, Hannington and Blunsdon townships did not come fully [to the inquest] etc., so they are in *mercy*. Let Walter's chattels be more fully inquired of in *Blackgrove* hundred.

405. Walter of Hardwick got himself into Highworth church, admitted that he was a thief and *abjured* the realm before the coroner. He had no chattels and was not in a tithing because he was a stranger. Highworth township did not arrest him, so it is in *mercy*. Richard of Pontefract got himself into Stanton Fitzwarren church, admitted that he had killed John of Ireland and *abjured* the realm before the coroner. He had no chattels and was not in a tithing because he was a stranger. Stanton Fitzwarren township did not arrest him when this happened in daytime, so it is in *mercy*.

406. Unknown malefactors came to the house of Emma Cotewy in Haydon Wick. They were pursuing William Cotewy, whom they killed. His sister Parnel, the first finder, has died. Four neighbours come and are not suspected. It is not known who they were. Walter Cubbel, Adam de Wytton and Nicholas de Wytton, accused of the death, were previously arrested, and Walter Cubbel was hanged before W. Brito, a justice[1] etc. His chattels *3s.*, the sheriff to answer. Adam le Gay took the said money without warrant, so he is in *mercy*.[2] He is pardoned because he previously paid those chattels in under a summons from the exchequer. Adam and Nicholas were delivered by the country before W. Brito. Parnel [Haydon] Wick, Blunsdon St. Andrew and Upper Stratton townships did not come fully [to the inquest] etc., so they are in *mercy*.

407. Thomas son of Walter de la Leghe, moved to anger against his father Walter, tried to strike him. Thomas's brother Richard came up and tried to help his father and Thomas attacked him, but Richard in self-defence struck Thomas with an axe[3] so that he died four days later. Richard fled immediately after the deed and is suspected, so let him be *exacted and outlawed*. His chattels *2s.*, the sheriff answer, and he was in Stanton 'Reynold son of Peter' tithing, which is in *mercy*. Marston, Stanton, Stratton and Haydon townships did not come fully to the inquest etc., so they are in *mercy*.

408. Nicholas of Wigmore got himself into Highworth church, admitted theft and *abjured* the realm before the coroner. He had no chattels and was not in a tithing because be was a stranger. Highworth township did not arrest him, so it is in *mercy*. Robert the miller of Wootton [Bassett] got himself into Rodbourne church, admitted theft and *abjured* the realm before the

---

1   William Brito, a justice on several eyres in the 1240s and 1250s, was doubtless here acting as a justice of gaol delivery, perhaps under his commission to deliver New Salisbury gaol, issued around 8 May 1257, C 66/71 m. 11d.

2   The margination, followed by ½ *mark*, has been scratched out.

3   *securis*, as distinct from the more usual *hachia*, which implies hatchet.

coroner. He had no chattels and was not in a tithing because he was a stranger. Rodbourne township did not arrest him, so it is in *mercy*.

409. As Roger Stony was leading a cart in Inglesham fields he was crushed by it and died instantly. Walter Hamund, the first finder, comes and is not suspected, nor is anyone else. Judgement *misadventure*. The value of the cart and mare (*deodand*) *6s. 8d.*, the sheriff to answer. Inglesham, Eastrop and Westrop townships valued the deodand falsely, so they are in *mercy*.

410. Alan of Wanborough was found killed in Marston fields. John Edolf, the first finder, has died. John Srethe and Roger son of Ellen of Highworth, accused of the death, have made off and are suspected, so let them be *exacted and outlawed*. They had no chattels, but John was in Marston 'Farleigh' tithing and Roger was in Hampton 'Turvile' tithing, so all the tithings are in *mercy*.

411. William Cut got himself into Blunsdon St. Andrew church, admitted theft and *abjured* the realm. He had no chattels and was not in a tithing, but he was in the mainpast of William Mauduyt of Widhill, who is in *mercy*.[1] Blunsdon St. Andrew township did not arrest him, so it is in *mercy*.

412. Thomas Gobelle struck William le Messager with a knife in the stomach so that he died four days later. Thomas fled immediately after the deed and is suspected, so let him be *exacted and outlawed*. He had no chattels and was not in a tithing, but he was in the mainpast of Constance, widow of Fulk Fitzwarine, who is in *mercy*.[2]

413. Sibyl Surhale was found dead in Stratton township in a ditch near the house of Adam de la Hyrne, who had the dead woman buried without a coroner's view. So let him be arrested (*taken into custody*).[3] Also, Lower Stratton township buried her without a coroner's view, so it is in *mercy*.[4]

414. Concerning serjeanties, they say that Eleanor de la Hose holds £10 worth of land in Inglesham of the king, by the serjeanty of keeping a goshawk etc.[5]

---

1 William Mauduyt was lord of the manor of West Widhill. He was himself hanged at Ilchester in Somerset, perhaps in March 1273, for stealing horses and for having broken out of Gloucester gaol. *VCH Wiltshire* xviii, 91; *Calendar of Inquisitions Miscellaneous i: 1219-1307* no. 949.

2 The Fitzwarines, a powerful family in the Welsh marches, were also mesne lords of North Widhill. Constance was the widow of Fulk (iv) Fitzwarine, who was killed in 1264 at the battle of Lewes. *VCH Wiltshire* xviii, 92; Frederick Suppe, 'Fitzwarine family (*per. c.* 1145-1315)', *ODNB* xix, 953-4.

3 In the margin *cap*[*iatu*]*r*, struck through, is followed by *c*[*ustodietu*]*r*. Presumably Adam was present at the eyre, making the order for his arrest superfluous.

4 The last two sentences are squeezed into the space before the next entry.

5 At the north-eastern tip of Wiltshire, Inglesham was sometimes treated as being

415. Concerning defaults, they say that the countess of the Isle[1] [of Wight], Reynold son of Peter, master William of Holborn, Richard de la More, Adam de Gay and Henry Tyeys did not come here on the first day, so they are in *mercy*.

416. Concerning indicted persons, they say that Robert Pulle (for the death of Robert Lucy),[2] William son of William Ylbert, Robert le Careter of Lydiard, John Nel of Hampton, Walter Wobode and John Adam of Highworth made off on suspicion of theft and are suspected, so let them be *exacted and outlawed*. They had no chattels. Robert [Pulle] was in Lydiard 'Clinton' tithing, and William in Stratton tithing. Robert [le Careter] was received outside a tithing in Lydiard 'Clinton' township. John [was] in Hampton tithing, Walter in Highworth tithing, and John Adam in the same, so all the tithings are in *mercy*.

417. Nicholas Pynke, arrested on suspicion of theft, comes and denies theft and all, and for good and ill puts himself on the country. The jurors say that he is not guilty, so he is quit.

THE HUNDRED OF CRICKLADE COMES BY TWELVE

418. Henry le Fulur was crushed by a cart in Eisey field. Laurence de la Lee, attached because he was present, comes and is not suspected, nor is anyone else. Judgement *misadventure*. The value of the cart and the horse 1 mark,[3] the sheriff to answer. Cricklade, Latton, Eisey and Shorncote townships valued the deodand falsely, so they are in *mercy*.

419. Walter Manning got himself into Cricklade church, where he admitted theft and *abjured* the realm before the coroner. He had no chattels and was not in a tithing because he was a stranger. Cricklade township did not arrest him, so it is in *mercy*.

420. Simon of Stanton got himself into Cricklade church, admitted theft

---

in Berkshire. Bartholomew de Husa, recorded as holding the serjeanty in 1243, by the service of mewing a goshawk, was also said to hold it in Great Faringdon, the estate consisting of two hides of land. In 1249 the serjeanty was valued at £5 per annum. In 1281, again worth £5, it was in the hands of Patrick de Cadurcis, who was performing the service, but although he was recorded as holding the manor of Inglesham at his death two years later, nothing was then said of a serjeanty. *Book of Fees* ii, 738, 866; *Wiltshire crown pleas, 1249* no. 82 and note; JUST 1/1005/2 m. 117; *CIPM* ii no. 477.

1 *de Insula*. The countess was Isabel, widow of William de Forz, count of Aumale (*d*. 1260), who now held the lordship of the Isle of Wight.

2 The words *pro morte Roberti Lucy* are inserted above a caret.

3 The price of the deodand appears to have been written in the margin as usual but to have been erased, perhaps because of the false estimate.

and *abjured* the realm. He had no chattels and was not in a tithing because he was a stranger.

421. From W[illiam le Dun], sheriff, for the chattels of Robert Davy, hanged before justices for gaol [delivery] etc., *14s.* Also from Hankerton tithing, for the same Robert's chattels, *10s.*[1]

422. Concerning wines sold, they say that John le Vineter of Cricklade, Robert le Mercer and John le Quer of the same have sold wine contrary to the assize, so they are in *mercy*.

423. Concerning defaults, they say that Robert de Gurnay and Laurence de St. Maur did not come here on the first day, so they are in *mercy*.

424. Concerning indicted persons, they say that William Hyldulf of Cricklade, William Bagge of Chelworth, Thomas Paucok, William Cut and Adam de Kytelby have made off on suspicion of theft and are suspected, so let them be *exacted and outlawed*. William Hyldulf's chattels *5s. 7d.*, the sheriff to answer. The same had land from which the [king's] year and waste [is worth] *½ mark*, the sheriff to answer. It is testified that William the smith of Cricklade has held that land and a messuage for eight years, so let him answer for the issues, namely for *16s.* Warin of Aylesbury seized the land after William's making off and later sold it to the said William the smith, so they are in *mercy* for doing this without warrant. William Bagge's chattels *8s.*, the sheriff to answer, and he was in Chelworth tithing, which is in *mercy*. The others had no chattels and were not in tithings because they were strangers etc.

425. The jurors present that 'Serneford' township used to do suit to the hundred every three weeks, but it has now been withdrawn through the might of the earl of Gloucester. So let this be discussed.

426. Nicholas Gangy of Shorncote was arrested for stealing pigs and imprisoned in Shorncote township.[2] In prison he admitted theft, became an approver and appealed Philip Stone, Richard Stone and Henry Stone of associating [with him], and later they were arrested through his appeal. They were later delivered by the country, after which he was allowed to leave the township's custody. So to judgement for the escape upon the township and upon Philip of Coughton, then the earl of Gloucester's bailiff, and Absolom the clerk and James of Fairford, then bailiff of that township, by whose orders Nicholas escaped. He is suspected, so let him be *exacted and outlawed*. His chattels 14s., the sheriff to answer.

---

1 Written in the main record as *xx s.* with the first *x* erased.

2 Shorncote, on the border between Wiltshire and Gloucestershire, was held by Robert de Gurnay of the earl of Gloucester. *CIPM* i no. 710. The earl is not recorded as claiming any franchises there.

m. 36 (IMG 0379, 0380)

THE HUNDRED OF STAPLE COMES BY TWELVE

427. Miles son of Henry killed Thomas son of Thomas de la Lee in Hailstone grove. He fled immediately after the deed and is suspected, so let him be *exacted and outlawed*. His father Thomas, the first finder, comes and is not suspected. Miles had no chattels and was not in a tithing, but he was in the mainpast of Henry le Brag, who is in *mercy*. Chelworth, Purton 'Abbot's', Somerford and Eaton townships did not come fully to the inquest etc., so they are in *mercy*.

428. Adam Guremund of Christian Malford got himself into Purton church, where he admitted theft and *abjured* the realm before the coroner. He had no chattels and was not in a tithing because he was a stranger. Christian of Montgomery got herself into the same church, where she admitted theft and *abjured* the realm before the coroner. She had no chattels. Purton township did not arrest them, so it is in *mercy*.

429. John Cogligan was arrested for the death of Peter of Wootton[1] and imprisoned in Chelworth township for that deed. Later he escaped from the township's custody, so to *judgement of the escape* upon Chelworth township. John is suspected, so let him be *exacted and outlawed*. He had no chattels and was not in a tithing because he was formerly a lay brother[2] in Gloucestershire. Calcutt, Eaton and Purton townships did not come fully to the inquest etc., so they are in *mercy*.

430. Roger le Wodewarde from Devonshire struck Geoffrey Child with a sword in the chest so that he died within three weeks. Roger fled immediately after the deed and is suspected, so let him be *exacted and outlawed*. He had no chattels and was not in a tithing, but he was in the mainpast of Hugh Peverel,[3] who is in *mercy*. Edith wife of John Page, accused of that death, made off and is suspected, so let her be *exacted and waived*. She had no chattels.

431. Walter Linghe from Gloucestershire struck Thomas Costard with a staff on the forehead, and Ellis, the servant of William Maudut, shot an arrow at Thomas and gave him a wound with it in the middle of the body from which he died instantly. Walter and Ellis fled immediately after the deed and are suspected, so let them be *exacted and outlawed*. They had no chattels and were not in a tithing, but Walter was in the mainpast of John Roydon and Ellis in

---

1 Perhaps the Peter son of John of Wootton for whose death George the smith of Ludgershall received a pardon on 22 May 1267. *CPR 1266-1272*, 63.

2 The employment of lay brothers implies a Cistercian house – the nearest one in Gloucestershire was Kingswood.

3 Peverel's having a Devon man in his household is explained by his having been lord of Sampford Peverell in Devon as well as of half of Staple hundred. The link is made clear by *CIPM* iii, nos. 339, 599.

that of William Maudut,[1] so they [John and William] are in *mercy*. Hugh de Maundeville and William Haghene, accused of that death, come and deny the death, felony and all, and for good and ill put themselves on the country. The twelve jurors of this hundred, together with the jurors of Highworth hundred and the twelve jurors of Cricklade hundred, say that Hugh and William are not guilty of the death, so they are quit, but they say that they came with force and arms to carry away some corn that was in dispute between William Haghene and Philip Unfrey. So let them be taken into *custody* for trespass, because they were in the first conflict when a quarrel arose between them. William Mauduyt and his employee[2] John, likewise accused of that death, do not come and are not suspected, so they are quit as to this, but because they came with Hugh and William in the manner aforesaid let them be *arrested* for trespass etc. Later Hugh came and made fine by *20s.*, pledges Roger of Writely and Peter of the mill.

432. Jordan the miller of Purton, intending to set up the mill-wheel, was crushed by it so that he died instantly. Adam son of Ida, the first finder, comes and is not suspected, nor is anyone else. Judgement *misadventure*. The value of the wheel and axle (*deodand*) *½ mark*, the sheriff to answer. Purton, Chelworth, Eaton and Charlton townships valued the deodand falsely, so they are in *mercy*.

433. Neil Edwyne of Purton and Richard of Blandford, Henry de Lacy's forester, quarrelled together in Braydon forest because Richard wanted to take a pledge from Neil. Neil struck Richard, who struck Neil back on the head with an axe so that he died instantly. Neil's son William, the first finder, comes and is not suspected. Richard fled immediately after the deed and is suspected, so let him be *exacted and outlawed*. He had no chattels and was not in a tithing because he was a stranger. Lydiard Millicent and Lydiard Tregoze townships did not come fully to the inquest, so they are in *mercy*.

434. Richard the whitesmith[3] of Hook and John son of Michael Uppehulle quarrelled together, and Richard attacked John and struck him with a stone on the head, felling him to the ground with that blow, and then tried to kill him, but John in self-defence struck him with an axe on the head, so that he later died. John fled immediately after the deed and is suspected, so let him be *exacted and outlawed*. He had no chattels and was not in a tithing, but he was received in Midgehall township in Blackgrove hundred, so it [the township] is in *mercy*.

435. Concerning serjeanties, they say that Robert son and heir of William de

---

1 *Maudut* is written after *Bardolph*, which is struck through. Slight differences in the handwriting suggest that a different clerk wrote the membrane from the heading to about this point, where the usual clerk took over.

2 *famulus*.

3 *albus faber* – also translatable as 'tinsmith'.

Kaynes, who is in the keeping of Robert Walerand, [and] Isabel de Welles, John Paynel and Hugh Peverel hold £15 worth of land in Chelworth by the serjeanty of providing one serjeant for the king in the army for forty days at their own expense.[1]

436. Concerning defaults, they say the abbot of St. Peter's, Gloucester, did not come on the first day, so he is in *mercy*.

437. Richard son of Alice of Purton and Richard de la Fayrhok wounded John Paynel in Purton fields so that he died instantly. They fled immediately after the deed and are suspected, so let them be exacted and outlawed.[2] They had[3] no chattels. Richard son of Alice was in Purton tithing, which is in mercy. The other was not in a tithing because he was a stranger wandering through the country. Calcutt township did not come fully [to the inquest] etc., so it is in mercy. William of Wilcot, accused of that death, and John le Waleys, accused of harbouring William, come and deny felony and all, and for good and ill put themselves on the country. The jurors say that neither William nor John is guilty, so they are quit.

438. Concerning indicted persons, they say that Geoffrey son of William Balle has made off on suspicion of theft and is suspected, so let him be exacted and outlawed. His chattels *3s.,* the sheriff to answer, and he was in Water Eaton tithing, which is in *mercy*.

439. Alexander Hog and his wife Isabel and Adam Hog, arrested on suspicion of theft, come and deny theft and all, and for good and ill put themselves on the country. The jurors say that they are not guilty, so they are quit.

THE HUNDRED OF HEYTESBURY COMES BY TWELVE

---

1 The manor of Chelworth came to have two serjeanties attached to it, one of providing a serjeant for the army, the other of keeping Braydon forest. In 1249 it was valued at £12 per annum, and was then held jointly by Hugh Peverel and Adam of Purton, who were also joint lords of the hundred. Peverel made a number of alienations from his portion. Adam died in 1266, leaving as his heirs his grandson Robert de Kaynes, lord of Tarrant Keynston, Dorset, and his daughters Isabel, widow of Robert de Welles, and Katherine, wife of John Paynel of Drax. Robert's wardship was granted to Robert Walerand later that year, with the custody of lands which included a quarter of Chelworth manor, valued at £4 1s.4½d. per annum. In 1274/5 Robert de Kaynes alone was said to be responsible for the forest serjeanty, which, however, went unmentioned in 1281 and 1289; in both those years the manor was valued at £30 per annum. *Book of Fees* ii, 1179, 1226; *Wiltshire crown pleas,* 1249, no. 61 and note; *CIPM* i no. 633; C 60/63 m. 4; *Rot. Hund.* ii, 270; JUST 1/1005/2 m. 120d; JUST 1/1011 m. 46d.

2 This entry has no margination, for no obvious reason.

3 The verb is in the singular, *habuit*, which is here treated as a mistake, but it may be that the intention was to refer only to the local man, not to the stranger.

440. A woman named Amice, a stranger, got herself into Hill Deverill church where she admitted theft and *abjured* the realm before the coroner. She had no chattels. Hill Deverill township did not arrest her, so it is in *mercy*.

441. Hugh the chaplain of Codford hanged himself in his house in Codford. John le Nywe, the first finder, comes and is not suspected, nor is anyone else. Judgement *suicide*. He had no chattels. Codford township took the dead body down and carried it out of the house into the field before it was viewed by the coroner (*in mercy*). And Ashton [Giffard], Sherrington and Boyton townships, with Philip le Ku, the coroner's clerk, and Adam of Codford, clerk,[1] in like manner buried the dead man without a coroner's view, so they are all are in *mercy*. The twelve jurors falsely presented that the coroner had held an inquest on the dead man, so they are in *mercy*. Knook township did not come to hold any inquest before the coroner, so it is in *mercy*.

442. William le Bor killed William Dunnyng in Ashton Giffard fields, and was later arrested and hanged before justices for gaol [delivery] etc. His chattels *10s. 6d.*, the sheriff to answer. Walter son of William le Bor, accused of that death, has made off and is suspected, so let him be *exacted and outlawed*. He had no chattels, but he was in Codford tithing, which is in *mercy*.

443. From W[illiam le Dun], sheriff, from the chattels of Robert le Malpe, hanged before justices for gaol [delivery] etc., *2s. 1d.*

444. Robert Gentyl of Pertwood wished to take a pledge from Roger of Puddletown, a shepherd, and a dispute having arisen between them, Robert Gentyl struck Roger with an arrow in the side so that he later died. Robert fled immediately after the deed and is suspected, so let him be *exacted and outlawed*. He had no chattels and was not in a tithing, but he was in the mainpast of Alexander of Pertwood, who is in *mercy*. Sutton, Bishopstrow,[2] Norton and Newnham townships did not come fully to the inquest, so they are in *mercy*. Let it be inquired of *Warminster* hundred concerning others who were present.[3]

445. John of Dartford got himself into Heytesbury church, where he admitted theft and *abjured* the realm before the coroner. He had no chattels and was not in a tithing because he was a stranger.

---

1 Adam appears in **360** as the sheriff's clerk, and it is possible that the scribe meant to indicate that he was acting in that capacity here, alongside the clerk of the coroner. But it is also possible, given his toponym, that he became involved in the concealment for no better reason than that Codford was where he lived.

2 Written as *Byssopeston* and faintly amended.

3 The entry is followed by a space of about two lines.

446.[1] (*Selkley*) Robert Edward, arrested for stealing sheep, comes and denies felony, theft[2] and all, and for good and ill puts himself on the country. The twelve jurors say on their oath that he is not guilty, so he is *quit*.

m. 36d (IMG 0460, 0461) *Continuing Heytesbury hundred*

447. Thomas le Kake intended to fish in the river Wylye, and Henry Grom came up and tried to take a pledge from him. Thomas tried to flee but Henry, catching up with him, struck him on the head with a pickaxe so that he died instantly. Henry fled immediately after the deed and is suspected, so let him be *exacted and outlawed*. He had no chattels and was not in a tithing, but he was received in 'Wattam Wyly', which is in *mercy*. Codford, Fisherton and Deptford townships did not come fully to the inquest, so they are in *mercy*.

448. Walter le Grom struck Robert le Hopere with an axe on the head so that he later died. Walter fled immediately after the deed and is suspected, so let him be *exacted and outlawed*. His chattels *1 mark*, the sheriff to answer, and he was in Chitterne tithing, which is in *mercy*. Boyton, East Corton and West Corton townships did not come fully to the inquest, so they are in *mercy*.

449. John the long of Tinhead struck John Eustace with an axe on the head on the head outside Tinhead township so that he later died. John the long fled immediately and is suspected, so let him be *exacted and outlawed*. He had no chattels but he was in Tinhead tithing in Whorwellsdown hundred, so it [the tithing] is in *mercy*. Imber, Chitterne and Ashton [Giffard] townships did not come fully to the inquest etc., so they are in *mercy*.

450. Richard of Leicester got himself into Horningsham church, where he admitted theft and *abjured* the realm before the coroner. He had no chattels and was not in a tithing because he was a stranger. Horningsham township did not arrest him when this happened in daytime, so it is in *mercy*.

451. James le Hyrde was leading a cart in Heytesbury fields when he was crushed to death by it. No one is suspected. Judgement *misadventure*. The value of the horse and cart *4s.*, the sheriff to answer.

452. Richard le Lestere and Roger de la More killed Robert Rudeman in Bishopstrow township and made off after the deed, so let them be arrested if they can be found. Richard's chattels *5s.*, the sheriff to answer. Roger's chattels *5s.*, the sheriff to answer. Later Richard and Roger came and they deny the death, felony and all, and for good and ill put themselves on the country. The twelve jurors of this hundred together with the jurors of Warminster hundred

---

1 The entry, written in two hands, has been added at the foot of the membrane. Below it, partly lost by trimming, are written *Catalla Ricardi Tylere, v s.'* and '*Catalla Ricardi*', apparently referring to **265**, above.

2 *furtum*, as against the usual *latrocinium*.

say on their oath that Richard and Roger are not guilty of the death, so they are quit. But they say that John Quintyn is guilty of it and has made off, so let him be exacted and outlawed. His chattels 2s., the sheriff to answer, and he was received in Warminster township, which is in *mercy*.

453. Concerning defaults, they say that John Mautravers, Ellis Owayn, John of Soley from Knook, Richard Syfrewast, William Leyr (poor)[1] and Henry Lyndeneys did not come here on the first day, so they are in *mercy*.

454. The jurors present that Knook township does not allow the king's bailiffs to levy debts to the king there. They also say that John Mautravers and Roger of Hinton likewise do not allow the king's bailiffs to enter their fees to make distraints, and they do not know by what warrant.[2] So to judgement.

455. Concerning suits withdrawn, they say that John Mautravers and Roger of Hinton and their men used to do suit to this hundred and now that suit has been withdrawn, by what warrant they do not know. So let this be *discussed*.

456. Concerning indicted persons, they say that John Goldhauek, Henry Pyfrey and William le Ballere have made off on suspicion of theft and are suspected, so let them be *exacted and outlawed*. William le Ballere's chattels 18d., the sheriff answer, and he was in Baycliff tithing, which is in *mercy*. John and [Henry][3] had no chattels, but they were in Great Horningsham tithing, which is in *mercy*.

457. Walter Turnepeny, Walter le Mul and Walter Orgaz, arrested on suspicion of theft, come and deny theft and all, and for good and ill put themselves on the country. The twelve jurors say that Walter and the others are not guilty, so they are quit.

THE HUNDRED OF WARMINSTER COMES BY TWELVE

458. As Hugh Bulymer was trying to catch a colt in the township of Rodden he was struck by the colt so that he died within a fortnight. No one is suspected. Judgement *misadventure*. The value of the colt (*deodand*) 4s., for which William Branche of Somersetshire is to answer because the accident happened in that county.[4]

---

1 Written above the name is *pp*, for *pauper*.

2 In 1242/3 John Maltravers and Thomas of Hinton (presumably Roger's father) held one knight's fee in Hill Deverill directly, and another half fee indirectly, from the earl of Gloucester. *Book of Fees* ii, 718, 724.

3 *Rogerus* is written in error, presumably taken from the preceding entry.

4 Since he died a fortnight after his fatal injury, Hugh was doubtless brought back into Wiltshire to die, explaining why his death was presented at the Wiltshire eyre. Rodden lay on the edge of Selwood forest just across the county boundary west of Warminster: *VCH Wiltshire* iv, 415–16. William Branche seems to have been

459. Isabel the widow of Ranulf Dunjoye appealed Hugh de la Forde in the county court of the death of her husband Ranulf, so that he was outlawed in the county court by Isabel's suit. He had no chattels and was not in a tithing because he was a stranger from overseas. It is testified by the coroners' rolls that Robert son of Hugh of Corsley came to the fourth county court and mainprised to have Hugh at the fifth county court and did not have him, so he is in *mercy*. Later it is testified that Hugh had chattels worth *3 marks*, of which Robert de Vernun is to answer for 2 marks and Hugh Puwyl and Walter le Clerk, who were with John,[1] for 1 mark. The sheriff answers for 1 mark.[2]

460. Two strangers were found killed in Norridge wood, having many wounds.[3] Robert Bayn, the first finder, has died. It is not known who killed them. No Englishry is presented. Judgement *murder*, upon the hundred. Warminster, Upton, Noridge and Great Corsley townships did not come fully to the inquest etc., so they are in *mercy*.

461. Roger Glendy of Wilton struck Adam Selyman with a knife in the stomach so that he died four days later. Roger fled immediately to Dinton church, admitted the deed and *abjured* the realm before the coroner. He had no chattels and was not in a tithing because he was a clerk. Dinton township did not arrest him, so it is in *mercy*. Teffont, Fisherton and Bapton townships did not come fully [to the inquest] etc., so they are in *mercy*.

462. John le Wyte struck his wife Denis with a sickle on the head so that she died instantly. Immediately after the deed he fled to Norton church, admitted the deed and *abjured* the realm before the coroner. His chattels 3s. 3d., the sheriff to answer, and he was in Bishopstrow tithing, which is in *mercy*. Middleton and Sutton [Veny] townships did not come fully [to the inquest] etc., so they are in *mercy*.

463. John son of Godfrey and Hugh son of Reynold de la More quarrelled together, and John struck Hugh with a pickaxe on the head so that he died instantly. John fled immediately after the deed and is suspected, so let him be *exacted and outlawed*. He had no chattels but was in Stockton tithing, so it is in *mercy*. Wylye 'Abbess' township did not come fully [to the inquest] etc., so it is in *mercy*.

---

involved in the keeping of Selwood forest: *CR 1268–1272*, 329, 333-4.

1 John has not been mentioned; he was presumably John de Vernun, the former sheriff for whose debts his son Robert was responsible.

2 The last sentence is added in a different hand, that of the writer of **466–7**, below.

3 It may have been for these deaths that Michael of Warminster was arrested, before being released to bail under an order issued around 7 November 1258. *CR 1256-1259*, 340-1.

464. Philip of Cranborne and William Bunye came from a tavern in Dinton, and a quarrel having arisen between them in that township's fields, Philip attacked William, who in self-defence struck Philip with an axe on the head so that he died four days later. William fled immediately after the deed and is suspected, so let him be *exacted and outlawed*. He had no chattels, but he was in Dinton tithing, which is in *mercy*. Compton township did not come fully [to the inquest] etc., so it is in *mercy*.

465. Martin of Shropshire fled to Boreham church, admitted that he was a thief and *abjured the realm* etc. He had no chattels and was not in a tithing because he was a stranger. Boreham township did not arrest him, so it is in *mercy*.

466.[1] Nicholas le Syur struck William the clerk of 'Wedmerelaund' with a staff in Warminister[2] township, and Ralph of Brockhurst similarly struck William with an axe on the head so that he died instantly. Immediately after the deed Nicholas fled to Manningford church, where he admitted the deed and *abjured* the realm before the coroner. He had no chattels but was in the mainpast of Robert Mauduyt, who is in *mercy*. And Ralph made off immediately after the deed and is suspected, so let him be *exacted and outlawed*. He had no chattels but was in the mainpast of the same Robert, who is in *mercy*. Warminster and Thoulstone townships did not come to the inquest, so they are in *mercy*.

467. Walter Aylwy encountered Walter Sturdy outside Cromhall wood with stolen withies and attacked him, striking him on the head with an axe so that he died instantly. Walter Aylwy fled immediately after the deed and is suspected, so let him be *exacted and outlawed*. He had no chattels but was in Little Sutton tithing, which is in *mercy*. Bugley township did not come to the inquest, so it is in *mercy*.

468. Hugh de Monte Acuto, the hayward of Peter Escudimor, struck William Halyman with an axe on the head so that he died. Immediately after the deed Hugh fled to Norridge church and *abjured* the realm etc. His chattels 4s., the sheriff to answer, and he was not in a tithing but was in the mainpast of Peter Escutemor, who is in *mercy*. Norridge township did not arrest him, so it is in *mercy*.[3]

469. Roger son of Alan of Durnford appealed John Doghet of Barford and

---

1 Entries **466** and **467**, and possibly the beginning of **468**, were written by another clerk in a perceptibly different hand.

2 Nicholas's taking sanctuary and abjuration are also recorded in **155**, above, where where he is said to have been in a tithing in Manningford and the death is apparently assumed to have happened in Manningford Abbots.

3 Peter de Scudamore was the son of Godfrey, sheriff of Wiltshire 1258-9, whose family gave its suffix to Upton Scudamore, the parish containing Norridge. On 2 June 1267 Adam de Greynville was appointed to inquire whether Hugh de Monte Acuto had killed William Haliman by misadventure. *CPR 1266-1272*, 135.

Walter le Butiller of Norton in the county court of wounding, robbery and breach of the king's peace. John and Walter do not come now. John was attached by Geoffrey de Chaucumbe and William of Berwick, and Walter by Henry of Tilshead, clerk, and Thomas of Sambourne, who are in *mercy*. Later it was testified that Roger has died. The jurors testify that they [the parties] were not agreed, but they say that they wounded Roger, so let them be arrested.

m. 37 (IMG 0381, 0382) *Continuing Warminster hundred*

470. John le Mur, miller of Cole Mill, appealed Ralph Crybbe of Sutton Mandeville and Robert Crybbe his brother in the county court of robbery, mayhem and breach of the king's peace, so that they were *outlawed* by his suit in the county court. They had no chattels and were in Sutton Mandeville tithing, which is in *mercy*.

471. John Tvyge of Chittterne appealed William of Henford, William Mete, William Muthe and Walter of Raesters[1] in the county court of wounding, robbery and breach of the king's peace. John does not come now, so let him be arrested, and his pledges for prosecuting are in *mercy*, namely Ralph Dygun and Reynold Grete of Bishopstrow. William and the others come. The jurors, asked if they [the parties] are agreed, say that they are not. They also say that Walter of Raesters is not guilty of that trespass, either in deed or in ordering it, so he is quit. They also say that William and the others beat and wounded John but took nothing from him in robbery, so let them be taken into *custody* for trespass. Later William of Henford came and made fine by 20s., pledges Thomas le Vineter of Warminster and David Durand. Later John came and made fine for himself and his pledges by ½ *mark*, pledge John Sprot. Later William [Mete] and William [Muthe] came and made fine by ½ *mark*, pledge David Duraund.

472. William Sunnepeny and Osbert Musard, arrested on suspicion of theft, come and deny theft and all, and for good and ill put themselves on the country. The jurors say that they are not guilty, so they are quit.

473. Concerning wines sold, they say that Richard le Nedlere has sold wine contrary to the assize, so he is in *mercy*.

474. Concerning indicted persons, they say that Stephen le Bloys of Upton and Walter le Butiller have made off on suspicion of theft and are suspected, so let them be *exacted and outlawed*. They had no chattels and were not in a tithing, but were paupers wandering through the country.

475. Concerning defaults they say that Peter at 'la Were' of Winterbourne,

---

1 After Walter's name that of William of Henford is repeated in error and struck through.

John de la Stane, John de Wateley, Roger Waspay and Ellis de la Mare did not come here on the first day. So they are in *mercy*.

THE BOROUGH OF WILTON COMES BY TWELVE

476. John Wynegod was arrested on suspicion of theft and imprisoned in Wilton township, and he escaped from prison to St Mary's church in Brede Street, where he admitted theft and abjured the realm etc. He had no chattels. Because he escaped from the township's custody, and there is only one prison in Wilton, to judgement for the *escape* on the whole township of Wilton, and be it known that there are eight aldermanries in Wilton.[1]

477. Nicholas le Wryke was likewise arrested and imprisoned in the same place, and he escaped from prison to St Michael's church and abjured the realm. He had no chattels. So to judgement for the *escape* as before.

478. Adam Plukerose got himself into St Peter's church in South Street, where he admitted theft and *abjured* the realm. His chattels *3s.*, the bishop of Salisbury[2] to answer.

479. Laurence the chaplain of Bristol and his servant Adam were lodged in the house of John le Croy in Wilton, and a dispute having arisen between them as they were together in a single chamber, Adam struck Laurence with an axe on the head so that he died instantly. Adam was immediately arrested, drawn and hanged.[3] His chattels *2s.*, the sheriff to answer.

480. Roger son of William le May struck Robert Cotele with a stone on the head so that he later died. Roger fled immediately after the deed and is suspected, so let him be *exacted and outlawed*. He had no chattels. The township did not arrest him, so it is in mercy.

481. An unknown woman, a stranger, was found killed in Wilton township outside Bulbridge. William Cappe, the first finder, has died. Later it was testified that she was called Maud, wife of Stephen of Bristol, and that William of Oxford killed her and was arrested and hanged immediately after the deed. His chattels *3s*, the sheriff to answer.

482. Austin of Ringwood burgled Ringwood church, where he took most of the wax.[4] He was later arrested at Wilton and imprisoned there, and he

---

1 The name is followed by a dash and the beginning of a letter erased.

2 'sheriff' is struck through

3 By killing his master Adam had committed petty treason and therefore suffered the prescribed penalty, being drawn - dragged by a horse along the ground - to the gallows, where he was hanged.

4 Ringwood is in south-west Hampshire, on the edge of the New Forest. Neither

escaped from that prison and fled to St. Mary's church in Salisbury and *abjured* the realm etc. He had no chattels. So to judgement for the *escape* upon Wilton township.

483. Robert le Duk appealed William le Feure of Wilton of wounding, beating and breach of the king's peace. Robert does not come now, so let him be arrested, and his pledges for prosecuting are in *mercy*, namely Richard Ryly and the other pledge has died. William comes and the jurors testify that they [the parties] are not agreed, but they say that they fought together and that William is not guilty as appealed, so he is quit. And the twelve jurors did not mention this appeal, so they are in *mercy*.

484. Concerning cloths sold contrary to the assize, [they say] that Richard le Agoyller and Walter le Mercer have sold cloths contrary to the assize, so they are in *mercy*.

485. Concerning wines sold, they say that Richard le Agoyller, Peter of Barford, John Isembert, Reynold of Bedford, Roger Dalerun[1] and Thomas the merchant have sold wines contrary to the assize, so they are in *mercy*.

THE BOROUGH OF MARLBOROUGH COMES BY TWELVE

486. Two strangers were lodged at the house of William Belami in Marlborough, and they killed William's wife Joan at night and carried off the goods found there. It is not known who they were.

487. John le Webbe of Blunsdon was arrested on suspicion of theft, and he was being led towards Salisbury castle prison by William de la Welle, William son of Henry, John Silverlok and William de Holonde and the whole tithing of Blunsdon St. Andrew in Highworth hundred, when he escaped from their custody. So to judgement of the *escape* upon Blunsdon tithing aforesaid. John fled and is suspected, so let him be *exacted and outlawed*. His chattels and tithing are unknown because he was a stranger.

488. Robert Corbyn of Ireland got himself into St. Mary's church in Marlborough, where he admitted theft and *abjured* the realm before the coroner. He had no chattels and was not in a tithing because he was a stranger.

489. Richard le Blund of Ogbourne and William of Gloucester wounded Robert le Knave in the king's street in Marlborough so that he later died. Richard le Blund[2] fled immediately after the deed and is suspected, so let him be *exacted and outlawed*. He had no chattels and was not in a tithing, but he was in the mainpast of the master of St. John's hospital in Marlborough, who is

---

Austin nor his crime was mentioned at the 1272 Hampshire eyre.

1 The name has been struck through.

2 The clerk has written *le Bolde*, clearly in error for *le Blund*.

in *mercy*. And William was arrested for the deed and hanged at Marlborough. He had no chattels. The aldermanry of John de Grey in the marsh, where this was done, did not arrest Richard, so it is in *mercy*.

490. Adam son of Richard of Winchester was arrested for theft committed at the house of Isaac the Jew and imprisoned in the prison of Marlborough borough. He escaped from prison to St. Mary's church in Marlborough, admitted the deed and *abjured* the realm. He had no chattels, and was in the aldermanry of William the smith in The Green, which is in *mercy*. John of Rockley the elder, accused of that theft, has made off and is suspected, so let him be *exacted and outlawed*. He had no chattels, and was in the same aldermanry, which is in *mercy*. Because Adam escaped from the township's prison, to judgement for the *escape* upon Marlborough township.

m. 37d (IMG 0462, 0463) *Continuing Marlborough*

491. John Turgys, a five-year-old boy, and Roger son of Robert le Taylur, a four-year-old, were playing together, and John shot Roger with a spindle and gave him a small wound on the head. Roger later became ill when a sickness came upon him, and died within a month . No one is suspected of the death. Judgement *misadventure*. John was seen in court and is under age, namely aged six.

492. Joan Dru, her daughter Maud and Christian Duge, arrested for stealing a strong-box which belonged to the king of France's messenger, come and deny theft, felony and all, and for good and ill put themselves on the country. The jurors say on their oath that Joan and the others are not guilty of stealing the strong-box or of any other evildoing, so they are quit.

493. Ralph son of Pycot[1] of Flexburgh and William Trypper of Marlborough, arrested on the indictment of Clarice Quintyn for the death of her brother James, and Everard de la Dene, likewise arrested on the indictment of Melida de St. Quintin for the death of her husband Richard de St. Quintin, come and deny the deaths, felonies and all, and for good and ill put themselves on the country. The jurors of Selkley hundred, together with the jurors of this borough, say on their oath that Ralph and William are not guilty of the death of James, nor is Everard guilty of the death of Richard, so they are quit.

494. Cecily the widow of Walter le Vacher appealed Reynold Wace and Robert le Frankeleyn in the county court of the death of her husband Walter. Later it is testified that this appeal was by royal writ sent before the justices of the Bench and determined there. So nothing of it here.[2]

---

1 Literally *Pycoteri*, but the faintness of the 'er' suspension mark suggests that it was written in error, and that the clerk tried to delete it.

2 The entry has in the margin the sign for an amercement, which has been struck through. The second sentence is partly written over a deletion, whose content

495. The jurors present that St. Mary's and St. Peter's churches in Marlborough used to be in the king's gift and are now in the gift of the bishop and dean of Salisbury.[1] William of Reading holds St. Mary's by gift of the dean of Salisbury, and it is worth 40s. Thomas of Marlborough holds St. Peter's by the king's gift, the see of Salisbury being vacant,[2] and it is worth 46s. 8d., and they do not know by what warrant. So let this to be discussed.

496. The jurors present that Henry Funtayne holds a plot of land which was formerly Ellis Cullebukke's, having escheated through felony, and he renders 1d. a year to the king, and it is worth *6d.* a year more. They also say that Thomas de la Grene holds a messuage which was William the baker's, having escheated through felony, and he renders 5d. a year to the king, and it is worth 19d. a year (*14d.*). They also say that Roger son of Adam holds a quarter virgate[3] of land, having escheated for lack of an heir to the fee which was formerly Thomas le Ludde's, and he renders 2d. a year to the king, and it is worth 6d. a year. They say also that William the smith holds half an enclosed plot of land[4] as an escheat from the same fee, and he renders 3½d. a year to the king, and it is worth 7d. a year. They also say that Richard son of Adam holds half an enclosed plot of land as an escheat from the same fee, and he renders 4d. a year to the king, and it is worth 8d. a year. They also say that Thomas Bruton holds a quarter virgate of land as an escheat from the same fee, and he renders 2d. a year to the king, and it is worth 4d. a year. They also say that Walter of Ramsbury holds a messuage which was formerly Eustace le Hattere's as an escheat through felony, and he renders 4½d. a year to the king, and it is worth 12d. more. They also say that Gillian Wodevol holds half an enclosed plot of land as an escheat from the aforesaid fee, and she renders 4d. a year to the king, and it is worth 4d. a year more. They also say that Gillian who the widow of Adam de la Rivere holds half an enclosed plot of land as an escheat for want of an heir, and she renders 5d. a year to the king and 12d. a year to the hospital of St. John, and it is worth 4d. a year more.

They also say that the holders of those escheats have hitherto paid their rents to the king's farmers and the keepers of his castle. But they hold them by permission of the farmers.[5]

---

presumably gave rise to the amercement which was later cancelled.

1 It was a long time since the Marlborough churches had been in the king's gift. Included in Bishop Osmund's endowment of Old Salisbury cathedral in 1091, they were confirmed to the diocese by Henry II in 1158. In 1255 St Mary's was valued at 10 marks per annum, St Peter's at £5. W.H.R. Jones (ed.), *The register of St Osmund*, 2 vols (Rolls Series, 1883-4), i, 199, 205. *Rot. Hund.* ii, 235.

2 The see was vacant from 13 December 1262 to 10 April 1263.

3 *quarteronem*, here and later in the entry.

4 *dimidiam wrthiam*, here and later in the entry.

5 This group of properties in Marlborough was also the subject of an inquest in 1256

497. Concerning wines sold, they say that Nicholas de Hampton, William the vintner and Ralph the marshal have sold wines contrary to the assize, so they are in *mercy*.

498. Concerning cloths sold, they say that William Delbowe and Gilbert Tryppe, drapers, have bought and sold cloths in breach of the assize so they are in *mercy*.

499. Concerning purprestures, they say that Richard of Alton holds a purpresture at 'Raenildewelle' which he took from Richard, constable of John de Mycegros,[1] and he pays the king 1d. It is a nuisance to its neighbours..

500. From William, son and heir of Stephen Fromund,[2] for the chattels of Eustace Baron, hanged, which his father Stephen took, 2s. 2d.

501. Adam son of Walter de la Dene, Agnes of Rockley and Edith Curteys, arrested on suspicion of theft and of harbouring thieves, come and deny theft and all, and for good and ill put themselves on the country. The jurors of this borough, together with the jurors of the Barton, say on their oath that Adam and Agnes and Edith are not guilty, so they are quit.

502. The jurors present that whereas the king had granted the bishop of Salisbury two fairs a year at Ramsbury and Sherborne in return for abolishing the market at Ramsbury, which was detrimental to the king, the bishop nevertheless holds that market on Sunday[3], causing greater damage and loss to the king, and to Marlborough borough and Hungerford and Bedwyn townships. So let this be *discussed*.

---

and a presentment at the 1281 eyre. There was no consistency in the number of holdings listed, or in the details provided concerning them, and only a few can be identified with any confidence from one record to another, suggesting that they changed hands frequently. In 1281 it was stated that the escheats were held on terms arranged by a former constable of Marlborough castle, following an inquest held on Henry III's orders. The justices ordered the bailiffs of Marlborough to answer to the crown for the rents in future, and nothing was said of them in 1289. E.A. Fry (ed.), *Abstracts of Wiltshire Inquisitiones Post Mortem, Henry III, Edward I and Edward II* (Index Library 37, 1908), 20; JUST 1/1005/2 m. 158d.

1 John de Mucegros became keeper or constable of Marlborough castle after the civil war and was replaced by Roger de Cheyne on 20 November 1267. Richard was evidently his deputy.

2 Keeper of Marlborough castle from July 1255 to March 1261, Stephen Fromund died in 1266, before 4 November. *CPR 1247-1258*, 418; *CPR 1258-1266*, 144; C 60/63 m. 7; *CPR 1266-1272*, 2.

3 For these fairs see **390** above, and note. The grant was in fact of two fairs at Ramsbury, and a third at Sherborne.

THE TOWNSHIP OF THE BARTON COMES BY SIX

503. Walter le Brode of Richardson made off because of the death of Walter Senglegeke and is suspected of it, so let him be *exacted and outlawed*. He had no chattels but was in Richardson tithing, which is in *mercy*.

504. From the heir of Stephen Fromund,[1] for the chattels of Edith wife of the said Walter [le Brode], which Stephen received, *5s.*

505. Richard Pycot was found killed in the warren outside Marlborough. The first finder has died. John le Hurd, accused of the death, has made off and is suspected, so let him be *exacted and outlawed*. He had no chattels but was in the tithing of William le Webbe of Manton, which is in *mercy*.

506. Roger son of Roger de la Penne and his brother James encountered John Caperun outside Rockley township, and a quarrel having arisen between them Roger killed John. Roger and James were arrested and imprisoned, and later before justices for gaol delivery etc. they were delivered to the bishop of Salisbury as clerks. The jurors presented no finder, so they are in *mercy*.

507. Thomas of the wood from Standen, Simon le Glover of Bedwyn and William of the wood from Standen were found killed on the road near Puthall. Everard de Putte, the first finder, comes and is not suspected. It is not known who killed them. No Englishry [is presented]. Judgement *murder*, upon Barton township.

508. Ralph Pycot appealed Robert of Hampton in the county court of mayhem, beating, robbery and breach of the king's peace etc. He comes now and does not sue against him using the words of an appeal, but says in complaint that on the Sunday next after the feast of the Annunciation of the blessed Mary in the 44th year [28 March 1260] he inflicted a wound on him through the middle of his arm, whereby he is maimed, and took 6d from him.

    Robert comes and denies mayhem, robbery and all, and asks that it be allowed him that he [Ralph] does not now sue against him in the words of an appeal, and with this allowed him he asks that the truth be inquired into by the country. Because Ralph does not sue against him in the proper manner it is decided that his appeal is null, whereby etc. The jurors say that they fought together, and that Robert wounded him in self defence, but he took nothing from him in robbery. So let Robert be taken into custody for trespass and let Ralph be taken into custody for a false appeal.[2]

509. Deulegard the Jew of Marlborough was outlawed in the county court for forging money. He had no chattels.

---

1 For Stephen Fromund see **500** above, and note.

2 There is an illegible abbreviation in the margin.

m. 38 (IMG 0383, 0384) Continuing the pleas of the crown at Wilton

THE HUNDRED OF DUNWORTH COMES BY TWELVE

510. The jurors present that about the feast of St. Thomas the Apostle in the 41st year [21 December 1256] Thomas son of Gervase bathed in a lead cistern in Donhead township and was drowned. No one is suspected. Judgement misadventure. The value of the cistern *2s. deodand*, the sheriff to answer. Be it known that the townships did not come to hold inquests as they should do, namely Donhead, Charlton, Coombe and 'Ersgrove', so they are in *mercy*.

511. The jurors present that about the feast of St. Peter in Chains in the 41st year [1 August 1257] in Donhead township William le Kute passed above the pond of William de Chirchmulle's mill and fell into the water, to be crushed under the mill's outer wheel so that he died immediately. No one is suspected. William de Chirchmulle, the first finder, comes and is not suspected. Judgement misadventure. The value of the wheel *12d. deodand*, the sheriff to answer.

512. The jurors present that on the Thursday next before the feast of St. Thomas the Apostle in the 44th year [18 December 1259] Thomas son of Walter was crossing a plank and fell into the water and was drowned. No one is suspected. Judgement misadventure. Berwick St Leonard, Fonthill Giffard, Hatch and Semley townships did not come [to the inquest], so they are in *mercy*.

513. And Tisbury and Chicksgrove townships did not come to hold inquests on the death of Alice Hender, so they are in *mercy*.

514. John Maheu[1] fled to Tisbury church and abjured the realm before William le Droes, the coroner. [His] chattels *6d.*, the sheriff to answer, and he was in Tisbury tithing, which is in *mercy*.

515. Swallowcliffe and Donhead townships did not come to hold an inquest on the death of William the ploughman, so they are in *mercy*.

516. William the goldsmith of Wilton struck William Puttepeyn with a pickaxe on the head in Chilmark township, so that he died three days later. He fled immediately. At the same township's fair[2] a stranger struck Richard

---

1 John Maheu's subsequent return, arrest and summary execution were recorded at the 1281 Wiltshire eyre. He was probably killed in 1276. JUST 1/1005/2 m. 122. R.B. Pugh (ed.), *Wiltshire gaol deliveries and trailbaston trials, 1275-1306* (Wiltshire Record Society 33, 1978 for 1977), no. 76.

2 No formal grant is known of a fair at Chilmark. The manor was held by Wilton Abbey from before the Norman Conquest, but in 1265 the sheriff accounted to the exchequer for 'pleas of Chilmark fair' from the morrow of the feast of St Margaret (21 July), she being the parish's patronal saint. E 389/137 m. 13.

Wyneman with a pickaxe on the head so that he died on the following Monday. He fled immediately. Judgement felony. Let William the goldsmith be *exacted and outlawed. Let his chattels be inquired of in Wilton,* and his tithing.

517. Peter of Bemerton was digging in Fonthill quarry, and a stone fell on him so that he died instantly. No one is suspected. Judgement misadventure. The value of the stone *1d.* (*deodand*), the sheriff to answer.

518. Concerning defaults, they say that[1] John son of Hugh of Ludwell, William Hendiman, Eustace Stoggy, William the forester, John le Despenser, John le Gentyl of Hatch, Robert of Hatch, Roger son of Pain, Ralph de Chaluns, Robert Mauduyt, Margery de Cantilupo, John de Furneis, Simon of Crowcombe, William of Bridzor, the abbess of St. Edward [Shaftesbury], Thomas de Chaluns, Bartholomew Turpin, Roger of Garston, Roger Kusyn, William Ernald, Thomas Ernalde and Adam Mydywynter are in good health and did not come on the first day, so they are in *mercy.*

THE HUNDRED OF KNOYLE COMES BY TWELVE

519. The jurors present that in the 46th year [1261–2] malefactors came to the house of Roger Hulloke, where they found William Balleheuede, the shepherd of John of Lussleigh, and they beat and wounded him and carried off what was found in the house, so that Roger raised the hue. The bailiff of Knoyle held an inquest on the robbery by which Henry the smith was[2] indicted. He fled and is suspected, and he was dwelling in Brixton Deverill[3] in Heytesbury hundred, so let it be *inquired* of that hundred about his chattels and tithing. And let Henry be *exacted and outlawed.* William le Flemenge, indicted of the same robbery, was arrested and hanged before justices assigned to gaol delivery. Let it be *inquired* of the same hundred about his chattels.

John Turbut, accused of that robbery, puts himself for good and ill on the country. The jurors say on their oath that John is not guilty of any evildoing, so he is *quit.*

Hindon and Fonthill Bishops townships do not come as they ought to do, so they are in *mercy.*

William the carpenter, accused of that robbery, has made off and is not suspected, so let him return to the peace. He had no chattels.

John Argaz and Richard Batecoke, accused of that robbery, put themselves on the country for good and ill. The jurors say on their oath that they are not guilty of any evildoing, so they are *quit.*

520. On the Thursday after the feast of All Saints in the 47th year [2 November

---

1 The introductory words *De defaltis dicunt quod* are added in the margin.

2 The verb is in the plural, referring to those named later.

3 The name reads 'Hytricheston', but no such place is recorded in Heytesbury hundred, and except for its capital letter the form is in perfect accord with other thirteenth-century spellings of Brixton Deverill. *PNS*, 165.

1262] Michael Purhoke and John Maheu came to the house of Agatha in Knoyle and [ ]¹ her, burgled the house, and thievishly carried off her goods and chattels. They fled and are suspected. The township did not pursue them, so it is in *mercy*. Michael was in Upton tithing, which is in *mercy*. [He had] *no chattels*. John Maheu fled to [Tisbury] church and abjured the realm, as appears in Dunworth² hundred. Let Michael be *exacted and outlawed*.

521. John of Bradley, John de Stapele and Michael son of Walter Purhog stole the tackle³ of two nuns of Shaftesbury in the bishop of Winchester's wood, and the nuns' servant, with the neighbouring townships and the hue raised, followed them to Knoyle, where the thieves, overcome by fear, threw away the tackle in Walter de la Forbure's curtilage. He comes and is not suspected, so he is quit. The thieves fled and are suspected. John of Bradley was later hanged before justices assigned to gaol delivery. John de Stapele and Michael were in the tithing of Nicholas le Ster in Upton, which is in *mercy*. Let them be *exacted and outlawed*. [They had] no chattels. John of Bradley was in Bradley tithing, which is in *mercy*.

522. William son of Shuna⁴ struck Godfrey Croke with a staff on the head so that he died instantly in Hindon township. He fled immediately and is suspected, so let him be *exacted and outlawed*. [He had] no chattels and was in the tithing of Robert Bruning of Fonthill Bishop, which is in *mercy*. Hindon township did not arrest him, so it is in *mercy*. No Englishry is presented. Judgement *murder*, upon the hundred.

523. Walter the smith of Fonthill Bishop met with John le Mouner, and as they played at wrestling they both fell so that John was wounded by an arrow which he had under his belt, so that he died next day. Walter fled immediately. Fonthill Bishop township did not arrest him, so it is in *mercy*. The jurors say that they were not wrestling in any spirit of evil intent, nor was there any previous quarrel between them, but by misadventure John fell and was wounded as they played. So let this be *discussed with the king*. Walter's chattels *8s.*, the bishop of Winchester to answer.

524. Richard, the rector of Fonthill church, was sleeping in his hall at the evening hour, and his servant William le Goggere <struck>⁵ him with an

---

1 A word appears to be omitted here, perhaps 'bound', since there is nothing to suggest homicide.

2 Above, **514**.

3 *harnesium*, meaning equipment for horses.

4 *Shune* is clearly written; it may be a surname, as in **527** below, the forename being omitted, rather than an unusual female given name.

5 Part of the membrane has been torn away, and angle brackets in this and the following entries indicate missing words.

axe[1] on the head so that he died instantly, and fled immediately. So let him be *exacted and outlawed*. He had <no> chattels. Fonthill township neither arrested him nor pursued him, so it is in mercy. Walter son of Evelotta, the first <finder>, comes and is not suspected, nor is anyone else.[2] He was not in a tithing.

525. <John . . .>yard, accused of the theft of horses and mares and of other evildoings, comes and puts himself for good and ill <on the country>. The jurors say on their oath that John is guilty of the theft of horses and mares and of <other> evildoing, so he has judgement [i.e. hanged]. Inquire about his chattels from Salisbury.

526. <Stephen> Hardinge, accused of burgling the house of Agatha of Upton and robbing the same,[3] comes and puts himself for good and ill <on> the country. The jurors say on their oath that Stephen is not guilty of any evildoing. So he is quit. The jurors are in mercy for concealment.

527. Roger Pavele of Deverill, who appealed Walter Coc of Fonthill and Alexander the shoemaker of Tisbury together with William Shune[4] of the death of his brother Godfrey Croke, withdrew in the county court. So let him be taken into custody, and his pledges for prosecuting, namely John Swotinge of Bishopstrow and David Duraunt of Sutton, are in *mercy*. The jurors testify that Walter and Alexander are not guilty of that death, so let them return safe.

528. The jurors present that the bishop of Winchester did not come before the justices on the first day, so he is in *mercy*.[5]

m. 38d (IMG 0464, 0465) *Continuing the crown [pleas] at Wilton, 52nd year*

THE HUNDRED OF MERE COMES BY TWELVE

529. John son of Roger le Mulnere struck John son of Geoffrey the smith with a staff on the head, so that he fell and died that same day at Maiden Bradley

---

1 *securis*, as distinct from the more usual *hachia*, hatchet.

2 The words 'nor is anyone else' – *nec aliquis alius* – have been struck through. Appropriately used in many cases of accidental death, the clerk presumably wrote them down automatically following the appearance of the first finder, and then drew a line through them after noticing his error.

3 Probably the same incident recorded in **520** above.

4 Presumably the man outlawed in **522** above.

5 John Gervase, bishop of Winchester, was in no position to attend the opening of the eyre, as he was in Italy at the time, having been suspended from office for his support of the barons during the civil wars, and died there on 19 or 20 January 1268. C.L. Kingsford, rev. Nicholas Vincent, 'Gervase, John (*d.* 1268)', *ODNB* xxi, 971-2.

fair.[1] He fled immediately and is suspected, so let him be *exacted and outlawed*. Bradley township did not arrest him, so it is in *mercy*. [He had] no chattels and was not in a tithing because he was from Flintford in Somersetshire. Stourton, Zeals, Bradley and Kingston townships did not [come] to hold the inquest as they should do, so they are in *mercy*.

530. Unknown malefactors [who] were in Conrish park[2] shot Philip le Parker with an arrow so that he died three days later and fled immediately. The townships came to hold the inquest but it could not be inquired [who] they were.

531. Edith Husful, accused of burning the house of Walter of the marsh, was arrested, and when she was to have been put in the stocks she slit her stomach with her own knife, so that she died three days later. Judgement suicide. [Her] chattels *12d.*, the sheriff to answer. No one else is suspected.

532. Walter le Turnur, his brother Nicholas and Jokyn the thresher quarrelled together, and Jokyn struck Walter on the head with a Danish axe in Stourton township [so that he died]. He fled immediately and is suspected, so let him be *exacted and outlawed*. Stourton township did not arrest him, so it is in *mercy*. Mere, Zeals, Kingston and Stourton townships did not come [to the inquest] as they ought to do. He was in the tithing of Robert Harpur of Stourton, which is in *mercy*.[3] Walter's brother Nicholas comes and is not suspected, so he is quit.

533. Richard the oxherd and William Duelye quarrelled, and Richard struck William on the head with an axe outside Dinton township so that he died three days later in Kingston Deverill township. He fled immediately and is suspected, so let him be *exacted and outlawed*. [His] chattels *2s.*, the sheriff to answer, and he was in the tithing of Roger Horner of Kingston, which is in *mercy*.

534. Roger Buke greased the cogs of the inner wheel of Stourton mill, and by misadventure the wheel crushed[4] him so that he died instantly. The value of the wheel *12d.*, the sheriff to answer. *Deodand*. No one is suspected.

---

1 Maiden Bradley fair was probably held on 14 May

2 Conrish is in Mere parish, and the park is likely to have belonged to Richard, earl of Cornwall, to whom Mere was granted on 25 December 1243. *CChR 1226-1257*, 276.

3 The townships which failed to come may have been in mercy along with the tithing.

4 The verb used is *contero* rather than the more usual *opprimo*.

535. Zeals tithing did not come on the first day before the justices. John of Holtby did not come,[1] nor the king of Germany.[2] So they are in *mercy*.

536. Walter of Hinton, accused of thefts and evildoing, puts himself for good and ill on the country. The jurors say on their oath that he is not guilty of any evildoing, so he is *quit*.

537. John le Graunt, accused of thefts and evildoing, puts himself for good or ill on the country, and the jurors say that he is not guilty, so he is *quit*.

538. The jurors did not present that John of Horsepool appealed John Galun of the death of his brother William of Horsepool, by which appeal John Galun was outlawed. So they are in *mercy* for concealment.

THE TOWNSHIP OF LONGBRIDGE DEVERILL COMES BY SIX

539. The jurors present that malefactors came at night to the house of John le Crockere in Raesters, burgled it and killed John and his wife. For which Walter Turnepeny of Knoyle and his wife Gillian and Nicholas le Heringmongere of S<...>ton,[3] arrested on suspicion of the deaths, previously came before justices assigned to gaol delivery, put themselves on the country and were quit. Henry Pefrei, Henry son of Thomas Pefrey and Joan Colette of Horningsham, accused of the deaths, do not come and are suspected, so let them be *exacted and outlawed* and let Joan be *waived*. No Englishry was presented. Judgement *murder*, upon the manor. Henry Pefrey's chattels *18s. 6d.*, Robert the son and heir of John de Vernun to answer. William Drueis the coroner did not make inquiry about the chattels, so he is in *mercy*. Henry son of Thomas and Joan had no chattels. Henry Pefrey and Henry son of Thomas were in the tithing of John de la Funteyne, which is in *mercy*. Horningsham township did not arrest them, so it is in *mercy*.

540. The jurors present that the abbot of Glastonbury, Hugh the black and John Turbut did not come on the first day before the justices. John Turbut was mainprised by Geoffrey Husee, who freely admitted that he mainprised him, and William of Whitecliff, Robert le Swon and Hugh le Neir likewise mainprised John. So they are in *mercy*.[4]

m. 39 (IMG 0385, 0386) *Continuing the crown [pleas] at Wilton*

---

1 John had been granted quittance from attendance at this eyre around 22 November 1267. *CR 1264-1268*, 494-5.

2 i.e. Richard earl of Cornwall; see **142** above, and note.

3 Reading uncertain.

4 The entry is followed by the word *Jur[atores]* ('The jurors'), clearly intended to be the first in another entry. A space of about 18 lines occupies the remainder of the membrane.

THE FOREIGN HUNDRED OF CHIPPENHAM WITH THE
TOWNSHIP OF CHIPPENHAM COME BY TWENTY-FOUR
BECAUSE THEY USED ALWAYS TO ANSWER THUS[1]

541. The jurors present that one William of Liddington came with a horse
to a wine-store at Sherston on a Sunday before the feast of the translation
of St. Thomas the Martyr in the 40th year [June or July[2] 1256]. One Peter
Daniel and Richard of Wick, then bailiff of Sherston manor, arrested and
imprisoned him, but he escaped from prison and fled towards the church.
Brito[3] le Porter, seeing this, tried to arrest him, and William took Brito's knife
and dealt him three wounds, whereupon Martin Tropinel came and arrested
him. William fatally wounded Martin, and was then straightway arrested and
in full court before the bailiff of sir [deleted] Mathias Besille[4] he was hanged
by judgement of the court, because he admitted theft and having wounded
Martin so that he died. [His] chattels a horse worth *20s.*, two oxen worth
14s., Mathias Besille to answer. Roger son of Edith owed him [William]
2s., the sheriff to answer, and Peter Daniel owed him *22s. 4½d.*, Richard le
Neuman, tithingman[5] of Sopworth, to answer. Likewise he had *100 sheep*
and *32 quarters of oats* in Runnington in Somersetshire, sown on the land of
John of Easton. So let John be distrained to come to answer for those chattels,
valued at 100s. (*To be discussed in Somersetshire.*)

Because the said court executed judgement on William on suspicion of
theft and for a man's death, which it could not do without justices assigned
to this, let the liberty be taken in the king's hand. And let the court come by
four men etc. on *Monday*. The sheriff is ordered to have the case recorded in
that court etc. and to have the record etc. Richard le Neuman, tithingman of
Sopworth, did not come and did not have the money, so he is in *mercy*. The
jurors are in *mercy* for presenting the tithingman of Sopworth falsely. Sherston,
Easton, Luckington and Alderton townships did not come sufficiently to hold
the inquest on Martin's death, so they are in *mercy*.[6]

---

1 Chippenham's privileged status as a borough led to its being distinguished from the
rest of the hundred – the 'foreign' hundred – to which it gave its name and with
which it originally formed a single administrative unit.

2 The date is not precise: the MS. has *quadam die dominica*.

3 *Breton'*. On the second occurrence, *Brito*.

4 The manor of Sherston was granted for life to Sir Mathias Besille, or Bezill, in
December 1240. A courtier and soldier who became Queen Eleanor's household
steward, Bezill tried to make his tenure of Sherston hereditary, but seemingly
without success. M. Ray, 'Three alien household stewards in thirteenth-century
England', M. Prestwich, R. Britnell and R. Frame (eds.), *Thirteenth-Century England*
x (Woodbridge, 2005), 51–67, at 56–7.

5 *dicenarius*, here and later in the entry, once as *dicennarium*. Richard's name is written
above that of Mathias, which is struck through.

6 Between this entry and the next there is a space of about 12 lines.

542. Ralph Shenne by night struck Walter Shene on the head with a staff at Lacock so that he later died. He fled immediately and is suspected, so let him be *exacted and outlawed*. [His] chattels 2s. 4d., the sheriff to answer. Lacock township did not arrest him, so it is in *mercy*. He was in the tithing of John le Net of Lacock, which is in *mercy*. Lacock township . . .[1]

543. Alexander of Dean struck John the miller on the head with a hammer in Avon mill in Bremhill manor, so that he died instantly. He fled immediately and is suspected, so let him be *exacted and outlawed*. He was dwelling outside a tithing in Bremhill for half a year, so the township is in *mercy*, and also because it did not arrest him. [He had] no chattels. No Englishry is presented. Judgement *murder*, upon the foreign hundred.

544. Walter Lesye was pursued from the park of the king of Germany in Corsham[2] to Box church, and he admitted the theft of three fawns and other evildoing and *abjured* the realm before the coroner. [His] chattels 1½d., the sheriff to answer.

545. John de Anesy, a beggar, was lodged at Thomas of Woodford's house in an old building, half of which fell on him so that he died instantly. No one is suspected. Judgement *misadventure*. The value of the building 2s. *deodand*, the sheriff to answer.

546. Peter Daniel struck William le Deveneis with a knife in Sopworth township so that he died three days later. He fled and is suspected. He had no chattels. Sopworth township did not arrest him, so it is in *mercy*. He was in the tithing of Richard le Neuman, which is in *mercy*. Much later he was arrested at Heytesbury and hanged before justices assigned to gaol delivery.

547. John Ive deliberately[3] drowned himself in the river[4] Were in Wraxall township. Judgement suicide. [His] chattels 25 acres of sown land, valued at 18d. each. Total 37s. 6d., Geoffrey of Wraxall to answer.[5] No Englishry was presented. Judgement *murder*, upon the hundred.[6] Wraxall, Slaughterford, Biddestone and Yatton townships [are] in *mercy* because they did not come

---

1 The entry breaks off incomplete.

2 The manor of Corsham was given by Henry III to his brother Richard, earl of Cornwall, on 9 March 1242; the grant was confirmed in detail on 25 December 1243. *CR 1237-1242*, 400; *CChR 1226-1257*, 276.

3 *gratis*.

4 *ripario*. In earlier entries the word for river is *aqua*.

5 The sentence about the total is an addition, partly interlined.

6 At first sight this second judgement seems an aberration, as inconsistent with the judgement of suicide. But it may have been justified by suicide having been a self-inflicted felony.

to hold the inquest as they should. The [king's] year and waste *15s.*, Geoffrey of Wraxall to answer.

548. A stranger was found killed by another stranger on the king's highway from Binsey, outside Biddestone township. William Stephen, the first finder, does not come, so John of the spring and Henry Herlewyn are in *mercy* as his pledges. He is not suspected. Biddestone, Allington, Hartham and 'Henton' townships did not come to hold the inquest, so they are in *mercy*. No Englishry is presented. Judgement *murder*, upon the hundred.

549. Emma de Putewelle came to a well in Box township, wanting to drink, and by chance she fell into the well and was drowned by *misadventure*. Peter of Box, the first finder, does not come, so Walter of Figheldean, [who has died,][1] and John le Blike are in *mercy* as his pledges. No one is suspected.

550. Six unknown thieves came at the evening hour to Edith of Bowden's house in Lacock. They broke into the house, carried off the goods found there, and killed Edith's daughter Edith and wounded her son R<. . .>[2] so that he later died. He was the finder of his sister Edith. Lacock, Stanley, Nethermore and Hardenhuish townships are in *mercy* because they did not come to hold the inquest.

551. Robert of Cowley from Preston parish in Buckinghamshire killed his wife Cecily [and] together with Christian le Fys dragged [the body] to the river.[3] They fled later and are suspected, so let Robert be *exacted and outlawed* and let Christian be *waived*. They were received after the deed in the house of master Henry de Biliby in Alderton, in whose mainpast Robert was previously. So he [Henry] is in *mercy*. [Robert and Christian had] no chattels. Sherston and <. . .> townships are in *mercy* because they did not arrest them. Richard Laundri, the first finder, comes and is not suspected. Great Sherston, Alderton, Luckington and Surrendell townships are in *mercy* because they did not come sufficiently <to the inquest> etc. Robert was dwelling outside a tithing in Alderton township, which is in *mercy*. <He was in> the mainpast of master Henry, whose lands are at Preston in Buckinghamshire.[4]

552. Roger le Mouner of Melksham[5] struck Ellis of Bowden with an axe,[6]

---

1 Walter's name is underlined for deletion and is followed by *obiit*, with *quia* interlined to show the reason.

2 The edge of the membrane has been crumpled and badly rubbed, and angle brackets in this and the following entries indicate doubtful and illegible words.

3 Presumably the Avon, here little more than a stream.

4 Henry de Biliby was patron of Preston Bissett church by 1252, and presented to it ten years later. Cowley is a hamlet in the parish. *VCH Buckinghamshire* iv, 219.

5 *Mouner de Melkesham* is written above *Goyz*, which has been struck through.

6 *securis*, as distinct from the more usual *hachia*, hatchet.

so that three days later (he died. Roger fled) and is suspected, so let him be *exacted and outlawed*. He was dwelling in Melksham township, which is in *mercy*. He was in the tithing of Alexander le Stuthe in Melksham, which is in *mercy*. Stanley, Tytherton, <. . .> and Hardenhuish townships did not come sufficiently to hold the inquest, nor did they pursue <Roger. So they are in *mercy*>.

m. 39d (IMG 0466, 0467) *Continuing Chippenham foreign hundred*

553. Robert of Colerne fled to Yatton church, admitted theft and *abjured* the realm before the coroner. He was dwelling at Colerne for a long time outside a tithing, so it is in *mercy*. Yatton township did not pursue him after he had burgled the house of master Nicholas of Malmesbury, so it is in *mercy*.

554. William Selewy fell from a boat into the river[1] Avon at Moor so that he drowned by misadventure. The value of the boat *6d.*, the sheriff to answer. *Deodand*.

555. William of Bradley, a merchant, fell from his horse onto his sword at Chapel Plaster and died instantly. Judgement misadventure. The value of the horse *½ mark*. The value of the sword *6d*. Let Roger Pipard[2] answer for the ½ mark. Hazelbury, Box, Rudloe and Hartham townships did not value the horse, so they are in *mercy*.

556. As one Henry le Vindere cut[3] a piece of wood he was crushed by it so that he died instantly. Judgement misadventure. The value of the wood *4d. deodand*.

557. John the miller killed Richard le King in Notton. He fled immediately and is suspected, so let him be *exacted and outlawed*. [He had] no chattels, but was in the tithing of Arnold le Byke of Bremhill, which is in *mercy*.

558. William of Hardingstone and his wife Margery fled to Great Sherston church and admitted theft and *abjured* the realm before the coroner. Sherston township did not arrest him[4], so it is in *mercy*. He was not in a tithing because he was a stranger.

559. Richard the cowman, Richard Beufrunt, Thomas son of Gunnilda, Walter Herberd and his brother Richard were going outside Chippenham under Lowden, and a dispute having arisen between them, Thomas son of Gunnilda struck Walter on the foot with an axe so that he died a month later. On that same day they encountered one Richard Beugraunt, and Richard

_____

1 *in ripariam*, as in **547** above.

2 One of the coroners in 1268: above, **1**.

3 *cecavit* for *secavit*.

4 *ipsum*, as though Margery was seen merely as an appendage.

Beufrunt struck him[1] on the head with an axe so that he died instantly. They fled immediately and are suspected, so let them be *exacted and outlawed.* Richard the cowman was in the tithing of Peter Saberis of Langley, which is in *mercy.* Richard Beufrunt was of the frankpledge of his father Ralph Page in Langley. Thomas son of Gunnilda was in the tithing of Richard of Campden in Hazelbury, which is in *mercy.* Thomas's chattels 23d., the sheriff to answer. Chippenham and Langley townships did not follow the hue to arrest the felons, so they are in *mercy.*

560. William Gorwy, arrested on suspicion of that death, comes and for good and ill puts himself on the country. The jurors say that he is not guilty, so he is quit.

561. One Gilbert from Weston in Somersetshire killed one Maud of Bath in 'Northlawe' field. He fled immediately and is suspected, so let him be *exacted and outlawed.* He had no chattels, but was in the mainpast of the abbot of Stanley, dwelling for a long time outside a tithing in Hazelbury township, which is in *mercy.* Pickwick, Hartham, Rudloe and Biddestone townships did not come to hold the inquest, so they are in *mercy.* No Englishry was presented. Judgement murder, upon the hundred.

562. William son of Giles of Kington 'Abbot's' struck William son of Christine with a knife on the arm so that he died within a month. William son of Giles fled and is suspected, so let him be *exacted and outlawed.* [His] chattels *18d.,* the bishop of Bath[2] to answer, and he was in the tithing of Roger Palling of Kington, which is in *mercy.* Leigh, Kington, Allington and Yatton townships did not come as they should to hold the inquest, so they are in *mercy.* Kington township did not arrest him, so it is in *mercy.*

563. William son of Richard Saman struck Benedict le Berker at Sopworth so that he died next day. He fled to Farleigh church and *abjured* the realm before the coroner. He had no chattels, and he was in the frankpledge of [ ].[3] Sopworth township did not arrest him, so it is in *mercy.* Little Sherston, Sopworth, Littleton and Alderton townships did not come sufficiently to hold the inquest, so they are in *mercy.* No Englishry is presented. Judgement *murder,* upon the hundred.

564. John of Taunton fled to Surrendell church, admitted theft and *abjured* the realm before the coroner. He had no chattels. Surrendell township did not arrest him, so it is in *mercy.*

---

1 *Ricardum Beufrunt* in the MS., clearly in error.

2 In this entry, and in **565** below, the clerk ignored the fact that the prelate in question had been styled bishop of Bath and Wells since 1244. David Gary Shaw, 'Salisbury, Roger of (c. 1185-1247)', [http://www.oxforddnb.com/view/article/95035, accessed 1 July 2012].

3 A space was left in the MS.

565. Philip Reyner struck William de la Hyde with his knife in Kington St Michael, [stabbing him] in the chest to the heart so that he died instantly. He was arrested and committed to gaol, and was later handed over to the bishop of Salisbury as convicted, because he was a clerk. He was in the tithing of Roger Pelling in Kington 'Abbot's', which is in *mercy*. Philip's chattels 2½ *marks*, the bishop of Bath to answer.

566. Ralph of Collingbourne killed John le Broke by night at Sopworth, and John of Norton, a shepherd, saw this, and having raised the hue he pursued Ralph into Gloucestershire, where he killed him and made off. [His] chattels are confiscated for his flight. He had no chattels and was in the tithing of [*blank*]¹ of Norton, which is in *mercy*. No Englishry is presented. Judgement *murder*, upon the hundred. Sherston, Luckington, Surrendell and Alderton townships did not come sufficiently to hold the inquest, so they are in *mercy*.

567. Hugh le Taylur of Malmesbury, [Roger of Ham the miller]² and John of Brokenborough at 'Blythemulne' in Kington 'Abbot's' killed Thomas Godwyne and his brothers Nicholas and Walter and threw them into the river.³ They fled and they are suspected, namely Hugh and John. Roger of Ham, accused of the death, is not suspected but does not come, so let his chattels be confiscated. Let his chattels and tithing be inquired of in Malmesbury. Hugh le Tayllur had no chattels, but he was in the aldermanry of the suburb of Malmesbury, which is in *mercy*. John of Brokenborough was unknown and had no chattels. So let Hugh and John be exacted and outlawed. Roger had no chattels but he may return to the peace because he is not suspected. No Englishry is presented. Judgement murder, upon the hundred. Kington 'Abbot's', Stanton St. Quintin, Tytherton Lucas and Langley Burrell townships did not come sufficiently [to the inquest], so they are in *mercy*.

568. Two nine-year-old boys, namely William of Shaw and Richard son of William of the water, were wrestling together,⁴ and William by chance fell under Richard and died instantly. The jurors, asked if there was any discord between them, say no, but that they were companions and were minding flocks⁵ in 'Bradlegh' pasture, and they know nothing else except that he died by misadventure. So Richard may return to the peace if wishes.

---

1 A large space was left for the name.

2 The name has been partly erased and struck through because Roger was innocent, but it can be read in ultra-violet light..

3 Order was given on 11 April 1266 that Hugh le Tailur and Roger le Moyn, arrested for the deaths of Thomas Godwyn and his brothers, should be released to bail. The river was presumably the Avon. *CR 1264-1268*, 186.

4 The edge of the membrane has been crumpled and badly rubbed, and angle brackets in this and the following entries indicate doubtful and illegible words.

5 *pecora*, a word with a wide range of possible meanings, but most likely meaning

569. Certain thieves, strangers, attacked Robert Tropynel in 'Colele' wood between Stanton and Christian Malford and wounded him so that he died next day. Likewise they killed Thomas le Deveneis as he came from Bradenstoke fair,[1] and fled immediately after the deed. It is not known who they were because they were strangers. Stanton township did not arrest them, <so it is in *mercy*.> Sopworth, Sherston, Luckington and Alderton townships did not come sufficiently to hold the inquest, so they are in *mercy*.

570. John de Cleyforde, accused of homicide and of harbouring thieves, puts himself for good and ill on the country. The jurors say that John is not guilty of any evildoing, <so he is quit. But they say that> Jordan le Breton of Trowbridge out of hatred imputed that < . . . > to him.

m. 40 (IMG 0387, 0388) *Continuing Chippenham foreign hundred*

571. Concerning defaults, they say that Wulfran de Burnewal, the prior of Marcigny (writ),[2] Nicholas de Caylewe, John of the garden from Tytherton, William de Valence (writ), Robert le Broc of Sopworth, William Hewe of Wraxall,[3] the abbot of Stanley (writ), Reynold de Grey, the abbot of Glastonbury (writ), Mathias Besil, Richard king of Germany,[4] Richard son of Avice of Sherston, Miles de Caynes, ill, and Thomas de Cancreswelle did not come on the first day.

572. William Kuisyn and John le Berker struck Walter the fisherman with a knife on the head at Kellaways[5] so that he died instantly. They fled immediately and the township did not arrest them, so it is in *mercy*. They were dwelling outside a tithing in Tytherton, which is in *mercy*. John le Berker was in the mainpast of John Kaylewey, who is in *mercy*. Tytherton Lucas, Kellaways, Langley Burrell and Cadenham townships did not come sufficiently to hold the

sheep here.

1 Bradenstoke fair was held on 8 September.

2 The four names followed by '(writ)' have *b*, for *breve*, written above them, indicating that each had a writ granting quittance from attendance. The 'prior' of Marcigny-sur-Loire was probably styled thus by mistake, instead of the prioress, since the nuns and monks of that house held their property – in this hundred the manor of Slaughterford - in common, and there is no evidence that the monks had a separate endowment. See **361** above.

3 The name is underlined, for deletion, and written above it is a note that he did not hold land at the beginning of the eyre.

4 i.e. Richard earl of Cornwall; see **142** above, and note.

5 'Tyderinton Kaylewey' in the manuscript, it was one of three manors originally named from Tytherton. But unlike Tytherton Lucas, in this case the manorial suffix completely superseded the original place-name, which seems to have disappeared by the early seventeenth century. *PNS*, 91-2, 99-100.

inquest, so they are in *mercy*. No Englishry was presented. Judgement *murder*. William and John le Berker had no chattels. Let them be *exacted and outlawed*.

573. William de Wrmle and four other unknown men beat Robert le Bencher of Grittleton at 'la Rode' in Gloucestershire so that he died in the third week following. They fled immediately and are suspected, so let them be *exacted and outlawed*. [They had] no chattels.

574. Ellis son of William de la Hele wished to give a drink to Ela la Hopere, but she did not want it, so he put his arms round her, and as though wrestling fell on her, and his knife wounded her so that she died. Ellis comes and denies the death. The jurors say that this was not done in a spirit of malice but only by misadventure. Ellis has found pledges, John le Flemeng, Peter de Malolacu, Roger le Grey and Walter Page, for his standing to right if anyone should wish to proceed against him.

575. The jurors present that Robert Steket, the sheriff's bailiff, arrested Agnes of Surendell on suspicion of harbouring her son John, accused of theft, and imprisoned her in his house at Chippenham, holding her for eight days until she made fine with him by a bull and a cow, worth 10s., and fifteen sheep, worth 11s. Robert is present and cannot deny this, so let him be taken into *custody*. He says that he made over the money to Richard of Worcester, then sheriff, because he attached Agnes on that sheriff's order. (*21s. 4d.*)[1]

576. Gillian the wife of Robert Bernard appeals Robert Stoket that at Lacock on Thursday the feast of the translation of St. Thomas the Martyr [7 July 1267] about midday at that township's fair,[2] between the two gates of the abbey of Lacock on the king's highway, in a premeditated assault he struck her son Roger Bernard with a squared ash staff on the left side of the head to the brain, so that he died instantly. And that he committed such a felony, and feloniously killed her son Roger, she is ready to sue and prove as a woman can and should do against felon to the king.

The same Gillian appealed Roger le Mareschal and John le Sumeter of aiding and abetting etc. by the same words.

Robert, Roger and John come and deny [causing] the death and all etc. They say Gillian has a husband Robert Bernard who is still living, who rather than Gillian ought to be admitted to make the appeal. They say that a woman cannot make an appeal except for the death of her husband killed in her arms, for the rape of her body, and for her child crushed in her womb,

---

1 The additional 4d. could represent an amercement on Robert, but may just be a mistake, since such a sum would have been an insignificant penalty for such a man. This allegation of extortion against Robert seems to have been repeated at the next eyre – R.E. Latham and C.A.F. Meekings (eds.), 'The veredictum of Chippenham hundred, 1281', N.J.Williams (ed.), *Collectanea* (Wiltshire Record Society 12, 1956), 50-128, at 94 (no. 132).

2 In 1237 Lacock abbey was granted an annual fair to be held on 7 July.

and they ask that this be allowed them. Gillian cannot deny this, so Robert, Roger and John are quit with regard to the appeal, and let Gillian be taken into *custody*. But for the maintenance of the king's peace Robert, Roger and John are asked how they wish to be acquitted, and for good and ill they put themselves on the country.

The jurors say that Roger le Mareschal struck Roger Bernard on the head with a stake so that he died instantly., and he has judgement. (*Hanged.*) They also say that Robert and John are not guilty, so they are quit. Roger had no chattels.

John Gille, accused of that death, has made off, so his chattels are confiscated. The jurors say that he is not guilty, so he may return to the peace if he wishes.

577. John Harding took his brother William's horse, surcoat[1] and a book and set off towards Oxford. William's men pursued him, and out of fear he got himself into a church in Oxfordshire, but left it as soon as he could. The jurors say that they do not suspect him, because he did this not with any intention of stealing, but only because he wished to go to the schools at Oxford and to send back the horse, book and surcoat when he was there, and they do not suspect him of any evildoing. So he may return to the peace, and let him find security to stand to right if anyone wishes to proceed against him.

578. The jurors present that John de Vivonne, son of Hugh de Vivonne, is under age and in the king's wardship, and his land is worth £10 a year.[2] Parnel de Vivonne holds it in West Kington.

579. Richard Payn has sold wine contrary to the assize, so he is in *mercy*.

580. The jurors present that Kington St. Michael, Grittleton and Nettleton manors[3] do not allow the king's bailiffs to make distraints for debts to the king as they used to do.[4] Throughout the whole time that Walter de Godarvile[5] had

---

1 *hergaudum.*

2 John's grandfather, another Hugh de Vivonne, was a Poitevin who enjoyed a distinguished career in the service of the crown, for instance as seneschal of Gascony and sheriff for several years of Somerset and Dorset. The manor of West Kington, granted to him in 1235, was valued at £15 per annum shortly before his death in 1249. When John came of age in 1273 he was said to have been brought up there. *Wiltshire crown pleas, 1249*, no. 216; Latham and Meekings, 'The veredictum of Chippenham hundred', 114-15; *CIPM* ii no. 43.

3 The MS. has the noun in the singular but the verb in the plural.

4 These three manors all belonged to Glastonbury Abbey. In 1321, together with the manor of Christian Malford, also a Glastonbury manor, they were brought together to form a new hundred, that of North Damerham. *PNS*, 65 n.1.

5 Chippenham was granted to Walter on 27 July 1231. When he died, around the end of 1249, manor and hundred were inherited by Geoffrey Gacelyn, who had married Joan, Walter's daughter and heir. *CChR 1226-1257*, 138; *CIPM* i nos. 181,

Chippenham hundred at fee farm from the king, his bailiffs for Chippenham used to make distraints and to arraign assizes and summonses in those townships, except when the men of those townships acted on the order of the bailiffs. And likewise in the whole time of Geoffrey Gacelyn, who now holds the hundred at fee farm from the king, until the time when Ralph Russel was sheriff of Wiltshire, when one Martin of Leigh, Ralph's under-sheriff, who was in the household and mainpast of the abbot of Glastonbury and took the abbot's robes,[1] made return of writs to the abbot's bailiffs at Damerham, and after that the [king's] bailiffs of Chippenham were always obstructed from making distraints etc. (*Let this be discussed with the king.*)

581. Reynold the cook of West Kington appealed Adam, the servant of Amisius the clerk (who was outlawed at the county court)[2], of mayhem, wounding and robberies, and Amisius of ordering it, and he is ready to pursue his appeal against him [Amisius], who does not come. He was mainprised[3] at the second county court after the appeal was lodged and the mainpernors have died. So he [Reynold] was told to sue from county court to county court until he [Amisius] is outlawed. The present eyre will be allowed him as one county court.[4]

The same Reynold appealed William Harre of aiding and abetting, and wishes to sue. William does not come, and he was mainprised at the second county court after the appeal was lodged by John Mussum of Little Bedwyn, Robert Robyne, Nicholas de la Strete, John of Ridge and Adam the clerk of Newnton, who are in *mercy*. Reynold was told to sue at the county court as above.[5]

m. 40d (IMG 0471, 0472)

201; *Rot. Hund.* ii, 231.

1 The syntax of this sentence is less than clear – '*Martinus de Leghe subvicecomes ipsius Radulfi qui fuit de familia et manupastu abbatis*' could be construed as saying that it was Ralph, not Martin, who was the abbot's retainer. But there is no evidence that Ralph Russel had any connection with Glastonbury, whereas Martin was not only the abbey's tenant but also appears frequently in its cartulary, often heading witness-lists, so it must have been the latter who was a member of the abbot's household. A Watkin (ed.), *The great chartulary of Glastonbury abbey*, 3 vols. (Somerset Record Society, 59, 63-4, 1947-56). This case is discussed in the introduction.

2 *qui utlagatus fuit ad comitatum* is inserted above a caret, evidently referring to Adam.

3 *fuerunt manucaptus*, muddling plural and singular

4 Reginald sued Amisius, Adam and William le Herre in the court *coram rege* in Trinity term 1258, alleging that they had cut off one of his ears and broken his arm. The accused did not appear, and Reginald evidently transferred his action to the county court. KB 26/158 m. 15.

5 It was presented at the next eyre that Reginald had duly continued his appeal until William was outlawed. JUST 1/1005/2 m. 134.

THE TOWNSHIP OF CHIPPENHAM COMES BY THE SAID JURORS

582. Walter son of Philip of Studley was found in Chippenham forest, killed by an arrow [shot] by malefactors [who were] strangers. His brother Richard, the first finder, does not come, so his pledges, namely his brother William and Alexander le Turnur of Studley, are in *mercy*. Englishry was presented by William son of Philip and his brother Richard, [and] on his mother's side by Alexander le Turnur.[1]

583. Unknown malefactors killed Alexander le Mazun with an arrow in a place called 'Inlond'. Robert of Redland who was with him fled out of fear and raised the hue. The malefactors fled, and Chippenham township did not arrest them, so it is in *mercy*. Chippenham, Stanley, Tytherton Lucas and Kellaways townships did not come sufficiently to the inquest etc., so they are in *mercy*. No Englishry is presented. Judgement *murder*. The first finder has died.

584. Ralph de Hoseby from Northamptonshire fled to Chippenham church and admitted theft and *abjured* the realm before the coroner. He had no chattels, and Chippenham township did not arrest him, so it is in *mercy*.

585. Unknown malefactors wounded one Wenciliana in Chippenham forest and took away her cloak. Wenciliana later died at Stanley. The township did not come to the inquest etc., so it is in *mercy*.

586. Thomas, the hayward of William de Torny,[2] struck Hugh the carter with a spade so that he died. He fled immediately and is suspected, so let him be exacted and outlawed. He had no chattels. Hardenhuish township did not arrest him, so it is in *mercy*. He was dwelling for a long time outside a tithing in Hardenhuish township, so it is in *mercy*. He was in the mainpast of William de Torny, who is in *mercy*.

587. John Smalred tried to beat his wife, and when his father Robert's wife Joan tried to prevent him she was injured by an arrow and later died. John fled to St. Andrew's church in Chippenham and *abjured* the realm before the coroner. Chippenham township did not arrest him, so it is in *mercy*. He was dwelling for a long time outside a tithing.in Chippenham township, which is in *mercy*.

CONTINUING THE FOREIGN HUNDRED OF CHIPPENHAM

588. The jurors present that William de Valence has withdrawn sheriff's aid

---

1 For Englishry see **3**, above. This is the only entry in the roll to name those who presented it.

2 In 1242/3 the holder of a knight's fee in Wroughton. *Book of Fees* ii, 723.

for Sopworth manor,[1] [worth] 3s. 6d. a year, and has withdrawn the three-weekly suit [owed] to Dunlow hundred.[2] Walter Dreu, William Plusbel and Walter the parson's son have withdrawn the same suit. Geoffrey Gascelin, who holds Chippenham hundred at fee farm has procured a royal writ against William Plusbel, Walter Dru and Walter the parson's son, that they should do suit to him at Dunlow hundred. And he procured another writ against Walter Dru, that he permit his villeins of Littleton Drew to do suit to his hundred of Dunlow etc. Whereupon Walter Dru, William Plusbel and Walter the parson's son came and admitted [owing] suit to Dunlow hundred, both for themselves and for Walter Dru's villeins, and for this etc. Geoffrey has remitted his damages to them.

589. Peter le Tukere, accused of stealing clothes, puts himself for good and ill on the country. The jurors say that he is not guilty of any evildoing, so he is *quit*. They also say that Peter was maliciously indicted by Jordan le Bretun, so let him be arrested.

Benedict of Slaughterford, accused by Jordan of the same theft, has made off. The jurors say that he is not guilty of this or of any other evildoing, so let him *return* to the peace (*quit*), but his chattels are confiscated for his flight. He had no chattels.

590. Maud Attechirchey of Grittleton, who appealed William Trendelove and Osbert the reeve of the same of felony and robbery, does not come. So let her be arrested, and her pledges for prosecuting are in *mercy*, namely John Kilston of Nettleton and Robert Wodie. William Trendelove does not come, and he was mainprised at the county court by Osbert Josep of Grittleton and Robert of Foxcote, who are in *mercy*. Maud withdrew against Osbert at the third county court after the appeal was lodged, so let her be arrested, and her pledges aforesaid are in *mercy*.

591. The jurors present that Parnel de Dunstanville has withdrawn the suit of Colerne manor to Chippenham hundred. Walter de Dunstanville now holds that manor.[3]

---

1 The manor of Sopworth formed part of the estate of Robert de Pont de l'Arche, and escheated to the crown following Robert's death early in 1246. After custody of all Robert's lands had been entrusted to Henry III's half-brother William de Valence in July 1247, they were provisionally granted to him and his heirs on 12 March 1249. Sopworth and the other properties were finally confirmed to William on 23 August 1252, when Robert's brother renounced his claim in return for a payment of 1000 marks. *CIPM*. i no. 76; *CR 1242-1247*, 524; *CChR 1226-1257*, 339, 402-3.

2 Dunlow hundred, having answered by itself at the 1194 Wiltshire eyre, had by 1249 been absorbed into Chippenham hundred, but clearly retained a separate identity within the latter. *PNS*, 75.

3 Colerne was one of five Wiltshire manors held by Walter de Dunstanville, the lord of the barony of Castle Combe, when he died on 14 January 1270. Parnel was the name of his daughter and heir, and perhaps also of his mother or grandmother.

592. Walter Mareschal of Trowbridge, who appealed William son of Philip Marmiun of burglary, wounding, robbery and breach of the king's peace, does not come. So let him be arrested, and his pledges for prosecuting are in mercy, namely William Lilie and William Russel. And William son of Philip[1] is dead.

593. Walter Burgeis of Corsham and his brother Hugh, arrested on suspicion of theft and for associating with John Galun, and imprisoned in Salisbury gaol, broke out of prison and escaped when John de Vernun was sheriff. Walter came to the house of his mistress Alice in Corsham, but she raised the hue, and he fled to the church, admitted theft and abjured the realm before the coroner. His chattels were a horse worth *12s.*, and a cow worth *5s.*, and the crop of three acres sown with oats, worth *7s.*, the sheriff to answer. And there were owed him *8s. 7d.*, the sheriff to answer. The jurors are in *mercy* for concealment.

Hugh made off immediately and is suspected, so let him be exacted and outlawed. He had no chattels. Both were in the tithing of Henry le Ku of Corsham, which is in *mercy*.

594. The inner wheel of Byde Mill in Corsham accidentally killed Gilbert son of Gilbert of Melksham. Judgement misadventure. The value of the wheel *18d. deodand*, the sheriff to answer.

m. 41 (IMG 0389, 0390)

595. Walter del boys appeals Stephen Mouhan that during the evening of Sunday the feast of Holy Trinity in the 51st year [12 June 1267], in a field called 'Lungchamp', in a premeditated assault he attacked Walter with a Scottish axe, and intending to strike him on the head he struck him with the axe on the left arm between the hand and the elbow, giving him a wound five inches long and in depth to the bone, and broke the small bone of the arm, whereby he was maimed. And immediately afterwards Stephen struck Walter with the axe on the right arm between the hand and the elbow, and gave him a wound whereby he was maimed, and in robbery feloniously took from him a silver brooch worth 9d. For this Walter immediately raised the hue and pursued it to the four townships, and from the townships to the coroner and from the coroner to the county court and from county court to county court until Stephen was attached to be before the justices here. And that he did him such felony he is ready to prove against him as against a felon to the king, as a maimed man can and should or as the court shall decide.

Stephen comes and denies wounding, robbery and all felony, and says that when he made his appeal in the county court he said that Stephen allegedly assaulted him in the king's street at a place called 'Neuwehay'. Again he said

---

CIPM i no. 729; I.J. Sanders, *English baronies: a study of their origin and descent, 1086-1327* (Oxford, 1960), 28.

1 The name is struck through.

in the county court that he broke the small bone and now does not specify it, and likewise does not now specify in what part of the field. For which he asks that there be allowed him both the variation and the omissions. Walter cannot deny this, so let him be taken into custody for a false appeal, and for the maintenance of the king's peace Stephen is asked how he wishes to be acquitted. He puts himself on the country that he is not guilty.

The jurors say that on that day and at that time a quarrel arose at first between Walter's wife [ ] and Stephen, and later between Stephen and Walter, and that Walter struck Stephen on the head with a rod, for which Stephen struck Walter with the axe and gave him those wounds. So it is decided that both be taken into *custody* for the trespass done to one another, and they are in mercy. Stephen's amercement is pardoned because he has long lain in prison.

596. Edith the widow of Nicholas of Rudloe, who appealed Ralph of Pinkney (he has died),[1] his son Thomas and his servant John of robbery and breach of the king's peace, does not come. So let her be arrested, and her pledges for prosecuting are in *mercy*, namely William of Biddestone and Peter of Lavington. Ralph has died, and Thomas and John do not come and were mainprised, Thomas by William Baylemund and Nicholas Lucas, John by Roger de la Hyde and John Kaym, who are in *mercy*. The jurors testify that they [the parties] are not agreed.

597. Thomas son of Geoffrey de la Grave fled to Lacock church and admitted theft and *abjured* the realm before the coroner. He had no chattels and was in the tithing of John le Net of Lacock, which is in *mercy*. The township did not pursue him, so it is in *mercy*.

598. Richard of Kent appeals William Trendelove that in premeditated assault on the eve of St. Andrew in the 43rd year [29 November 1258] he feloniously attacked Richard's father, Richard of Kent, at nightfall in his chief house of Hartham, by the north side of the hearth of the house, and in felony held his right hand while Nicholas Pusye struck Richard on the head between the crown and his left ear with a Danish axe of steel, and dealt him a wound five inches in length and six inches in depth through the middle of his brainbox[2] so that he died instantly, for which felony Nicholas was later hanged. Coming on the scene, Richard saw this felony and immediately raised the hue and pursued it to four neighbours, and from the neighbours to the four nearest townships, from the townships to the coroner, from the coroner to the county court, and from county court to county court until by his suit he was attached to be here. And that he did him such a felony he is ready to prove against him as against a felon to the king by his body as the court shall decide.

William comes and denies the death and all felony and all etc., and offers a sufficent defence against him, and as he is ready to defend this against him by his body as the court shall decide, it is decided that William should give

---

1 Ralph's forename has been struck through and *obiit* is written above it.

2 *per medium teye cerebri.*

a pledge to defend and Richard should give a pledge to prove. William's pledges to defend [are] Roger Godine of Kington, Roger the bailiff of the same, Ralph of Grittleton and Henry Michel of Nettleton. Richard's pledges for proving [*a line and a half left blank*]. (*Duel.*)[1]

A day has been given them on Tuesday next after the feast of St. Peter's Chair [24 Feb. 1268], at Wilton. Let them come equipped[2] etc.[3]

[*At the foot of the membrane*] William Gog, whom Richard appealed of that death, dwells at Wolverton in Somersetshire.

m. 41d (IMG 0473) *Continuing Chippenham foreign hundred*

599. Isabel of Chalfield, accused of the death of Richard of Kent, comes and for good and ill puts herself on the country. The jurors say that she is not guilty of this, so she is *quit*.

600. The king has sent his writ to the justices in these words:

H. by God's grace etc. to his dear and faithful Nicholas de Turri and his fellow justices in eyre in Wiltshire, greetings. Know that it was provided by us and our council and others our liegemen who lately convened with us at Marlborough, that if appeals or complaints are made to you, or to others of our itinerant justices, of robbery and breach of the peace, or homicide, or other offences committed in the recent time of war both against those who were opposed to us and against others, or if presentments of such acts are made according to the articles of the [pleas of the] crown, as is customarily done, then no one should for that reason lose life or members, or incur the penalty of perpetual imprisonment, but justice and punishment should be done in some other way with regard to damages and goods taken and trespasses, according to the discretion of our justices. Moreover, let the justices carefully attend to and uphold the contents of the dictum of Kenilworth, and let them have at every eyre a transcript of the dictum, so that in those cases which have been or should be concluded by other of our justices assigned to this, our itinerant justices are do nothing without our special order, if perchance we send them some instruction. And be it known that the time of war began on the 4th day of April in the 48th year of our reign [1264], when with banners unfurled we departed from Oxford with our army for Northampton, and lasted continuously until the 16th day of September in the 49th year of our

---

1 The word, written in the margin in a flamboyant hand, has been struck through: Trendelove was granted a royal pardon around 24 March 1268, both for killing Richard of Kent and for escaping from prison: *CPR 1266–1272*, 211.

2 The word translated as 'equipped' – *coured* – presumably refers to the white leather armour – *de albo coreo* – traditionally worn by combatants in judicial duels. M.T. Clanchy, 'Highway robbery and trial by battle in the Hampshire eyre of 1249', R.F. Hunnisett and J.B. Post (eds.), *Medieval legal records edited in memory of C.A.F. Meekings* (1978), 25-61, at 33-4.

3 There is a space of about six lines.

reign [1265], when after the battle of Evesham we had our peace confirmed and proclaimed at Winchester in the presence of our barons convened there. It was also provided that no one should lose life or limbs for robbery or homicide or other offences committed under the guise of war by those who were opposed to us from the 4th day of June in the 47th year of our reign [1263], when with banners unfurled they began to commit robberies, homicides and imprisonments against both ecclesiatical and secular persons, until that time when with our army we departed from Oxford to Northampton. For other offences, however, which were committed at that time without being under the guise of war, let that period be regarded as a time of peace. As for the time when we had our peace confirmed and proclaimed at Winchester, let the law run as it used to run in time of peace, as long as those who were at Axholme or at Kenilworth or in the isle of Ely or at Chesterfield or later at Southwark have our peace fully observed as they should have it, either under the dictum of Kenilworth or by our charters granted to them for our peace. For those, however, who were with the earl of Gloucester in the latest unrest, let the peace made between us and the earl be observed, so that the justices do not proceed against him or those who were in his party, between the time when the earl departed from Wales towards London and the day on which he left that city, and let this be understood as applying only to them. As to depredations committed on either side during that period, let the peace made between us and the earl be observed. And so we order you that in your eyre aforesaid, and in other counties in which you go on eyre, you observe all these things and have them observed. Myself witness at Westminster the 4th day of February in the 52nd year of our reign [1268]. Furthermore we are sending to you the tenor of the dictum of Kenilworth and the form of the peace lately made between us and the earl of Gloucester, sealed with the foot of our seal.[1]

m. 42 (IMG 0391, 0392)

Pleas of the Crown of the city of Salisbury in the 52nd year [of Henry III, 1268]

THE CITY OF NEW[2] SALISBURY COMES BY TWELVE[3]

601. The city of Salisbury comes by twelve who say that they know nothing

---

1 This writ, which is discussed in the introduction, was clearly the model for the instructions issued by Edward I's government in 1276 concerning offences against the peace committed during the Barons' Wars. A second, abbreviated, version of it was enrolled among the civil pleas. JUST 1/998A m. 18; *CCR 1272-1279*, 333.

2 *Novar[um]*, as though agreeing with a genitive plural *Sar[um]*.

3   The heading is written in a very large bold and flamboyant hand. It is followed by a space of about 16 lines.

about the old pleas of the crown, and [of those that] were before justices in another fashion they know nothing.[1]

602. Of new pleas of the crown which have subsequently emerged in peacetime, they say that Richard the bishop of Salisbury's miller was drowned,[2] and no one is suspected. Judgement misadventure. Geoffrey horilog,[3] the first finder, does not come. So he is in *mercy*.

603. Agnes the widow of Turgis died suddenly in her own house. No one is suspected. Judgement misadventure. One Dulcia, the first finder, does not come, so she is in *mercy*.

604. John of Inkpen got himself into the church of the Friars Minor of Salisbury, admitted being a thief and abjured the realm. No chattels.

605. One Walter of Tawstock escaped from Wilton[4] prison, and he got himself into St. Mary's church in New Salisbury, admitted being a thief and abjured the realm. (*Upon Wilton.*) No chattels.

606. William Pumerey was attached on suspicion of [harbouring] his son, who was hanged at Fordingbridge for theft, and was put in prison at Salisbury, where he died. He was not convicted, so nothing from his chattels.

607. Nicholas of Powick got himself into the church of St. Thomas the Martyr in Salisbury, admitted being a thief and abjured the realm. Chattels 7*d.*, which the aldermany of the south side of the market took. It is in *mercy* for not having the money before the justices.

608. Robert le Clop came to the house of William of Wanstrow and was coming down there from an upper room[5] when he broke his neck. No one is suspected. *Deodand 6d.*

609. John Pitewine, who appealed Ralph Payn of robbery and theft, does

---

1 The phrasing of the second part of this presentment is obscure – *et alias fuerunt coram justiciariis nihil sciunt* – but seems to be part of a general disclaimer of knowledge of other proceedings involving Salisbury.

2 *emersus*, for *submersus*, perhaps through confusion with *emerserunt* earlier in the sentence.

3 The name suggests involvement with a *horologium*, a time-keeping device of some kind. Salisbury Cathedral is not known to have had a mechanical clock before 1306, but Geoffrey could have been responsible for a water-clock. J. North, *God's clockmaker: Richard of Wallingford and the invention of time* (2005), 145-69.

4 In the margin is written *sr*, apparently for *supra* ('above'), referring to the entries for Wilton at **476–85**.

5 *solio*, apparently for *solario*.

not come, so let him be arrested, and his pledges for prosecuting are in *mercy*, namely Richard Pidewine, Walter Grom, William Buttevile, William Laurence, Herbert of Wilton, Richard Bachet (he has died)[1] and William le Taylur. Ralph, who comes and is asked how he wishes to be acquitted of that robbery and theft, puts himself for good and ill on the country. Because the deed was done on the border of the counties of Hampshire and Wiltshire the sheriff of Hampshire is ordered to make come twelve from Thorngate hundred in his county, and the sheriff of Wiltshire is ordered to make come twelve from the hundreds of Amesbury and Alderbury in his county, and the four nearest townships, on Monday next after the Purification of the Blessed Mary [6 Feb. 1268] at Salisbury. Those twelves[2] come on that day, and being sworn they say that he is suspected neither of the robbery and theft nor of any other evildoing, so it is decided that Ralph be quit etc.[3]

610. John Rocelin,[4] arrested on suspicion of the death of Jospin the Jew, who was killed at Salisbury, puts himself on the twelve of the city of Salisbury for good and ill. They say on their oath that he is not guilty, so John is quit.

611. Malefactors came to the house of Michael, vicar of Salisbury, and wounded one Jordan of Devon, Michael's servant, so that he died next day. No one [else] is suspected, nor is Michael who was in the house, so Michael is quit.

612. Thomas le Engleys Fox[5] of Quidhampton got himself into St. Mary's church in Salisbury, admitted having killed John de Cumbe and abjured the realm. Let his chattels be investigated *in Quidhampton*.

613. Michael of Tytherley and his brother Richard [were] arrested and imprisoned on suspicion of stealing a bullock. Michael acknowledged that and of other thefts, and by judgement of Salisbury township both were imprisoned

---

1 The name is struck through and *obiit* is written in the margin.

2 The MS. has just *xij*, but 'twelves' is probably meant; no townships are mentioned.

3 There is a gap of about six lines between this entry and the next. No reference has been noticed to this case among Thorngate hundred's pleas at the 1272 Hampshire eyre. JUST 1/780 mm. 9, 9d.

4 An order was issued on 15 March 1266 that John Rocelyn of Wilton, imprisoned for the death of Jospin of Fisherton (a suburb of Salisbury), a Jew, should be released to bail. *CR 1264-1268*, 179. He may have been identical with Rocelin of Wilton, a subdeacon who was convicted of theft at a gaol delivery in 1276. R.B. Pugh (ed.), *Wiltshire gaol deliveries and trailbaston trials, 1275-1306* (Wiltshire Record Society 33, 1978 for 1977), no. 74.

5 Cf. above, **327**, recording (apparently inaccurately) that Thomas le Fox was outlawed for the death of John de Cumbe. Either he had alternative surnames or 'Fox' was a nickname.

and died in prison. So to judgement on the township. Value of the bullock 2s., for which Walter,[1] bishop of Salisbury, must answer.

614. John Harang of Laverstock and the men of Laverstock brawled with the men of Milford at Salisbury. Stephen son of Richard de Dorsere came between them to calm the fight, and John Harang struck Stephen with a knife and killed him. Christian, the first finder, raised the hue, and she comes and is not suspected. John Harang is committed to *prison*. Later John came and put himself on Salisbury township and six of Underditch hundred [. . .][2] that John Harang, Edmund son of John, Reynold de Drumar and Thomas le Dun, who were accused of the death and put themselves on that jury for good and ill. The jurors say that they are not guilty. So they are quit.

615. Walter son of Augustine le Buss came to the house of William of Amesbury, where he struck him with a stake so that he died three days later. The hue was raised and the township did not arrest him, and to *judgement* on it.

616. Adam Porterose came to the house of Robert Porterose in Salisbury and they fought there, so that Adam killed Robert with a bar so that he died [*sic*]. Adam fled to Wilton, where he got himself into St Peter's church, admitted the evildoing and abjured the realm. And because he was dwelling in that city without love and without law[3], the whole township is in mercy. Chattels 2s. 6d., Walter bishop of Salisbury to answer.

617. Isabel the wife of John Page and Felice la Grosse killed John Page with a cowl-staff[4] and immediately after the deed they fled and are suspected. So let them be exacted and waived. Nicholas de Lenna has Isabel's chattels, worth 4s, so he is in *mercy*.[5]

m. 42d (IMG 0474)

618. John of Church Hill and John of Andover quarrelled. John of Andover struck John of Church Hill through the middle of the arm and pursued him to kill him, and John of Church Hill struck him with a knife so that he died.

---

1 Walter de la Wyle, bishop from 1263 to 1271.

2 This entry is particularly carelessly written. Either something has been omitted, or the clerk left in words which he intended to delete. Proceedings were doubtless complicated by John Harang's having been already acquitted by the Alderbury jury, **47**.

3 *sine love et sine lawe*, i.e. out of frankpledge.

4 *tinello*. A 'cowl' in this context was a tub, carried by two people on a staff passed through its handles.

5 A second margination, further down the membrane, appears to be *v[e]r[t]e f[olium]* (turn the leaf).

John of Church Hill is suspected, so let him be exacted and waived.[1] Later[2] it is testified that John was arrested and imprisoned in the city of Salisbury, and he was handed over to John Robuk, Robert le Turnur, Walter of Banbury, Stephen the goldsmith, Thomas Dunkenal and Richard Dunstaple. He escaped from their custody, so to judgement upon them for the *escape*.

619. William le Barbur, accused of clipping coins, has fled. He is not suspected, so he may return if he wishes. Because he found pledges that he would come before the justices and does not come, his pledges are in mercy, namely John of Wootton, Nicholas his brother, Hamon de Lisewis, John le Scut the younger, William Batecok (poor),[3] Robert Farlif (poor), Robert le Cupere the younger, Henry of Dilton, Richard of Blakemoor and William le Taylur.

620. Concerning those who have sold cloths contrary to the assize, they say Robert la Warre, John of Honiton, William of Langford, Henry the long, Roger of Stoke, Richard de Anne, Robert of Pentrich, Gilbert Chinne, William of Clatford, Richard of Ludgershall, and Robert of Wallop have sold cloths contrary to the assize, so they are in *mercy*.

621. Concerning wines sold contrary to the assize, they say that William Pinnok, Robert le Cupere, William le Boteler, Gilbert Chinne, Robert of Newnham (poor),[4] John of Wootton, John Isemberd, Henry le Dun and Giles[5] le Fleming of Southampton have sold wines contrary to the assize, so they are in *mercy*.

622. Thomas Susanne, John Bertram, Thomas Tutebrege, John Biset, William de Estre, William Samson, Adam le Lade, Robert le Markant, William le Macekreu, Adam le Blake, John le Cule and Adam le Knythe, all of Hampshire, who appealed Robert le Frаunceys, clerk, Reynold le Drumar the younger and Hugh Brun have not prosecuted. So let them be arrested, and their pledges for prosecuting are in mercy, namely William Pinnok, Richard of Romsey, Richard de Anne, Robert le Cupere, Richard of Bedford, John Debuk (poor),[6] John Scut, Herbert of Wilton, Salomon le Pescur (poor), Robert of Newnham (poor), John Winstan, William le Limbrenere (poor), John of Homington, Walter of Shipton, Hugh le Nuch, Walter of Downton, Bartholomew le Pessuner, Matthew of St. Edward and William Kotin.

---

1 Waiver normally applied only to women. The word *wayvetur* is clearly written.

2 The last two sentences are squeezed into the space before the next entry.

3 Written above each of the two names followed by '(poor)' is *pp*, for *pauper*.

4 Written above his name is *pp*, for *pauper* ('poor').

5 *Egid*[*ius*] is interlined to replace *Gilbertus*.

6 Written above each of the three names followed by '(poor)' is *pp*, for *pauper*.

623. Maurice of Wilton of Salisbury,[1] William de Hamton of Salisbury, Peter the wheelwright of the same,[2] Richard the spicer, William Pinnok the little, William of Ford, James of Britford, William of Winterslow, Robert le Lewede, John Chirpede, Richard of Whiteparish and Walter Comin are all in *mercy*, because they did not have Peter le Retundur, whom they mainprised, at Wilton on the first day.

THE BOROUGH OF LUDGERSHALL COMES BY TWELVE

624. An unknown man was found killed in the road outside Ludgershall township. Adam Buket, the first finder, comes and is not suspected. It is not known who killed him. No Englishry is presented. Judgement *murder*, upon Ludgershall township.

625. Walter Burel was arrested and imprisoned in the king's prison of Ludgershall, and he escaped from it when Ralph de Warderoba of Biddesden was keeper of that manor and of its prison.[3] Walter fled and is suspected, so let him be *exacted and outlawed*. His chattels and tithing are unknown because he was a stranger. To judgement for the *escape* upon Ralph and (. . .)

1 The first two names are followed by *in Sarum*, the preposition *in* being presumably used to show that they were living in Salisbury, whatever their place of origin..

2 *de eadem* ('of the same') is repeated after the name of each of the mainpernors.

3 Ralph de Warderoba, or de la Garderobe, was referred to as bailiff of Ludgershall in November 1267, when he and others were given oaks for repairs to their houses lately burnt there. *CR 1264-1268*, 406. More information about this case was given at the 1281 eyre, when it was presented that following his arrest Walter admitted involvement in the killing of Peter Kene (**18**) and in many thefts and became an approver. But he secured his release by paying £5 to Ralph, who by 1281 was living in Southampton. He may have been identical with the Walter Burel recorded in 1281 as abjuring the realm for stealing sheepskins in Whorwellsdown hundred. JUST 1/1005/2 mm. 141, 157d.

GLOSSARY

Abjuration: the process licensing a suspect who had fled to a church for sanctuary to leave the realm after confessing his offences to a coroner.

Aldermanry: the basic unit of frankpledge [see below] in Wiltshire's principal boroughs.

Amercement: a financial penalty, the medieval equivalent of the modern fine.

Appeal: a formal accusation, made in an elaborate set form and usually offering battle as the means of proof.

Approver: a self-confessed criminal who attempted to save his own life by securing the conviction of his associates.

Assize: (1) a regulation or ordinance (2) a form of legal action.

Attach: to oblige a man or woman to find guarantors of their future appearance in court.

Carucate: a unit of land, variable in size, but usually in the region of 120 acres.

[Tenure in] Chief: land held directly from the crown.

Deodand: the material cause of an accidental death, given to God – that is, to some charitable institution – by way of propitiation.

Englishry: the proof that a dead man or woman was English, rather than French, which enabled a community to avoid a murder fine [see below].

Escheat: the reversion of property to the crown, either for lack of heirs or through forfeiture.

Exact to outlawry/exigent: the process whereby people charged with felony were summoned to attend at successive meetings of the county court, and outlawed if they had failed to do so after five summonses.

Fee: an estate held of a superior lord; a knight's fee was the basic unit of feudal tenure, granted in return for military service

Felony: a serious crime, punishable by death or mutilation.

Franchise: an office or function of government in private hands.

Frankpledge: a system of collective responsibility, fundamental to law enforcement in thirteenth-century England, implemented through tithings in townships and aldermanries in boroughs.

Gaol Delivery: a judicial session at which the prisoners in a royal gaol were presented for trial.

Hue: the alarm obligatorily raised against suspicious and/or violent behaviour, or when evidence of crime was discovered.

Hundred: an ancient administrative unit, varying in extent, which with its court and bailiff constituted an essential component of medieval local government.

Kalendar: a list or register, for instance of juries.

Lawday: the six-monthly meeting of a hundred court, coinciding with the tourn [see below], to which presentments of offences were made.

Liberty: the area within which a privileged lord enjoyed franchises [see above].

Mainpast: the dependents of a lord – literally the eaters of his bread – for whose good behaviour he was held responsible.

Mainpernor: the surety, by the process of mainprise, for a man or woman's appearance in court.

Mark: a monetary unit of account, valued at 13s. 4d. (66p.).

Mayhem: maiming

Murder: the archaic fine levied on a community which failed to prove the Englishry [see above] of a man who had died by violence.

Novel disseisin: an action for the recovery of land of which the plaintiff claimed to have been deprived 'unjustly and without judgment'.

Parcener: partner.

Purpresture: an encroachment or intrusion upon the property or rights of another.

Replevin: the action for the recovery of goods taken in distraint, and still withheld after the distrainee had offered pledges for the performance or payment for which the distraint had been made.

Serjeanty: a form of tenure, whereby the holder of land performed specified, usually non-military, services in return for his estate.

Sheriff's aid: a customary due, perhaps originating in an obligation to provide the sheriff with hospitality when he performed his duties, which by the thirteenth century had become a crown revenue.

Stot: a draught animal, sometimes an ox but more often a horse.

Suit: the duty of attendance at a court.

Tithing: the basic unit of frankpledge [see above] in the townships, usually a whole community, but sometimes a group of some ten men, whose members were sworn to keep each other law-abiding.

Tourn: the sheriff's twice-yearly circuit of the hundreds of his shire, at which he received presentments of offences against the peace.

Virgate: a unit of land, usually of around thirty acres.

Waiver: the equivalent of outlawry for women.

Year and waste: the king's right to take a year's revenue from any free land held by a convicted felon, along with every movable asset which could be found on it at the end of that year.

INDEX OF PERSONS AND PLACES

References in arabic figures are to entry numbers, those in roman figures to the introduction. People of the same surname and forename are sometimes indexed together even if the context shows them to be distinct. Two or more than references appended to a name do not necessarily relate to the same person. All names of the offspring are indexed under the parent's name (eg Adam son of Ida as Ida, Adam son of). One surname lacking the initial letters is added at the end of the index.

county of, 577
king's departure from, 600
Merton College, lxxxv
schools at, lx, 577
Oxford (Oxon', Oxn), John of, 372,
William of, 481;
oxherd, Richard the, 533
Oyslelur (Oysel'), Henry le, 37
John, 167

Pache, Walter, 63 *and see* Pak
Pacok, Adam, 263
John, 12, *and see* Paucok
Page, Edith wife of John, 430
Isabel wife of John, lvi, 617
John, 430, 617
Ralph, 559
Walter, 574
William, 59, 353
Pain, monk of Reading, *see* Leominster,
Pain of
Pain, Robert son of, 248
Pain, Roger son of, 518
Pak (Pakke), Adam, 283
Roger, 70 *and see* Pache
Palling, Robert, lvi, 179
Roger, 562
Parche, Geoffrey, 325
Parele, Ralph, 389
park, John of the, 387
Parker, Adam le, 168, 321
Philip le, lxv, 530
William le, 246
William son of Adam le, 321
Parmenter, Roger le, xxi, lxxxvii, 8
parson, Walter son of the, 588
Patelot, Richard, 167
Thomas, 163
Patney (Patenee, Pateny), xxiv, 315–16
Patney (Pateny), Clement, 317
Paucoke, (Pokoc) Geoffrey, 55, 81
Thomas, 424; *and see* Pacok
Paumer, John le, 244
Maud daughter of Walter le, lxxiv, 109
Reynold son of John le, 244
Walter le, 109
William le, 191
Pavely (Pavele), Reynold de, 338
Roger, 527
Walter, xxxv
Payn, Hugh, 146
Ralph, 609
Richard, 579
Richard son of Hugh, 146
Paynel, John, 435, 437

Thomas brother of William son of William,
401
William, 396, 401
William son of William, 401
Pechur, Thomas le, 339; *and see* Fisherman
Pede, William son of Walter, 182
Pefrey (Pefrei), Henry, 539
Henry son of Thomas, 539
Thomas, 539
and see Pyfrey
Pek, John le, xxx, 213
Peleter, Robert le, 271; *and see* Skinner
Pelling, Roger, 565
Penant, W. le, 305
Penaund, William le, 364
Penleigh (Penlee), in Dilton, lxv, 300–1
Penne, James brother of Roger son of Roger
de la, 506
Roger de, 191, 506
Roger son of Roger de, 506
Pensworth (Pendeleswrth', Pendeswrth), in
Redlynch, 78, 81, 83
Pentecoste, Henry, 97
Ralph, 327
Pentridge (Pentrich), Robert of, 620
Pepercorn, William, 10
Perceval, Richard, 50, 74
Peree, Henry, 164, Walter, 164
Perham, Thomas son of Thomas of, 167
Perrel, Thomas, 28
Pers, Michael, 167
Pertryke, William, 240
Pertwood (Portewrth'), in East Knoyle, 444
Pertwood (Pertewrth'), Alexander of, 444
Perungel, Peter, 24
Pescur, Salomon le, 622
Pesse, Maud, 54
Pessuner, Bartholomew le, 622
Pestur, John son of Thomas le, 130
Thomas le, 130
and see baker
Peter, parson of Laverstock, 53
Peter, Reynold son of, 155n, 158, 317, 407, 415
Peter of the mill, *see* mill
Peter servant of the treasurer of Salisbury, 42
Petit, (Petyt), Henry le, 280, 286
Petitot, Dycun, 167
Petyt, *see* Petit
Peverel, Hugh, lxii, 430, 435
Pewsey (Peueseye), 385
Pewsham (Peusam), forest, 177
and see Nethermore
Peytevin (Peytevyn, Pidewine, Pitewine),
Clarice, see Merchant
Henry, 167

William le, 150, 609, 619
William son of Robert le, 70
and see tailor
Teffont (Tefhunte, Tefunte) [*unspecified*], 21, 461
Templer, John le, 101
Terot, Richard, and William his son, 250
Thachere (Thechere), Thomas le, lxxiv, 108–9
Theyn, Andrew le, 102
Thomas, parson of Whiteparish, xlvi, 66
Thomas son of the priest of Little Durnford and
    Thomas his brother, 331
Thony, Ralph de, lxxv, lxxix
Thorngate, Hants., hundred, 609
Thornhill (Thornhull', Thornull'), in Broad
    Town, 188, 192, 206
  hundred, xxi, 133, 216, **349–64**
Thoughe, Gillian daughter of Margery, 223
Thoulstone (Toluest'), in Upton Scudamore,
    466
thresher, Adam the, 350
  Jokyn the, 532
Thunt, Richard le, 231
Thurbern, John, xxxviii–xxxix, 396
Tidcombe (Tydecumbe), 366, 381; *and see*
    Fosbury
Tidpit (Tudeputte), in Martin, 95
Tidworth (Tudeford, Tudeswrth', Tudewr',
    Tudewrth'), 10, 12, 18, 23, 24
  North Tidworth (Norttudewrth'), lxxxviii,
    10
Tidworth (Tudewrth', Tudeswrth'), Christian
    of, 12
  Ellen of, 12
  Gilbert son of Christian of, 12
  Isabel of, 10, 23
  Reynold son of Robert and Isabel of, 10,
    23
  Robert of, 23
  Roger son of Ellen of, 12
  Simon son of Ellen, 12
Tiffany, (Thefania) wife of William, *see*
    William
Till, river, 252 *n*
Tilshead (Tydolveshyde), xxiv, 341, 345
  church, 343
Tilshead (Tydolveshyde, Tydolvesyde), Henry,
    469
  Walter of, 345
Tinhead (Tynehyd', Tynehyde), in Edington,
    288, 449
Tisbury (Tissebir', Tissebur', Tissebyr',
    Tyssebur'), 513–14, 527
  church, xxxiii, 514, 520
  and see Chicksgrove; Hatch; Nippard
Toc, William, 75

Tockenham (Tokeham, Tokenham), 188,
    193, 209
  East Tockenham (Est Tokeham, Estokeham),
    205, 209–10
  West Tockenham (West Tokham), 204
Tockenham (Tokeham), Denis of, 213
Tony, Geoffrey, 376
Tormauntel, Geoffrey, 236
Torny, William of, 586
Torp, Walter le, 360
Torre, Edward le, 333
Tosh, Thomas, and Gillian his daughter, 371
Tracy, Henry de, *see* Henry de la Mare
Trat, Edward, 260
Traventer, Walter le, 190–1
Tredegold, Adam, 246
Tregoz, John, 200
  Robert, xxvi, 196, 200, 221, 317
Trenchefoyle, (Trenchfoylle), Nicholas, 72
  Roger, 75
  Simon, 291; William his servant, *see* William
Trendelove, William, 590, 598
Trepas, Thomas, and Emma his wife, lxv, 246
Tristram, master Henry, 21
Tronmere, John de, and his son John, l
Tropenell (Tropinel, Tropynel), Martin, 541
  Robert, 569
Trot, Richard, 250
Trowbridge (Treubreg', Treubregg', Treubrig',
    Treubrige, Trobrige, Troubrige), xxiv,
    167, 265, 280, 286, 570, 592
Trowbridge (Troubrygh'), Gilbert, and
    Robert his son, 265
Trow, Alexander of, lxx, 105
  Geoffrey of, 104
Trowle (Trolle), in Bradford on Avon, 165, 171
Troye (Trowe), Adam de la, 188, 213
Trudebus, Adam, 172
Truer, John, wife of, *see* Edith, daughter of
    John Humphrey
Trug, John le, 318
Tryp (Tryppe), Gilbert, 198
  William, 121
Trypper, William, 493
Tukeman, John, 327
Tukere, Peter le, xxiii, 589
Tumbere, John le, lxxxi
Tur, Richard le, 65
Turberville, Thomas of, xliv
  William de, 63
Turburne, William, 307
Turbut, John, 519, 540
Turgis, Agnes wife of, 603
Turgys, John, lviii, 491
  Roger, 167

SELECTIVE INDEX OF SUBJECTS

References in arabic figures are to entry numbers, those in roman figures to the introduction.

abbess, 5, 100, 132, 200, 279, 298, 305, 361, 518
abbey, gates of, 576; robbery allegedly done in, 75
abbot, 53, 94, 97, 120, 158, 172, 186, 317, 342, 361, 383, 436, 540, 561, 571, 580
abetting, 27, 166
abjuration:
  on admission of homicide, xxx, lii, lxi, lxiv, 47, 57, 59, 155, 169, 193, 220, 225, 358, 405, 461–2, 466, 468, 563, 587, 612, 616
  on admission of larceny or theft, lxiii, lxxxvi, 4, 7, 38, 41, 46, 48, 57–9, 71, 79, 99, 102, 113, 119, 123, 174, 180, 218–19, 252, 254, 270, 272, 290, 308, 350, 354, 367–9, 372, 377–8, 391, 395, 402–3, 405, 408, 411, 419–20, 428, 440, 445, 450, 465, 476–8, 482, 488, 490, 514, 520, 544, 553, 558, 564, 584, 593, 597, 604–5, 607
accomplice, 7
accusations, false or malicious, 42, 66, 74, 98, 202, 215, 263, 266, 380, 386 570, 589
acres, *see* land
advowsons, *see* churches in the king's gift
aldermen or aldermanries, xxxvii, 476, 489–90, 567, 607
almoner, 167
amercement, lxxxiii, lxxxvii–lxxxviii:
  of aldermanry, for failing to arrest, 489; for inhabitant abjured or outlawed, 490, 567; for not having money for chattels, 607
  of appellant for withdrawing from appeal, 105
  of bishop, for default of suit, 528
  of coroner's clerk, 441
  of first finder for not appearing, 602–3
  of holders of knights' fees for failing to become knights, 347
  of hundred juries, lxxxviii–lxxxix
  of jurors:
    for concealment, 243, 526, 593; for concealing or failing to mention appeal, 10, 130, 276, 306, 334, 483, 538; for concealing chattels, 358; for escape from custody, lxxxix; for failing to mention chattels, 179; for failing to present finding of body,

179; for failing to present first finder, 114, 506; for failing to take the oath, 341, 348; for false presentment, 541; for false statement, 41, 77, 441; for false valuation, 48; for leaving without permission, 131; for trespass, 259
  of neighbours, for not appearing, 30
  of parson for taking convict's chattels, 84
  of person or persons:
    for entering land without warrant, 266
    for failing to arrest, 60, 121–2, 170, 185
    for false claim, 338
    for refusing to serve as juror, 90
    for taking chattels, 266, 396, 406, 617
    for taking deodand, 295
    for trespass, 27, 66, 260, 264, 595
    for withholding dues, 19
  of persons in whose frankpledge mainpast offenders were, 16, 21, 126, 130, 146, 170, 196, 221, 255, 259, 291, 411–12, 427, 430–1, 444, 466, 468, 489, 551, 559, 561, 572, 586
  of persons standing bail, 112
  of pledges (mainpernors) for (attached) persons not appearing, 10, 18, 21, 30, 70, 93, 105, 109, 167, 187, 190–1, 194, 223, 237, 246–7, 250–1, 275–6, 307, 332, 355, 359, 388–9, 459, 469, 540, 548–9, 582, 590, 596, 619, 623
  of pledges for prosecuting, 12, 22, 62, 105 109, 130, 167–8, 191, 223, 259, 264, 275, 306–7, 328, 334, 353, 387, 389, 401, 471, 483, 527, 581, 590, 592, 596, 609, 622
  of tithingman for not attending eyre with money due, 541
  of tithings:
    for failing to attend eyre on first day, 535; for mainprised witness not appearing, 326; for malicious accusation, xxxix, 263; for members outlawed or abjured, 10, 13, 18, 24, 34, 38, 47, 49, 55, 60, 68–9, 76, 100, 108, 119–20, 122, 124–5, 129, 138, 146, 151, 155, 160, 175, 182, 185, 207, 210, 225, 229, 231, 243–4, 261, 263, 265, 283, 293, 296, 311, 314, 316, 319, 322–3, 325,

combat, trial by, lxviii–lxix; preparation
for, 598
commission, xxvii
constable, 499
coram rege court, xxvi
corn, stolen, 102, 191
coroners:
coroner's clerk, 441
inquest, xxxi, xxxii, xxxiii, xxxiv, xlii; *and
see* amercement, of townships: for failing
to attend *and* for refusing to attend
named, xxxi, 1
removed from office, xxxi, 1
rolls of, xlix, lxviii, 11, 133, 189, 364, 459
view by, body moved before, 441; burial
without, 227, 269, 413, 441
countess, 279, 285, 361, 415
county court, xxxi, xlvii, lxviii:
appeals begun in, 10, 12, 21–3, 62, 105, 127,
129–30, 167–8, 190–1, 216, 223, 264–5,
267, 275, 307, 334, 353, 469–71, 590, 595
eyre allowed as, 581
outlawry declared in, lxviii, 10, 21, 23, 265,
267, 327–8, 389, 459, 470, 509, 538, 581
outlawry not proceeded to, 12
courts, *see* bishop; *coram rege*; county court;
hanging, before justices *and* in other
courts; hundred; King's Bench; lawdays;
lord's court; manor court
cows (calves), stolen, lxi, 189; bull and cow
wrongly exacted, 575; bullock, stolen,
613
crimes, *see* abetting; arson; burglary; death:
homicide; larceny; mayhem; robbery
crown pleas held without warrant, *see* gallows;
pleas of replevin
curtilage, *see* land
custody ordered:
for breaking into house, 191
for burying without coroner's view, 413
for false accusation, 42, 74, 98, 202, 215, 266
for false appeal, 20, 189, 216, 327, 345, 364,
508, 576, 595
for false complaint, 268
for felony, 20
for involvement in robbery, 167
for mayhem, 133
for presence at jurors' deliberation without
taking oath, 348
for rape, 359
for superfluous distraint, 189
for trespass, 20, 22, 80, 189, 216, 259, 345,
364, 387, 431, 471, 508, 595
for unjust exaction, 360, 575
for withdrawing from appeal, 259, 328, 527

and see arrest

damages for loss of suit, 588
death:
causes of:
accidental, liv; arrow, wounded by, in
wrestling, 523; building, fall of, 545; cart
or cart's wheel, crushed by, 14, 43, 45, 67,
192, 198, 230, 374, 409, 418, 451; draught
animal, crushed by, 330; drowning, 6,
54, 77, 96, 139, 163–4, 228, 250, 269,
295, 326, 510, 512, 549, 554, 602; falling,
breaking neck, in coming down from
upper room, 608; found dead in house,
194; freak hailstorm, liv; horse or mare,
fall from, 91, 96, 228, 238, 295, 309, 555;
horse, colt or mare, struck or crushed by,
5, 176, 300, 329, 458; hurdle, crushed by,
355; knife, as though in wrestling, 574;
mill–wheel, crushed by, 432, 511, 534,
594; misadventure, lxxxiii, lxxxv; press,
crushed by, 310; sail–yard of mill, struck
by, 352; spindle, wound from, 491; stone
falling in quarry, 517; sword, falling on,
from horse, 555; timber (piece of wood),
crushed by, 50, 556; tree, falling from,
184, 376; tree, struck by branch of, 85,
381; wrestling, fall during, 568
hunger and cold, 187
killed by child, xlviii
lunatic, xlviii, li, lv; killing by, 365
natural, 8; disease, illness, 80, 388
sudden, at home, 603
unspecified cause, 513
homicide, xxvii, 34, 44, 61, 92–4, 120, 122,
124, 126, 130, 152, 169–70, 177, 185, 188,
199, 221, 226, 234, 239–40, 271, 291, 311,
321–3, 333, 341, 364–5, 373, 375, 404, 410,
412, 416, 427, 429–31, 437, 442, 448–9,
452, 461, 466–8, 480–1, 489, 503, 505,
516, 522, 524, 529, 541–3, 546, 552, 557,
561–2, 565–7, 572–3, 586, 615
accused not guilty, 47, 80–1, 112, 130, 244,
265–6, 277, 321, 327, 353, 362, 380, 401,
406, 431, 437, 452, 493, 527, 539, 560 570,
576, 599, 610, 614
accused unjustly held, 213
admitted by abjurer, *see* abjuration
after dispute or fight, lviii, 13, 15–16, 18,
49, 60, 68–70, 80, 95, 100–1, 117, 121,
125, 138, 166, 171, 179, 182, 196, 207–10,
231–3, 237, 244, 247, 251, 289, 292–3,
296, 302, 314, 316, 325, 331, 356, 380,
392, 433–4, 444, 447, 463–4, 479, 506,
532–3, 559, 614, 616, 618

WILTSHIRE RECORD SOCIETY
(AS AT AUGUST 2012)

President: DR NEGLEY HARTE
Honorary Treasurer: IVOR M. SLOCOMBE
Honorary Secretary: MISS HELEN TAYLOR
General Editor: DR V. BAINBRIDGE
Assistant Joint Editor: S.D. HOBBS

Committee:
D. CHALMERS
DR A. CRAVEN
DR D.A. CROWLEY
DR J. LEE
MRS S. THOMSON
K.H. ROGERS

Honorary Independent Examiner: C.C. DALE
Correspondent for the U.S.A.: SENIOR JUDGE R.W. OGBURN

PRIVATE MEMBERS

ADAMS, Ms S, 23 Rockcliffe Avenue, Bathwick, Bath BA2 6QP

ANDERSON, MR D M, 6 Keepers Mews, Munster Road, Teddington, Middlesex TW11 9NB

BADENI, COUNTESS JUNE, Garden Cottage, Norton, Malmesbury SN16 0JX

BAINBRIDGE, DR V, 60 Gloucester Road, Lower Swainswick, Bath BA1 7BN

BANKS, MR B H, 16 Velley Hill, Gastard, Corsham, SN13 9PU

BARNETT, MR B A, 3 The Orangery, Academy Drive, Corsham, SN13 0SF

BATHE, MR G, Byeley in Densome, Woodgreen, Fordingbridge, Hants SP6 2QU

BAYLIFFE, MR B G, 3 Green Street, Brockworth, Gloucester GL3 4LT

BENNETT, DR N, Hawthorn House, Main Street, Nocton, Lincoln LN4 2BH

BERRETT, MR A M, 10 Primrose Hill Road, London NW3 3AD

BERRY, MR C, 17 Fore Street, Hayle, Cornwall TR27 4DX

BLAKE, MR P A, 18 Rosevine Road, London SW20 8RB

BOX, MR S D, 73 Silverdale Road, Earley, Reading RG6 2NF

BRAND, DR P A, 155 Kennington Road, London SE11 6SF

BROWN, MR D A, 36 Empire Road, Salisbury SP2 9DF

BROWN, MR G R, 6 Canbury Close, Amesbury, Salisbury SP4 7QF

BROWNING, MR E, 58 Stratton Road, Swindon SN1 2PR

BRYANT, MRS D, 1 St John's Ct, Devizes SN10 1BJ

BRYSON, DR A, Humanities Research Institute, 34 Gell Street, Sheffield S3 7QW

BURGESS, MR I D, 29 Brackley Avenue, Fair Oak, Eastleigh, Hants SO5 7FL

CARRIER, MR S, 9 Highfield Road, Bradford on Avon BA15 1AS

CARTER, MR D, Docton Court, 2 Myrtle Street, Appledore, Bideford EX39 1PH

CAWTHORNE, MRS N, 45 London Road, Camberley, Surrey GU15

3UG

CHALMERS, MR D Bay House West, Bay House, Ilminster, Somerset TA19 0AT

CHANDLER, DR J H, Jupe's School, The Street, East Knoyle, Salisbury SP3 6AJ

CHURCH, MR T S, 12 Cathedral View, Winchester SO23 0PR

CLARK, MR G A, Highlands, 51a Brook Drive, Corsham SN13 9AX

CLARK, MRS V, 29 The Green, Marlborough SN8 1AW

COBERN, MISS A M, 4 Manton Close, Manton, Marlborough SN8 4HJ

COLCOMB, MR D M, 38 Roundway Park, Devizes SN10 2EO

COLES, MR H, Ebony House, 23 Lords Hill, Coleford, Glos GL16 8BG

COLLINS, MR A, 22 Innox Mill Close, Trowbridge BA14 9BA

COLLINS, MR A T, 36 Wasdale Close, Horndean, Waterlooville PO8 0DU

CONGLETON, LORD, West End Farm, Ebbesbourne Wake, Salisbury SP5 5JW

COOMBES-LEWIS, MR R J, 45 Oakwood Park Road, Southgate, London N14 6QP

COOPER, MR S, 12 Victory Row, Wootton Bassett, Swindon SN4 7BE

COWAN, MRS E, 24 Lower Street, Harnham, Salisbury SP2 8EY

CRAVEN, DR A, 17 Steamship House, Gasferry Road, Bristol BS1 1GL

CROOK, MR P H, Bradavon, 45 The Dales, Cottingham, E Yorks HU16 5JS

CROUCH, MR J W, 25 Biddesden Lane, Ludgershall, Andover SP11 5PJ

CROWLEY, DR D A, 7 Eversley Court, Wymering Road, Southwold IP18 6BF

CUNNINGTON, MS J, 1177 Yonge Street, #214, Toronto, Ont. M4T 2Y4, Canada

DAKERS, PROF C, Ferneley Cottage, Water Street, Berwick St John, Shaftesbury SP7 0HS

D'ARCY, MR J N, The Old Vicarage, Edington, Westbury BA13 4QF

DAVIES, MRS A M, Barnside, Squires Lane, Old Clipstone, Mansfield

NG21 9BP

DUNFORD, MRS J, 6 Round Chimneys, Glanvilles Wootton, Sherborne DT9 5QQ

DYSON, MRS L, 1 Dauntsey Ct, Duck St, West Lavington, Devizes SN10 4LR

EDE, DR M E, 12 Springfield Place, Lansdown, Bath BA1 5RA

EDWARDS, MR P C, 33 Longcroft Road, Devizes SN10 3AT

FIRMAGER, MRS G M, 72b High Street, Semington, Trowbridge BA14 6JR

FLOWER-ELLIS, DR J G, Kyrkogatan 2A, SE-815, 38 TIERP, Sweden

FOSTER, MR R E, Cothelstone, 24 Francis Way, Salisbury, SP2 8EF

FOWLER, MRS C, 10 Ullswater Road, Wimborne, Dorset, BH21 1QT

FOY, MR J D, 28 Penn Lea Road, Bath BA1 3RA

FROST, MR B C, Red Tiles, Cadley, Collingbourne Ducis, Marlborough SN8 3EA

GAISFORD, MR J, 9 Dudley Road, London NW6 6JX

GALE, MR J, PO Box 1015, Spit Junction, NSW 2088, Australia

GHEY, MR J G, Little Shute, Walditch, Bridport DT6 4LQ

GODDARD, MR R G H, Sinton Meadow, Stokes Lane, Leigh Sinton, Malvern, Worcs WR13 5DY

GOODBODY, MR E A, Stockmans, Rectory Hill, Amersham HP7 0BT

GOSLING, REV DR J, 1 Wiley Terrace, Wilton, Salisbury SP2 0HN

GOUGH, MISS P M, 39 Whitford Road, Bromsgrove, Worcs B61 7ED

GRIFFIN, D, C J, School of Geography, Queen's University, Belfast BT7 1NW

GRIST, MR M, 38 Springfield, Bradford on Avon BA15 1BB

HARDEN, MRS J O, The Croft, Tisbury Road, Fovant, Salisbury SP3 5JU

HARE, DR J N, 7 Owens Road, Winchester, Hants SO22 6RU

HARTE, DR N, St Aldhelm's Cottage, 5 Stokes Road, Corsham SN13 9AA

HEATON, MR R J, 16 St Bernard's Crescent, Harlow Road, High Wycombe HP11 1BL

HELMHOLZ, PROF R W, Law School, 1111 East 60th Street, Chicago, Illinois 60637 USA

HENLY, MR C R G, 27 Harden's Close, Chippenham SN15 3AA

HERRON, MRS Pamela M, 25 Anvil Crescent, Broadstone, Dorset BH18 9DY

HICKMAN, MR M R, 184 Surrenden Road, Brighton BN1 6NN

HICKS, MR I, 153 Cornbrash Rise, Trowbridge BA14 7TU

HICKS, PROF M A, King Alfred's College, Winchester SO22 4NR

HILLMAN, MR R B, 20 West Ashton Road, Trowbridge BA14 7BQ

HOBBS, MR S, 63 West End, Westbury BA13 3JQ

HORNBY, MISS E, 70 Archers Court, Castle Street, Salisbury SP1 3WE

HOWELLS, DR Jane, 7 St Mark's Rd, Salisbury SP1 3AY

HUMPHRIES, MR A G, Rustics, Blacksmith's Lane, Harmston, Lincoln LN5 9SW

INGRAM, DR M J, Brasenose College, Oxford OX1 4AJ

JAMES, MR & MRS C, 20 The Willows, Yate, Bristol, BS37 5XL

JEACOCK, MR D, 16 Church Street, Wootton Bassett, Swindon SN4 7BQ

JOHNSTON, MRS J M, Greystone House, 3 Trowbridge Road, Bradford on Avon BA15 1EE

KENT, MR T A, Rose Cottage, Isington, Alton, Hants GU34 4PN

KITE, MR P J, 13 Chestnut Avenue, Farnham GU9 8UL

KNEEBONE, MR W J R, Rose Cottage, Barbican Hill, Looe PL13 1BB

KNOWLES, MRS V A, New Woodland Cottage, Stanton St Bernard, Marlborough SN8 4LP

LANSDOWNE, MARQUIS OF, Bowood House, Calne SN11 0LZ

LAURENCE, MISS A, 1a Morreys Avenue, Oxford OX1 4ST

LAWES, MRS G, 48 Windsor Avenue, Leighton Buzzard LU7 1AP

LEE, DR J, 66 Kingshill Road, Bristol, BS4 2SN

LUSH, DR G J, 5 Braeside Road, West Moors, Ferndown, Dorset BH22 0JS

MARSH, REV R, 67 Hythe Crescent, Seaford, East Sussex BN25 3TZ

MARSHMAN, MR M J, 13 Regents Place, Bradford on Avon BA15 1ED

MARTIN, MS J, 21 Ashfield Road, Chippenham SN15 1QQ

MATHEWS, MR R, 57, Anthony Road, Denistone, NSW 2114, Australia

MOLES, MRS M I, 40 Wyke Road, Trowbridge BA14 7NP

MONTAGUE, MR M D, 115 Stuarts Road, Katoomba, NSW 2780, Australia

MOODY, MR R F, Fair Orchard, South Widcombe, East Harptree, Bristol BS40 6BL

MORIOKA, PROF K, 3-12, 4-chome, Sanno, Ota-ku, Tokyo, Japan

MORLAND, MRS N, 33 Shaftesbury Road, Wilton, Salisbury SP2 0DU

MOULTON, DR A E, The Hall, Bradford on Avon BA15 1AH

NAPPER, MR L R, 9 The Railway Terrace, Kemble, Cirencester GL7 6AU

NEWBURY, MR C COLES, 6 Leighton Green, Westbury BA13 3PN

NEWMAN, MRS R, Tanglewood, Laverstock Park, Salisbury SP1 1QJ

NICOLSON, MR A, Sissinghurst Castle, Cranbrook, Kent TN17 2AB

NOKES, MR P M A, 3 Rockleaze Avenue, Bristol BS9 1NG

OGBOURNE, MR J M V, Dale View, Redmire, Leyburn, N Yorks DL8 4EH

OGBURN, MR D A, 110 Libby Lane, Galena, Missouri 65656, USA

OGBURN, SENIOR JUDGE R W, 303 West Hahn's Peak Avenue, Pueblo West, Colorado, 81007, USA

PARKER, DR P F, 45 Chitterne Road, Codford St Mary, Warminster BA12 0PG

PATIENCE, MR D C, 29 Priory Gardens, Stamford, Lincs PE9 2EG

PERRY, MR W A, Noads House, Tilshead, Salisbury SP3 4RY

POWELL, MRS N, 4 Verwood Drive, Bitton, Bristol BS15 6JP

PRICE, MR A J R, Littleton Mill, Littleton Pannell, Devizes SN10 4EP

RAYBOULD, MISS F, 20 Radnor Road,

Salisbury SP1 3PL

RAYMOND, MR S, 38 Princess Gardens, Trowbridge BA14 7PT

ROBINSON, MRS S, The Round House, 109 Chitterne, Warminster BA12 0LH

ROGERS, MR K H, Silverthorne House, East Town, West Ashton, Trowbridge BA14 6BE

ROLFE, MR R C, 4 The Slade, Newton Longville, Milton Keynes MK17 0DR

ROOKE, MISS S F, The Old Rectory, Little Langford, Salisbury SP3 4NU

SAUNT, MRS B A, The Retreat, Corton, Warminster, BA12 0SL

SHARMAN-CRAWFORD, MR T, One Mapledurham View, Tilehurst, Reading RG31 6LF

SHELDRAKE, MR, B, The Coach House, 4 Palmer Row, Weston super Mare, BS23 1RY

SHEWRING, MR P, 73 Woodland Road, Beddau, Pontypridd, Mid-Glamorgan CF38 2SE

SINGER, MR J, 49 Bradwall Road, Sandbach, Cheshire CW11 1GH

SLOCOMBE, MR I, 11 Belcombe Place, Bradford on Avon BA15 1NA

SMITH, MR P J, 6 Nuthatch, Longfield, Kent DA3 7NS

SNEYD, MR R H, Court Farm House, 22 Court Lane, Bratton, Westbury BA13 4RR

SPAETH, DR D A, School of History and Archaeology, 1 University Gardens, University of Glasgow G12 8QQ

STEVENAGE, MR M R, 49 Centre Drive, Epping, Essex CM16 4JF

STONE, MR M J, 26 Awdry Close, Chippenham SN14 0TQ

SUTER, MRS C, 16 Swindon Road, Highworth, Swindon, SN6 7SL

SUTTON, A E, 3 Meadow Court, 24 Deckenham Grove, Bromley BR2 0XA

TATTON-BROWN, MR T, Fisherton Mill House, Mill Road, Salisbury, SP2 7RZ

TAYLOR, MR C C, 11 High Street, Pampisford, Cambridge CB2 4ES

TAYLOR, MISS H, 14 Pampas Court, Warminster BA12 8RS

THOMPSON, MR & MRS J B, 1 Bedwyn Common, Great Bedwyn, Marlborough SN8 3HZ

THOMSON, MRS S M, Home Close, High St, Codford, Warminster BA12 0NB

TIGHE, MRS D, Strath Colin, Pettridge Lane, Mere, Warminster BA12 6DG

VINE, MR R E, 11 Brocks Mount, Stoke sub Hamdon, Somerset, TA14 6PJ

WAITE, MR R E, 18a Lower Road, Chinnor, Oxford OX9 4DT

WARREN, MR P, 6 The Meadows, Milford Mill Road, Salisbury SP1 2SS

WILLIAMSON, B, 40 Florence Park, Bristol BS6 7LR

WILTSHIRE, MR J, Cold Kitchen Cottage, Kingston Deverill, Warminster BA12 7HE

WILTSHIRE, MRS P E, 23 Little Parks, Holt, Trowbridge BA14 6QR

WOODWARD, A S, 35 West Ridge Drive, Stittsville, Ontario K2S 1S4, Canada

WRIGHT, MR D P, Gerrans, Coast Road, Cley-next-the-Sea, Holt NR25 7RZ

YOUNGER, MR C, The Old Chapel, Burbage, Marlborough SN8 3AA

UNITED KINGDOM INSTITUTIONS

Aberystwyth
    National Library of Wales
    University College of Wales
Bath. Reference Library
Bristol
    University of Bristol Library
    University of the West of England

Cambridge. University Library
Cheltenham. Bristol and
    Gloucestershire Archaeological
    Society
Chippenham
    Chippenham Museum & Heritage
    Centre

Wiltshire and Swindon History
  Centre
Coventry. University of Warwick
  Library
Devizes
  Wiltshire Archaeological & N.H.
    Soc.
  Wiltshire Family History Society
Durham. University Library
Edinburgh
  National Library of Scotland
  University Library
Exeter. University Library
Glasgow. University Library
Leeds. University Library
Leicester. University Library
Liverpool. University Library
London
  British Library
  College of Arms
  Guildhall Library
  Inner Temple Library
  Institute of Historical Research
  London Library
  The National Archives
  Royal Historical Society
  Society of Antiquaries
  Society of Genealogists
Manchester. John Rylands Library
Marlborough

Memorial Library, Marlborough
  College
Merchant's House Trust
Savernake Estate Office
Norwich. University of East Anglia
  Library
Nottingham. University Library
Oxford
  Bodleian Library
  Exeter College Library
Reading
  University Library
St Andrews. University Library
Salisbury
  Bemerton Local History Society
  Bourne Valley Historical Society
  Cathedral Library
  Salisbury and South Wilts Museum
Southampton. University Library
Swansea. University College Library
Swindon
  English Heritage
  Swindon Borough Council
Taunton. Somerset Archaeological and
  Natural History Society
Trowbridge: Wiltshire Libraries &
  Heritage
Wetherby. British Library Document
  Supply Centre
York. University Library

INSTITUTIONS OVERSEAS

AUSTRALIA
Crawley. Reid Library, University of
  Western Australia
Melbourne
  Victoria State Library

CANADA
Halifax, Killam Library, Dalhousie
  University
London, Ont. D.B.Weldon Library,
  University of Western Ontario
Ottawa, Ont. Carleton University
  Library
Toronto, Ont
  Pontifical Inst of Medieval Studies
  University of Toronto Library
Victoria, B.C. McPherson Library,
  University of Victoria

EIRE
Dublin. Trinity College Library

GERMANY
Gottingen. University Library

JAPAN
Sendai. Institute of Economic History,
  Tohoku University
Tokyo. Waseda University Library

NEW ZEALAND
Wellington. National Library of New
  Zealand

UNITED STATES OF AMERICA
Ann Arbor, Mich. Hatcher Library,
  University of Michigan
Athens, Ga. University of Georgia
  Libraries
Atlanta, Ga. The Robert W Woodruff
  Library, Emory University
Binghampton, NY, Glenn Bartle
  Library, State University of New

York

Bloomington, Ind. Indiana University
    Library

Boston, Mass. New England Historic
    and Genealogical Society

Boulder, Colo. University of Colorado
    Library

Cambridge, Mass.
    Harvard College Library
    Harvard Law School Library

Charlottesville, Va. Alderman Library,
    University of Virginia

Chicago.
    Newberry Library
    University of Chicago Library

Dallas, Texas. Public Library

Davis, Calif. University Library

East Lansing, Mich. Michigan State
    University Library

Evanston, Ill. United Libraries, Gar-
    rett/Evangelical, Seabury

Fort Wayne, Ind. Allen County Public
    Library

Houston, Texas. M.D. Anderson Li-
    brary, University of Houston

Iowa City, Iowa. University of Iowa
    Libraries

Ithaca, NY. Cornell University Library

Los Angeles.

Public Library

Young Research Library, University
    of California

Minneapolis, Minn. Wilson Library,
    University of Minnesota

New York.
    Columbia University of the City of
    New York
    Public Library

Piscataway, N.J. Rutgers University
    Libraries

Princeton, N.J. Princeton University
    Libraries

Salt Lake City, Utah. Family History
    Library

San Marino, Calif. Henry E. Hunting-
    ton Library

Santa Barbara, Calif. University of
    California Library

South Hadley, Mass. Williston Me-
    morial Library, Mount Holyoke
    College

Urbana, Ill. University of Illinois
    Library

Washington. The Folger Shakespeare
    Library

Winston-Salem, N.C. Z.Smith
    Reynolds Library, Wake Forest
    University

LIST OF PUBLICATIONS

The Wiltshire Record Society was founded in 1937, as the Records Branch of the Wiltshire Archaeological and Natural History Society, to promote the publication of the documentary sources for the history of Wiltshire. The annual subscription is £15 for private and institutional members. In return, a member receives a volume each year. Prospective members should apply to the Hon. Secretary, c/o Wiltshire and Swindon History Centre, Cocklebury Road, Chippenham SN15 3QN. Many more members are needed.

The following volumes have been published. Price to members £15, and to non-members £20, postage extra. Most volumes up to 51 are still available from the Wiltshire and Swindon History Centre, Cocklebury Road, Chippenham SN15 3QN. Volumes 52-65 are available from Hobnob Press, PO Box 1838, East Knoyle, Salisbury SP3 6FA.

1. *Abstracts of feet of fines relating to Wiltshire for the reigns of Edward I and Edward II*, ed. R.B. Pugh, 1939
2. *Accounts of the parliamentary garrisons of Great Chalfield and Malmesbury, 1645-1646*, ed. J.H.P. Pafford, 1940
3. *Calendar of Antrobus deeds before 1625*, ed. R.B. Pugh, 1947
4. *Wiltshire county records: minutes of proceedings in sessions, 1563 and 1574 to 1592*, ed. H.C. Johnson, 1949
5. *List of Wiltshire boroughs records earlier in date than 1836*, ed. M.G. Rathbone, 1951
6. *The Trowbridge woollen industry as illustrated by the stock books of John and Thomas Clark, 1804-1824*, ed. R.P. Beckinsale, 1951
7. *Guild stewards' book of the borough of Calne, 1561-1688*, ed. A.W. Mabbs, 1953
8. *Andrews' and Dury's map of Wiltshire, 1773: a reduced facsimile*, ed. Elizabeth Crittall, 1952
9. *Surveys of the manors of Philip, earl of Pembroke and Montgomery, 1631-2*, ed. E. Kerridge, 1953
10. *Two sixteenth century taxations lists, 1545 and 1576*, ed. G.D. Ramsay, 1954
11. *Wiltshire quarter sessions and assizes, 1736*, ed. J.P.M. Fowle, 1955
12. *Collectanea*, ed. N.J. Williams, 1956
13. *Progress notes of Warden Woodward for the Wiltshire estates of New College, Oxford, 1659-1675*, ed. R.L. Rickard, 1957
14. *Accounts and surveys of the Wiltshire lands of Adam de Stratton*, ed. M.W. Farr, 1959
15. *Tradesmen in early-Stuart Wiltshire: a miscellany*, ed. N.J. Williams, 1960
16. *Crown pleas of the Wiltshire eyre, 1249*, ed. C.A.F. Meekings, 1961
17. *Wiltshire apprentices and their masters, 1710-1760*, ed. Christabel Dale, 1961
18. *Hemingby's register*, ed. Helena M. Chew, 1963
19. *Documents illustrating the Wiltshire textile trades in the eighteenth century*, ed. Julia de L. Mann, 1964
20. *The diary of Thomas Naish*, ed. Doreen Slatter, 1965
21-2. *The rolls of Highworth hundred, 1275-1287*, 2 parts, ed. Brenda Farr, 1966, 1968
23. *The earl of Hertford's lieutenancy papers, 1603-1612*, ed. W.P.D. Murphy, 1969
24. *Court rolls of the Wiltshire manors of Adam de Stratton*, ed. R.B. Pugh, 1970
25. *Abstracts of Wiltshire inclosure awards and agreements*, ed. R.E. Sandell, 1971
26. *Civil pleas of the Wiltshire eyre, 1249*, ed. M.T. Clanchy, 1971
27. *Wiltshire returns to the bishop's visitation queries, 1783*, ed. Mary Ransome, 1972
28. *Wiltshire extents for debts, Edward I - Elizabeth I*, ed. Angela Conyers, 1973
29. *Abstracts of feet of fines relating to Wiltshire for the reign of Edward III*, ed. C.R. Elrington, 1974
30. *Abstracts of Wiltshire tithe apportionments*, ed. R.E. Sandell, 1975

31. *Poverty in early-Stuart Salisbury,* ed. Paul Slack, 1975
32. *The subscription book of Bishops Tounson and Davenant, 1620-40,* ed. B. Williams, 1977
33. *Wiltshire gaol delivery and trailbaston trials, 1275-1306,* ed. R.B. Pugh, 1978
34. *Lacock abbey charters,* ed. K.H. Rogers, 1979
35. *The cartulary of Bradenstoke priory,* ed. Vera C.M. London, 1979
36. *Wiltshire coroners' bills, 1752-1796,* ed. R.F. Hunnisett, 1981
37. *The justicing notebook of William Hunt, 1744-1749,* ed. Elizabeth Crittall, 1982
38. *Two Elizabethan women: correspondence of Joan and Maria Thynne, 1575-1611,* ed. Alison D. Wall, 1983
39. *The register of John Chandler, dean of Salisbury, 1404-17,* ed. T.C.B. Timmins, 1984
40. *Wiltshire dissenters' meeting house certificates and registrations, 1689-1852,* ed. J.H. Chandler, 1985
41. *Abstracts of feet of fines relating to Wiltshire, 1377-1509,* ed. J.L. Kirby, 1986
42. *The Edington cartulary,* ed. Janet H. Stevenson, 1987
43. *The commonplace book of Sir Edward Bayntun of Bromham,* ed. Jane Freeman, 1988
44. *The diaries of Jeffery Whitaker, schoolmaster of Bratton, 1739-1741,* ed. Marjorie Reeves and Jean Morrison, 1989
45. *The Wiltshire tax list of 1332,* ed. D.A. Crowley, 1989
46. *Calendar of Bradford-on-Avon settlement examinations and removal orders, 1725-98,* ed. Phyllis Hembry, 1990
47. *Early trade directories of Wiltshire,* ed. K.H. Rogers and indexed by J.H. Chandler, 1992
48. *Star chamber suits of John and Thomas Warneford,* ed. F.E. Warneford, 1993
49. *The Hungerford Cartulary: a calendar of the earl of Radnor's cartulary of the Hungerford family,* ed. J.L. Kirby, 1994
50. *The Letters of John Peniston, Salisbury architect, Catholic, and Yeomanry Officer, 1823-1830,* ed. M. Cowan, 1996
51. *The Apprentice Registers of the Wiltshire Society, 1817- 1922,* ed. H. R. Henly, 1997
52. *Printed Maps of Wiltshire 1787–1844: a selection of topographical, road and canal maps in facsimile,* ed. John Chandler, 1998
53. *Monumental Inscriptions of Wiltshire: an edition, in facsimile, of Monumental Inscriptions in the County of Wilton, by Sir Thomas Phillipps,* ed. Peter Sherlock, 2000
54. *The First General Entry Book of the City of Salisbury, 1387-1452,* ed. David R. Carr, 2001
55. *Devizes Division income tax assessments, 1842-1860,* ed. Robert Colley, 2002
56. *Wiltshire Glebe Terriers, 1588-1827,* ed. Steven Hobbs, 2003
57. *Wiltshire Farming in the Seventeenth Century,* ed. Joseph Bettey, 2005
58. *Early Motor Vehicle Registration in Wiltshire, 1903-1914,* ed. Ian Hicks, 2006
59. *Marlborough Probate Inventories, 1591-1775,* ed. Lorelei Williams and Sally Thomson, 2007
60. *The Hungerford Cartulary, part 2: a calendar of the Hobhouse cartulary of the Hungerford family,* ed. J.L. Kirby, 2007
61. *The Court Records of Brinkworth and Charlton,* ed. Douglas Crowley, 2009
62. *The Diary of William Henry Tucker, 1825-1850,* ed. Helen Rogers, 2009
63. *Gleanings from Wiltshire Parish Registers,* ed. Steven Hobbs, 2010
64. *William Small's Cherished Memories and Associations,* ed. Jane Howells and Ruth Newman, 2011

VOLUMES IN PREPARATION

Wiltshire papist returns and estate enrolments, 1705-87, edited by J.A. Williams; *The parish registers of Thomas Crockford, 1613-29,* edited by C.C. Newbury; *Wiltshire rural industry organiser surveys and reports, c. 1938 - c. 1957,* edited by Ian Hicks; *Public health in 19th-century Wiltshire,* edited by Negley Harte; *The churchwardens' accounts of St. Mary's, Devizes, 1600-1700,* edited by Alex Craven. *Wiltshire Quarter Sessions order book, 1642-52,* edited by Ivor Slocombe. The volumes will not necessarily appear in this order.

A leaflet giving full details may be obtained from the Hon. Secretary, c/o Wiltshire and Swindon History Centre, Cocklebury Road, Chippenham, Wilts. SN15 3QN.